Guns
Recognition Guide

Richard Jones &
Andrew White

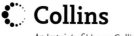

Collins

An Imprint of HarperCollins*Publishers*

Contents

Jane's

Guns
Recognition Guide

www.collins.co.uk

ISBN: 978-0-00-726645-6

www.harpercollins.com

ISBN: 978-0-06-137408-1 (in the United States)

FIFTH EDITION Published in 2008.
HarperCollins books may be purchased for educational, business, or sales promotional use. For information in the United States, please write to: Special Markets Department, HarperCollins Publishers, 10 East 53rd Street, New York, NY 10022.

The name of the "Smithsonian," "Smithsonian Institution," and the sunburst logo are registered trademarks of the Smithsonian Institution.

Text © HarperCollins*Publishers*, 2008

www.janes.com

Layout: Susie Bell
Editorial: Louise Stanley, Jodi Simpson

Printed and bound by Printing Express, Hong Kong

15 14 13 12 11
7 6 5 4

Acknowledgements:

Thanks to the MoD Pattern Room, the Infantry Museum, Edgar Brothers, the Royal Military College of Science, the West Midlands Constabulary, M. J. McBride (p. 96), and Jane's/Patrick Allen (pp. 56, 64, 99, 103, 204, 235, 255, 314) for their invaluable assistance in providing access to and photography of various weapons in their care.

Disclaimer:

The information in the book is derived from examination of weapons, weapon handbooks, and other authoritative sources, but it cannot be guaranteed. Neither the authors nor the publisher can be held responsible for any accident arising during the examination of any firearm, whether described in this book or not.

51	Walther P5	Germany
52	Walther P38	Germany
53	Walther PP	Germany
54	Walther PPK	Germany
55	Walther P88	Germany
56	Walther P99	Germany
57	Desert Eagle	Israel
58	Jericho 941	Israel
59	Beretta M951	Italy
60	Beretta Model 84	Italy
61	Beretta Model 92	Italy
62	Beretta Model 93R	Italy
63	Beretta Model 1934	Italy
64	Beretta Px4 Storm	Italy
65	Bernardelli P-018	Italy
66	Tanfoglio TA90	Italy
67	Poland P-64	Poland
68	Radom	Poland
69	Vanad P-83	Poland
70	Makarov	Russia
71	PSM	Russia
72	PSS	Russia
73	SPP-1	Russia
74	Stechkin	Russia
75	Tokarev	Russia
76	Yarygin "Grach" 6P35	Russia
77	Model 70	Serbia
78	Vektor SP	South Africa
79	Daewoo DP51	South Korea
80	Astra 300	Spain
81	Astra 400	Spain
82	Astra A-50	Spain
83	Astra A-75	Spain
84	Astra A-100	Spain
85	Star M40 Firestar	Spain
86	Star Megastar	Spain
87	SIG P 210	Switzerland
88	SIG P 220	Switzerland
89	SIG P 225	Switzerland
90	SIG P 226	Switzerland
91	SIG P 230	Switzerland
92	SIG P 232	Switzerland
93	SIG Sauer P 228	Switzerland
94	SIG Sauer P 229	Switzerland
95	SIG Sauer P 239	Switzerland
96	Sphinx AT2000/3000	Switzerland
97	Kirrikale	Turkey
98	Welrod Mark 1	UK
99	Fort 14 TP	Ukraine
100	AMT Hardballer	USA
101	Colt Double Eagle	USA
102	Colt Government Model .380	USA
103	Colt M1911/M1911A1	USA
104	Colt Mark IV Series 70/80	USA
105	Colt Officers' ACP/ ACP LW	USA
106	Coonan	USA
107	LAR Grizzly Win Mag	USA
108	Liberator	USA
109	Ruger P-85	USA
110	Ruger Standard	USA

Revolvers

Submachine Guns

Bolt-Action Rifles

Automatic Rifles

272	**FN FAL**	Belgium
273	**FN FNC**	Belgium
274	**Type 56**	China
275	**Type 63**	China
276	**Type 95**	China
277	**VZ52**	Czech Republic
278	**VZ58**	Czech Republic
279	**Sako M90**	Finland
280	**Valmet M76**	Finland
281	**FAMAS**	France
282	**MAS-49**	France
283	**Heckler & Koch G3**	Germany
284	**Heckler & Koch G36**	Germany
285	**Heckler & Koch G41**	Germany
286	**Heckler & Koch HK33E**	Germany
287	**Heckler & Koch HK53**	Germany
288	**Heckler & Koch HK 416**	Germany
289	**Heckler & Koch MSG90**	Germany
290	**Heckler & Koch PSG1**	Germany
291	**MP 44**	Germany
292	**Gepard M2/M2A1**	Hungary
293	**Gepard M3**	Hungary
294	**INSAS**	India
295	**Galil**	Israel
296	**Magal**	Israel
297	**SR-99**	Israel
298	**Tavor**	Israel
299	**Beretta AR 70/.223**	Italy
300	**Beretta BM59**	Italy
301	**Type 64**	Japan
302	**Type 89**	Japan
303	**Beryl**	Poland
304	**AK-47/AKM/variants**	Russia
305	**AK-47 Kalashnikov/ variants**	Russia
306	**Kalashnikov 1974 (AK-74)**	Russia
307	**Kalashnikov AKS-74U**	Russia
308	**APS**	Russia
309	**AS**	Russia
310	**Dragunov SVD**	Russia
311	**OSV-96**	Russia
312	**OTs-14 (Groza)**	Russia
313	**Simonov SKS**	Russia
314	**SR88**	Singapore
315	**SR88A**	Singapore
316	**ST Kinetics SAR 21**	Singapore
317	**NTW 20/14.5**	South Africa
318	**Vektor R4**	South Africa
319	**Daewoo K2**	South Korea
320	**Santa Barbara CETME Model L**	Spain
321	**AK5**	Sweden
322	**Ljungman AG42**	Sweden
323	**SIG SG 540/542/543**	Switzerland
324	**SIG SG 550/551 (Stgw 90)**	Switzerland
325	**SSG 550 Sniper**	Switzerland
326	**Stgw 57**	Switzerland
327	**Type 65**	Taiwan
328	**Type 86**	Taiwan
329	**L85A1/L85A2 Individual Weapon**	UK
330	**ArmaLite AR-18**	USA/UK

Foreword

The object of this book is to enable appropriate authorities, and others who might be called upon to confront firearms, to examine and recognize them with a fair degree of accuracy. This term has to be approached with caution, for although a firearm may fall within a particular recognition bracket, it could well happen that within that bracket fall numerous variants, calibre differences, manufacturers' names, and other details that might pass outside the outlines included in these pages. There is also the complication that other enterprises rather than their original manufacturer may copy designs (officially or unofficially), and may either be marked accordingly or have their own alterations from the original. Numerous variations can be encountered, especially among the most widely distributed firearms, so caution is needed when identifying or examining any firearm.

It also has to be stressed that the contents of this book cannot be encyclopaedic. Any attempt to provide suitable details and illustrations for every firearm likely to be examined would need a large library, rather than a single book. Some "sifting" has therefore been done: choices have made in favor of the types and models of firearm most likely to be encountered in law enforcement, military, freedom fighter, or criminal hands—and these days, that covers a wide array of potential types. It is also worth noting that the markings of guns (where given) are indicative of what might be found on a particular type or model, and can vary greatly.

This sifting has resulted in many once-common types, such as interwar Spanish pistols and the many American "Saturday Night Specials," being omitted. Most firearms have protracted potential service lives, but these two types seldom lasted long, and better weapons are now usually accessible from current sources, both official and unofficial.

Despite these comments, it must be appreciated that even antique firearms in a worn condition can be lethal in incautious hands. Users of this book are therefore strongly recommended to read and act upon the safety guidelines provided below. Firearms are meant to inflict harm and are very likely to harm their users if treated carelessly or in a cavalier fashion. The same applies to their ammunition.

Safety Warning

This book deals with the examination and identification of firearms.

Firearms are designed to kill.

Therefore:

1. Never pick up, accept, or hand over a firearm without removing any magazine or emptying any cylinder, and opening the action so as to expose the chamber and demonstrate that the weapon is empty. If you do not know how to do this, leave the weapon alone or ask someone else to do it fo you.
2. If circumstances dictate that you must hand over a loaded firearm, make sure that the safety catch is applied and inform the recipient without any ambiguity: "This weapon is loaded. The safety catch is on." If there is no safety catch, ensure the recipient knows.
3. Always assume that any firearm is loaded until you have positively proved that it is not. No matter how old, corroded, rusted, obsolete, decrepit, or dirt-covered a firearm may be, it is still possible that it is loaded. And that goes for muzzle-loaded antiques as well.
4. Always use an unloading box if one is available, and always point the firearm in a safe direction while unloading it.
5. Do not be overawed by "experts" who decry these rules; you will outlive them.

Pistols

Ballester Molina ARGENTINA

At first sight, the 0.45 Ballester Molina pistol closely resembles the Colt M1911. This is not too surprising as Colt technicians assisted its development, but there are some differences. One is the absence of a butt grip safety, another is the contours of the external hammer, and the trigger is pivoted instead of sliding, as on the M1911; other differences are internal. Even with these differences, the Ballester Molina is visually very similar to the M1911; the magazines are identical. As a rule, the finish is not as good as on most M1911s, but the pistol is reliable and rugged. Also known as the Hafdasa, after the concern involved in manufacture, numbers of Ballester Molina pistols were procured by Allied forces in 1939–43. Substantial numbers remained in Argentinian service until the Falklands War.

SPECIFICATION:

CARTRIDGE:
0.45 ACP

DIMENSIONS:
LENGTH O/A: 228 mm (9 in)
WEIGHT, UNLOADED: 1.1 kg (2 lb 8 oz)
BARREL: 127 mm (5 in)
RIFLING: 6 grooves, rh
MAGAZINE CAPACITY: 7 rounds

IN PRODUCTION:
1927–55

MARKINGS:
Prolifically marked on left of the slide is "PISTOLA AUTOMATICA CAL .45 FABRICADA PER 'HAFDASA' PATENTES INTERNACIONALES 'BALLESTER MOLINA' INDUSTRIA ARGENTINA." Serial number on left side of grip strap.

SAFETY:
Manual safety catch on left rear of frame. Up for safe, down to fire. Hammer may be drawn to half-cock position.

UNLOADING:
Magazine catch on left side behind trigger. Press in to release magazine. Remove magazine. Pull back slide to eject any round in chamber. Inspect chamber through ejection port in slide. Release slide. Pull trigger.

Glock 17/17L/19/20/21/31/34/35 AUSTRIA

Now one of the most widely used self-loading pistols, the Glock 17 (the base model for a host of basically similar Glock pistols) appeared during 1983. It is still in production in significant numbers. From this base model came the Glock 19, essentially the same as the Glock 17 but in compact form, while the Glock 17L has a longer barrel (153 mm/6 in). These three models are chambered for 9 x 19 mm Parabellum, but visually identical (apart from the caliber markings and model number) to the Glock 17 are the Glock 20 (10 mm Auto), Glock 21 (0.45 ACP), Glock 31 (0.357 SIG), and the target-shooting Glock 34 and 35. All these models have compact and subcompact equivalents.

SPECIFICATION:

CARTRIDGE:
9 x 19 mm Parabellum or 0.45 cal

DIMENSIONS:
LENGTH O/A: 186 mm (7.3 in)
WEIGHT: 620 g (1 lb 5 oz)
BARREL: 114 mm (4.5 in)
RIFLING: Hexagonal, rh
MAGAZINE CAPACITY: 17 rounds

IN PRODUCTION:
1983–

MARKINGS:
"GLOCK 17 AUSTRIA 9X19" on left side of slide. Serial number on right side of slide.

SAFETY:
No manual safety devices. Trigger safety bar protrudes from trigger face and is automatically pressed in when taking pressure on trigger. This unlocks an internal safety device, and further pressure on trigger cocks the striker and then releases it.

UNLOADING:
Magazine catch on left side of butt behind trigger. Remove magazine. Pull back slide to eject any round in chamber. Inspect chamber through ejection port; release slide. Pull trigger.

Glock 26/27/28/29/30/33/36 AUSTRIA

In 1995, Glock introduced the first of their subcompact pistols intended for ease of concealment. The overall dimensions were much reduced and the magazine contents limited to nine or 10 rounds, according to caliber, but the basic Glock outline and operating methods remain as for the Glock 17. The Glock 26 fires the 9 x 19 mm Parabellum cartridge. This model was followed by the visually identical Glock 27 (0.40 S&W), Glock 28 (0.380 Auto), Glock 29 (10 mm Auto), Glock 30 (0.45 ACP), Glock 33 (0.357 SIG), and (in 1999) the reduced-width "slimline" Glock 36 (0.45 ACP), holding only six rounds.

SPECIFICATION:

CARTRIDGE:
9 x 19 mm Parabellum or 0.45 cal

DIMENSIONS:
LENGTH, SLIDE: 160 mm (6.3 in)
WEIGHT: 616 g (1 lb 5 oz)
BARREL: 88 mm (3.5 in)
RIFLING: Hexagonal, rh
MAGAZINE CAPACITY: 10 rounds

IN PRODUCTION:
1995–

MARKINGS:
"GLOCK [model number] AUSTRIA 9X19" on left side of slide. Serial number on right side of slide.

SAFETY:
No manual safety devices. Trigger safety bar protrudes from trigger face and is automatically pressed in when taking pressure on trigger. This unlocks an internal safety device, and further pressure on trigger cocks striker and then releases it.

UNLOADING:
Magazine catch at left side of butt behind trigger. Remove magazine. Pull back slide to eject any round in chamber. Inspect chamber through ejection port. Release slide. Pull trigger.

Steyr 1912 AUSTRIA

One of the most robust and reliable service pistols ever made, it fired a cartridge unique to the Austro–Hungarian Empire. Unusually, it was backed using a charger-dip system, a system that had fallen into disuse some years earlier with the introduction of the detatchable magazine. When Austria was assimilated into the Third Reich in 1938, the service pistols were re-barrelled for the 9 mm Parabellum cartridge, and will be found marked "P-08" on the left side of the slide to indicate their conversion; however, 9 mm Steyr ammunition is still made.

SPECIFICATION:

CARTRIDGE:
9 mm Steyr or 9 x 19 mm Parabellum

DIMENSIONS:
LENGTH O/A: 216 mm (8.5 in)
WEIGHT: 1 kg (2 lb 4 oz)
BARREL: 128 mm (5 in)
RIFLING: 4 grooves, rh
MAGAZINE CAPACITY: 8 rounds

IN PRODUCTION:
1912–45

MARKINGS:
"STEYR [date of manufacture]" (Austrian military)
"STEYR MOD 1912" (Hungarian military)
"OESTERREICHISCHE WAFFENFABRIK STEYR M1911 9m/m" (Austrian commercial)
"EJERCITO DE CHILE" (Chilean military)
Serial number on left of slide and left side of frame in all models.

SAFETY:
Manual safety catch at left rear of frame. Forward for safe, down to fire.

UNLOADING:
Magazine is integral and loaded from a charger. Pull back slide and, while holding it open, press catch on right side at top of butt. This retracts a keeper and allows the magazine spring to push out all cartridges. (Do this over a table or some receptacle to catch rounds.) Once magazine is seen to be empty, release slide; if it does not close, depress cartridge catch again. Pull trigger.

Steyr M-Series/S-Series AUSTRIA

Steyr-Mannlicher went to considerable trouble to improve handling and natural pointing during aiming their M-Series self-loading pistol. The pistol is constructed using smooth, tough, molded polymers with ergonomic contours, and the pistol grip is distinctly angled to make holding the pistol as natural as possible. Other features include a self-cocking trigger action; safety actions are further enhanced by a Limited Access integrated key-lock in the pistol grip, preventing unauthorized use. The base M9 is chambered for the 9 x 19 mm Parabellum cartridge, while the similar M40 is chambered for the 0.40 S&W. The current model is the Steyr M-AI.

SPECIFICATION:

CARTRIDGE:
9 x 19 mm Parabellum, or 0.40 S&W, or 0.357 SIG

DIMENSIONS:
LENGTH O/A: 180 mm (7 in)
WEIGHT: 780 g (1 lb 12 oz)
BARREL: 102 mm (4.1 in) (S Model, 92 mm)
RIFLING: 4 grooves, rh
MAGAZINE CAPACITY: 12 (0.40 S&W and
0.357 SIG) or 14 rounds (9 x 19 mm Parabellum)

IN PRODUCTION:
1999–

MARKINGS:
"AUSTRIA [serial number] STEYR-MANNLICHER"
on right side of slide. "STEYR M40 40 S&W" or
"STEYR M9 9x19" on left side of slide

SAFETY:
Trigger reset catch in front edge of trigger. Manual safety: Press button above trigger in frame to set safe; press up on arm inside trigger guard to set to fire. Integrated keylock safety on right side of frame above trigger.

UNLOADING:
Magazine catch on forward edge of butt (both sides). Remove magazine. Pull back slide to eject any round in chamber. Inspect feedway and chamber to ensure both are empty. Release slide. Press trigger.

Steyr SPP AUSTRIA

The SPP (Special Purpose Pistol) is a self-loading version of the TMP (Tactical Machine Pistol). It uses the same synthetic frame and receiver and operates in the same delayed blowback mode by means of a rotating barrel. The principal difference is that the pistol has no forward handgrip and a slightly greater length of exposed barrel and jacket in front of the receiver. Another prominent feature is a short downward spur at the front of the frame, which positions the non-firing hand when using a two-handed hold and also prevents the fingers slipping in front of the barrel when firing. Manufacturing rights were purchased by Brügger & Thomet in Germany, and the SPP is now marked under their name.

SPECIFICATION:

CARTRIDGE:
9 x 19 mm Parabellum

DIMENSIONS:
LENGTH O/A: 282 mm (11.1 in)
WEIGHT: 1.3 kg (2 lb 14 oz)
BARREL: 130 mm (5.1 in)
RIFLING: 6 grooves, rh
MAGAZINE CAPACITY: 15 or 30 rounds

IN PRODUCTION:
1993–

MARKINGS:
"MADE IN AUSTRIA" on right side of receiver.
"STEYR-MANNLICHER" and Steyr badge on left side of receiver.

SAFETY:
Manual push-through safety catch at top of pistol grip; push through from left to right to fire.

UNLOADING:
Magazine release button on left side of pistol grip behind trigger. Remove magazine. Grasp cocking handle at rear of receiver and below rear sight and pull back to open breech. Inspect chamber through ejection port to ensure it is empty. Release cocking handle. Press trigger.

Browning 1903 BELGIUM

Designed by John Browning, who sold the rights to Colt for the USA and to FN for the rest of the world. Colt produced the Browning as a home-defense pistol in 7.65 mm, FN as a military pistol in 9 mm Browning Long caliber. It was widely copied in Spain from 1905 onward, and in various calibers. Most 1905–35 cheap Spanish automatic pistols are copies of this weapon, due to its simple design and manufacture. It has long been obsolete as a service-issue weapon.

SPECIFICATION:

CARTRIDGE:
9 x 20 mm SR Browning Long or 7.65 mm Browning (0.32 ACP)

DIMENSIONS:
LENGTH O/A: 205 mm (8. in)
WEIGHT: 910 g (2 lb)
BARREL: 127 mm (5.0 in)
RIFLING: 6 grooves, rh
MAGAZINE CAPACITY: 7 (9 mm) or 8 rounds (7.65 mm)

IN PRODUCTION:
1903–39

MARKINGS:
"FABRIQUE NATIONALE D'ARMES de GUERRE HERSTAL BELGIQUE / BROWNING'S PATENT / DEPOSE" on left side of slide. Serial number on right side of frame (Belgian model). "COLT'S PT FA MFG CO HARTFORD CT USA / PATENTED APR 20 1897 DEC 22 1903" on left side of slide. Serial number on left side of frame. "COLT AUTOMATIC / CALIBER .32 RIMLESS SMOKELESS" on right side of slide (US model).

SAFETY:
Safety catch at left rear of frame: up to fire, down for safe. Grip safety in rear edge of butt must be squeezed in to release firing mechanism. Magazine safety is fitted.

UNLOADING:
Magazine catch in heel of butt. Remove magazine. Pull back slide to eject any round in chamber. Inspect chamber through ejection port; release slide. Pull trigger.

Browning 1910 BELGIUM

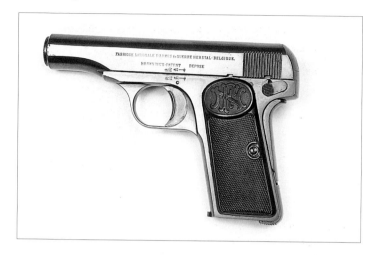

An improved version of the M1903, in which the recoil spring is placed around the barrel instead of beneath it, giving the unique tubular appearance to the slide. It was copied in Spain in 1920–35, though not to the extent of the M1903, and also in Germany as the Rheinmetall and DW pistols, easily distinguished by their markings. In 1922, it was given a longer barrel and the slide lengthened by a bayonet-jointed extension, remaining otherwise the same.

SPECIFICATION:

CARTRIDGE:
7.65 mm Browning (0.32 ACP)

DIMENSIONS:
LENGTH O/A: 153 mm (6 in)
WEIGHT: 600 g (1 lb 5 oz)
BARREL: 89 mm (3.5 in)
RIFLING: 6 grooves, rh
MAGAZINE CAPACITY: 7 rounds

IN PRODUCTION:
1910–39

MARKINGS:
"FABRIQUE NATIONALE D'ARMES de GUERRE HERSTAL BELGIQUE / BROWNING'S PATENT DEPOSE" on left side of slide. "CAL 7m/m.65" on barrel, visible through ejection opening. Serial number on right side of frame, right side of slide and barrel; on 1922 model, also on slide extension.

SAFETY:
Safety catch at left rear of frame: up for safe, down for fire. Grip safety in rear of pistol grip must be depressed to fire. Magazine safety is fitted; pistol cannot be fired if magazine is withdrawn.

UNLOADING:
Magazine catch at heel of butt. Remove magazine. Pull back slide to eject any round in chamber, release slide. Pistol will remain cocked and trigger cannot be pressed unless emptied magazine is replaced.

Browning BDA (Browning Double Action) 380 BELGIUM

This is little more than a Beretta 84 with a Belgian accent. FN wanted a blowback-operated pistol for the police market, and since they owned a piece of Beretta, it made sense to take an existing successful design and make a few minor cosmetic changes. The most obvious difference is the plastic grip plate with the FN monogram. This was one of the first pistols of this size to feature a double-column or high-capacity magazine.

SPECIFICATION:

CARTRIDGE:
9 mm Short (0.380 Auto) or 7.65 mm (0.32 Auto)

DIMENSIONS:
LENGTH O/A: 173 mm (6.8 in)
WEIGHT: 640 g (1 lb 6 oz)
BARREL: 96 mm (3.8 in)
RIFLING: 6 grooves, rh
MAGAZINE CAPACITY: 13 (9 mm) or 12 rounds (7.65 mm)

IN PRODUCTION:
1980–

MARKINGS:
"FABRIQUE NATIONALE" or "FN HERSTAL SA" on left side of slide. "BDA-380" and serial number on left side of frame. If made in Beretta factory, will have PB monogram on right side of slide.

SAFETY:
Manual safety catch at left rear of slide, which acts as a decocking lever. Press down for safe (hammer will be released to fall safely on a loaded chamber).

UNLOADING:
Magazine catch at left side of butt behind trigger. Remove magazine. Pull back slide to eject any round in chamber. Inspect chamber through ejection port; release slide. Pull trigger.

Browning High Power Mark 2/Mark 3/BDA9/BDAO

BELGIUM

The Browning High Power Mark 2 appeared during the 1960s but differed little from the original Model 35, other than a few detail changes and ergonomic pistol grips. It was replaced by the Browning Mark 3, with more detail changes and some strengthening, plus more easily adjustable sights, ambidextrous safety levers, and an automatic firing pin safety. The Mark 3 (shown) was followed by a Mark 3S with fully adjustable sights, although it has been supplemented by the Browning BDA9. There is also a Browning BDAO model intended for police use and meant to be carried loaded with no manual safety; only a determined pressure on the trigger will fire the pistol. Compact versions of both the BDA9 and BDAO exist, both having a 10-round magazine capacity. Norinco of China have copied the Mark 2 model for their Type 88SP.

SPECIFICATION:

CARTRIDGE:
9 x 19 mm Parabellum

DIMENSIONS:
LENGTH O/A: 200 mm (7.9 in)
WEIGHT, UNLOADED: 930 g (2 lb)
BARREL: 118 mm (4.6 in)
RIFLING: 6 grooves, rh
MAGAZINE CAPACITY: 6 rounds

IN PRODUCTION:
1990–

MARKINGS:
"FABRIQUE NATIONALE [or FN] HERSTAL BELGIUM" on slide. Serial number on right side of frame (position may vary).

SAFETY:
On both sides of frame at rear: up for safe.

UNLOADING:
Magazine catch at left side behind trigger. Remove magazine. Pull back slide to eject any round in chamber. Inspect chamber through ejection port, release slide. Pull trigger.

Browning High Power Model 1935 BELGIUM

This is still one of the most widely used of all service pistols, having been in continuous production since it was introduced by FN back in 1935. During World War II, the Model 35 was kept in production in Belgium as the 9 mm P 640(b) for the German forces; these are marked accordingly. Other wartime Model 35s can be found marked "J Inglis." After 1945, in addition to production by what is now FN Herstal in Belgium, licensed manufacture (or direct copying) has been carried out in Argentina (Domingo Mathieu), Bulgaria (ARCUS), Hungary (FEG), India (Ordnance Factories), Indonesia (PT Pindad), and Israel (KSN Industries). The number of user countries has reached over 50. Due to this widespread service, numerous detail differences between pistols can be found.

SPECIFICATION:

CARTRIDGE:
9 x 19 mm Parabellum

DIMENSIONS:
LENGTH O/A: 200 mm (7.9 in)
WEIGHT UNLOADED: 882 g (1 lb 15 oz)
BARREL: 118 mm (4.6 in)
RIFLING: 6 grooves, rh
MAGAZINE CAPACITY: 13 rounds

IN PRODUCTION:
1935–

MARKINGS:
"FABRIQUE NATIONALE HERSTAL BELGIUM BROWNING'S PATENT DEPOSE FN [year]" on left side of slide. Military models may have NATO stock number.

SAFETY:
Manual at left rear of frame; recent models have it duplicated on both sides of frame. Up for safe.

UNLOADING:
Magazine catch at left side of butt behind trigger. Remove magazine. Pull back slide to eject any round in chamber. Inspect chamber through ejection port, release slide. Pull trigger.

FN Five-seveN

This is a self-cocking, self-loading pistol. The trigger action is rather unusual, in that pressure on the trigger first loads the firing pin spring and then releases the firing pin. Unless the trigger is pressed, the firing pin is not under any pressure, and thus there is no safety catch of the normal type. The cartridge is longer than the average pistol round, but the grip nevertheless fits the hand well.

The Five-seveN operates on the delayed-blowback principle. On firing, the barrel and slide both move back, but the barrel is under a forward impulse due to the bullet's friction. The slide is held after a short movement, until the pressure on the barrel is released as the bullet leaves. There is also a Five-seveN Tactical pistol with a single-action trigger mechanism and added safeties. It is intended primarily for issue to law-enforcement agencies.

SPECIFICATION:

CARTRIDGE:
5.7 x 28 mm FN

DIMENSIONS:
LENGTH O/A: 208 mm (7.8 in)
WEIGHT: 618 g (2 lb 5 oz)
BARREL: 122.5 mm (4.4 in)
RIFLING: 6 grooves, rh
MAGAZINE CAPACITY: 20 rounds

IN PRODUCTION:
1998–

MARKINGS:
"FN HERSTAL BELGIUM" on left side of slide, "CAL 5.7x28" on right side. Serial number on barrel, visible through ejection port, and on right side of slide, below foresight.

SAFETY:
No applied safety. Weapon is safe until final movement of trigger.

UNLOADING:
Magazine catch in front edge of grip. Remove magazine. Pull back slide to eject any round in chamber. Release slide. No need to pull trigger.

Imbel M973/MD1

The M973 in its original form was simply a copy of the US Colt M1911A1 in 0.45 caliber. It was then reworked into 9 x 19 mm Parabellum caliber but was still known as the M973. In 1990, it was again reworked, this time into 0.38 Super Auto caliber, primarily for the civil and export markets, though it is believed a number have gone to police and some army units. Most parts are interchangeable among all three pistols.

SPECIFICATION:

CARTRIDGE:
0.45 ACP, 9 x 19 mm Parabellum, or 0.38 Super Auto

DIMENSIONS:
LENGTH O/A: 216 mm (8.5 in)
WEIGHT: 1 kg (2 lb 4 oz)
BARREL: 128 mm (5 in)
RIFLING: 6 grooves, rh
MAGAZINE CAPACITY: 7 (0.45), 8 (9 mm), or 9 rounds (0.38 Super)

IN PRODUCTION:
1973–?

MARKINGS:
"FABRICA ITJUBA BRASIL" on left side of slide. "EXERCITO BRASILIERO" and serial number on right side of slide. "Pist 9 [or 45] M973" and serial number on right side of frame above trigger, or "Pist 38 MD1" and serial number on right side of frame.

SAFETY:
Manual safety catch on left rear side of frame: up for safe.

UNLOADING:
Magazine catch on front left side of butt behind trigger. Press in; remove magazine. Pull back slide to eject any round in breech. Inspect chamber through ejection port. Release slide. Pull trigger.

Taurus PT 52 S BRAZIL

A compact straight blowback pistol modeled on the larger PT 92 AF with identical control levers and takedown. Like the larger 9 mm pistols, the PT 52 S is available with a stainless-steel or carbon-steel slide/barrel assembly on an aluminum frame.

SPECIFICATION:

CARTRIDGE:
0.380 Auto (9 mmK)

DIMENSIONS:
LENGTH O/A: 180 mm (7.1 in)
WEIGHT: 800 g (1 lb 12 oz)
BARREL: 102 mm (4 in)
RIFLING: 6 grooves, rh
MAGAZINE CAPACITY: 12 rounds

MARKINGS:
"TAURUS" on left side of slide. "TAURUS BRASIL" in circle with bull's head motif inside. Serial number on left of frame. "FORJAS TAURUS S.A., MADE IN BRAZIL" and "PT 52 S, .380 ACP" on right side of slide. Earlier models did not have "Int Mfg Miami Fl" on slide.

SAFETY:
Manual safety catch/decocking lever on both sides of frame at rear: up for safe, which will lock hammer in cocked and uncocked position; down to fire, and continued downward movement releases hammer to fall onto intercept notch. When lever is removed, it returns to fire position. Trigger-released firing-pin block.

UNLOADING:
Magazine catch at left side of butt behind trigger. Press in; remove magazine. Pull back slide to eject any round in chamber. Inspect chamber through ejection port. Release slide.

Arcus 94/98DA
BULGARIA

The Bulgarian company Arcus, a new entry in the handgun market, produced a series of single-action Arcus 94 and double-action Arcus 98DA pistols based on the Browning design. The pistols are of all steel construction with a high-capacity magazine. Three safeties are fitted: manually applied, half-cock, and magazine. A .22 in caliber adapter for the Arcus 98M is available for reduced-cost training. A variety of grip styles and combat sights are offered.

SPECIFICATION:

CARTRIDGE:
9 x 19 mm

DIMENSIONS:
LENGTH O/A: 203 mm (8 in)
WEIGHT: 970 g (2 lb 2 oz)
BARREL: 118 mm (4.7 in)
MAGAZINE CAPACITY: 13 (Arcus 94) or 15 rounds (Arcus 98DA)

IN PRODUCTION:
2003–

MARKINGS:
"ARCUS" on right side of slide and frame. Serial number on barrel, ejection port, frame, and slide.

SAFETY:
Manual safety locks slide and hammer. Up for safe.

UNLOADING:
Magazine release catch on left side behind trigger-guard. Remove magazine. Pull slide to rear to eject any round in chamber. Inspect chamber through ejection port; release slide. Replace empty magazine. Pull trigger.

Para Ordnance P14 CANADA

A high-capacity Canadian-made version of the Colt Government pistol with a double-column magazine and supported chamber barrel. The company originally produced aftermarket high-capacity frame kits in aluminum and later in carbon steel. Complete pistols are available with aluminum alloy or steel frames. Compact models are also listed (P13-45 and P12-45), along with a similar-sized range in 0.40 S&W with slightly higher capacities. The combination of high-capacity and powerful cartridges with the steel frame makes for a formidable if weighty pistol.

SPECIFICATION:

CARTRIDGE:
0.45 ACP

DIMENSIONS:
LENGTH O/A: 216 mm (8.5 in)
WEIGHT: 1.1 kg (2 lb 5 oz)
BARREL: 127 mm (5 in)
RIFLING: 6 grooves, rh
MAGAZINE CAPACITY: 13 rounds

IN PRODUCTION:
1991–

MARKINGS:
"PARA-ORDNANCE" on left of slide. "P-14-45" on right of slide. "PARA-ORDNANCE INC, FT. LAUDERDALE FL, MADE IN CANADA," and serial number on right of frame.

SAFETY:
Grip safety. Manual safety catch lever on top left of frame at rear: up for safe, down to fire. Firing-pin safety blocks firing-pin movement unless trigger is pulled fully to rear.

UNLOADING:
Magazine catch at left side of butt behind trigger. Press in to remove magazine. Pull back slide to eject any round in chamber. Inspect chamber; release slide.

Type 64 CHINA

An unusual silenced pistol, easily recognized by the bulbous integral silencer. The breech slide can be locked closed to prevent ejection of the spent case after firing, which could make more noise than the shot itself. Alternatively, it can be unlocked when the weapon operates in the normal blowback self-loading mode. Note that the cartridge for this weapon is peculiar to it; the pistol will not chamber 7.65 mm or 0.32 ACP cartridges, which are of similar dimensions, because they are semirimmed and will prevent the breech closing.

SPECIFICATION:

CARTRIDGE:
7.65 x 17 mm rimless

DIMENSIONS:
LENGTH O/A: 222 mm (8.8 in)
WEIGHT: 810 g (1 lb 12 oz)
BARREL: 95 mm (3.7 in)
RIFLING: 4 grooves, rh
MAGAZINE CAPACITY: 9 rounds

IN PRODUCTION:
1964–

MARKINGS:
"64" with factory number in an oval and serial number on left side of slide.

SAFETY:
Manual safety catch at top of left butt grip: up for safe. Cross-bolt in upper part of slide will lock slide to barrel and prevent self-loading action and thus prevent any mechanical noise after firing a silent shot.

UNLOADING:
Magazine catch at heel of butt. Remove magazine. Pull back slide to eject any round in chamber. Inspect chamber through ejection port. Release slide. Pull trigger.

Type 67 CHINA

An improved version of the Type 64, this has a rather less clumsy silencing system that fits better into a holster and gives the weapon better balance. There is no provision for locking the breech closed on this model, normal blowback operation being the only option. The Type 67 fires a special low-powered 7.62 mm round known as the Type 64. The illustration shows the Type 67 with the slide held in open position.

SPECIFICATION:

CARTRIDGE:
7.62 x 17 mm Type 64 rimless

DIMENSIONS:
LENGTH O/A: 226 mm (8.9 in)
WEIGHT: 1.1 kg (2 lb 5 oz)
BARREL: 89 mm (3.5 in)
RIFLING: 4 grooves, rh
MAGAZINE CAPACITY: 9 rounds

IN PRODUCTION:
1968–

MARKINGS:
Factory identifying number in oval, "67" followed by Chinese character and serial number on left side of slide.

SAFETY:
Manual safety catch at top of left butt grip: up for safe. Cross-bolt in upper part of slide will lock slide to barrel and prevent self-loading action and thus prevent any mechanical noise after firing a silent shot.

UNLOADING:
Magazine catch at heel of butt. Remove magazine. Pull back slide to eject any round in chamber. Inspect chamber through ejection port. Release slide. Pull trigger.

The HS 95 is a conventional all-steel self-loading pistol of modern design. It uses the Browning locking system and can be fired in either the single- or double-action mode. It has a similar double-action and decocking system, though with a rather more rounded contour to the butt. The mechanism is also similar, using Browning cam and locking into the ejection opening and having an automatic firing-pin safety. It is apparently issued to Croatian Army personnel and is also offered for export.

SPECIFICATION:

CARTRIDGE:
9 x 19 mm Parabellum

DIMENSIONS:
LENGTH O/A: 180 mm (7.1 in)
WEIGHT, UNLOADED: 1 kg (2 lb 4 oz)
BARREL: 102.5 mm (4 in)
RIFLING: 6 grooves, rh
MAGAZINE CAPACITY: 15 rounds

IN PRODUCTION:
1995–

MARKINGS:
"Cal 9 mm Para" on barrel, visible in ejection port.
"Made in CROATIA" on right side of slide, together
with serial number.

SAFETY:
Decocking lever only; no manual safety catch.
Automatic firing-pin safety.

UNLOADING:
Magazine catch is duplicated on both sides of butt
behind trigger. Remove magazine. Pull back slide.
Inspect chamber through ejection opening. Release
slide. Press trigger or depress decocking lever.

HS 2000 CROATIA

The Croatian 9 mm HS 2000 is manufactured by IM-METAL and is an updated version of the HS 95 manufactured by the same concern. It differs from the earlier HS 95 pistol in having a high-impact molded polymer frame. The XD series of this model was developed for the US market.

SPECIFICATION:

CARTRIDGE:
9 x 19 mm Parabellum, or 0.40 S&W, or 0.357 SIG

DIMENSIONS:
LENGTH O/A: 180 mm (7.1 in)
WEIGHT, UNLOADED: 775 g (1 lb 11 oz)
BARREL: 102.5 mm (4 in)
RIFLING: 6 grooves, rh
MAGAZINE CAPACITY: 15 rounds (9 mm) or 12 (0.40 S&W, 0.357 SIG) rounds

IN PRODUCTION:
2000–

MARKINGS:
"Cal 9 mm Para [or appropriate caliber]" on barrel, visible through ejection port. "Made in CROATIA" or sometimes "IM-METAL" on left side of slide (these markings may vary). Serial number on right side of slide.

SAFETY:
Grip safety only; no manual safety catch. Automatic firing-pin safety. Pinhead protrudes from recess in rear of slide when round is in chamber.

UNLOADING:
Magazine catch is duplicated on both sides of butt behind trigger. Remove magazine. Pull back slide. Inspect chamber through ejection opening. Release slide. Grip butt firmly and pull trigger.

This replaced the prewar M38 design; it is intended to fire the Czech M48 cartridge, which is reportedly more powerful than the normal 7.62 mm Soviet pistol round. It uses a complicated roller-locked breech. It can also fire dimensionally similar 7.63 mm Mauser pistol cartridges.

SPECIFICATION:

CARTRIDGE:
7.62 mm Czech M48 (7.62 x 25 mm)

DIMENSIONS:
LENGTH O/A: 209 mm (8.2 in)
WEIGHT: 960 g (2 lb 1 oz)
BARREL: 120 mm (4.7 in)
RIFLING: 4 grooves, rh
MAGAZINE CAPACITY: 8 rounds

IN PRODUCTION:
1953–70

MARKINGS:
Serial number on left side of frame. No other markings.

SAFETY:
Safety catch at left rear of slide. Three-position switch: down to fire; backward for safe; and when pushed up from this position, cocked hammer drops safely onto rebound notch. Safety catch can then be moved to "fire" position and pistol can be quickly brought into use by thumbing back hammer.

UNLOADING:
Magazine catch at heel of butt. Remove magazine. Pull back slide to eject any round in chamber. Inspect chamber through ejection port. Release slide. Pull trigger.

CZ75

The Czech 9 mm CZ75 pistol is the foundation of a family of pistols, based around a Browning-derived action, similar to that used with the Browning High Power Model-35. This family has gained an enviable reputation for reliability and robustness and has been procured by several nations, including Turkey, where it is license-produced by Rocketsan. It has also been copied by Norinco of China as their 9 mm NZ75 for commercial sales. The base CZ75 has now been largely replaced by the CZ75B (shown) with an additional firing pin safety. Also produced are compact and semi-compact models, both with 10-round magazines. Other models include a suppressed version (the Tarantule), a double-action-only variant, and the CZ75 POLICE, with decocking levers according to application.

SPECIFICATION:

CARTRIDGE:
9 x 19 mm Parabellum, 9 x 21 mm, or 0.40 S&W

DIMENSIONS:
LENGTH: 206 mm (8.1 in)
WEIGHT, UNLOADED: 1 kg (2 lb 8 oz)
BARREL: 120 mm (4.7 in)
RIFLING: 6 grooves, rh
MAGAZINE CAPACITY: 15 (9 mm) or 10 (0.40) rounds

IN PRODUCTION:
1976–

MARKINGS:
"CZ75B CAL. 9 PARA" on left side of slide. "MADE IN CZECH REPUBLIC" or "MADE IN CZECHOSLOVAKIA" on left side of frame. Serial number on right side of slide and frame, also visible through ejection opening.

SAFETY:
Manual safety catch at left rear of frame: up for safe.

UNLOADING:
Magazine catch on left side rear of trigger guard. Press and remove magazine. Pull slide to rear to eject any round in chamber. Inspect chamber and magazine well through ejection port. If no cartridges present, point weapon in safe direction. Release slide. Pull trigger.

A conventional double-action blowback-operated pocket self-loading pistol, which can be thought of as the Czech Republic's answer to the Makarov. It fills the same niche in Czech services and has a few refinements, such as an automatic firing pin safety system, an ambidextrous safety catch and magazine release, and a trigger guard large enough to take a gloved hand. Note that in 7.65 mm and 9 mm short calibers the rifling is conventional, but in 9 mm Makarov it is polygonal, that is, the barrel section resembles a circle that has been slightly flattened on four sides.

SPECIFICATION:

CARTRIDGE:
7.65 mm ACP, or 9 mm Short (0.380 Auto), or 9 mm Makarov

DIMENSIONS:
LENGTH O/A: 172 mm (6.8 in)
WSEIGHT, UNLOADED: 750 g (1 lb 10 oz)
BARREL: 97 mm (3.8 in)
RIFLING: 6 grooves, rh (9 mm Makarov, polygonal)
MAGAZINE CAPACITY: 15 (7.65 mm) or 12 (9 mm) rounds

IN PRODUCTION:
1984–

MARKINGS:
"CZ83 CAL. 9 MAKAROV [or alternative caliber]" on left side of slide. "MADE IN CZECH REPUBLIC" or "MADE IN CZECHOSLOVAKIA" on left side of frame. Serial number on right side of slide and frame and also visible through ejection opening.

SAFETY:
Ambidextrous manual safety catch at rear of frame locks hammer and trigger. Automatic firing-pin safety system locks pin until trigger is pressed.

UNLOADING:
Magazine catch at either side of butt behind trigger. Remove magazine. Pull back slide to eject any round in chamber. Inspect chamber through ejection port. Release slide. Pull trigger.

CZ100/101 CZECH REPUBLIC

Introduced in 1995, this chunky pistol brings synthetic materials into CZ construction. The slide is steel, and the frame is constructed of polymer. The pistol grip has a reduced width and provides a comfortable hold. The pistol is self-cocked, the firing system being under no tension unless the trigger is pulled. There is an automatic firing pin safety device. An unusual protrusion on the top of the slide, just behind the ejection port, is intended to permit one-handed cocking by placing this part against a hard surface and pushing down on the grip so the slide is forced back to load the first round. The action is the usual Browning cam, locking the chamber top into the ejection port. A laser spot can be fitted. The Model 101 is similar but has a smaller magazine capacity: seven rounds of 9 mm or six rounds of 0.40.

SPECIFICATION:

CARTRIDGE:
9 x 19 mm Parabellum or 0.40 S&W

DIMENSIONS:
LENGTH O/A: 177 mm (7 in)
WEIGHT: 645 g (1 lb 7 oz)
BARREL: 95 mm (3.7 in)
RIFLING: 6 grooves, rh
MAGAZINE CAPACITY: 13 (9 mm) or 10 rounds (0.40)

IN PRODUCTION:
1995–

MARKINGS:
"CZ 100 Cal .40 S&W MADE IN CZECH REPUBLIC" on left side of slide. "CZ" and symbol of a pistol in a circle molded into lower part of grips.

SAFETY:
Manual safety catch on frame locks trigger. Automatic firing-pin safety.

UNLOADING:
Magazine catch in grip, behind trigger aperture; may be on either side. Press to release magazine. Draw back slide to empty chamber; verify chamber empty; release slide. No need to pull trigger.

Lahti L-35 FINLAND

Although the Lahti L-35 resembles the Parabellum, its mechanism is totally different. These pistols were manufactured both in Sweden and in Finland and were made in small batches, which differed in minor details. The Swedish version also differs from the Finnish in minor details. A highly reliable pistol, it became available on the surplus market in the 1970s. Do not attempt to dismantle this gun without expert guidance and a full toolkit.

SPECIFICATION:

CARTRIDGE:
9 x 19 mm Parabellum

DIMENSIONS:
LENGTH O/A: 245 mm (9.7 in)
WEIGHT: 1.2 kg (2 lb 11 oz)
BARREL: 107 mm (4.2 in)
RIFLING: 6 grooves, rh
MAGAZINE CAPACITY: 8 rounds

IN PRODUCTION:
1939–85

MARKINGS:
"VKT" inside a diamond on top of receiver and molded into butt plates (Finnish). "USQVARNA VAPENFABRIKS AB" on left side of receiver (Swedish). Serial number on left side of receiver and left side of frame (all models).

SAFETY:
Manual safety catch at left rear of frame.

UNLOADING:
Magazine catch at toe of butt. Remove magazine. Grasp end of bolt and pull back to eject any round in chamber. Inspect chamber through ejection port. Release bolt. Press trigger.

MAB PA-15 FRANCE

A militarized model of a commercial pistol, adopted by the French Army in the 1960s and also sold commercially. Unusual for its time in using a rotating barrel to lock the barrel and slide together for firing, the barrel turning during recoil to release the slide. A long-barrel target model was also produced.

SPECIFICATION:

CARTRIDGE:
9 x 19 mm Parabellum

DIMENSIONS:
LENGTH O/A: 203 mm (8 in)
WEIGHT: 1.1 kg (2 lb 6 oz)
BARREL: 114 mm (4.5 in)
RIFLING: 6 grooves, rh
MAGAZINE CAPACITY: 15 rounds

IN PRODUCTION:
1975–90

MARKINGS:
"Pistol Automatique MAB Brevete SGDG" on left side of slide. "MODELE PA-15" on right side of slide. "P.A.P. Mle F1 Cal 9m/m" on right side of slide (military models); "MADE IN FRANCE" on right side of frame (both military and commercial models). Serial number on right side of frame above trigger.

SAFETY:
Manual safety catch at left rear of frame.

UNLOADING:
Magazine release button on left side behind trigger. Remove magazine. Pull back slide to eject any round in chamber. Inspect chamber through ejection port. Release slide. Pull trigger.

Heckler & Koch HK4 GERMANY

This was Heckler & Koch's first production pistol of blowback-operated design, based on the prewar Mauser HSc pistol. It was available with a kit of four inter-changeable barrels, allowing the pistol to be converted to any of the four calibers: 9 mm Short, 7.65 mm (0.32 ACP), 6.35 mm or 0.22 rimfire. For the latter, an adjustment was provided to alter the strike of the firing pin.

SPECIFICATION:

CARTRIDGE:
9 mm Browning Short (0.380 Auto), 7.65 mm Browning (0.32 ACP) and .22 RF

DIMENSIONS:
LENGTH O/A: 157 mm (6.2 in)
WEIGHT: 480 g (1 lb 1 oz)
BARREL: 85 mm (3.3 in)
RIFLING: 6 grooves, lh
MAGAZINE CAPACITY: 7 (9 mm) or 8 rounds (7.65 mm, 6.35 mm, and 0.22)

IN PRODUCTION:
1964–90

MARKINGS:
"HECKLER & KOCH GmbH OBERNDORF/N MADE IN GERMANY Mod HK4" on left side of slide.

SAFETY:
Safety catch on left rear of slide: down for safe, up to fire.

UNLOADING:
Set safety catch to safe. Press back magazine catch at heel of butt. Remove magazine. Pull back slide to eject any round in chamber. Slide will stay open when released. Inspect chamber. Press trigger; this will allow slide to close, leaving hammer cocked. Press trigger again to drop hammer.

Heckler & Koch P7 GERMANY

Developed in response to a German police demand for a pistol that would be safe at all times but without needing to be set to fire before using it. It has a unique grip catch that engages the trigger with the cocking and firing mechanism. To fire, the user simply grips the weapon and pulls the trigger, which then cocks and releases the firing pin. If the weapon is dropped, the grip is released and the weapon is instantly made safe. It uses an unusual gas piston delay system to slow down the opening of the breech after firing.

Various models of this pistol were manufactured, the P7M8 with the box magazine holding eight rounds and the P7M13 holding 13 rounds. The P7K3 version was a blowback-operated weapon offered in 9 mm Short or 7.65/0.32 ACP.

SPECIFICATION:

CARTRIDGE:
9 x 19 mm Parabellum, or 0.40 S&W

DIMENSIONS:
LENGTH O/A: 171 mm (6.7 in)
WEIGHT, LOADED: P7M8, 950 g (2 lb 1 oz); P7M13, 1.1 kg (2 lb 8 oz)
BARREL: 105 mm (4.1 in)
RIFLING: 4-groove polygonal
MAGAZINE CAPACITY: 8 (P7M8) or 13 rounds (P7M13)

IN PRODUCTION:
1980–

MARKINGS:
"HECKLER & KOCH GmbH Oberndorf/Neckar US Pat No 3,566,745 Made in Germany, [serial number]" on left side of slide. Serial number on left side of frame. "P7M8" or "P7M13" in panel on lower part of butt grip.

SAFETY:
No applied safety. Grip control in butt prevents firing unless weapon is properly held.

UNLOADING:
Magazine catch at left side of butt, behind trigger. Remove magazine. Pull back slide to eject any round in chamber. Inspect chamber through ejection port. Release slide. Squeeze grip and pull trigger.

Heckler & Koch P9/P9S GERMANY

Heckler & Koch's first locked-breech military pistol, this uses a complex roller-locked delayed-blowback system similar to that used on the company's rifles and machine guns. The P9 pistol came first but was soon followed and then replaced by the P9S, the difference being that the P9 was single-action only, whereas the P9S was double action.

SPECIFICATION:

CARTRIDGE:
9 x 19 mm Parabellum

DIMENSIONS:
LENGTH O/A: 192 mm (7.6 in)
WEIGHT: 880 g (1 lb 15 oz)
BARREL: 102 mm (4 in)
RIFLING: Polygonal, 4 grooves, rh
MAGAZINE CAPACITY: 9 rounds

IN PRODUCTION:
1970–90

MARKINGS:
"HK MOD P9 HECKLER & KOCH GmbH OBERN-DORF/NECKAR Made in Germany" on left side of slide. Serial number on left side of slide and right side of frame.

SAFETY:
Manual safety catch on left rear of slide: down for safe, up to fire. Lever beneath left grip offers control of hammer. When hammer is down, pressing this lever will cock it; when the hammer is cocked, pressing this lever, then pulling trigger, will allow pressure on lever to be gently released and hammer safely lowered.

UNLOADING:
Magazine catch at heel of butt. Remove magazine. Pull back slide to eject any round from chamber. Inspect chamber through ejection port. Release slide (it will remain open). Press down on cocking lever under left grip to release slide. Pull trigger.

Heckler & Koch SOCOM, Mark 23 Mod 0 GERMANY

In 1990, the US Special Operations Command (SOCOM) requested proposals for an automatic pistol in 0.45 caliber of superior accuracy to the M1911A1 and with an accessory silencer and a laser aiming spot projector. The result was a double-action design, hammer fired, with the breech locked by the Browning dropping-barrel system. An additional recoil buffer is incorporated into the buffer spring assembly to reduce the felt recoil and thus improve the accuracy. The muzzle protrudes from the slide and is threaded to accept the sound suppressor, which is said to reduce noise by 25 dB. A slide lock is provided so that the noise of the slide and the ejected cartridge do not negate the silencing of the shot. The front of the frame is grooved to accept the laser-spot projector, which can project either visible or infrared light.

SPECIFICATION:

CARTRIDGE:
0.45 ACP

DIMENSIONS:
LENGTH O/A: 245 mm (9.7 in); with suppressor 421 mm (16.6 in)
WEIGHT: 1.2 kg (2 lb 10 oz); with suppressor and full magazine, 1.9 kg (4 lb 4 oz)
BARREL: 149 mm (5.9 in)
RIFLING: 4 grooves, polygonal, rh
MAGAZINE CAPACITY: 12 rounds

IN PRODUCTION:
1995–

MARKINGS:
"U.S.PROPERTY Mk 23 Mod 0." Serial number on left side of slide.

SAFETY:
Manual safety on both sides of frame. Manual decocking lever in front of safety will lower cocked hammer silently.

UNLOADING:
Magazine catch at rear edge of trigger guard. Remove magazine. Ensure slide lock is unlocked. Draw back slide. Inspect chamber through ejection opening. Release slide. Press trigger or depress decocking lever.

Heckler & Koch USP GERMANY

The USP (Universal Self-loading Pistol) was designed to incorporate all the various features that military and law-enforcement agencies appeared to find vital. It uses the Browning cam system of breech locking, together with a patented recoil-reduction system that forms part of the recoil spring and buffer assembly. The frame is of a polymer synthetic material, and metal components are given an anti-corrosion finish.

The pistol was originally designed and produced in 0.40 Smith & Wesson caliber, after which variants in 0.45 ACP (shown) and 9 x 19 mm Parabellum were produced. All models have a variety of options including a manual safety catch, a decocking lever, a self-cocking, double-action, and ambidextrous controls.

SPECIFICATION:

CARTRIDGE:
0.40 S&W, or 9 x 19 mm Parabellum, or 0.45 ACP

DIMENSIONS:
LENGTH O/A: 194 mm (7.6 in)
WEIGHT: 830 g (1 lb 13 oz)
BARREL: 108 mm (4.3 in)
RIFLING: Polygonal, rh
MAGAZINE CAPACITY: 13 (0.40) or 15 rounds (9 mm)

IN PRODUCTION:
1992–

MARKINGS:
"H&K USP 9x19mm [serial number]" on left side of slide. "Heckler & Koch GmbH Made In Germany" on right side of frame.

SAFETY:
Safety lever at rear of frame; normally on left, but can be moved to right side if desired. "S" for safe and "F" to fire. Appropriate letter should align with white line on frame.

UNLOADING:
Magazine release lever below triggerguard. Recesses in butt permit gripping magazine to make removal easier. Remove magazine. Pull back slide. Inspect chamber through ejection port. Release slide. Press trigger.

Mauser 1910/1934 GERMANY

An enlarged version of a design that appeared in 6.35 mm caliber in 1910, this became an officers' pistol during World War I and was then sold commercially as the Model 1914. In 1934, a small change in the shape of the butt and some other minor improvements brought the Model 1934, which was sold commercially and then adopted by the German armed forces in World War II.

SPECIFICATION:

CARTRIDGE:
7.65 mm Browning (0.32 ACP)

DIMENSIONS:
LENGTH O/A: 153 mm (6 in)
WEIGHT: 600 g (1 lb 5 oz)
BARREL: 87 mm (3.4 in)
RIFLING: 6 grooves, rh
MAGAZINE CAPACITY: 8 rounds

IN PRODUCTION:
1914–34; 1934–45

MARKINGS:
"WAFFENFABRIK MAUSER A.G. OBERNDORF aN MAUSER'S PATENT" on left side of slide. Mauser badge on left side of frame. Serial number on left front of slide and rear of frame (1914). "MAUSER-WERKE AG OBERNDORF aN" on left side of slide. "CAL 7,65 DRPuAP" on right side of slide. Serial numbers on left front of slide and rear of frame (1934).

SAFETY:
Manual catch at front edge of left butt grip: up to fire; when pressed down for safe, it locks in this position and can be released by pressing in button beneath it. Will then rise to fire position.

UNLOADING:
Magazine catch at heel of butt. Remove magazine. Pull back slide to eject any round in chamber. Inspect chamber through ejection port. Release slide. Pull trigger.

Mauser HSc GERMANY

A double-action, blowback-operated weapon introduced in response to Walther's PP model. Most pre-1945 production was taken for military use. Post-1964 production was sold commercially, but in 1984 Mauser ceased manufacture and licensed the design to Renato Gamba of Italy; they ran into difficulties and re-organized in the early 1990s as Societa Armi Bresciana (SAB) and again set about putting the HSc back into production, but few appear to have been made.

SPECIFICATION:

CARTRIDGE:
7.65 mm Browning (0.32 ACP)

DIMENSIONS:
LENGTH O/A: 152 mm (6 in)
WEIGHT: 600 g (1 lb 5 oz)
BARREL: 86 mm (3.4 in)
RIFLING: 6 grooves, rh
MAGAZINE CAPACITY: 8 rounds

IN PRODUCTION:
1937–45; 1964–84

MARKINGS:
"MAUSERWERKE AG OBERNDORF aN Mod HSc KAL 7,65mm" on left side of slide. Serial number on front edge of butt.

SAFETY:
Manual safety catch on left rear of slide: up for safe, down to fire. Magazine safety.

UNLOADING:
Magazine catch at heel of butt. Remove magazine and empty it. Pull back slide to eject any round in chamber. Inspect chamber through ejection port. Release slide. Replace empty magazine. Pull trigger.

Mauser Military Model 1912 GERMANY

There were several variations on the basic "broomhandle" Mauser (so called because of its grip), but this Model 12, or c/12 to give it its military designation, is probably the most commonly found and, apart from the safety catch, is representative of all models. Note that this model was also made in 9 x 19 mm Parabellum caliber in 1914–18 and these have a large figure 9 cut into the grips and colored red.

SPECIFICATION:

CARTRIDGE:
7.63 mm Mauser

DIMENSIONS:
LENGTH O/A: 318 mm (12.5 in)
WEIGHT: 1.3 kg (2 lb 12 oz)
BARREL: 140 mm (5.5 in)
RIFLING: 6 grooves, rh
MAGAZINE CAPACITY: 10 rounds

IN PRODUCTION:
1912–45

MARKINGS:
"WAFFENFABRIK MAUSER OBERNDORF A NECKAR" on right side of frame. Serial number in full on left side of chamber and rear of bolt; last two digits repeated on almost every removeable part.

SAFETY:
Safety lever alongside hammer: up for safe, down to fire. Note: Earlier models worked in opposite direction. BE CAREFUL.

UNLOADING:
Integral charger-loaded box magazine ahead of trigger. Unlike with Mannlicher and Roth designs, there is no short cut to unloading. Grasp pistol and pull back bolt, gripping "wings" at rear end to eject any round from chamber. Release bolt to load next round from magazine, pull back to eject, and carry on loading and ejecting until magazine is empty. Inspect magazine chamber. Release bolt. Pull trigger.

Parabellum Pistole '08

There are many variations on the Parabellum (Luger) pistol, but the German Army Pistole '08 can be taken as representative of the type. Foreign (Persian, Finnish, Portuguese, etc.) markings can also be found.

SPECIFICATION:

CARTRIDGE:
9 x 19 mm Parabellum

DIMENSIONS:
LENGTH O/A: 223 mm (8.8 in)
WEIGHT: 850 g (1 lb 10 oz)
BARREL: 102 mm (4 in)
RIFLING: 8 grooves, rh
MAGAZINE CAPACITY: 8 rounds

IN PRODUCTION:
1908–45

MARKINGS:
Maker's name "DWM-ERFUR-KRIEGHOFF-SIMSON" or identifying code "-S/42-42-byf-" engraved on toggle. Year of manufacture engraved over chamber. Mauser pistols of 1934 and 1935 are marked "K" and "G." Serial number on left side of barrel extension. Note: These can be duplicated; each of three factories making this pistol used the same numbering system, relying on the factory marking to distinguish them. Each year saw the start of a fresh series of numbers, distinguished by a prefix or suffix letter. It is therefore quite possible to have six pistols all bearing the number 1234, but they would be distinguished by having a letter behind the number and by the maker's mark. Figures stamped on the front end of the barrel extension beneath the rear end of the barrel are the actual (as opposed to the nominal) diameter of the bore across the grooves. Why the makers thought this important enough to stamp on the pistol is a mystery.

SAFETY:
Manual safety catch on left side of frame; operation of this has varied between models, sometimes up for safe, sometimes down. However, frame is stamped with the word "GESICHERT" or "SAFE" or "SEGURANCA," which will be visible when catch is set to safe position, and with the word "FEUER" or "FIRE" which will be visible when catch is set to fire position. Some models have grip safety device in rear edge of butt which must be squeezed in before pistol can be fired.

UNLOADING:
Magazine catch is a push-button behind trigger on left side. Remove magazine. Pull up and back on two grips on breech toggle to eject any round in chamber. Inspect chamber. Release toggle. Pull trigger.

Parabellum "Long '08"

This is the standard Pistole '08 with a long barrel and adjustable rear sight, introduced for support troops in place of the normal artillery or engineer carbines. They were also used by the German Navy. The "snail" drum magazine was not entirely effective and is now rarely encountered in these pistols. Both the artillery and navy models have a cutout on the lower rear of the pistol grip to fit a wooden stock, which also functioned as a holster. Shown here is the artillery model.

SPECIFICATION:

CARTRIDGE:
9 x 19 mm Parabellum

DIMENSIONS:
LENGTH O/A: 313 mm (12.3 in)
WEIGHT: 1.1 kg (2 lb 5 oz)
BARREL: 200 mm (7.9 in)
RIFLING: 6 grooves, rh
MAGAZINE CAPACITY: 8-round box or 32-round "snail" magazine

IN PRODUCTION:
1913–45

MARKINGS:
Maker's name—"DWM" or "Erfurt"—on forward toggle link. Serial numbers on left side of barrel extension; last three or four digits repeated on almost every removeable part.

SAFETY:
Manual safety catch at left rear of frame: up for safe, down to fire.

UNLOADING:
Magazine catch is a push-button behind trigger on left side. Remove magazine. Pull up and back on two grips on breech toggle to eject any round in chamber. Inspect chamber. Release toggle. Pull trigger.

Sauer M38H GERMANY

The M38H is a modernized version of the M30, of more streamlined appearance and with a double-action trigger.

SPECIFICATION:

CARTRIDGE:
7.65 mm Browning (0.32 ACP)

DIMENSIONS:
LENGTH O/A: 171 mm (6.7 in)
WEIGHT: 720 g (1 lb 9 oz)
BARREL: 83 mm (3.3 in)
RIFLING: 4 grooves, rh
MAGAZINE CAPACITY: 8 rounds

IN PRODUCTION:
1938–45

MARKINGS:
"J.P.SAUER & SOHN SUHL CAL 7,65" on left side of slide. "PATENT" on right side of slide. "S&S" monogram on left buttgrip. "S&S Cal 7,65" on magazine bottom plate. Serial number on rear of frame.

SAFETY:
Manual safety catch on left rear of slide: up for safe, down to fire. Cocking/decocking lever behind trigger on left side of frame; when pistol is cocked, pressure on this lever releases hammer so it can be lowered safely onto a loaded chamber. When pistol is uncocked, pressure on this lever will cock hammer.

Walther P5

This is another of the designs that appeared in response to a German police requirement in the early 1970s for a safe but fast-acting pistol. To achieve this, the firing pin of the P5 normally lies lined up with a recess in the hammer; if the hammer falls, it hits the slide but does not touch the firing pin. Only at the instant of hammer release, with the trigger drawn fully back, does a pawl push the entire firing pin up and align it with the solid portion of the hammer. There is also a safety notch in the hammer, and the trigger is disconnected from the firing mechanism unless the slide is fully forward.

SPECIFICATION:

CARTRIDGE:
9 x 19 mm Parabellum

DIMENSIONS:
LENGTH O/A: 181 mm (7 in)
WEIGHT: 795 g (1 lb 12 oz)
BARREL: 90 mm (3.5 in)
RIFLING: 6 grooves, rh
MAGAZINE CAPACITY: 8 rounds

IN PRODUCTION:
1975–90

MARKINGS:
"Walther Banner/P5/Carl Walther Waffenfabrik Ulm/Do." on left side of slide. Serial number on right side of frame.

SAFETY:
Decocking lever on left side of frame drops hammer safely on loaded chamber. All other safety devices are automatic.

UNLOADING:
Magazine catch at heel of butt. Remove magazine. Pull back slide to eject any round in chamber. Inspect chamber through ejection port. Release slide. Pull trigger.

Walther P38 GERMANY

The P38 became the Wehrmacht's official sidearm in 1938 to replace the Luger; it was readopted when the Bundeswehr was formed in the 1950s, now known as the P1. As with the other Walther pistols, there are slight dimensional differences between the pre- and post-1945 models. There is also a short-barrel model known as the P38K, though this is uncommon. The P38 was the first locked-breech pistol to use the double-action lock, allowing the user to carry the weapon loaded with the hammer down and then pull through on the trigger to fire the first shot.

SPECIFICATION:

CARTRIDGE:
9 x 19 mm Parabellum

DIMENSIONS:
First figure pre-1945; second figure current production
LENGTH O/A: 213/218 mm (8.4/8.6 in)
WEIGHT: 840/772 g (1 lb 13 oz/1 lb 11 oz)
BARREL: 127/124 mm (5/4.9 in)
RIFLING: 6 grooves, rh
MAGAZINE CAPACITY: 8 rounds

IN PRODUCTION:
1938–

MARKINGS:
Pre-1945: (a) "WALTHER (banner)/Waffenfabrik Walther Zella Mehlis (Thur)/Walther's Patent Kal 9m/m/Mod P38" on left side of slide (very early production); (b) "480 P-38" (late 1939 production); (c) "ac P-38" (1939–45 production); (d) "WALTHER (banner)/Carl Walther Waffenfabrik Ulm/Do/P-1" (current production). Serial number on left side of slide and left side of frame ahead of trigger guard.

SAFETY:
Safety catch on left rear of slide: up to fire; down for safe, when it locks safety pin and drops cocked hammer.

UNLOADING:
Magazine catch at left side of butt behind trigger. Remove magazine. Pull back slide to eject any round in chamber. Inspect chamber through ejection port. Release slide. Pull trigger.

Walther PP GERMANY

Introduced as a pistol for uniformed police. The abbreviation stands for "Polizei Pistole." It was the first successful application of the double-action principle, which Walther then adapted to the P38. There is no significant mechanical difference between pre- and postwar models, though the postwar weapons are a few millimeters longer and slightly lighter, and the design has been widely copied, with and without benefit of license.

SPECIFICATION:

CARTRIDGE:
7.65 mm Browning, 9 mm Short and .22 LR

DIMENSIONS:
First figure pre-1945; second figure current production
LENGTH O/A: 162/173 mm (6.4/6.8 in)
WEIGHT: 710/682 g (1 lb 9 oz/1 lb 8 oz)
BARREL: 85/99 mm (3.4/3.9 in)
RIFLING: 6 grooves, rh
MAGAZINE CAPACITY: 8 rounds

IN PRODUCTION:
1929–

MARKINGS:
"WALTHER (banner)/Waffenfabrik Walther Zella-Mehlis (Thur)/Walther's PatentCal 7.65m/m/Mod PP" on left side of slide (pre-1945). "WALTHER (banner)/Carl Walther Waffenfabrik Ulm/Do/Model PP Cal 7.65mm" on left side of slide (post-1945). Serial number on right side of frame behind trigger. May also be found bearing the "MANURHIN" name; this French company made these pistols under license from about 1948 to 1956.

SAFETY:
Safety catch on left rear of slide: up to fire; down for safe, when it locks safety pin and drops cocked hammer.

UNLOADING:
Magazine catch at left side of butt behind trigger. Remove magazine. Pull back slide to eject any round in chamber. Inspect chamber through ejection port. Release slide. Pull trigger.

Walther PPK GERMANY

The PPK (Polizei Pistole Kurtz, or 'short') was simply the PP scaled down for use by plainclothes police; there are some fundamental design differences in the frame, but mechanically the two models work the same way. As with the PP, the postwar models are slightly larger. Easily recognized by the finger extension on the bottom of the magazine to give a better grip for the hand. A hybrid model, the PPK/S, used the slide and barrel of the PPK and the frame of the PP in order to circumvent the US Gun Control Act of 1968 by increasing its depth dimension, it was restricted to sales in the USA.

SPECIFICATION:

CARTRIDGE:
6.35 mm Browning, or 7.65 mm Browning, or 9 mm Short

DIMENSIONS:
First figure pre-1945; second figure current production
LENGTH O/A: 148/155 mm (5.7/6.1 in)
WEIGHT: 580/590 g (1 lb 4 oz/1 lb 4 oz)
BARREL: 80/83 mm (3.2/3.3 in)
RIFLING: 6 grooves, rh
MAGAZINE CAPACITY: 7 rounds

IN PRODUCTION:
1930–

MARKINGS:
"WALTHER (banner)/Waffenfabrik Walther Zella-Mehlis (Thur)/Walther's PatentCal 7.65m/m/Mod PPK" on left side of slide (pre-1945). "WALTHER (banner)/Carl Walther Waffenfabrik Ulm/Do/Model PPK Cal 7.65mm" on left side of slide (post-1945). Serial number on right side of frame behind trigger. May also be found bearing the "MANURHIN" name; this French company made these pistols under license from about 1948 to 1956.

SAFETY:
Safety catch on left rear of slide: up to fire; down for safe, when it locks safety pin.

UNLOADING:
Magazine catch at heel of butt. Remove magazine. Pull back slide to eject any round in chamber. Inspect chamber through ejection port. Release slide. Pull trigger.

Walther P88 GERMANY

The P88 compact self-loading pistol marked Walther's move away from the wedge system of locking the breech, introduced with the P-38 and continued in several other designs. This pistol uses a Browning dropping barrel, controlled by a cam and locking the squared-off area of the chamber into the ejection opening in the slide, a system easier and cheaper to manufacture. The safety system is the same as that adopted in the P5 pistol, described above, and relies upon a nonaligned firing pin; should the hammer accidentally fall, the end of the firing pin is lined up with a recess in the hammer face. Only by pulling the trigger all the way through will the firing pin be lifted to line up with the solid portion of the hammer.

SPECIFICATION:

CARTRIDGE:
9 x 19 mm Parabellum

DIMENSIONS:
LENGTH O/A: 187 mm (7.4 in)
WEIGHT: 900 g (1 lb 15 oz)
BARREL: 102 mm (4 in)
RIFLING: 6 grooves, rh
MAGAZINE CAPACITY: 15 rounds

IN PRODUCTION:
1988–98

MARKINGS:
"Walther Banner/P88/Made in Germany" on left side of slide. Serial number on right side of frame.

SAFETY:
Ambidextrous decocking lever on both sides of frame above butt; depressing this allows hammer to fall safely. All other safety devices are automatic.

UNLOADING:
Magazine catch on both sides of butt behind trigger. Remove magazine. Pull back slide to eject any round in chamber. Inspect chamber through ejection port. Release slide. Pull trigger.

Walther P99 GERMANY

The Walther P99 is a self-loading pistol developed for law enforcement use. It features a steel slide and polymer frame. It is hammerless to prevent snagging on clothing and is offered with three trigger options: double action only (DAO); quick action (QA) with a partially preloaded striker; and antistress (AS) mode, is engaged after reloading. All controls, slide-stop, magazine release, and decocking button are ambidextrous. A loaded-chamber indicator is fitted to the slide and can be both seen and felt. An interchangeable back-strap to suit the size of the user's hand is provided. Both full-size P99 and compact P99 C models are offered.

SPECIFICATION:

CARTRIDGE:
9 x 19 mm or 0.40 S&W

DIMENSIONS:
LENGTH O/A: 181 mm (7.1 in)
WEIGHT: 690 g (1 lb 8 oz)
BARREL: 102 mm (4 in)
MAGAZINE CAPACITY: 15 rounds (P99), or 10 rounds (P99C)

IN PRODUCTION:
1999–

MARKINGS:
"WALTHER" banner and model number on left side of slide. Serial number on barrel, ejection port, slide, and metal witness plate at rear of frame.

SAFETY:
The P99 uses an internal striker system. DAO mode has trigger at rest and requires a long steady pull to the rear to fire. QA mode has a partially preloaded striker allowing a short light trigger pull. AS mode, used with both double- and single-action modes, engages after reloading.

UNLOADING:
Remove magazine. Pull slide to rear. Check chamber is clear. Release slide. Press decocking lever.

Desert Eagle ISRAEL

A large and heavy pistol that can be found chambered for a variety of cartridges, all of them powerful. It originally appeared in 0.357 Magnum chambering, and others were later added. Such powerful loads demand a well-locked breech and the pistol uses a three-lug rotating bolt, which is unlocked by gas tapped from the fixed barrel acting on a piston that drives the slide back. This movement of the slide first rotates and then opens the bolt. The pistol may be found with a steel or an alloy frame and with varying barrel lengths.

SPECIFICATION:

CARTRIDGE:
0.357 Magnum, or 0.44 Magnum, or 0.50 Action Express

DIMENSIONS (0.357 MAGNUM):
LENGTH O/A: 260 mm (10.3 in) with 152 mm barrel
WEIGHT: 1.7 kg (3 lb 12 oz) with steel frame; 1.4 kg (3 lb 4 oz) with alloy frame
BARREL: 152 mm (6 in); also available with 203, 254, and 350 mm (6, 10, and 14 in) barrels
RIFLING: 6 grooves, rh
MAGAZINE CAPACITY: 9 rounds

IN PRODUCTION:
1983–

MARKINGS:
"DESERT EAGLE .357 MAGNUM PISTOL. ISRAEL MILITARY INDUSTRIES." on left side of slide.

SAFETY:
Ambidextrous manual safety catch on slide locks firing pin and disconnects hammer from trigger.

UNLOADING:
Magazine catch on butt, behind trigger. Remove magazine. Pull back slide, exposing chamber. Inspect chamber. Release slide. Pull trigger.

Jericho 941

This originally appeared as a "convertible" pistol in 9 mm with a spare barrel, recoil spring, and magazine for 0.41 Action Express cartridges. (The 0.41AE had the same rim dimensions as the 9 mm.) However, it failed to gain much of a following, and later models dropped the "941" appellation. Subsequently, the pistol was offered in 0.40 S&W caliber, which had become popular with US law-enforcement agencies. There are variant models: the F model has the safety on the frame, while the R model has it on the slide and uses it as a decocking lever. The Jericho FL model differs in having a polymer frame, to which combat accessories may be attached.

SPECIFICATION:

CARTRIDGE:
9 x 19 mm Parabellum or 0.40 S&W

DIMENSIONS:
LENGTH O/A: 207 mm (8.2 in)
WEIGHT: 1.3 kg (2 lb 13 oz)
BARREL: 112 mm (4.4 in)
RIFLING: 6 grooves, rh, polygonal
MAGAZINE CAPACITY: 13 (9 mm) or 9 rounds (0.40)

IN PRODUCTION:
1990–

MARKINGS:
"JERICHO 941/ISRAEL MILITARY INDUSTRIES" on left side of slide. "MADE IN ISRAEL" on right side of frame. Serial number on right side of frame and right side of slide; last four digits on barrel, visible through ejection opening.

SAFETY:
Manual safety catch/decocking lever at left rear of slide which locks firing pin, disconnects trigger and drops hammer when applied: down for safe. Later models may have plain safety catch on frame or a safety catch/decocking lever on slide.

UNLOADING:
Magazine catch is a button on front left side of butt, behind trigger; press in, remove magazine. Pull back slide to eject any round in breech. Inspect chamber through ejection port. Release slide. Pull trigger.

Beretta M951 ITALY

Recognizably Beretta by the cutaway slide top, the M951 was their first locked-breech military pistol. It was also adopted by the Egyptian and Israeli armies, the Nigerian police forces, and others. It was also marketed commercially as the "Brigadier," shown in the Egyptian produced "Helwan" model.

SPECIFICATION:

CARTRIDGE:
9 x 19 mm Parabellum

DIMENSIONS:
LENGTH O/A: 203 mm (8 in)
WEIGHT: 870 g (1 lb 14 oz)
BARREL: 114 mm (4.5 in)
RIFLING: 6 grooves, rh
MAGAZINE CAPACITY: 8 rounds

IN PRODUCTION:
1953–90

MARKINGS:
"P BERETTA - CAL 9 m/m MOD 1951 - PATENT GARDONE VT ITALIA" (Italian service models); "HELWAN CAL 9 m/m A.R.E." (Egyptian versions). Serial number on right side of slide.

SAFETY:
Safety device is a push-through button at top of grip: push to left for safe, right to fire.

UNLOADING:
Magazine catch is a button at lower left of grip; push in and remove magazine. Pull back slide to eject round in chamber. Examine breech. Release slide. Pull trigger.

Beretta Model 84 ITALY

The Model 84 represents Beretta's unlocked-breech blowback design in modern form and is accompanied by several variant models. The Model 81 is the same pistol but in 7.65 mm ACP caliber; both are double-action pistols and use double-row magazines with a slot in the rear face that allows the contents to be checked. The Models 81BB, 82BB, 83F, 84BB, 84F, 85F, 87BB, and 87BB/LB are all variants. The BB models have a smaller magazine, a single-column type allowing a thinner butt, a loaded chamber indicator, and improved safety with an automatic firing pin safety system. F models have all the BB features but also have a decocking mechanism that allows the hammer to be dropped safely on a loaded chamber. The 87BB/LB has a long barrel (150 mm). The Model 84 is also made by FN Herstal as the Browning BDA380.

SPECIFICATION:

CARTRIDGE:
9 mm Short (0.380 Auto)

DIMENSIONS:
LENGTH O/A: 172 mm (6.8 in)
WEIGHT: 660 g (1 lb 7 oz)
BARREL: 97 mm (3.8 in)
RIFLING: 6 grooves, rh
MAGAZINE CAPACITY: 13 rounds

IN PRODUCTION:
1976–95

MARKINGS:
"PIETRO BERETTA GARDONE V.T." on left side of slide. "MODEL 84 9m/m" on right side of slide. Serial number on left front of frame.

SAFETY:
Manual safety catch at left rear of frame: up for safe.

UNLOADING:
Magazine catch at left side of butt behind trigger. Remove magazine. Pull back slide to eject any round in chamber. Inspect chamber through ejection port. Release slide. Pull trigger.

Beretta Model 92 ITALY

The Beretta 92, adopted by the US Army as the M9, is offered in many different versions, each denoted by a suffix. The 92S has a decocking lever; the B has an ambidextrous decocking lever; the C is a compact version 197 mm long; the F has the trigger guard modified for two-handed grip; the G has no manual safety, just a decocker on the slide. The 92D is double action only: the hammer cannot be single-action cocked, and after each shot the hammer follows the slide back and falls to a safe position. The DS is similar, but without manual safety. The 92M is stainless steel, with a thinner butt and smaller magazine capacity. The Beretta 96 series is a 0.40 S&W version of the same family and uses the same suffixes.

SPECIFICATION:

CARTRIDGE:
9 x 19 mm Parabellum

DIMENSIONS:
LENGTH O/A: 217 mm (8.5 in)
WEIGHT: 850 g (1 lb 14 oz)
BARREL: 125 mm (4.9 in)
RIFLING: 6 grooves, rh
MAGAZINE CAPACITY: 15 rounds

IN PRODUCTION:
1976–

MARKINGS:
"Pist Mod 92 Cal 9 Para BERETTA" on left side of slide. Serial number on left front of frame.

SAFETY:
Manual or other safety depends on model.

UNLOADING:
Magazine catch at left side of butt behind trigger. Remove magazine. Pull back slide to eject any round in chamber. Inspect chamber through ejection port. Release slide. Pull trigger.

Beretta Model 93R ITALY

This is a selective-fire pistol with a selector switch allowing automatic fire at about 1100 rounds per minute in three-round bursts for each pull of the trigger. There is a fold-down grip in front of the trigger guard, and an extendible steel shoulder stock that can be attached to the rear of the butt. The basic design is that of the Model 92 but with an extended barrel with a compensator to reduce muzzle climb when firing bursts. The alternative 20-round magazine extends some distance below the bottom of the butt when fitted.

SPECIFICATION:

CARTRIDGE:
9 x 19 mm Parabellum

DIMENSIONS:
LENGTH O/A: 240 mm (9.5 in)
WEIGHT: 1.1 kg (2 lb 7 oz)
BARREL: 156 mm (6.1 in) incl. muzzle brake
RIFLING: 6 grooves, rh
MAGAZINE CAPACITY: 15 or 20 rounds

IN PRODUCTION:
1986–

MARKINGS:
"PIETRO BERETTA GARDONE V.T. Cal 9 Parabellum" on left side of slide. Serial number on right side of frame.

SAFETY:
Manual safety catch behind trigger. Fire selector lever above left grip: one white dot = single shots, three white dots = three-round burst fire.

UNLOADING:
Magazine catch at heel of butt. Remove magazine. Pull back slide to eject any round in chamber. Inspect chamber through ejection port. Release slide. Pull trigger.

Beretta Model 1934 ITALY

Probably the most common of the small Berettas, having been widely issued to the Italian armed forces during World War II. Similar to the Model 1931 and best identified by its open-top slide and marking. The year mark in Roman figures indicates the year of the Fascist regime.

SPECIFICATION:

CARTRIDGE:
9 mm Short or 0.380 Auto

DIMENSIONS:
LENGTH O/A: 150 mm (5.9 in)
WEIGHT: 750 g (1 lb 10 oz)
BARREL: 88 mm (3.5 in)
RIFLING: 6 grooves, rh
MAGAZINE CAPACITY: 7 rounds

IN PRODUCTION:
1934–50

MARKINGS:
"P BERETTA CAL 9 CORTO Mo 1934 BREVETTATO GARDONE V.T. 1937 - XVI [or other year]" on left side of slide. Serial number on right side of slide and frame. "PB" monogram on bottom of butt plates.

SAFETY:
Manual safety catch on left side above trigger: forward for safe, rearward to fire.

UNLOADING:
Magazine catch at heel of butt. Remove magazine. Pull back slide to eject any round in the chamber. Inspect chamber through ejection port. Release slide. Pull trigger.

Beretta Px4 Storm ITALY

The Px4 Storm is a self-loading pistol developed to meet the needs of a changing law-enforcement environment. The fully enclosed barrel breaks the Beretta tradition of open-topped slides. The frame is constructed of polymer with a short length of Picatinny rail at the front end for mounting a tactical light or aiming device. Interchangeable backstraps are provided to suit different hand sizes. Three model types are offered: the FS, in single action (SA) and double action (DA) with decocking lever and manual safety; the G, in SA and DA with decocking lever and no manual safety, and the D in double action only (DAO) with spurless hammer. Extended-capacity magazines are available: 20 rounds (9 mm) and 17 rounds (0.40 S&W).

SPECIFICATION:

CARTRIDGE:
9 x 19 mm or 0.40 S&W

DIMENSIONS:
LENGTH O/A: 193 mm (7.6 in)
WEIGHT: 780 g (1 lb 11 oz)
BARREL: 102 mm (4 in)
MAGAZINE CAPACITY: 17 (9 mm) or 14 rounds (0.40 S&W)

IN PRODUCTION:
2003–

MARKINGS:
"Px4 Storm" on right side of slide and pistol grip.

SAFETY:
Varies with model type. Ambidextrous manually applied safety at rear of slide: up for on.

UNLOADING:
Magazine catch on right behind trigger guard. Remove magazine. Pull slide to rear. Check chamber is clear; allow slide to go forward. Point weapon in safe direction and press either decocking lever or trigger.

Bernardelli P-018 ITALY

A conventional double-action self-loading pistol. There is also a compact version 109 mm long with a 102 mm barrel and a 14-shot magazine. Although specifically designed for police and military use, it appears to have had more success on the commercial market.

SPECIFICATION:

CARTRIDGE:
9 x 19 mm Parabellum

DIMENSIONS:
LENGTH O/A: 213 mm (8.4 in)
WEIGHT: 998 g (2 lb 3 oz)
BARREL: 122 mm (4.8 in)
RIFLING: 6 grooves, rh
MAGAZINE CAPACITY: 15 rounds

IN PRODUCTION:
1986–

MARKINGS:
"VINCENZO BERNARDELLI SpA Gardone V.T. Made in Italy" on left side of slide. "Mod P-018 9 Para" on left side of frame. Serial number on right side of frame and on barrel, visible in ejection opening.

SAFETY:
Manual safety catch at left rear of frame: up for safe.

UNLOADING:
Magazine catch at heel of butt. Remove magazine. Pull back slide to eject any round in chamber. Inspect chamber through ejection port. Release slide. Pull trigger.

Tanfoglio TA90 ITALY

This began more or less as a license-built CZ75, but improvements have been made and variations introduced, and it is now an independent and original design. The standard model came first; the combat model differs only in its safety arrangements, which allow it to be carried "cocked and locked." There are also Baby Standard and Baby Combat models, which are some 25 mm shorter and use 9-round magazines. In addition to 9 x 19 mm Parabellum, these pistols are available in 9 mm IMI, 0.40 S&W, 0.41AE, 10 mm Auto, and 0.45 ACP chamberings.

SPECIFICATION:

CARTRIDGE:
9 x 19 mm Parabellum

DIMENSIONS:
LENGTH O/A: 202 mm (8 in)
WEIGHT: 1 kg (2 lb 4 oz)
BARREL: 120 mm (4.7 in)
RIFLING: 6 grooves, rh
MAGAZINE CAPACITY: 15 rounds

IN PRODUCTION:
1983–

MARKINGS:
"Fratelli Tanfoglio SpA Gardone V.T. Italy Mod TA-90 Cal 9 mm Parabellum" on left side of slide.

SAFETY:
Standard models have a manual safety catch on left side of slide that locks firing pin and drops hammer. Combat models have a manual safety catch on left side of frame above butt that simply locks trigger; there is also an automatic firing-pin safety that holds the firing pin locked until trigger is correctly pulled through.

UNLOADING:
Magazine catch at left side of butt behind trigger. Remove magazine. Pull back slide to eject any round in chamber. Inspect chamber through ejection port. Release slide. Pull trigger.

Poland P-64 POLAND

Yet another Walther PP derivative, with elements of the Makarov thrown in, notably the simplified double-action firing mechanism. Like the Makarov, the double-action trigger pull is not very smooth or crisp, but in this type of pistol it is not critical.

SPECIFICATION:

CARTRIDGE:
9 x 18 mm Makarov

DIMENSIONS:
LENGTH O/A: 155 mm (6.1 in)
WEIGHT: 635 g (1 lb 5 oz)
BARREL: 84 mm (3.3 in)
RIFLING: 4 grooves, rh
MAGAZINE CAPACITY: 6 rounds

IN PRODUCTION:
1964–84

MARKINGS:
"9 mm P-64" on left side of slide. Serial number on right side of frame.

SAFETY:
Manual safety catch/decocking lever on left rear of slide: press down for safe. Firing pin is blocked, trigger disconnected, and hammer is allowed to fall safely.

UNLOADING:
Magazine release on heel of butt. Remove magazine. Pull back slide to eject any round in chamber. Inspect chamber through ejection port. Release slide. Pull trigger.

Radom POLAND

An excellent combat pistol, made for the Polish Army pre-1939; during the German occupation, it was made for German use, but the quality gradually deteriorated. During the 1990s, the Radom was placed back into production, not as a service weapon but for sale to collectors. When compared with the original war-years production examples, these models can be recognized only by their superior finish.

SPECIFICATION:

CARTRIDGE:
9 x 19 mm Parabellum

DIMENSIONS:
LENGTH O/A: 211 mm (8.3 in)
WEIGHT: 1.1 kg (2 lb 5 oz)
BARREL: 115 mm (4.5 in)
RIFLING: 6 grooves, rh
MAGAZINE CAPACITY: 8 rounds

IN PRODUCTION:
1936–45

MARKINGS:
"F.B. RADOM [year] [Polish eagle] VIS Mo 35 Pat Nr 15567" on left side of slide (Polish models); "F.B. RADOM VIS Mod 35 Pat Nr 15567/P. 35(p)" on left side of slide (German occupation models). Serial number on right side of frame above trigger.

SAFETY:
Grip safety let into rear of butt; this must be pressed in before pistol can be fired. Catch at left rear of slide is a decocking lever; when depressed it will withdraw firing pin into safe position and allow hammer to fall safely. Weapon can then be readied by simply thumbing back hammer.

UNLOADING:
Magazine catch is a button behind trigger on left side. Remove magazine. Pull back slide to eject any round in chamber. Inspect chamber through ejection port. Release slide. Pull trigger.

Vanad P-83 POLAND

Development of the P-83 began in the late 1970s as a replacement for the P-64 pistol already in Polish service. To reduce production costs, much use was made of metal pressings, welding, and forged components. However, it retained the simple fixed-barrel blowback system of operation. The trigger is single or double action, and the external safety lever drops the cocked hammer when applied; at the same time, the rear of the firing pin is lowered and cannot strike a cartridge in the chamber. A loaded-chamber indicator is located the left rear of the slide and can be both seen and felt. A variant, the P-83G, is a conversion to blank-firing or, with a muzzle attachment, is capable of projecting gas pellets. The civilian caliber of 9 x 17 mm (9 mm Short) was also offered.

SPECIFICATION:

CARTRIDGE:
9 x 18 mm or 9 x 17 mm

DIMENSIONS:
LENGTH O/A: 165 mm (6.5 in)
WEIGHT: 730 g (1 lb 10 oz)
BARREL: 90 mm (3.5 in)
RIFLING: 4 grooves, rh
MAGAZINE CAPACITY: 8 rounds

IN PRODUCTION:
1980?–

MARKINGS:
"9mm P-83" on left side of slide. Serial number on right side of frame behind trigger.

SAFETY:
Manual safety on left side rear of slide.

UNLOADING:
Magazine catch is at rear of butt behind magazine baseplate. Remove magazine. Pull back slide to eject any round in chamber. Inspect chamber through ejection port. Release slide. Point weapon in safe direction and pull trigger.

Makarov

This is generally assumed to be based upon the Walther PP, though various other versions of its origin exist. The trigger mechanism is simpler than that of the Walther and has a trigger pull. The 9 x 18 mm Makarov cartridge was designed to obtain the maximum performance from an unlocked breech pistol; though nominally the same size as the Western 9 mm Police round, the two are not interchangeable.

In addition to continued production within Russia, Makarov (sometimes referred to as the PM) copies have been made (and are still being made) in Bulgaria and China. The latter are made by Norinco and are chambered for either the 9 x 18 mm Makarov (Type 59) or 0.380 (Type 59A). Commercially available models with the trade name Baikal are now being produced.

SPECIFICATION:

CARTRIDGE:
9 x 18 mm Makarov

DIMENSIONS:
LENGTH O/A: 161 mm (6.3 in)
WEIGHT: 730 g (1 lb 13 oz)
BARREL: 93 mm (3.7 in)
RIFLING: 4 grooves, rh
MAGAZINE CAPACITY: 8 rounds

IN PRODUCTION:
1952–

MARKINGS:
Serial number, factory identifying mark, and year of manufacture on left side of frame.

SAFETY:
Manual safety catch/decocking lever at left rear of slide. Moved up for safe, it places a block between hammer and firing pin, then releases hammer.

UNLOADING:
Magazine release at heel of butt. Remove magazine. Pull back slide to eject any round in chamber. Inspect chamber through ejection port. Release slide. Pull trigger.

This is a simple blowback-operated pistol that has been made as slim as possible and without any surface excrescences so that it can be easily concealed. It fires a bottle-necked cartridge with non-expanding bullet, which has considerable penetrative capabilities against "soft" body armors. Although originally intended strictly as a service-issue pistol for Soviet security forces, there are now several commercial models, including a personal defense model firing a rubber ball and a variant chambered for 6.35 mm (0.25 ACP) ammunition. These commercial models can be recognized by their molded pistol grips and are sold under the trade name of Baikal.

SPECIFICATION:

CARTRIDGE:
5.45 x 18 mm, 6.35 mm or .25 ACP

DIMENSIONS:
LENGTH O/A: 155 mm (6.1 in)
WEIGHT: 460 g (1 lb oz)
BARREL: 85 mm (3.4 in)
RIFLING: 6 grooves, rh
MAGAZINE CAPACITY: 8 rounds

IN PRODUCTION:
1980–

MARKINGS:
Factory identifying mark and serial number on left side of slide.

SAFETY:
Manual safety catch at left rear of slide: pull back for safe.

UNLOADING:
Magazine release in heel of butt. Remove magazine. Pull back slide to eject any round in chamber. Inspect chamber through ejection port. Release slide. Pull trigger.

The 7.62 mm PSS silent pistol (also known as the Vul) is a close-range, special-forces recoil-operated pistol with an unusual method of suppressing the firing signature. It does not have the usual muzzle-mounted suppressor but instead fires a special 7.62 x 42 mm cartridge. The flat-nosed projectile sits flush with the top of the cartridge case and, on firing, is propelled into the barrel by an internal piston that is then arrested by a recess at the mouth of the case so that all the firing flash and noise is confined within the case. Most PSS pistols examined have a basic finish, indicating a short anticipated service life, and none have been seen bearing any markings other than serial numbers on left side.

SPECIFICATION:

CARTRIDGE:
7.62 x 42 mm Special

DIMENSIONS:
LENGTH O/A: 165 mm (6.5in)
WEIGHT, UNLOADED: 700 g (1 lb 8 oz)
BARREL: ca. 60 mm (2.4 in)
RIFLING: 4 grooves, rh
MAGAZINE CAPACITY: 6 rounds

IN PRODUCTION:
1995–?

MARKINGS:
Serial number on left side.

SAFETY:
Unmarked safety catch on left side of receiver.
A partially shrouded external hammer indicates when pistol is cocked.

UNLOADING:
Push latch at base of magazine to release magazine. Pull back slide to eject any round in chamber. Inspect chamber and feedway. Release slide. Pull trigger.

SPP-1 RUSSIA

The SPP-1 is a multibarrel four-shot pistol designed for underwater use by naval combatants. It is loaded using four-round clips. Unlike conventional pistol-caliber projectiles fired from a rifled barrel, the SPP-1 fires a long dart-like projectile, which is stabilized by the flow of water along its length. This is a short-range weapon, and effective range is dependent on water depth, with a range of 17 m at 5 m depth and 6 m at 40 m depth.

SPECIFICATION:

CARTRIDGE:
4.5 x 39 mm

DIMENSIONS:
LENGTH O/A: 244 mm (9.6 in)
WEIGHT: 950 g (2 lb 1 oz)
BARREL: 178 mm (7 in)
RIFLING: Smoothbore
MAGAZINE CAPACITY: 4 x round clip

IN PRODUCTION:
circa 1970s–

MARKINGS:
"Safe" and "fire" on left side of pistol grip. Serial number on left rear side of barrel.

SAFETY:
Manual safety on left side.

UNLOADING:
Release barrel assembly. Withdraw 4 x round clip. Close action.

Stechkin RUSSIA

The Stechkin (also known as the APS) could be considered an overgrown Walther PP modified to permit selective full-automatic fire; the cyclic rate is about 850 rounds/min, though the practical rate is more like 80 rounds/min, fired in short bursts. It was issued to officers and NCOs of various Soviet units and also exported. It was claimed to be an effective submachine gun, but like all such conversions it was difficult to control and was withdrawn in the 1970s when the AKSU shortened version of the AK47 rifle appeared. Terrorists tend to regard it with some favor, and it is likely to be encountered for some time to come.

The pistol can be fitted with a suppressor (as shown) and can use either a folding wire stock or a wooden holster as a butt stock. Despite being withdrawn from Soviet/Russian service, it is still available from Russian sources and is now marketed chambered for 9 x 18 mm Makarov.

SPECIFICATION:

CARTRIDGE:
9 x 18 mm Makarov

DIMENSIONS:
LENGTH O/A: 225 mm (8.9 in)
WEIGHT: 1 kg (2 lb 4 oz)
BARREL: 140 mm (5.5 in)
RIFLING: 4 grooves, rh
MAGAZINE CAPACITY: 20 rounds

IN PRODUCTION:
1951–

MARKINGS:
Serial number and factory identifying number on left side of slide.

SAFETY:
Safety/selector lever on left side of slide; it has three positions: safe (np), semiautomatic (OA), and full automatic (ABT). When set at safe, slide cannot be retracted.

UNLOADING:
Magazine catch at heel of butt. Remove magazine. Move selector lever off safe. Pull back slide to eject any round in chamber. Inspect chamber through ejection port. Release slide. Pull trigger.

Tokarev RUSSIA

First produced in 1930, the Tokarev uses the Browning dropping-barrel locking system and is unusual in having the hammer and its spring and other components in a removable module in the upper rear of the frame. Unusually, it has no form of applied safety when cocked and loaded. Also, the magazine lips are machined into the frame, so that slight malformation of the actual magazine does not interfere with feeding. In 1933, the design was modified to have locking lugs all around the barrel, rather than simply on top, a change that sped up manufacture; this became the TT-33 model. The T-33 was not in use in large numbers during World War II, but replaced the Nagant revolver thereafter and was widely exported to fellow-Communist countries. Also made in China, Egypt, and Yugoslavia from the 1950s. Yugoslavian M57 illustrated.

SPECIFICATION:

CARTRIDGE:
7.62mm Soviet Pistol (also fires 7.63 mm Mauser)

DIMENSIONS:
LENGTH O/A: 196 mm (7.7 in)
WEIGHT: 840 g (1 lb 13 oz)
BARREL: 116 mm (4.6 in)
RIFLING: 4 grooves, rh
MAGAZINE CAPACITY: 8 rounds

IN PRODUCTION:
1930–

MARKINGS:
Serial number on frame or slide; may have a factory number but generally does not. Copies made in other countries can usually be identified by badge molded into butt grips.

SAFETY:
No manual safety; only half-cock notch on hammer.

UNLOADING:
Magazine catch at left side of butt behind trigger. Remove magazine. Pull back slide to eject any round in chamber. Inspect chamber through ejection port. Release slide. Pull trigger.

Yarygin "Grach" 6P35

The Yarygin or "Grach" (Rook) pistol manufactured by the Izhevsky Mekhanichesky Zavod was selected by the Russian Army to replace the long-serving Makarov pistol. It has a steel frame and slide with a wrap-around polymer pistol grip. When engaged, the ambidextrous manual safety lever blocks sear, hammer, and slide. The cartridge extractor also acts as a visual and tactile loaded-chamber indicator. The magazine release is reversible for left- or right-handed shooters. The Yarygin has been designed to fire the enhanced-performance 7H21 high-impulse armor-piercing cartridge. Variants include the commercially available MP-446 and MP-446P (Viking), the latter for law-enforcement use.

SPECIFICATION:

CARTRIDGE:
9 x 19 mm or 9 x 19 mm 7H21

DIMENSIONS:
LENGTH O/A: 196 mm (7.7 in)
WEIGHT: 850 g (1 lb 13 oz)
BARREL: 112.5 mm (4.1 in)
MAGAZINE CAPACITY: 17 rounds

IN PRODUCTION:
2002–

MARKINGS:
Serial number repeated on barrel (ejection port), slide, and frame. Manufacturer's logo molded into grip panels.

SAFETY:
Ambidextrous manual safety.

UNLOADING:
Magazine catch behind trigger guard. Remove magazine. Pull slide to rear. Check chamber is clear. Allow slide to go forward. Point weapon in safe direction and press trigger.

Model 70 SERBIA

The Model 70 is a scaled-down version of the M57, itself a copy of the Russian Tokarev TT-33. It has been offered as the CZ Model 10 in the past. There is no need for a locked breech in this caliber, or in 9 mm Short, for which the pistol can also be chambered, and it has been dispensed with, the pistol operating on the blowback principle. A magazine safety is fitted in addition to the manually applied safety on the frame. The pistol is well finished, from good materials, and is widely distributed throughout the Balkans.

SPECIFICATION:

CARTRIDGE:
7.65 mm Browning or 0.32 ACP

DIMENSIONS:
LENGTH O/A: 165 mm (6.5 in)
WEIGHT: 740 g (1 lb 10 oz)
BARREL: 94 mm (3.7 in)
RIFLING: 6 grooves, rh
MAGAZINE CAPACITY: 8 rounds

IN PRODUCTION:
1977–

MARKINGS:
"CRVENA ZASTAVA of ZAVOD CRVENA ZASTAVA" or "ZASTAVA ARMS. Kal [or Cal] 7.65mm Mod 10 [or Mod 70]" on left side of slide. Serial number on right side of slide.

SAFETY:
Manual safety catch on left side locks firing pin, hammer and slide. Magazine safety prevents operation of trigger when magazine is out.

UNLOADING:
Magazine catch on left side of butt behind trigger. Press in, remove magazine. Pull back slide to eject any round in chamber. Inspect chamber through magazine opening. Release slide. Empty magazine if necessary. Replace empty magazine in pistol. Press trigger.

Vektor SP

There are two pistols in this group, the SP1, chambered for the 9 x 19 mm Parabellum cartridge, and the SP2, chambered for the 0.40 S&W cartridge. Both are to the same design, which uses the same dropping-wedge breech-locking system as the Walther P38 and Beretta 92. The slide is made of steel, and the frame of alloy. An automatic firing pin safety system is used, plus a manual safety catch. The SP2 has an accessory conversion kit consisting of a barrel, return spring, and magazine, allowing it to be reconfigured in 9 x 19 mm Parabellum caliber.

Two compact versions, known as the SP1 and SP2 General Officer's Pistols, are also produced. These are 20 mm shorter in overall length, with 103 mm barrels, and weigh 850 g, but are otherwise identical to the full-sized weapons.

SPECIFICATION:

CARTRIDGE:
9 x 19 mm Parabellum or 0.40 S&W

DIMENSIONS:
LENGTH O/A: 210 mm (8.3 in)
WEIGHT: 995 g (2 lb 3 oz)
BARREL: 118 mm (4.7 in)
RIFLING: 4 grooves, polygonal, rh
MAGAZINE: 15-round detachable box (11-round in 0.40 caliber)

IN PRODUCTION:
1995–

MARKINGS:
"VEKTOR SP1 9 mm P MADE IN SOUTH AFRICA" on left side of slide. Serial number on left side of frame.

SAFETY:
Manual safety catch that locks both slide and sear, duplicated on both sides of pistol. Automatic firing-pin safety system.

UNLOADING:
Magazine catch is on butt grip behind trigger; normally on left but can be transferred to right side if required. Remove magazine. Pull back slide to eject any round in chamber. Inspect chamber to ensure it is empty. Release slide. Pull trigger.

Daewoo DP51 SOUTH KOREA

The DP51 is a self-loading pistol in 9 x 19 mm Parabellum caliber, operating on an unusual delayed-blowback system. The interior of the chamber has a number of shallow annular grooves; on firing, the cartridge brass expands, under the high chamber pressure, into these grooves and thus prevents the case from being extracted and the breech from being opened. After the bullet leaves the barrel, the pressure drops, the brass contracts to its normal dimensions, and the breech can then open. Designed for police and military use, the double-action trigger is better than most, providing a very even trigger pull.

SPECIFICATION:

CARTRIDGE:
9 x 19 mm Parabellum

DIMENSIONS:
LENGTH O/A: 190 mm (7.5 in)
WEIGHT: 800 g (1 lb 12 oz)
BARREL: 105 mm (4.1 in)
RIFLING: 6 grooves, rh
MAGAZINE CAPACITY: 13 rounds

IN PRODUCTION:
1993–

MARKINGS:
"DP51 9MM PARA DAEWOO" on left side of slide. Serial number on right side of frame.

SAFETY:
Manual safety catch at left rear of frame: up for safe.

UNLOADING:
Magazine catch at left side of butt behind trigger. Remove magazine. Pull back slide to eject any round in chamber. Inspect chamber through ejection port. Release slide. Pull trigger.

Astra 300 SPAIN

This is a smaller version of the Astra 400, introduced in 9 mm in 1922 for the Spanish Prison Service, and in 7.65 mm and 9 mm in 1923 for commercial sales. It was adopted by the Spanish Navy in 9 mm in 1928. A total of 85,390 (both calibers) were supplied to the German Army in 1939–44; these will have German property marks (WAA and Nazi eagle). Manufacture ceased in 1947, 171,300 having been made. A considerable number of Astra 300s were sold as surplus in the USA in the 1960s and 1970s.

SPECIFICATION:

CARTRIDGE:
9 mm Short or 7.65 mm ACP

DIMENSIONS:
LENGTH: 165 mm (6.5 in)
WEIGHT: 560 g (1 lb 4 oz)
BARREL: 90 mm (3.5 in)
RIFLING: 6 grooves, rh
MAGAZINE CAPACITY: 7 rounds

IN PRODUCTION:
1922–47

MARKINGS:
"UNCETA y COMPANIA." Serial number on right rear of frame and right rear of slide. Astra trademark behind front sight blade.

SAFETY:
Manual, above trigger: up for safe, down to fire. Magazine safety. Grip safety.

UNLOADING:
Magazine catch at heel of butt. Remove magazine. Pull back slide to eject any round in chamber. Inspect chamber through ejection port. Release slide. Pull trigger.

Astra 400 SPAIN

This is a Spanish service pistol manufactured between 1921 and 1950. It was sold commercially, and also used by the French Army in the 1920s. Total production was 106,175. It is based on an earlier Campo-Giro model, which it resembles in its tubular receiver and barrel. Copies of the Astra 400 were made during the Spanish Civil War and may be found marked "F. ASCASO TARASA" or simply "RE" (Republica Espana). Chambered for the 9 mm Largo cartridge, this pistol will reportedly fire a variety of cartridges of a nominal 9 mm diameter; this is not correct—it is neither safe nor desirable to do so. Pistols in 7.65 mm and 7.63 mm calibers are known but extremely rare and were probably made only as samples.

SPECIFICATION:

CARTRIDGE:
9 mm Largo (Bergmann-Bayard), or 7.65 mm ACP (rare), or 7.63 mm Mauser (rare)

DIMENSIONS:
LENGTH: 235 mm (9.3 in)
WEIGHT: 880 g (1 lb 15 oz)
BARREL: 150 mm (5.9 in)
RIFLING: 6 grooves, rh
MAGAZINE CAPACITY: 8 rounds

IN PRODUCTION:
1921–50

MARKINGS:
"UNCETA Y COMPANIA" on slide top. Astra trademark behind front sight. Serial number on right rear of frame.

SAFETY:
Manual behind trigger: up for safe; down to fire. Magazine safety. Grip safety.

UNLOADING:
Magazine catch at heel of butt. Remove magazine. Pull back slide to eject any round in chamber. Inspect chamber through ejection port. Release slide. Pull trigger.

Astra A-50 SPAIN

This is an updated version of an earlier model known as the Constable and, in spite of its appearance, is a simple single-action fixed-barrel blowback-operated pistol. It can also be found chambered for either 7.65 mm Browning or 9 mm Short cartridges.

SPECIFICATION:

CARTRIDGE:
9 mm Short (0.380 Auto)

DIMENSIONS:
LENGTH: 168 mm (6.6 in)
WEIGHT: 650 g (1 lb 7 oz)
BARREL: 89 mm (3.5 in)
RIFLING: 6 grooves, rh
MAGAZINE CAPACITY: 7 rounds

IN PRODUCTION:
1960–85

MARKING:
"ASTRA UNCETA CIA Guernica Spain Mod A-50" on left side of slide. Serial number on right side of frame.

SAFETY:
Manual safety catch at left rear of frame: up for safe.

UNLOADING:
Magazine catch at left side of butt behind trigger. Remove magazine. Pull back slide to eject any round in chamber. Inspect chamber through ejection port. Release slide. Pull trigger.

Astra A-75 SPAIN

This is more or less a double-action version of the earlier A-70, a compact and robust weapon firing a pair of potent cartridges. Primarily intended for police and military use, it had seen some success in the commercial market. In 1994, an aluminum-framed version was announced, and a version chambered in 0.45 ACP was expected to enter production during late 1995, but Astra went out of business soon after that.

SPECIFICATION:

CARTRIDGE:
9 x 19 mm Parabellum or 0.40 S&W

DIMENSIONS:
LENGTH O/A: 166 mm (6.5 in)
WEIGHT: 880 g (1 lb 15 oz)
BARREL: 89 mm (3.5 in)
RIFLING: 6 grooves, rh
MAGAZINE CAPACITY: 8 (9 mm) or 7 rounds (0.40)

IN PRODUCTION:
1993–96

MARKINGS:
"ASTRA GUERNICA SPAIN A-75" on left side of slide. Serial number on right side of frame.

SAFETY:
Manual safety catch at left rear of frame: up for safe. Half-cock notch on hammer. Automatic firing pin safety device.

UNLOADING:
Magazine catch at left side of butt behind trigger. Remove magazine. Pull back slide to eject any round in chamber. Inspect chamber through ejection port. Release slide. Pull trigger.

Astra A-100 SPAIN

With the introduction of the A-90 model, the A-80 was discontinued, but there was still a demand for a pistol without manual safety. In addition, overseas markets preferred the magazine release in the butt, behind the trigger. The A-100 attended to these requirements, improved the safety mechanisms, and introduced the 0.45 chambering. It also adopted the larger magazine of the A-90.

SPECIFICATION:

CARTRIDGE:
9 x 19 mm Parabellum or 0.45 ACP

DIMENSIONS:
LENGTH O/A: 180 mm (7.1 in)
WEIGHT: 985 g (2 lb 3 oz)
BARREL: 96.5 mm (3.8 in)
RIFLING: 6 grooves, rh
MAGAZINE CAPACITY: 15 (9 mm) or 9 rounds (0.45)

IN PRODUCTION:
1990–

MARKINGS:
"ASTRA UNCETA CIA SA GUERNICA SPAIN MOD A-100" on left side of slide. Serial number on left side of frame.

SAFETY:
No manual safety is provided. Decocking lever and automatic firing pin safety allow pistol to be carried loaded with hammer down and fired simply by pulling trigger.

UNLOADING:
Magazine catch at left side of butt behind trigger. Remove magazine. Pull back slide to eject any round in chamber. Inspect chamber through ejection port. Release slide. Pull trigger.

Star M40 Firestar SPAIN

An extremely compact pistol for this caliber, the M40 is slimmer than a comparable revolver and smaller than most automatics of this power. It is easily concealed. It also has the slide running in internal rails in the frame, which helps reliability and accuracy. It was among the first of the new-generation Star pistols to have this feature. There is also an M45 Firestar, which is the same pistol but chambered for the 0.45 ACP cartridge; the only noticeable difference lies in the slide: the M45 slide is the same width end to end, while the M40 slide has the front section rebated. However, the 0.45 model is some 5 mm longer and weighs 1025 g. Star ceased production in the late 1990s.

SPECIFICATION:

CARTRIDGE:
0.40 S&W

DIMENSIONS:
LENGTH O/A: 165 mm (6.5 in)
WEIGHT: 855 g (1 lb 14 oz)
BARREL: 86 mm (3.4 in)
RIFLING: 6 grooves, rh
MAGAZINE CAPACITY: 6 rounds

IN PRODUCTION:
1993–96

MARKINGS:
"STAR EIBAR ESPANA" on left side of slide. Serial number on right side of frame.

SAFETY:
Manual safety catch on both sides of frame above butt: up for safe. If hammer is down, applying catch locks both hammer and slide. If hammer is cocked, only hammer is locked and slide can be withdrawn to check chamber. Automatic firing pin safety. Magazine safety. Half-cock notch on hammer.

UNLOADING:
Magazine catch at left side of butt behind trigger. Remove magazine. Pull back slide to eject any round in chamber. Inspect chamber through ejection port. Release slide. Pull trigger.

Star Megastar SPAIN

This is a full-sized heavy-caliber weapon that has an unusually large magazine capacity: the 0.45 version holds 12 rounds; the 10 mm holds 14 rounds and is fractionally heavier. As with the Firestar models, the slide runs inside the frame, giving it good support and contributing to accuracy. Star ceased production in the late 1990s.

SPECIFICATION:

CARTRIDGE:
0.45 ACP or 10 mm Auto

DIMENSIONS:
LENGTH O/A: 212 mm (8.4 in)
WEIGHT: 1.4 kg (3 lb oz)
BARREL: 116 mm (4.6 in)
RIFLING: 6 grooves, rh
MAGAZINE CAPACITY: 12 (0.45) or 14 rounds (10 mm)

IN PRODUCTION:
1993–98

MARKINGS:
"STAR EIBAR ESPANA" on left side of slide. Serial number on right side of frame.

SAFETY:
Manual safety catch/decocking lever on both sides of slide at rear: up to fire, down for safe, continued downward movement will lock firing pin and release hammer. When lever is released it moves back to safe position. Magazine safety.

UNLOADING:
Magazine catch at left side of butt behind trigger. Remove magazine. Pull back slide to eject any round in chamber. Inspect chamber through ejection port. Release slide. Pull trigger.

SIG P 210 SWITZERLAND

One of the world's finest pistols, the P 210 was developed during World War II by SIG and was adopted by the Swiss Army in 1949 and by the Danish Army shortly afterward. Though widely sold, particularly in target versions, military adoption has fallen off due to the high price. The slide runs in rails inside the frame; the P 210 was one of the first production pistols to use this system, which contributes to its renowned accuracy and reliability. There are several variations: the P 210 has a polished finish and wooden grips; the P 210-2 has a sand-blasted finish and plastic grips; the P 210-4 was a special model for the West German Border Police; and the P 210-5 and -6 are target models, the -5 having an extended barrel. Production of the final model ceased in late 2006.

SPECIFICATION:

CARTRIDGE:
9 x 19 mm Parabellum

DIMENSIONS:
LENGTH O/A: 215 mm (8.5 in)
WEIGHT: 900 g (1 lb 15 oz)
BARREL: 120 mm (4.7 in)
RIFLING: 6 grooves, rh
MAGAZINE CAPACITY: 8 rounds

IN PRODUCTION:
1949–2006

MARKINGS:
SIG badge, model number and serial number on right side of slide.

SAFETY:
Manual safety catch on left side behind trigger: up for safe.

UNLOADING:
Magazine release at heel of butt. Remove magazine. Pull back slide to eject any round in chamber. Inspect chamber through ejection port. Release slide. Pull trigger.

SIG P 220 <small>SWITZERLAND</small>

Sales of the SIG P 210 suffered because of its high price, so the company set about simplifying the design and manufacturing in order to lower the price, resulting in the P 220. Even so, the quality is still outstanding. This, and subsequent models, are properly known as "SIG-Sauer" pistols, because SIG collaborated with J. P. Sauer of Germany so that sales restrictions imposed by Swiss law could be avoided.

To assist export sales, versions of the P 220 were also made in 0.45 ACP, 7.65 mm Parabellum, and 0.38 Super Auto, though examples chambered for the latter two cartridges are rarely encountered. To assist sales of the entire SIG range in the USA, SIG established SIGARMS Inc. Pistols sold this way are marked accordingly.

SPECIFICATION:

CARTRIDGE:
9 x 19 mm Parabellum

DIMENSIONS:
LENGTH O/A: 198 mm (7.8 in)
WEIGHT: 750 g (1 lb 10 oz)
BARREL: 112 mm (4.4 in)
RIFLING: 6 grooves, rh
MAGAZINE CAPACITY: 9 rounds

IN PRODUCTION:
1975–2002

MARKINGS:
"SIG SAUER" on left forward area of slide. Model number and serial number on right side of slide. Serial number on right side of frame.

SAFETY:
Decocking lever on left side of butt, with thumb-piece just behind trigger: pressing down will drop hammer into safety notch. Automatic firing pin safety locks pin at all times except during last movement of trigger when firing. Note: Catch above left grip is a slide lock, used when dismantling pistol, and is not a safety device.

UNLOADING:
Magazine release at heel of butt. Remove magazine. Pull back slide to eject any round in chamber. Inspect chamber through ejection port. Release slide. Pull trigger.

SIG P 225

This model, which is more or less a compact version of the P 220, was developed in response to a German police demand in the mid-1970s for a 9 mm pistol that could be safely carried but brought into action without the need to set or operate any safety devices. It relies on the same automatic firing pin safety and decocking lever as do the other SIG models, which was sufficient to meet the German requirement, and it was adopted by a number of Swiss and German police forces.

SPECIFICATION:

CARTRIDGE:
9 x 19 mm Parabellum

DIMENSIONS:
LENGTH O/A: 180 mm (7.1 in)
WEIGHT: 740 g (1 lb 10 oz)
BARREL: 98 mm (3.9 in)
RIFLING: 6 grooves, rh
MAGAZINE CAPACITY: 8 rounds

IN PRODUCTION:
1978–2002

MARKINGS:
"SIG SAUER" on left forward area of slide. Model number and serial number on right side of slide. Serial number on right side of frame.

SAFETY:
Decocking lever on left side of butt, with thumb-piece just behind trigger: pressing down will drop hammer into safety notch. Automatic firing pin safety locks pin at all times except during last movement of trigger when firing. Note: Catch above left grip is a slide lock, used when dismantling pistol, and is not a safety device.

UNLOADING:
Magazine catch at left side of butt behind trigger. Remove magazine. Pull back slide to eject any round in chamber. Inspect chamber through ejection port. Release slide. Pull trigger.

SIG P 226 SWITZERLAND

The P 226 was developed in late 1980 as an entrant for the US Army's pistol contest and came within an ace of winning it, being beaten, reportedly, solely on price. In effect, it was the P 220 with an enlarged magazine and an ambidextrous magazine release in the forward edge of the butt behind the trigger, instead of at the base of the butt. About 80% of the parts are from the P 220 and P 225 pistols. Although turned down by the US Army, several US federal agencies have purchased this pistol, and it has been sold widely in the commercial market, almost half a million having been made by 1995.

SPECIFICATION:

CARTRIDGE:
9 x 19 mm Parabellum

DIMENSIONS:
LENGTH O/A: 196 mm (7.7 in)
WEIGHT: 750 g (1 lb 10 oz)
BARREL: 112 mm (4.4 in)
RIFLING: 6 grooves, rh
MAGAZINE CAPACITY: 15 rounds

IN PRODUCTION:
1981–2002

MARKINGS:
"SIG SAUER" on left forward area of slide. Model number and serial number on right side of slide. Serial number on right side of frame.

SAFETY:
Decocking lever on left side of butt, with thumb-piece just behind trigger: pressing down will drop hammer into safety notch. Automatic firing pin safety locks pin at all times except during last movement of trigger when firing. Note: Catch above left grip is a slide lock, used when dismantling pistol, and is not a safety device.

UNLOADING:
Magazine catch at left side of butt behind trigger. Remove magazine. Pull back slide to eject any round in chamber. Inspect chamber through ejection port. Release slide. Pull trigger.

SIG P 230

The P 230 is the smallest of the SIG family, a blowback-operated pocket or small holster pistol widely used by police and security forces. It was originally produced in 7.65 mm Browning caliber, but the 9 mm Short version proved more popular, and production of the smaller-caliber mode ceased in the 1980s. The pistol is double action, with a decocking lever on the left grip, and is fitted with the usual SIG automatic firing pin safety system. Production of the 9 mm model ended in 1996.

SPECIFICATION:

CARTRIDGE:
9 x 17 mm Short (0.380 Auto)

DIMENSIONS:
LENGTH O/A: 168 mm (6.6 in)
WEIGHT: 460 g (1 lb)
BARREL: 92 mm (3.6 in)
RIFLING: 6 grooves, rh
MAGAZINE CAPACITY: 7-round detachable box

IN PRODUCTION:
1972–2002

MARKINGS:
"MADE IN W. GERMANY [or GERMANY] P230" and serial number on right side of slide. Late production merely has P230 and serial number. "SIG-SAUER 9 mm KURZ" on left side of slide.

SAFETY:
No manual safety catch. Decocking lever on left side of frame allows cocked hammer to be lowered safely. Automatic firing pin safety system only allows firing pin to move during last movement of trigger when firing.

UNLOADING:
Magazine release at heel of butt. Remove magazine. Pull back slide to eject any round in chamber. Inspect chamber through ejection port. Release slide. Pull the trigger or depress decocking lever.

SIG P 232 SWITZERLAND

This design was introduced in 1997 as the replacement for the P 230 and is really little more than a redesign of the 230 to take advantage of modern manufacturing techniques. The general shape is the same, with very slight changes in the slide contours. Variant models include one with a stainless-steel slide, one with a black slide and a blued-steel frame, and one that is self-cocking (double action only). The 7.65 mm caliber has also been reintroduced.

SPECIFICATION:

CARTRIDGE:
7.65 mm Browning or 9 x 17 mm Short

DIMENSIONS:
LENGTH O/A: 168 mm (6.6 in)
WEIGHT: 500 g (1 lb 2 oz)
BARREL: 92 mm (3.6 in),
RIFLING: 6 grooves, rh
MAGAZINE CAPACITY: 7 rounds (8 rounds in 7.65 mm caliber)

IN PRODUCTION:
1997-2002

MARKINGS:
"SIG-SAUER MADE IN GERMANY P232" on left side of slide. Serial number on right side of slide and right side of frame.

SAFETY:
No manual safety catch. Decocking lever on left side of frame allows cocked hammer to be lowered safely. Automatic firing pin safety system only allows firing pin to move during last movement of trigger when firing.

UNLOADING:
Magazine release at heel of butt. Remove magazine. Pull back slide to eject any round in chamber. Inspect chamber through ejection port. Release slide. Pull trigger or depress decocking lever.

SIG Sauer P 228

The P 228 appeared in 1988 and was intended to round off the SIG line with a compact pistol with a large magazine capacity. Most parts are from the P 225 and P 226, and it uses the same automatic firing pin safety and decocking double-action system. The magazine catch can be mounted on either side of the frame as the user wishes.

Optional extras for the P 228 (and other SIG pistols) include an ergonomically molded grip and a laser target indicator or tactical light assembly. The P 228 was selected by the US Army and designated the M11. It was issued to military police units.

SPECIFICATION:

CARTRIDGE:
9 x 19 mm Parabellum

DIMENSIONS:
LENGTH O/A: 180 mm (7.1 in)
WEIGHT: 830 g (1 lb 13 oz)
BARREL: 98 mm (3.9 in)
RIFLING: 6 grooves, rh
MAGAZINE CAPACITY: 13 rounds

IN PRODUCTION:
1988–?

MARKINGS:
"SIG-SAUER" on left forward part of slide. "P228 MADE IN GERMANY [or W. GERMANY]" on right side of slide with serial number. Serial number on right side of frame. "CAL 9 PARA" on barrel, visible in ejection port.

SAFETY:
Decocking lever on left side of butt, with thumb-piece just behind trigger: pressing down will drop hammer into safety notch. Automatic firing pin safety locks firing pin at all times except during final movement of trigger when firing. Note: Catch above left grip is a slide lock, used when dismantling pistol, and is not a safety device.

UNLOADING:
Magazine catch at left side of butt behind trigger. Remove magazine. Pull back slide to eject any round in chamber. Inspect the chamber through ejection port. Release slide. Pull trigger or depress decocking lever.

SIG Sauer P 229 SWITZERLAND

The P 229 is, except for slight changes in the contours of the slide, the P 228 chambered for the 0.40 S&W cartridge. The standard model uses a steel slide and alloy frame; a variant is the P 229SL with stainless-steel slide. The principal visible change is in the upper surface of the slide, which is distinctly rounded rather than the usual SIG angular appearance. The frame and controls are exactly as for other SIG pistols, so that familiarity with any one of them ensures easy operation of the remainder. It may be found with alloy frame and carbon steel slide, or alloy frame and stainless steel slide. The latter version is also produced in 9 x 19 mm Parabellum chambering.

The P 229 may also be encountered chambered for the 0.357 SIG cartridge. There is also a P 239 that is exactly the same as the P 229 but in a lighter, compact form with a reduced-capacity magazine.

SPECIFICATION:

CARTRIDGE:
0.40 S&W, or 9 x 19 mm Parabellum, or 0.357 SIG

DIMENSIONS:
LENGTH O/A: 180 mm (7.1 in)
WEIGHT: 870 g (1 lb 10 oz)
BARREL: 98 mm (3.9 in)
RIFLING: 6 grooves, rh
MAGAZINE CAPACITY: 12 rounds

IN PRODUCTION:
1991–2002

MARKINGS:
"SIG-SAUER MADE IN GERMANY" or "W.GERMANY" on early production on left side of slide. Model number on right side of slide and molded into left grip plate. Serial number on right side of slide and right side of frame.

SAFETY:
Decocking lever on left side of butt, with thumb-piece just behind trigger: pressing down will drop hammer into safety notch. Automatic firing pin safety locks firing pin at all times except during final movement of trigger when firing. Note: Catch above left grip is a slide lock, used when dismantling pistol, and is not a safety device.

UNLOADING:
Magazine release normally on left side of butt, behind trigger, but can be moved to right. Remove magazine. Pull back slide to eject any round in chamber. Inspect chamber through ejection port. Release slide. Pull trigger or depress decocking lever.

SIG Sauer P 239 SWITZERLAND

The SIG Sauer P 239 family contains three pistols of varying calibers: 9 x 19 mm Parabellum, 0.40 S&W, and 0.357 SIG—all intended primarily for the US market. Apart from the calibers they are essentially the same as the P 229 pistol with the addition of a decocking lever on the left side of the receiver, just behind the trigger. This lever allows the hammer to be locked in the forward position when a round is chambered. Just pulling the trigger is then sufficient to fire the pistol. In addition to this feature, the P 239 is slimmer than the P 229.

Reportedly, the P 239 was also intended for use by persons with small hands who found a single-stack magazine housing more comfortable.

SPECIFICATION:

CARTRIDGE:
9 x 19 mm Parabellum, or 0.40 S&W, or 0.357 SIG

DIMENSIONS:
LENGTH O/A: 172 mm (6.8 in)
WEIGHT, UNLOADED: 9 mm, 780 g (1 lb 11 oz); 0.40 and 0.357, 820 g (1 lb 12 oz)
BARREL: 92 mm (3.6 in)
RIFLING: 6 groove, rh
MAGAZINE CAPACITY: 8 (9 mm) or 7 rounds (0.40/0.357)

IN PRODUCTION:
Circa 1995–2002

MARKINGS:
Model number molded into both sides of pistol grip. "SIG SAUER P239" and "SIGARMS INC EXETER-NH-USA INC" on left side of slide. Serial numbers on right side of slide and receiver caliber engravings on barrel visible through ejection slot.

SAFETY:
Usual safety at rear top of pistol grip. Thumb-actuated decocking lever above left side of grip: pressing down drops hammer into safety notch. Automatic firing-pin safety locks firing pin at all times except during final movement of trigger when firing.

UNLOADING:
Magazine release may be on either left or right of butt, just behind trigger. Remove magazine. Pull back slide to eject any round in chamber. Release slide. Pull trigger.

Sphinx AT2000/3000 SWITZERLAND

This pistol originally appeared in the 1980s as the ITM AT 84; the ITM company was later absorbed by Sphinx Engineering, and the pistol was renamed. Originally it was little more than a copy of the CZ75 but the Swiss makers made a number of design changes and patented improvements, including an automatic firing pin safety system and a magazine dimensioned to accept different calibers of ammunition, so that caliber conversion was quickly achieved by changing the barrel and/or slide. Various trigger options and finishes are available, as well as a competition model. The AT2000 series was followed by the Series 3000, with further improvements to handling and accuracy.

SPECIFICATION:

CARTRIDGE:
9 x 19 mm, or 9 x 21 mm, or 0.40 S&W

DIMENSIONS:
LENGTH O/A: 204 mm (8 in)
WEIGHT: 1 kg (2 lb 4 oz)
BARREL: 115 mm (4.5 in)
RIFLING: 6 grooves, rh
MAGAZINE CAPACITY: 15 rounds

IN PRODUCTION:
1985–

MARKINGS:
"+SOLOTHURN+ AT 2000" on left side of slide.
"SPHINX MADE IN SWITZERLAND" and serial number on left side of frame.

SAFETY:
Manual safety catch on left side of frame can be applied when hammer is cocked or uncocked. Ambidextrous safety was fitted after 1990. Automatic firing-pin safety locks firing pin except during final movement of trigger when firing.

UNLOADING:
Magazine release catch on left side behind trigger guard. Remove magazine. Pull slide to rear to eject round in chamber. Inspect chamber through ejection port. Release slide. Point weapon in safe direction and pull trigger.

Kirrikale TURKEY

This is a Turkish-made copy of the Walther PP and is almost identical to the German product. Kirrikale Tufek became Makina ve Kimya Endustrisi in 1952, and the final two years production carried the MKE badge. It is frequently found with the American dealer's name, "FIREARMS CENTER INC VICTORIA, TEXAS," marked on the left side of the slide.

SPECIFICATION:

CARTRIDGE:
7.65 mm Browning or 9 mm Short

DIMENSIONS:
LENGTH O/A: 168 mm (6.6 in)
WEIGHT: 700 g (1 lb 8 oz)
BARREL: 95 mm (3.7 in)
RIFLING: 6 grooves, rh
MAGAZINE CAPACITY: 7 rounds

IN PRODUCTION:
1948–54

MARKINGS:
"Kirrikale Tufek FB Cap 7,65 [9]mm" on left side of slide. Serial number and year of manufacture on right side of slide. Late models marked "MKE MADE IN TURKEY" on left side of slide.

SAFETY:
Safety catch/decocking lever on left rear of slide: press down to make safe and drop hammer.

UNLOADING:
Magazine catch at heel of butt. Remove magazine. Pull back slide to eject any round in chamber. Release slide. Pull trigger.

Welrod Mark 1 UK

The Welrod was a very efficient silent pistol developed by the British Special Operations Executive at their workshops in Welwyn Garden City in 1942 and subsequently manufactured by BSA Ltd. It was a single-shot weapon, with a magazine in the butt. To operate it, the knurled cap at the rear end of the receiver was turned and drawn back, opening the bolt, and then pushed forward to load a cartridge and cock the striker, after which it was turned to lock. Grasping the pistol depressed the grip safety at the rear of the butt, and pulling the trigger fired the cartridge. An integral silencer in the forward part of the gun body ensured that the sounds of both propellant and bullet were effectively muffled.

Shown is the 9 mm Mark 1 Welrod, identifiable by the foresight located midway down the barrel. Both calibers carried the designation Mark 1; the most common 7.65 mm version was the Mark 2 without the trigger guard and magazine release at the back of the butt.

SPECIFICATION:

CARTRIDGE:
7.65 mm Browning or 0.32 ACP or 9 x 19 mm Parabellum

DIMENSIONS:
LENGTH O/A: 312 mm (12.3 in)
WEIGHT: 1.1 kg (2 lb 6 oz)
BARREL: 111 mm (4.4 in)
RIFLING: 6 grooves, rh
MAGAZINE CAPACITY: Single shot—up to 7 rounds stored in butt for hand loading

IN PRODUCTION:
1942–45

MARKINGS:
Serial number on front face of silencer and underneath rear end of receiver. No other identifying marks.

SAFETY:
Grip safety at top rear of butt must be pressed in to permit trigger movement.

UNLOADING:
Magazine catch is horizontal lever beneath trigger. Press down and entire butt (containing magazine) will come away from receiver. Grasp silencer portion, rotate rear cap anticlockwise until it unlocks. Pull sharply back to extract and eject any round in chamber. Inspect chamber and feedway via ejection port. Close bolt, rotate end cap to lock, press grip safety forward and press back trigger to release striker. Empty magazine if necessary. Replace butt unit on gun.

Fort 14 TP UKRAINE

With the collapse of the former Soviet Union, the Ukraine developed its own arms industry, and the Fort 14 TP self-loading pistol has replaced the Makarov. It is of all-steel construction with the blow-back system of operation. It can be fired either single or double action; the manually applied safety locks the hammer in either mode. Accessories include the Fort-4 sound suppressor and LT-6 tactical light. The Fort 12 is the compact version. Since its introduction, it has been offered in 9 mm (blank/gas) caliber for personal protection.

SPECIFICATION:

CARTRIDGE:
9 x 18 mm

DIMENSIONS:
LENGTH O/A: 222 mm (8.7 in)
WEIGHT: 890 g (2 lb 3 oz)
BARREL: 135 mm (5.3 in)
RIFLING: 6 grooves, rh
MAGAZINE CAPACITY: 14 rounds

IN PRODUCTION:
2005–

MARKINGS:
"Fort 14 TP 9 x 18 mm Made in Ukraine" (in Ukrainian) on left side of slide. Serial number on right side of frame.

SAFETY:
Manual safety on left side rear of slide.

UNLOADING:
Magazine catch at left side of butt behind trigger. Remove magazine. Pull back slide to eject any round in chamber. Inspect chamber through ejection port; release slide. Point weapon in safe direction and pull trigger.

AMT Hardballer USA

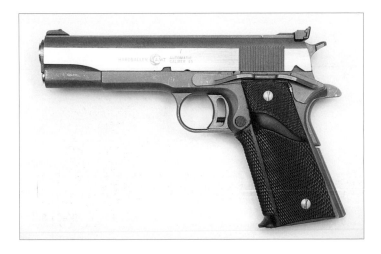

This is a faithful stainless steel copy of the full-sized Colt Government 1911A1 pistol with a magazine capacity of seven rounds of 0.45 ACP. Also available in a Longslide version with a 178 mm barrel and a weight of 1303 g. This pistol has an extended slide-release cover and safety catch to facilitate one-handed operation.

SPECIFICATION:

CARTRIDGE:
0.45 ACP

DIMENSIONS:
LENGTH: 216 mm (8.5 in)
WEIGHT: 1076 g (2 lb 6 oz)
BARREL: 127 mm (5 in)
RIFLING: 6 grooves, rh
MAGAZINE CAPACITY: 7 rounds

IN PRODUCTION:
1977–

MARKINGS:
"HARDBALLER, AMT" with circled "AUTOMATIC CALIBER .45" on left side of slide. "STAINLESS - MADE IN USA" on right side of slide. "AMT" and serial number on right side of frame.

SAFETY:
Manual safety catch lever on top left of frame at rear: up for safe, down to fire. Grip safety incorporated into rear of frame blocks trigger movement unless is gripped correctly.

UNLOADING:
Magazine catch at left side of butt behind trigger; press in to release magazine. Remove magazine. Pull back slide to eject any round in the chamber. Inspect chamber through ejection port. Release slide. Pull trigger.

Colt Double Eagle USA

This is based on the Government Model M1911A1 but has the added feature of double-action firing. The shape is more streamlined and the trigger guard is reverse-curved for two-handed firing. Variations include the Combat Commander which is more compact (114 mm barrel) and also available in 0.40 S&W caliber, and an Officer's Model with an 89 mm barrel available only in 0.45 caliber.

SPECIFICATION:

CARTRIDGE:
10 mm Auto or 0.45 ACP

DIMENSIONS:
LENGTH O/A: 216 mm (8.5 in)
WEIGHT: 1.1 kg (2 lb 6 oz)
BARREL: 127 mm (5 in)
RIFLING: 6 grooves, lh
MAGAZINE CAPACITY: 8 rounds

IN PRODUCTION:
1990–95

MARKINGS:
"COLT DOUBLE EAGLE/MK II SERIES 90" on left side of slide. Serial number on right side of frame.

SAFETY:
Decocking lever behind left grip: press down to secure safety pin and drop hammer. Pull trigger to cock and fire.

UNLOADING:
Magazine catch on left side behind trigger; press in to release magazine. Remove magazine. Pull back slide to eject any round in chamber. Inspect chamber through ejection opening in slide. Release slide. Pull trigger.

Colt Government Model .380 USA

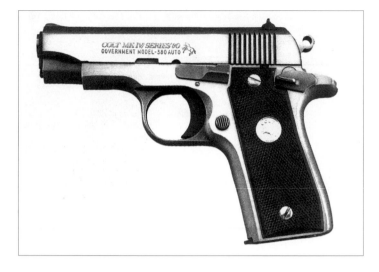

Derived from the 0.45 ACP Colt Government Model with a similar barrel-locking system, the Government .380 is built with a much smaller frame, slide, and barrel. The characteristic Model 1911A1 grip safety is not fitted. A number of variations of the Model .380 are made: the Mustang Plus II, with a shorter slide, and the 0.380 Mustang, with shorter slide and frame. In addition, aluminum-alloy-framed versions are available with the suffix "Pocketlite," the heaviest of which weighs only 418 g.

SPECIFICATION:

CARTRIDGE:
0.380 Auto (9 mmK)

DIMENSIONS:
LENGTH O/A: 152 mm (5 in)
WEIGHT: 730 g (1 lb 10 oz)
BARREL: 82.6 mm (3.3 in)
RIFLING: 6 grooves, lh
MAGAZINE CAPACITY: 7 rounds

IN PRODUCTION:
1983–

MARKINGS:
"COLT MKIV SERIES 80, GOVERNMENT MODEL .380 AUTO" on left side of slide. Serial number on left side of frame. "COLT'S PT. F .A. MFG. CO. HARTFORD, CONN, U.S.A." on right side of frame.

SAFETY:
Manual safety catch lever on top left of frame at rear: up for safe, down to fire. Firing-pin safety blocks firing-pin movement unless trigger is pulled fully rearwards.

UNLOADING:
Magazine catch at left side of butt behind trigger; press in to release magazine. Remove magazine. Pull back slide to eject any round in chamber. Inspect chamber through ejection port. Release slide.

Colt M1911/M1911A1 USA

This pistol is made commercially, carrying the Colt name and "rampant colt" badge. There are many look-alikes: the Spanish Llama and Star, Argentine Hafdasa, and Mexican Obregon can be confused with this Colt; the easiest method of distinguishing between them is to look at the markings. The Norwegian forces used a modified version, made under license, and marked "Mo 1912;" the slide release catch (on the left side of the frame above the trigger) is longer. A model marked "RAF" or "ROYAL AIR FORCE" may be found; this is chambered for the 0.455 Webley & Scott cartridge, which is NOT interchangeable with 0.45 ACP.

The M1911 and M1911A1 have been widely copied, clones being available from Norinco of China and ARMS-COR of the Philippines. Updated copies are also manufactured by the commercial Springfield Armory.

SPECIFICATION:

CARTRIDGE:
0.45 ACP

DIMENSIONS:
LENGTH O/A: 216 mm (8.5 in)
WEIGHT: 1.1 kg (2 lb 7 oz)
BARREL: 127 mm (5 in)
RIFLING: 6 grooves, lh
MAGAZINE CAPACITY: 7 rounds

IN PRODUCTION:
1911–

MARKINGS:
"MODEL OF 1911 U.S. ARMY PATENTED APRIL 29 1907 COLT'S PT FA MFG CO." "M1911A1 U.S. ARMY ITHACA GUN CO INC ITHACA N.Y." "REMINGTON RAND INC SYRACUSE N.Y. U.S.A." "M1911A1 U.S. ARMY U.S.& S.CO SWISSVALE PA USA." All models will also be marked "UNITED STATES PROPERTY." Serial number on right side of frame.

SAFETY:
Grip safety. Manual safety catch at left rear of frame: up for safe, down to fire. Hammer may be drawn to half-cock position.

UNLOADING:
Magazine catch on left side behind trigger; press in to release magazine. Remove magazine. Pull back slide to eject any round in chamber. Inspect chamber through ejection opening in slide. Release slide. Pull trigger.

Colt Mark IV Series 70/80 USA

A continuation of the powerful 0.45 ACP Colt 1911/1911A1 pistol line, the Series 70 and 80 were improved versions with a firing pin block safety, also available in 0.38 Super with a higher magazine capacity and 28 g greater weight. Models have been manufactured from blued carbon steel and stainless steel. A low-price, matte finish, carbon steel version was introduced in 1993 as the model 1991 with slightly different markings, most notably "COLT M1991 A1" on the left side of the slide, shown upper right in the Series 70 Gold Cup National Match model.

SPECIFICATION:

CARTRIDGE:
0.45 ACP or 0.38 Super

DIMENSIONS:
LENGTH O/A: 216 mm (8.5 in)
WEIGHT: 1.1 kg (2 lb 6 oz)
BARREL: 127 mm (5.5 in)
RIFLING: 6 grooves, lh
MAGAZINE CAPACITY: 8 (0.45) or 9 rounds (0.38 Super)

IN PRODUCTION:
1983–

MARKINGS:
"COLT MK IV - SERIES 70 [or 80]" - on left side of slide. "GOVERNMENT MODEL" on right side of slide. "COLT'S PT.F.A. MFG. CO. HARTFORD, CONN, U.S.A." and serial number on right side of frame.

SAFETY:
Manual safety catch lever on top left of frame at rear: up for safe, down to fire. Grip safety incorporated into rear of frame blocks trigger movement unless butt is gripped correctly. Firing-pin safety blocks firing-pin movement unless trigger is pulled fully rearwards.

UNLOADING:
Magazine catch at left side of butt behind trigger; press in to release magazine. Remove magazine. Pull back slide to eject any round in chamber. Inspect chamber through ejection port. Release slide.

Colt Officers' ACP/ACP LW USA

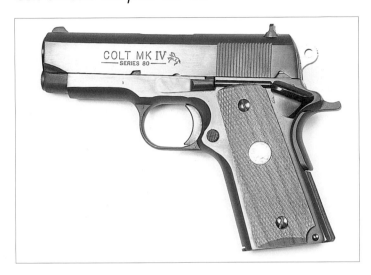

A very compact version of the 0.45 ACP Colt Mk IV Government Model with a 37.5 mm shorter slide and 10 mm shorter frame. The standard models are produced in carbon steel and stainless steel, with the lightweight version having an aluminum alloy frame that reduces the weight by 283 g. This makes for a potent combination: extremely light and concealable yet still chambered for a major-caliber round.

SPECIFICATION:

CARTRIDGE:
0.45 ACP

DIMENSIONS (ACP LW):
LENGTH O/A: 184 mm (7.3 in)
WEIGHT: 680 g (1 lb 8 oz)
BARREL: 89 mm (3.5 in)
RIFLING: 6 grooves, lh
MAGAZINE CAPACITY: 6 rounds

IN PRODUCTION:
1985–

MARKINGS:
"COLT MK IV - SERIES 80" on left side of slide. "OFFICERS ACP" on right side of slide. "COLT'S PT.F.A. MFG. CO. HARTFORD, CONN, U.S.A." and serial number on right side of frame.

SAFETY:
Manual safety catch lever on top left of frame at rear: up for safe, down to fire. Grip safety incorporated into rear of frame blocks trigger movement unless butt is gripped correctly. Firing-pin safety blocks firing-pin movement unless trigger is pulled fully rearwards.

UNLOADING:
Magazine catch at left side of butt behind trigger; press in to release magazine. Remove magazine. Pull back slide to eject any round in chamber;. Inspect chamber through ejection port. Release slide.

Coonan USA

An all-stainless-steel pistol built on the Colt Government pattern but lengthened and internally modified to accommodate the rimmed 0.357 Magnum revolver cartridge. Approximately 5000 were made in the first 10 years of production, mainly with the B-series linkless barrel. A limited number were produced to order with a 153 mm bull barrel and standard slide. Other options included a shortened and cropped Cadet model.

SPECIFICATION:

CARTRIDGE:
0.357 Magnum

DIMENSIONS:
LENGTH O/A: 266 mm (10.5 in)
WEIGHT: 1.4 kg (3 lb)
BARREL: 165 mm (6.5 in)
RIFLING: 6 grooves, rh
MAGAZINE CAPACITY: 7 rounds

IN PRODUCTION:
1980–

MARKINGS:
"COONAN .357 MAGNUM AUTOMATIC" on left side of slide. Serial number on right side of frame.

SAFETY:
Manual safety catch lever on top left of frame at rear: up for safe, down to fire. Grip safety incorporated into rear of frame blocks trigger movement unless butt is gripped correctly.

UNLOADING:
Magazine catch at left side of butt behind trigger; press in to release magazine. Remove magazine. Pull back slide to eject any round in chamber. Inspect chamber through ejection port. Release slide.

LAR Grizzly Win Mag USA

As is very obvious from the shape, this pistol is based upon the Colt M1911A1, the significant external differences being the extended barrel, the squared-off trigger guard, and the micrometer-adjustable rear sight. The pistol is chambered for a unique cartridge, which is arrived at by necking-down the 0.45 ACP case to accept a 0.357 bullet. Conversion kits are available to permit changing the caliber to 0.357 Magnum, 0.45 ACP, 0.44 Magnum, and various 9 mm cartridges. The pistol can also be found with the frame, slide, and barrel extended to cater for 8 and 10 in barrels, and the barrel may also be cut into the form of a compensator.

SPECIFICATION:

CARTRIDGE:
0.357 or 0.44 Grizzly Win Mag

DIMENSIONS:
LENGTH: 266 mm (10.5 in)
WEIGHT: 1.4 kg (3 lb)
BARREL: 165 mm (6.5 in)
RIFLING: 6 grooves, rh
MAGAZINE CAPACITY: 7 rounds

IN PRODUCTION:
Circa 1985–

MARKINGS:
"L.A.R. MFG INC WEST JORDAN UT 84084 U.S.A." and serial number on right rear side of frame. L.A.R. logo and "GRIZZLY WIN MAG" on left side of slide.

SAFETY:
Manual safety catch on both sides of frame: up for safe.

UNLOADING:
Magazine catch at left front edge of butt behind trigger. Remove magazine and empty it if necessary. Pull back slide to eject any round left in chamber. Inspect chamber through ejection port to ensure it is empty. Release slide, pull trigger. Replace the empty magazine in pistol.

Liberator usa

This was a mass-produced smooth-bore pistol that was dropped to resistance groups and guerilla forces in various theaters of war in 1944–45. A million short-range, single-shot weapons were made and distributed freely. Rarely encountered today, they are now collector's pieces. Five loose cartridges can be carried in the hollow butt; a pencil or some similar implement is needed to eject the empty case.

SPECIFICATION:

CARTRIDGE:
0.45 ACP

DIMENSIONS:
LENGTH O/A: 141 mm (5.6 in)
WEIGHT: 445 g (1 lb)
BARREL: 102 mm (4 in)
RIFLING: None; smoothbore
MAGAZINE CAPACITY: Nil; single-shot weapon

IN PRODUCTION:
1942–43

MARKINGS:
None.

SAFETY:
None.

UNLOADING:
Pull back striker, at rear of pistol, and turn through 90° to lock. Lift plate closing rear end of barrel and check that chamber is empty. Replace plate. Turn striker back through 90°. Press trigger. Pull out sliding plate at bottom of butt and check that there are no loose cartridges inside.

Ruger P-85 USA

This pistol first appeared as the P-85, but since then the model number has changed periodically with the year as minor improvements have been made. There are now several variations on the basic design, offering single action, double action, double action only, and decocker models in which the safety catch also releases the hammer. Models in 0.45 ACP and 0.40 S&W chambering are also available, differing only slightly from the basic model's dimensions, and there is also a "convertible" model that allows changing the caliber to 7.65 mm Parabellum.

SPECIFICATION:

CARTRIDGE:
9 x 19 mm Parabellum

DIMENSIONS:
LENGTH O/A: 200 mm (7.9 in)
WEIGHT: 910 g (2 lb)
BARREL: 114 mm (4.5 in)
RIFLING: 6 grooves, rh
MAGAZINE CAPACITY: 15 rounds

IN PRODUCTION:
1987–

MARKINGS:
"RUGER P[XXX]" (according to model number) on left side of slide. Serial number on right side of frame. "BEFORE USING THIS GUN READ WARNINGS IN INSTRUCTION MANUAL AVAILABLE FREE FROM STURM, RUGER & CO INC" on right side of frame. "STURM, RUGER & CO INC/SOUTHPORT CONN USA" on right side of slide.

SAFETY:
Ambidextrous safety catch at rear of slide: press down to secure firing pin, interpose block between hammer and pin, and disconnect trigger.

UNLOADING:
Magazine release latch on both sides behind trigger. Remove magazine. Pull back slide to eject any round in chamber. Inspect chamber through ejection port. Release slide. Pull trigger.

Ruger Standard USA

This was the pistol that founded Ruger's business, and it has been in constant production since 1949. A Mark 2 introduced in 1982 has some small improvements, including a hold-open latch and a new magazine catch, a new safety catch, and a modified trigger system. Both pistols were supplemented by target models with longer barrels, and a 'bull barrel' model with a heavier cylindrical barrel replacing the normal tapered barrel. The Government Target Model Mark 2 has a heavy 175 mm barrel.

SPECIFICATION:

CARTRIDGE:
0.22 Long Rifle rimfire

DIMENSIONS:
LENGTH O/A: 222 mm (8.7 in)
WEIGHT: 1 kg (2 lb 4 oz)
BARREL: 120 mm (4.7 in)
RIFLING: 6 grooves, rh
MAGAZINE CAPACITY: 9 rounds

IN PRODUCTION:
1949-

MARKINGS:
"RUGER .22 CAL AUTOMATIC PISTOL MARK 1" on left side of receiver. "STURM, RUGER & CO SOUTHPORT CONN USA" and serial number on right side of receiver.

SAFETY:
Sliding button on left rear side of frame: push up for safe. Note: This only works when the gun is cocked. Safety catch can also be used to hold bolt to rear.

UNLOADING:
Magazine release at heel of butt; push backwards to remove magazine. Pull back bolt, using "wings" at rear end of receiver, to eject any round in chamber. Inspect chamber through ejection port. Release bolt. Pull trigger.

Savage USA

All Savage pistols look similar, though there are three different models: the 1907, with large grip serrations on the slide and a serrated hammer; the 1915, with similar slide serrations, a grip safety, and no hammer; and the 1915, with thinner grip serrations, a spur hammer, and a wedge-shaped grip. Numbers of 1915 models, an American commercial product, were bought by the Portuguese Army and passed on to the Guarda Nacional de Republica, and were then sold off in the 1950s—so that they are rather more common in Southern Europe than might otherwise be expected.

SPECIFICATION:

CARTRIDGE:
7.65 mm Browning (0.32 ACP) or 9 mm Short (0.380 Auto)

DIMENSIONS:
LENGTH O/A: 167 mm (6.6 in)
WEIGHT: 625 g (1 lb 6 oz)
BARREL: 96 mm (3.8 in)
RIFLING: 6 grooves, rh
MAGAZINE CAPACITY: 10 rounds

IN PRODUCTION:
1907–28

MARKINGS:
"SAVAGE" on left side of frame or top of slide. 1917 models have "Savage 1917 Model" on left side of frame. All models have company trademark (an Indian head) with "Savage Quality" around it molded into butt grips.

SAFETY:
Manual safety catch at left rear of frame: up for safe.

UNLOADING:
Magazine catch at toe of butt. Remove magazine. Pull back slide to eject any round in chamber. Inspect chamber through ejection port. Release slide. Pull trigger.

Smith & Wesson 0.45 Third Generation   USA

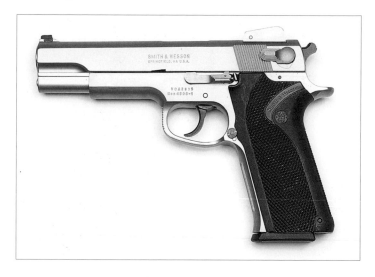

This is a generic title for a series of automatic pistols developed by Smith & Wesson and introduced in 1988. Designed in consultation with law enforcement and military experts, these pistols incorporate double-action triggers, triple safety systems, fixed barrel bushings for greater accuracy and simpler take-down, three-dot sights for quick alignment, bevelled magazine well for quicker changing, and greatly improved trigger pull. The pistols are available in a variety of calibers and finishes. The pistol illustrated is the Model 4506, the number indicating 0.45 caliber and a stainless steel slide and frame.

SPECIFICATION:

CARTRIDGE:
0.45 ACP

DIMENSIONS:
LENGTH O/A: 200 mm (7.9 in)
WEIGHT: 1.1 kg (2 lb 7 oz)
BARREL: 101 mm (4 in)
RIFLING: 6 grooves, rh
MAGAZINE CAPACITY: 11 rounds

IN PRODUCTION:
Ca. 1990–

MARKINGS:
"SMITH & WESSON SPRINGFIELD MA. U.S.A." on left side of slide. "MODEL 4506" and serial number on left side of frame. S&W monogram on right side of frame.

SAFETY:
Ambidextrous manual safety catch at rear of frame: up for safe. Magazine safety prevents firing when magazine is removed. Automatic firing-pin safety locks pin except when trigger is pulled fully through.

UNLOADING:
Magazine catch in front left edge of butt behind trigger. Press in; remove magazine; empty magazine if necessary. Draw back slide to eject any round in chamber. Inspect chamber to ensure the weapon is empty. Release slide. Replace magazine. Pull trigger.

Smith & Wesson Model 39 USA

The Model 39, Smith & Wesson's first modern self-loading pistol, this was accompanied by the short-lived Model 44, essentially the same but single-action only. The Model 39 was the progenitor of several similar improved models that followed it. Numbers were taken into service by the US Navy and Special Forces.

SPECIFICATION:

CARTRIDGE:
9 x 19 mm Parabellum

DIMENSIONS:
LENGTH O/A: 188 mm (7.4 in)
WEIGHT: 750 g (1 lb 10 oz)
BARREL: 101 mm (4 in)
RIFLING: 6 grooves, rh
MAGAZINE CAPACITY: 8 rounds

IN SERVICE DATES:
1954–80

MARKINGS:
"SMITH & WESSSON MADE IN U.S.A. MARCAS REGISTRADAS SMITH & WESSON SPRINGFIELD MASS" and S&W monogram on left side of slide. Serial number on left side of frame above trigger.

SAFETY:
Magazine safety. Manual safety catch at rear left of slide retracts firing pin and lowers hammer when applied.

UNLOADING:
Magazine catch at left side of butt behind trigger. Remove magazine. Pull back slide to eject any round in chamber. Inspect chamber through ejection port. Release slide. Pull trigger.

Smith & Wesson Model 59 USA

Basically the same pistol as the Model 39 but with a larger double-column magazine, the Model 59 can be quickly distinguished because the rear edge of the butt is straight, and not curved as on the Model 39.

SPECIFICATION:

CARTRIDGE:
9 x 19 mm Parabellum

DIMENSIONS:
LENGTH O/A: 189 mm (7.4 in)
WEIGHT: 785 g (1 lb 11 oz)
BARREL: 101 mm (4 in)
RIFLING: 6 grooves, rh
MAGAZINE CAPACITY: 14 rounds

IN SERVICE DATES:
1954–80

MARKINGS:
"SMITH & WESSON MADE IN U.S.A. MARCAS REGISTRADAS SMITH & WESSON SPRINGFIELD MASS" on left side of slide. Serial number on left side of frame above trigger.

SAFETY:
Magazine safety. Manual safety catch at rear left of slide retracts firing pin and lowers hammer when applied.

UNLOADING:
Magazine catch at left side of butt behind trigger. Remove magazine. Pull back slide to eject any round in chamber. Inspect chamber through ejection port. Release slide. Pull trigger.

Smith & Wesson Sigma USA

The Sigma is Smith & Wesson's venture into synthetic materials for gun construction, with a high-strength polymer material used for the frame. It also incorporates the currently fashionable self-cocking (double action only) firing mechanism, so that the pistol can be fired without delay or preparation. The basic model is chambered for the 0.40 S&W cartridge, but it is also available in 9 x 19 mm Parabellum; a subcompact model in 9 mm Short is also manufactured.

SPECIFICATION:

CARTRIDGE:
0.40 S&W

DIMENSIONS:
LENGTH O/A: 188 mm (12.3 in)
WEIGHT: 737 g (1 lb 10 oz)
BARREL: 111 mm (7.4 in)
RIFLING: 6 grooves, rh
MAGAZINE CAPACITY: 15 rounds

IN PRODUCTION:
1994–

MARKINGS:
"SMITH & WESSON Model SW40" on left side of slide. Serial number on right side of frame.

SAFETY:
No manual safety catch, all safety being automatic. Safety device built into trigger. Automatic firing pin safety system prevents firing pin from moving unless trigger is fully pulled through.

UNLOADING:
Magazine catch on left front edge of but behind trigger. Remove magazine and empty it if necessary. Pull back slide to eject any round left in chamber. Inspect chamber through ejection port to ensure it is empty. Release slide. Replace magazine.

Smith & Wesson Third-Generation Pistols 9 mm ^{USA}

This series appeared in 1989 and consists of models in 9 x 19 mm Parabellum, 10mm Auto, 0.40 S&W, and 0.45 ACP calibers. They are identified by a numbering system: the first two digits indicate the caliber, the third indicates features such as compact size or the presence of a decocking lever, and the final figure indicates the material and finish. Thus, the 4043 is a 0.40 S&W with double action only and an alloy frame with stainless steel slide. The Model 1076 was a special 10 mm model developed for the FBI.

SPECIFICATION:

CARTRIDGE:
9 x 19 mm Parabellum, or 10 mm Auto, or 0.40 S&W or 0.45 ACP

DIMENSIONS (MODEL 4000):
LENGTH O/A: 190.5 mm (7.5 in)
WEIGHT: 1.1 kg (2 lb 6 oz)
BARREL: 101.6 mm (4 in)
RIFLING: 6 grooves, rh
MAGAZINE CAPACITY: 11 rounds

IN PRODUCTION:
1989–

MARKINGS:
"SMITH & WESSON SPRINGFIELD MA. USA" on left side of slide. "MOD 40XX" and serial number on left side of frame.

SAFETY:
Ambidextrous safety catch on both sides of slide at rear: up for safe. Automatic firing pin safety system. Magazine safety system. Some models may have decocking lever, some may be double action only.

UNLOADING:
Magazine catch at left side of butt behind trigger. Remove magazine. Pull back slide to eject any round in chamber. Inspect chamber through ejection port. Release slide. Pull trigger.

Springfield P9 USA

This was actually the Czech CZ75 pistol made for Springfield Armory (a private company, not the government establishment, which had closed in 1975). There were some slight differences, such as the adoption of a ring hammer instead of the spur type used on the CZ75, and some changes in the frame contours. The P9 was available in three calibers, and in compact and longslide versions too.

SPECIFICATION:

CARTRIDGE:
9 x 19 mm Parabellum

DIMENSIONS:
LENGTH O/A: 206 mm (8.1 in)
WEIGHT: 1 kg (2 lb 3 oz)
BARREL: 120 mm (4.7 in)
RIFLING: 6 grooves, rh
MAGAZINE CAPACITY: 16 rounds

IN PRODUCTION:
1989–93

MARKINGS:
"MODEL P9 Cal 9 mm" on left side of slide.
"SPRINGFIELD ARMORY" on right side of slide.
Serial number on right side of frame.

SAFETY:
Manual safety catch on left side of frame above butt: up for safe.

UNLOADING:
Magazine catch at left side of butt behind trigger. Remove magazine. Pull back slide to eject any round in chamber. Inspect chamber through ejection port. Release slide. Pull trigger.

Revolvers

Nagant Russian Model 1895 BELGIUM/RUSSIA

A solid-frame revolver that may be found as a single action or double action, the latter being the more common. An unusual weapon; as the hammer is cocked, the cylinder is pushed forward so that the mouth of the chamber engages around the rear of the barrel. This, together with a specially long cartridge with the bullet concealed inside the case, makes a gas-tight joint between cylinder and barrel. This revolver can be found all over Europe and in any other country that was subjected to Soviet influence. Modern revolvers using the same principle are produced for target shooting in Russia and the Czech Republic, and ammunition is available in many countries. A modified, blank-firing version firing a rubber ball for self-protection was offered in 2005.

SPECIFICATION:

CARTRIDGE:
7.62 mm Russian Revolver

DIMENSIONS:
LENGTH O/A: 230 mm (9.1 in)
WEIGHT: 750 g (1 lb 10 oz)
BARREL: 114 mm (4.5 in)
RIFLING: 4 grooves, rh
CHAMBERS: 7 rounds

IN PRODUCTION:
1895–1942

MARKINGS:
Russian inscription in oval form, with date of manufacture beneath on left side of frame (pre-1917). Under Soviet control a large star and factory number may be stamped anywhere on weapon. Commercial models will be marked "L NAGANT BREVETE LIEGE" with a date prior to 1902. Serial number on frame in front of cylinder and possibly on barrel; some commercial models also have it on the cylinder, trigger guard, and butt.

SAFETY:
None.

UNLOADING:
Open loading gate on right side behind cylinder; this will disconnect hammer and allow cylinder to be rotated freely by hand. Withdraw ejector rod forward from its resting place in axis of cylinder; swing it to right and then push back to eject cartridge from chamber. Repeat for all chambers. Replace ejector rod. Close loading gate.

Taurus 76 BRAZIL

Offered either as a target model with adjustable rear sight or a duty gun with fixed rear sight and Patridge front sight, the Taurus 76 is built on a medium frame the equivalent of that used in Smith & Wesson's K-frame revolvers, of which it is an external copy. Internal parts of the trigger group are different, however, with a coil mainspring, floating firing pin, and transfer bar safety. It is shown above in a compact carry model with simple groove rear sight. The Taurus 76, although long out of production, was followed by newer models in this caliber: the M731 Ultra-Lite in 0.32 H&R is an example.

SPECIFICATION:

CARTRIDGE:
0.32 S&W Long

DIMENSIONS:
LENGTH O/A: 284 mm (11.2 in)
WEIGHT: 1.2 kg (2 lb 10 oz)
BARREL: 155 mm (6.1 in)
RIFLING: 5 grooves, rh
CHAMBERS: 6 rounds

IN PRODUCTION:
1975–

MARKINGS:
"TAURUS BRASIL" on left side of barrel. ".32 LONG" on right side of barrel. Serial number and "MADE IN BRAZIL" on right side of frame below front of cylinder. "TAURUS BRASIL" in circle with bull's head motif inside on right side of frame behind recoil shield.

SAFETY:
Trigger-operated transfer bar to transmit hammer force to floating firing pin.

UNLOADING:
Cylinder latch is on left of frame behind cylinder. Push cylinder latch forwards. Swing out cylinder to left. Eject any live or spent cartridges by pushing cylinder ejector rod to rear.

Manurhin MR73 FRANCE

Manurhin were primarily machinery manufacturers but took to making Walther automatic pistols under license after World War II. In the early 1970s, they began developing a line of revolvers of which the MR73 is the backbone. Though generally based on Smith & Wesson's pattern, it has a few features of its own, such as a roller-bearing trigger system that gives a remarkably smooth action. There are various models—specifications for the Defense are given here—for competition, sport, and service use. They are widely sold in Europe and used by many French police forces.

SPECIFICATION:

CARTRIDGE:
0.357 Magnum

DIMENSIONS:
LENGTH O/A: 195 mm (7.7 in)
WEIGHT: 880 g (1 lb 15 oz)
BARREL: 63mm (2.5 in); other barrel lengths available
RIFLING: 6 grooves, rh
CHAMBERS: 6 rounds

IN PRODUCTION:
1973–

MARKINGS:
"MR 73 Cal 357 MAGNUM" on right or left side of barrel. Manurhin (MR) monogram badge set into grips.

SAFETY:
No applied safety device.

UNLOADING:
Push forward thumb catch on left side of frame behind cylinder; allow cylinder to swing out to left of frame. Press in ejector rod to force out ejector plate and eject contents of chambers. Return cylinder to frame, ensuring catch locks.

Arminius Model 10 GERMANY

This is shown as an example of a wide range of cheap revolvers made by Friedrich Pickert of Zella St. Blasii/Zella Mehlis, Germany, from the 1890s until 1945. Although cheap and simple, they were made of sound material, and untold numbers survive in working order. They can be found in "hammerless" (actually with a concealed hammer) or hammer designs, with varying barrel lengths, and in calibers of 0.22 RF, 5.5 mm Velo-Dog, 6.35 mm ACP, 7.65 mm ACP, 0.320, 7.5 mm Swiss, 7.62 mm Nagant, and 0.380. Cylinders can be five, seven, or eight shot, according to caliber, and some models have no ejector rod but require the removal of the cylinder (by pulling out the axis rod) to unload.

SPECIFICATION:

CARTRIDGE:
7.65 mm Browning

DIMENSIONS:
LENGTH O/A: 155 mm (6.1 in)
WEIGHT: 460 g (1 lb)
BARREL: 65 mm (2.6 in)
RIFLING: 4 grooves, rh
CHAMBERS: 5 rounds

IN PRODUCTION:
1895–1945

MARKINGS:
"F PICKERT DEUTSCHE INDUSTRIE" on top strap. "Kal .380" on left side of barrel. Warrior's head trademark molded into butt grips.

SAFETY:
Manual safety catch on left side of frame above butt: press forward to fire, back for safe. Locks hammer when applied and also disconnects it from cylinder to permit unloading.

UNLOADING:
Apply safety catch. Depress latch on right side beneath barrel and pull out ejector rod from hollow cylinder axis pin. Swing ejector about its hinge until it is aligned with the "one o'clock" chamber; thrust out empty case. Retract ejector rod, turn the cylinder to next chamber and repeat until cylinder is empty.

Weihrauch HW-9 GERMANY

This is actually a 0.38 frame carrying a 0.22 barrel, which makes for a heavy pistol of good accuracy. An inexpensive weapon, it and its various derivatives (different barrel lengths, sights, and grips) may be found in some numbers in Western Europe.

SPECIFICATION:

CARTRIDGE:
0.22LR

DIMENSIONS:
LENGTH O/A: 295 mm (11.6 in)
WEIGHT: 1.1 kg (2 lb 7 oz)
BARREL: 150 mm (5.9 in)
RIFLING: 8 grooves, rh
CHAMBERS: 6 rounds

IN PRODUCTION:
1970–

MARKINGS:
Warrior's head trademark or "ARMINIUS" or both, and "HW9" on left side of frame. Serial number on right side of frame. "CAL .22 LR" on left side of barrel.

SAFETY:
No applied safety device.

UNLOADING:
Grasp sleeve surrounding ejector rod beneath barrel and pull it forward to unlock cylinder, which will then swing out to left on a crane. Push ejector rod back to eject contents of chambers; swing cylinder back into frame, where it will lock and the spring sleeve will reengage.

Miroku .38 Special Police JAPAN

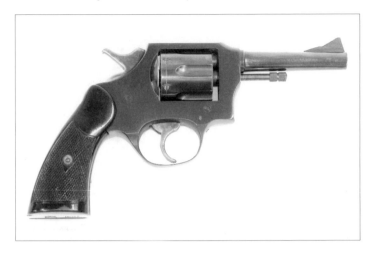

This appears to have been intended to attract Japanese police, who had been armed with revolvers during the US occupation after 1945. They preferred to return to self-loading models once they were given the chance, and Miroku therefore exported almost their entire output to the USA under the EIG and Liberty Chief badges. Cheap but serviceable, they survived for about 20 years. There was also a six-shot model, slightly larger, using the same names.

SPECIFICATION:

CARTRIDGE:
0.38 Special

DIMENSIONS:
LENGTH O/A: 195 mm (7.7 in)
WEIGHT: 485 g (1 lb 1 oz)
BARREL: 64 mm (2.5 in)
RIFLING: 6 grooves, rh
CHAMBERS: 5 rounds

IN PRODUCTION:
1967–84

MARKINGS:
Japanese markings unknown; those exported carry either an EIG monogram on left side of frame or "LIBERTY CHIEF" on left side of frame over trigger. ".38 SPECIAL CALIBER" on left side of barrel. Serial number on right side of frame.

SAFETY:
No applied safety device.

UNLOADING:
Pull back thumb catch on left side of frame behind cylinder; allow cylinder to swing out to left of frame. Press in ejector rod to force out ejector plate and eject contents of chambers. Return cylinder to frame, ensuring catch locks.

Astra 357 Police SPAIN

This replaced an earlier model, the 357, and has a stronger hammer, a smoothed-out front sight that is less liable to snag in the holster, and a nonadjustable rear sight better adapted to instinctive shooting. The short barrel tends to deliver a good deal of muzzle blast due to the powerful cartridge. The manufacturer has ceased business.

SPECIFICATION:

CARTRIDGE:
0.357 Magnum

DIMENSIONS:
LENGTH O/A: 212 mm (8.4 in)
WEIGHT: 1 kg (2 lb 4 oz)
BARREL: 77 mm (3 in)
RIFLING: 6 grooves, rh
CHAMBERS: 6 rounds

IN PRODUCTION:
1980–95

MARKINGS:
"ASTRA SPAIN" and badge on right side of frame above butt. "357 MAGNUM CTG" on left side of barrel. Serial number on left side of frame behind trigger. Astra badges on grips.

SAFETY:
No safety device.

UNLOADING:
Press forward thumb catch on left side of frame behind cylinder; allow cylinder to swing out to left of frame. Press in ejector rod to force out ejector plate and eject contents of chambers. Return the cylinder to frame, ensuring catch locks.

Astra Cadix SPAIN

The Cadix is a double-action revolver with swing-out cylinder and can be found in four calibers. The dimensions differ accordingly; data given here is for the 0.38 Special model. Models in 0.22 caliber have a nine-chambered cylinder, 0.32 models a six-chambered cylinder. The ejector rod shroud and trigger guard have very distinctive shapes. The manufacturer has ceased business.

SPECIFICATION:

CARTRIDGE:
0.22LR, or 0.22 Magnum, or 0.32 S&W Long, or 0.38 Special

DIMENSIONS:
LENGTH O/A: 229 mm (9 in)
WEIGHT: 715 g (1 lb 9 oz)
BARREL: 102 mm (4 in)
RIFLING: 6 grooves, rh
CHAMBERS: 5 rounds

IN PRODUCTION:
1958–73

MARKINGS:
"ASTRA SPAIN" and badge on right side of frame above butt. Caliber at left front of ejector rod shroud beneath barrel. Serial number on left side of frame behind trigger. Astra badge on grips.

SAFETY:
None.

UNLOADING:
Press forward thumb catch on left side of frame behind cylinder; allow cylinder to swing out to left of frame. Press in ejector rod to force out ejector plate and eject contents of chambers. Return cylinder to frame, ensuring catch locks.

Astra Model 960 SPAIN

This is a modern double-action revolver for police or commercial use. It is a rework of the earlier Cadix model to conform to the US 1968 Gun Control Act, the essential change being the adoption of a transfer-bar mechanism to prevent the hammer striking the firing pin unless the trigger is correctly pulled through. The front sight has a larger ramp, the trigger guard is somewhat more smoothly streamlined and the hammer was made larger. The back sight is adjustable and the main-spring can be regulated for strength of hammer blow. It can be found with a 152 mm barrel. The manufacturer has ceased business.

SPECIFICATION:

CARTRIDGE:
0.38 Special

DIMENSIONS:
LENGTH O/A: 241 mm (9.5 in)
WEIGHT: 1.2 kg (2 lb 8 oz)
BARREL: 102 mm (4 in)
RIFLING: 6 grooves, rh
CHAMBERS: 6 rounds

IN PRODUCTION:
1973–95

MARKINGS:
"ASTRA SPAIN" with badge on right side of frame. ".38 SPECIAL" on left side of barrel. Serial number on bottom of butt grip.

SAFETY:
None

UNLOADING:
Press forward thumb catch on left side of frame behind cylinder; allow cylinder to swing out to left of frame. Press in ejector rod to force out ejector plate and eject contents of chambers. Return cylinder to frame, ensuring catch locks.

Llama Comanche SPAIN

A thoroughly conventional modern revolver, quite obviously based upon the Smith & Wesson design and none the worse for that. It is well made of good material and excellently finished, widely sold throughout Europe as well as being exported in substantial numbers. The company, which has ceased trading, made several similar revolvers that only differ in size and caliber. The Comanche was available with barrels 4 in (see Specification) or 6 in (152 mm) long.

SPECIFICATION:

CARTRIDGE:
0.357 Magnum

DIMENSIONS:
LENGTH O/A: 235 mm (9.3 in)
WEIGHT: 1 kg (2 lb 4 oz)
BARREL: 102 mm (4 in)
RIFLING: 6 grooves, rh
CHAMBERS: 6 rounds

IN PRODUCTION:
1970–

MARKINGS:
"GABILONDO y CIA VITORIA ESPANA" on left side of barrel. "LLAMA .357 MAG CTG" on right side of barrel. Serial number on bottom of grip frame.

SAFETY:
No applied safety device.

UNLOADING:
Push forward thumb catch on left side of frame behind cylinder; allow cylinder to swing out to left of frame. Press in ejector rod to force out ejector plate and eject contents of chambers. Return cylinder to frame, ensuring catch locks.

Llama Ruby Extra SPAIN

Ruby was a brand name of the Gabilondo Company of Eibar, Spain, first applied to a cheap copy of the Browning 1903 pistol made for the French Army in 1915. The name was allowed to lapse and was replaced by Llama in the 1920s. It was revived in the early 1950s for a series of revolvers that were of generally cheaper construction and finish than their regular Llama range. The Ruby Extra appeared as Models 12, 13, and 14, varying in caliber from 0.22 to 0.38 Special and with barrel lengths from 2 to 6 in. Some had ventilated ribs on the barrel and micrometer sights, others had plain barrels with fixed sights. Manufacture of this particular range of revolvers appears to have ended around 1970.

SPECIFICATION:

CARTRIDGE:
0.32 S&W Long

DIMENSIONS:
LENGTH O/A: 162.5 mm (6.4 in)
WEIGHT: 1.1 kg (1 lb 2 oz)
BARREL: 51 mm (2 in)
RIFLING: 6 grooves, rh
CHAMBERS: 6 rounds

IN PRODUCTION:
Ca. 1953–70

MARKINGS:
"GABILONDO y CIA ELGOEIBAR ESPANA" on barrel. "RUBY EXTRA" in oval on left side of frame. "RUBY" in medallions at top of grips. "0.32 S & W L" on left side of barrel.

SAFETY:
None: double-action revolver.

UNLOADING:
Press forward catch on left side of frame alongside hammer; swing cylinder out to left side. Push back on ejector rod to expel any rounds or empty cases in chambers. Inspect chambers. Swing cylinder back into frame and ensure it locks. Lower hammer if cocked.

Bulldog UK

This is a class of revolver rather than a specific make. Originated by Webley as a small, heavy-caliber personal-defense weapon, it was widely copied by European makers, especially in Belgium. All exhibit the same appearance: a solid-frame double-action revolver with a large butt and short, stubby barrel, often oval in section, though round and octagonal barrels will be met. Usually in 0.44 or 0.45, specimens in 0.380 are not uncommon, and some European versions may be found chambered for 10.6 German Ordnance and similar metric calibers.

SPECIFICATION:

CARTRIDGE:
0.44 or 0.45

DIMENSIONS:
LENGTH O/A: 159 mm (6.3 in)
WEIGHT: 525 g (1 lb 2 oz)
BARREL: 64 mm (2.5 in)
RIFLING: 7 grooves, rh
CHAMBERS: 6 rounds

IN PRODUCTION:
1878–1939

MARKINGS:
Various. Original Webley designs have "WEBLEY PATENT" on left side of frame in front of cylinder and may also have Webley "winged bullet" trademark. Others will have maker's name, usually on top of barrel, or simply "BULLDOG" or "BRITISH BULLDOG" on the barrel.

SAFETY:
Not usually found on these revolvers, though some continental makes can be found with safety catch on left side of frame above butt.

UNLOADING:
Usually with a swinging ejector rod and loading gate on right side. Open loading gate to disconnect hammer, allowing cylinder to be rotated; push the ejector rod back to empty each chamber in turn. Cheaper models will have no ejector system: remove axis pin to allow cylinder to drop out of frame, use axis pin to punch case out of each chamber.

Pistol, Revolver, No. 2, Mks I/I*/I** (.38 Enfield Revolver) UK

As a result of World War II experience, the British Army decided that the Mk VI revolver was too heavy for machine gunners, etc., carrying substantial loads and developed recoil that was a hindrance to rapid training. Webley and ICI then produced a version of the .38 S&W round with a 200 g bullet, and the Webley Mk IV revolver was designed around it. The ammunition was adapted, but the War Office–designed .38 in Enfield (Pistol, Revolver, No. 2) was preferred to the .38 in Webley. The .38 in Enfield Mk I was a double- and single-action revolver, while Mks I* and I** were double action only (to simplify training). Mk I** had no hammer safety stop. Later, grips were fuller and made of wood or plastic.

SPECIFICATION:

CARTRIDGE:
0.38 Mark 1 or 2 British service; will also chamber 0.38 S&W, 0.38 Short Colt, and 0.380 Revolver

DIMENSIONS:
LENGTH O/A: 260 mm (10.2 in)
WEIGHT: 780 g (1 lb 11 oz)
BARREL: 127 mm (5 in)
RIFLING: 7 grooves, rh
CHAMBERS: 6 rounds

IN PRODUCTION:
1931–45

MARKINGS:
"Mk I [or I*]" on right side of frame below hammer. These pistols were also made by the Albion Motor Company and may be found marked "ALBION." Parts may be found stamped "SSM," indicating manufacture of these parts by the Singer Sewing Machine Company. Serial number on bottom of butt frame.

SAFETY:
No manual safety device.

UNLOADING:
Press down thumb catch alongside hammer to release stirrup lock above standing breech; hinge barrel down to expose cylinder. This will cause extractor plate to come out of cylinder and extract any rounds or cases. Once clear, raise barrel until top strap engages with stirrup lock.

Webley .38 Mark III UK

Production of this revolver began in about 1896, and the last examples were assembled just after WWII. Most examples appear to have been made in .38 in S&W, with a 3 in or 4 in barrel and a small, round butt. There was a target version with a 6 in barrel and a frame with a square butt. Numerous other versions appeared, including a .32 in variant with a rebated cylinder. Oversize grips in wood or vulcanite were not uncommon. Indian government purchases included the Mk III*— a .38 in variant with a square butt frame like that of the .38 in Mk IV revolver.

SPECIFICATION:

CARTRIDGE:
0.38 S&W

DIMENSIONS:
LENGTH O/A: 205 mm (8.1 in)
WEIGHT: 540 g (1 lb 3 oz)
BARREL: 76 mm (3 in)
RIFLING: 7 grooves, rh
CHAMBERS: 6 rounds

IN PRODUCTION:
1896–1939

MARKINGS:
"WEBLEY'S PATENT" and serial number on right side of frame. "MK III .38" on left side of top strap. May have "MADE IN ENGLAND" on right side of top strap. Weapons purchased by Indian government will have broad arrow and "I" mark with the year of purchase on right side of frame in front of trigger.

SAFETY:
Not normally fitted, but could be obtained as an optional extra, in which case it is a small lever on right side of frame alongside hammer: push up for safe.

UNLOADING:
Press down thumb catch on left side of frame, withdrawing stirrup lock and allowing top strap to rise. Hinge down barrel, and ejector plate will be forced out, ejecting contents of chambers. Hinge barrel back until top strap reengages with stirrup lock.

Webley .38 Mark IV UK

Webley developed this revolver to meet the British requirement for a 0.38 model, but the Army chose the Enfield design, and therefore Webley produced this commercially. But in World War II over 100,000 were taken by the British Army and remained in use until 1956. It differs from the Enfield—which was based on the Webley design—only in its lockwork and some minor details, and the two can be easily confused at first glance. A target model, with adjustable back sight, was also sold commercially.

SPECIFICATION:

CARTRIDGE:
0.38 British Service, or 0.38 S&W, or similar

DIMENSIONS:
LENGTH O/A: 266 mm (10.5 in)
WEIGHT: 760 g (1 lb 11 oz)
BARREL: 127 mm (5 in)
RIFLING: 7 grooves, rh
CHAMBERS: 6 rounds

IN PRODUCTION:
1929–45

MARKINGS:
"MARK IV .38 145/200" on left side of top strap above cylinder. Webley "winged bullet" trademark or "PAT 186131" on right side of frame below cylinder. Serial number on right side of frame below cylinder.

SAFETY:
No safety device.

UNLOADING:
Press down thumb catch alongside hammer to release stirrup lock above standing breech; hinge barrel down to expose cylinder. This will cause extractor plate to come out of cylinder and extract any rounds or cases. Once clear, raise barrel until top strap reengages with stirrup lock.

Webley .320 Pocket Hammerless UK

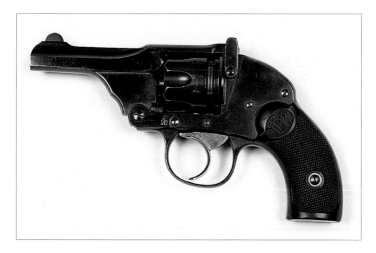

In addition to being chambered for the 0.320 revolver cartridge, these pistols could also be chambered and regulated for the 0.32 Long or Short Colt or 0.32 S&W cartridges if desired. Nickel plating and mother-of-pearl grips are also to be found. Although produced for many years, it is doubtful if more than 10,000 were made, but they still turn up quite regularly.

SPECIFICATION:

CARTRIDGE:
0.320 Revolver or similar cartridges

DIMENSIONS:
LENGTH O/A: 178 mm (7 in)
WEIGHT: 480 g (1 lb 1 oz)
BARREL: 76 mm (3 in)
RIFLING: 7 grooves, rh
CHAMBERS: 6 rounds

IN PRODUCTION:
1901–36

MARKINGS:
"WEBLEY'S PATENT" and serial number on right side of frame.

SAFETY:
Sliding manual safety catch is fitted over hammer position. Slide back to lock hammer and expose word "safe."

UNLOADING:
Press down thumb catch on left side of frame, withdrawing stirrup lock and allowing top strap to rise. Hinge down barrel; ejector plate will be forced out, ejecting contents of chambers. Hinge barrel back until top strap reengages with stirrup lock.

Webley .455 WG

These revolvers were the work of a new Webley designer, Michael Kaufman, and his initials and a number are stamped on the gun, largely to ensure that he got his royalties for every pistol. Many improvements that later became standard on other Webley designs first appear on this model, and it was widely bought by British officers and travelers going to the wilder parts of the world. The WG is generally held to mean "Webley Government" model, though others say it means "Webley-Green," Green being the original designer of the stirrup lock.

SPECIFICATION:

CARTRIDGE:
0.455 British Service

DIMENSIONS:
LENGTH O/A: 286 mm (11.3 in)
WEIGHT: 1.1 kg (2 lb 8 oz)
BARREL: 152 mm (6 in)
RIFLING: 7 grooves, rh
CHAMBERS: 6 rounds

IN PRODUCTION:
1885–1912

MARKINGS:
"WEBLEY PATENTS" and "winged bullet" on left side of frame. Caliber of cartridge on left side of barrel assembly in front of cylinder. Serial number on right side of frame. "WG MODEL" and year on left side of top strap. Letters "MK" in a triangle, together with a number on right side of frame.

SAFETY:
No applied safety device.

UNLOADING:
Press down thumb catch alongside hammer to release stirrup lock above standing breech; hinge barrel down to expose cylinder. This will cause extractor plate to come out of cylinder and extract any rounds or cases. Once clear, raise barrel until top strap reengages with stirrup lock.

Webley .455 Mark IV/V UK

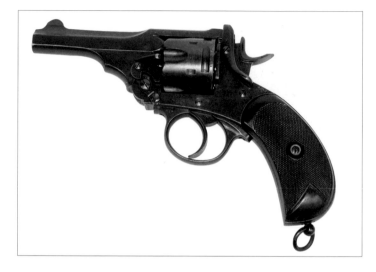

The Mark IV revolver was in production from 1889 to 1913 and was essentially the .455 in Mark III made from an improved steel. It was one of the main pistols used by the British Army during the South African War. British government contract pistols (about 37,000) had 4 in barrel, but 6 in was an option on commercial examples, which were also made in .230 in or .476 in. The Mark V revolver, in production from 1913 to 1915, was basically the Mark IV with a cylinder .027 in longer in diameter. Government and commercial examples were made with 4 in and 6 in barrels. Some commercial examples had 7.5 in barrels, a few of which incorporated Metford rifling. Government contract production was about 28,000.

SPECIFICATION:

CARTRIDGE:
0.455 British Service

DIMENSIONS:
LENGTH O/A: 235 mm (9.3 in)
WEIGHT: 1 kg (2 lb 3 oz)
BARREL: 102 mm (4 in)
RIFLING: 7 grooves, rh
CHAMBERS: 6 rounds

IN PRODUCTION:
1889–1913 (Mk IV); 1913–1915 (Mk V)

MARKINGS:
"WEBLEY/MARK V/PATENTS" on left side of frame below cylinder. "MARK V" on left side of top strap above cylinder. Serial number usually on right side of frame above trigger.

SAFETY:
No manual safety device.

UNLOADING:
Press down thumb catch alongside hammer to release stirrup lock above standing breech; hinge barrel down to expose cylinder. This will cause extractor plate to come out of cylinder and extract any rounds or cases. Once clear, raise barrel until the top strap reengages with stirrup lock.

Webley .455 Mark VI   UK

This Mark VI is the last version of the Webley WS Army Model commercial revolver. The Mark VI designation superseded the commercial designation when the revolver was adopted by the British Army in 1915. The chief difference from the earlier service revolvers is that the Mark VI has a frame with a square grip rather than an angled bird's-head grip. About 127,000 government contract examples, with 6 in barrels, were made in 1915–1919 and RSAF Enfield made about 40,000 in 1921–1926. Webley continued to offer it commercially until 1940, and a 4 in barrel was available after World War I. A 7.5 in barrel target version was also made, although most of these target examples were designated WS Target Model, not Mark VI.

SPECIFICATION:

CARTRIDGE:
0.455 British Service

DIMENSIONS:
LENGTH O/A: 286 mm (11.3 in)
WEIGHT: 1.1 g (2 lb 6 oz)
BARREL: 152 mm (6 in)
RIFLING: 7 grooves, rh
CHAMBERS: 6 rounds

IN PRODUCTION:
1915–1939

MARKINGS:
"WEBLEY/MARK V/PATENTS" on left side of frame below cylinder. "MARK VI" on left side of top strap above cylinder. Serial number on right side of frame above trigger or underneath frame in front of trigger guard.

SAFETY:
No manual safety device.

UNLOADING:
Press down thumb catch alongside hammer to release stirrup lock above standing breech; hinge barrel down to expose cylinder. This will cause extractor plate to come out of cylinder and extract any rounds or cases. Once clear, raise barrel until top strap reengages with stirrup lock.

Charter Arms Pathfinder USA

This design is typical of a number of small revolvers made by Charter Arms in calibers from 0.22 to 0.44 under names such as Undercover, Undercoverette, and Off Duty and in 0.44 S&W as the Bulldog and Pathfinder. All were side-opening double-action weapons of medium quality, intended to be carried concealed by police officers or for personal defense.

SPECIFICATION:

CARTRIDGE:
0.22LR

DIMENSIONS:
LENGTH O/A: 188 mm (7.5 in)
WEIGHT: 525 g (1 lb 2 oz)
BARREL: 76 mm (3 in)
RIFLING: 6 grooves, rh
CHAMBERS: 6 rounds

IN PRODUCTION:
1964–

MARKINGS:
"PATHFINDER .22" on left side of barrel. "CHARTER ARMS CORP/BRIDGEPORT CONN" on left side of barrel. Serial number on right side of frame.

SAFETY:
No safety device.

UNLOADING:
Press forward thumb catch on left side of frame behind cylinder; allow cylinder to swing out to left of frame. Press in ejector rod to force out ejector plate and eject contents of chambers. Return cylinder to frame, ensuring catch locks.

Colt Anaconda USA

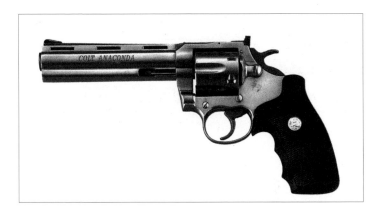

This is Colt's largest double-action revolver and is made entirely from stainless steel. It is chambered for the formidable 0.44 Magnum cartridge, with 6 in and 8 in barrel versions also produced, chambered for 0.45 Colt.

SPECIFICATION:

CARTRIDGE:
0.44 Magnum

DIMENSIONS (WITH 203 MM/ 8 IN BARREL):
LENGTH O/A: 345 mm (13.6 in)
WEIGHT: 1.7 kg (3 lb 11 oz)
BARREL: 203 mm (8 in); also available with 102 mm (4 in) and 152 mm (6 in) barrels
RIFLING: 6 grooves, lh
CHAMBERS: 6 rounds

IN PRODUCTION:
1990–

MARKINGS:
"COLT ANACONDA 44 MAGNUM" on left side of barrel. Rampant colt motif on left side of frame. "DOUBLE-ACTION REVOLVER, COLT'S PT. F. A. MFG. CO. HARTFORD, CONN, USA" on right side of barrel. Serial number on frame under cylinder crane.

SAFETY:
Trigger-retracted hammer block.

UNLOADING:
Cylinder latch is on left of frame behind cylinder. Pull cylinder latch to rear; swing out cylinder to left, eject any live or spent cartridges by pushing cylinder ejector rod to rear.

Colt Detective Special USA

The Detective Special was simply a shortened version of the standard Police Positive Special revolver, designed to provide plainclothes police with a concealable but powerful pistol. It is very similar to the Banker's Special that appeared in 1928, the principal difference being that the Banker had a full-sized butt with squared-off end, whereas the Detective had a smaller butt with rounded end, again for better concealment. With something in the order of 1.5 million of these two models made, they are relatively common.

SPECIFICATION:

CARTRIDGE:
0.38 Special

DIMENSIONS:
LENGTH O/A: 171 mm (6.7 in)
WEIGHT: 595 g (1 lb 5 oz)
BARREL: 54 mm (2.1 in)
RIFLING: 6 grooves, lh
CHAMBERS: 6 rounds

IN PRODUCTION:
1927–86

MARKINGS:
".38 DETECTIVE SPECIAL" on left side of barrel.
Rampant colt badge on left side of frame.

SAFETY:
None.

UNLOADING:
Pull back thumb catch on left side of frame behind the cylinder; allow cylinder to swing out to left of frame. Press in ejector rod to force out ejector plate and eject contents of chambers. Return cylinder to frame, ensuring catch locks.

Colt King Cobra USA

A budget double-action stainless steel revolver with two barrel lengths and adjustable sights introduced to succeed the Trooper series. Built on a rugged frame with extensive use of cast parts, the Cobra was a competitor for the Ruger GP 100 and Smith & Wesson L-frame 0.357 Magnum revolvers.

SPECIFICATION:

CARTRIDGE:
0.357 Magnum

DIMENSIONS (WITH 152 MM/ 6 IN BARREL):
LENGTH O/A: 280 mm (11 in)
WEIGHT: 1.3 kg (2 lb 14 oz)
BARREL: 152 mm (6 in); also available with 102 mm (4 in) barrel
RIFLING: 6 grooves, lh
CHAMBERS: 6 rounds

IN PRODUCTION:
1986–

MARKINGS:
"KING COBRA" and Cobra-head motif on left of barrel. Rampant colt motif on left side of frame. "- 357 MAGNUM CARTRIDGE - & COLT'S PT. F. A. MFG. CO. HARTFORD, CONN, USA" on right side of barrel. Serial number on frame under cylinder crane.

SAFETY:
Trigger-retracted hammer block.

UNLOADING:
Cylinder latch is on left of frame behind cylinder. Pull cylinder latch to rear, swing out cylinder to left, eject any live or spent cartridges by pushing cylinder ejector rod to rear.

Colt Model 1917 USA

In 1917, the US Army, short of pistols, called on Colt (and Smith & Wesson) to fill the gap using their stock heavy revolver but chambering it for the 0.45 Auto cartridge fired by the Colt automatic pistol, which was the approved sidearm. The M1917 is therefore the New Service with a shortened cylinder so that the rimless 0.45 ACP cartridge will load with the aid of two three-shot clips, positioning the rounds in the chamber and giving the ejector something to push against. It remained in service throughout World War II.

SPECIFICATION:

CARTRIDGE:
0.45 ACP

DIMENSIONS:
LENGTH O/A: 273 mm (10.8 in)
WEIGHT: 1.1 kg (2 lb 8 oz)
BARREL: 140 mm (5.5 in)
RIFLING: 6 grooves, lh
CHAMBERS: 6 rounds

IN PRODUCTION:
1917–45

MARKINGS:
"COLT D.A. 45" on left side of barrel. "COLT'S PAT FA CO HARTFORD CONN" on top of barrel, with various patent dates. "UNITED STATES PROPERTY" on right side of frame. Serial number on bottom of butt.

SAFETY:
No applied safety device.

UNLOADING:
Pull back thumb catch on left side of frame behind cylinder; allow cylinder to swing out to left of frame. Press in ejector rod to force out ejector plate and eject the contents of chambers. Return cylinder to frame, ensuring catch locks.

Colt New Navy/Army/Marine Corps USA

Three variant models: the New Army has smooth walnut buttplates, the New Navy has hard rubber buttplates; the New Marine Corps has checkered walnut buttplates with a slightly rounded butt. The New Navy had five rifling grooves. The New Marine Corps is chambered the 0.38 Special cartridge instead of the 0.38 Long Colt. All cylinders revolve anticlockwise. These models are distinguishable from Smith & Wesson revolvers by the unsupported ejector rod.

SPECIFICATION:

CARTRIDGE:
0.38 Long Colt

DIMENSIONS:
LENGTH O/A: 280 mm (11 in)
WEIGHT: 965 g (2 lb 2 oz)
BARREL: 152 mm (6 in)
RIFLING: 6 grooves, lh
CYLINDER: 6 chambers

IN PRODUCTION:
1889–1919

MARKINGS:
"COLT .38 DA" on left side of barrel. "US ARMY/NAVY/MARINE CORPS" on top of barrel. Serial number on bottom of butt frame.

SAFETY:
No manual safety devices. Trigger will not operate unless cylinder is closed and locked.

UNLOADING:
Pull back thumb catch on left side of frame, releasing cylinder to open to left. Push back on ejector rod to eject cases; load chambers individually; swing chamber into frame.

Colt New Service USA

Developed in the 1890s primarily as a military revolver, it was not officially adopted until 1917 but then continued in production until 1944, some 360,000 being made. The greater part were in 0.45 Colt or 0.44 S&W Russian, though such odd calibers as 0.44/40 Winchester and 0.476 Eley were produced in small numbers.

SPECIFICATION:

CARTRIDGE:
0.45 Colt and 17 other calibers

DIMENSIONS:
LENGTH O/A: 275 mm (10 in)
WEIGHT: 1.2 kg (2 lb 9 oz)
BARREL: 140 mm (5.5 in)
RIFLING: 6 grooves, lh
CHAMBERS: 6 rounds

IN PRODUCTION:
1898–1944

MARKINGS:
"NEW SERVICE 45 COLT [or other caliber]" on left side of barrel. "Colt's Pat FA Co Hartford Conn" and various patent dates on top of barrel. Serial number on bottom of butt frame.

SAFETY:
No applied safety device.

UNLOADING:
Pull back thumb catch on left side of frame behind the cylinder; allow cylinder to swing out to left of frame. Press in ejector rod to force out ejector plate and eject contents of chambers. Return cylinder to frame, ensuring catch locks.

Colt Pocket Positive USA

This was the continuance of the earlier New Pocket Model, with the addition of the Positive Safety feature of the Police Positive model. Serial numbers continued, but any serial number above 30,000 has the Positive Safety device. These pistols can be found chambered either for the 0.32 Long Colt or for the 0.32 Police Positive and 0.38 S&W Long cartridges. The chambers differ slightly in order to obtain the optimum performance from each round; it is possible to interchange ammunition quite safely.

SPECIFICATION:

CARTRIDGE:
0.32 Long Colt

DIMENSIONS:
LENGTH O/A: 215 mm (8.5 in)
WEIGHT: 455 g (1 lb)
BARREL: 115 mm (4.5 in)
RIFLING: 6 grooves, lh
CHAMBERS: 6 rounds

IN PRODUCTION:
1895–1943

MARKINGS:
"POCKET POSITIVE/32 POLICE CTG" on left side of barrel. "COLT'S PAT FA CO" on right side of barrel. Rampant colt motif on left side of frame.

SAFETY:
No applied safety device.

UNLOADING:
Pull back thumb catch on left side of frame behind cylinder; allow cylinder to swing out to left of frame. Press in ejector rod to force out ejector plate and eject contents of chambers. Return cylinder to frame, ensuring catch locks.

Colt Python USA

Colt's premier double-action revolver in the postwar years with a fine reputation for accuracy with its 1:14 twist rifling. Early models were available with a nickel-plated finish, but this was dropped with the introduction of stainless steel to supplement the existing blued carbon steel models. A very limited number were made with 203 mm (8 in) barrels and chambered for 0.38 S&W Special only.

SPECIFICATION:

CARTRIDGE:
0.357 Magnum (& 0.38 S&W Special)

DIMENSIONS:
LENGTH O/A: 343 mm (13.5 in)
WEIGHT: 1.4 kg (3 lb)
BARREL: 203 mm (8 in); also available with 102 mm (4 in) and 152 mm (6 in) barrels
RIFLING: 6 grooves, rh
CHAMBERS: 6 rounds

IN PRODUCTION:
1955–

MARKINGS:
"PYTHON 357, 357 MAGNUM CTG" on left side of barrel. Rampant colt motif on left side of frame. "COLT'S PT. F. A. MFG. CO. HARTFORD, CONN, USA" on right side of barrel. Serial number on frame under cylinder crane.

SAFETY:
Trigger-retracted hammer block.

UNLOADING:
Cylinder latch is on left of frame behind cylinder. Pull cylinder latch to rear, swing out cylinder to left, eject any live or spent cartridges by pushing cylinder ejector rod to rear.

Dan Wesson USA

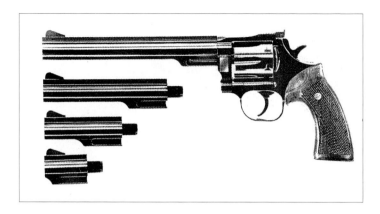

Although of conventional appearance, the Dan Wesson revolvers were unique in having interchangeable barrels and grips, so that the user could change the configuration of the pistol to suit the particular requirements of the moment, whether it be hunting, target shooting, or self-defense. Basic calibers available run from 0.22 Long Rifle to 0.45 Colt, and the range of barrels from 52 mm (2 in) to 381 mm (15 in), though all lengths are not necessarily available in all calibers. The system uses a removable barrel, screwed into the frame in the usual manner, with a removable shroud, all locked in place by a special key. When properly assembled, the cylinder-breech clearance is ensured by feeler gauges, and the barrel is held in tension by the shroud. The rest of the revolver is a conventional solid frame with side-opening cylinder.

SPECIFICATION:

CARTRIDGE:
0.22LR, 0.22WMR, 0.32 S&W, 0.38 Special, 0.357 Magnum, 0.41 Magnum, 0.44 Magnum, or 0.45 Colt

DIMENSIONS (MODEL 15-2 0.357 MAG):
LENGTH O/A: 305 mm (12 in)
WEIGHT: 1.1 kg (2 lb 6 oz)
BARREL: 152 mm (6 in); also available with 64 mm (2.5 in), 102 mm (4 in) and 203 mm (8 in) barrels
RIFLING: 6 grooves, rh
CHAMBERS: 6 rounds

IN PRODUCTION:
1968–

MARKINGS:
None.

SAFETY:
No applied safety. Double-action revolver.

UNLOADING:
Press down on thumb latch on left side of frame in front of cylinder to release cylinder. Swing cylinder out to left and press in on ejector rod to eject any rounds in chambers. Inspect chambers. Return cylinder to its place, allowing catch to spring back and lock.

Harrington & Richardson .38 Auto Ejector USA

Another of the popular pocket revolvers of the early years of the twentieth century, though this one lasted in production for longer than all its competitors and, with some changes in the butt contours, even reappeared after 1945. Commonly found nickel plated, it can also be seen in 0.22 and 0.32 calibers and with barrels from 2 to 6 in, though the 3.35 in and 4 in barrels are most common, since they are more pocketable.

SPECIFICATION:

CARTRIDGE:
0.38 S&W

DIMENSIONS:
LENGTH O/A: 187 mm (7.4 in)
WEIGHT: 420 g (15 oz)
BARREL: 83 mm (3.3 in)
RIFLING: 5 grooves, rh
CHAMBERS: 5 rounds

IN PRODUCTION:
1897–1940

MARKINGS:
"AUTO EJECTING .38 S&W" on left side of barrel. "HARRINGTON & RICHARDSON ARMS COMPANY WORCESTER MASS USA" and various patent dates on top of barrel rib. "H&R" pierced target trademark on both grips. Serial number on left side of butt frame, concealed by grips.

SAFETY:
No applied safety device.

UNLOADING:
Grasp knurled ends of spring catch above standing breech; lift and hinge barrel down. This will cause ejector plate to move out and eject contents of chambers. Close barrel and ensure spring catch engages.

Hopkins & Allen .38 Safety Police USA

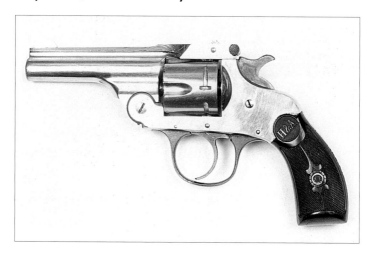

Apart from the catch securing the barrel closed, there is little to distinguish this revolver from any of its contemporaries, but the trigger action is unique. The hammer is mounted on an eccentric axis pin and if it is thumbed back and released, it strikes the pistol frame and not the firing pin in the standing breech. Pulling the trigger rotates the axis pin and lowers the hammer so that it will strike the firing pin. It was this that inspired the Safety portion of the name. It was a well-made and sound design but is less common than the others shown here since it was made for only seven years.

SPECIFICATION:

CARTRIDGE:
0.38 S&W

DIMENSIONS:
LENGTH O/A: 185 mm (7.3 in)
WEIGHT: 460 g (1 lb)
BARREL: 83 mm (3.3 in)
RIFLING: 6 grooves, rh
CHAMBERS: 5 rounds

IN PRODUCTION:
1907–14

MARKINGS:
"HOPKINS & ALLEN ARMS CO NORWICH CONN" and various patent dates on top barrel rib. Serial number on butt frame beneath grips.

SAFETY:
No applied safety device.

UNLOADING:
Squeeze together two ribbed catches on each side of top strap; hinge down barrel to eject contents of cylinder. Return barrel, ensuring that spring catch engages.

Iver Johnson Safety Automatic   USA

As with most revolvers of this period, the word "Automatic" means automatic ejection of the spent cases as the barrel is opened. Also as usual, the word "hammerless" means a concealed hammer, though in this case the frame of the pistol is designed to conceal it, while other makers often used the frame of their hammer models and added a light metal shroud. The "Safety" in the title comes from the Iver Johnson "Hammer the Hammer" transfer bar system, which prevents the hammer striking the frame-mounted firing pin unless the trigger is correctly pulled, sliding a transfer bar between the two and thus transfering the blow. Dropping the pistol or letting the hammer slip during cocking could not cause the weapon to fire.

SPECIFICATION:

CARTRIDGE:
0.32 S&W

DIMENSIONS:
LENGTH O/A: 191 mm (7.5 in)
WEIGHT: 440 g (15.5 oz)
BARREL: 76 mm (3 in)
RIFLING: 5 grooves, rh
CHAMBERS: 6 rounds

IN PRODUCTION:
1894–1917

MARKINGS:
"IVER JOHNSON'S ARMS & CYCLE WORKS FITCHBURG MASS USA" on left side of barrel. Serial number on butt frame beneath grips.

SAFETY:
No applied safety device.

UNLOADING:
Grasp knurled ends of spring catch above standing breech and lift; hinge barrel down. This will cause ejector plate to move out and eject contents of chambers. Close barrel and ensure spring catch engages.

Ruger GP 100 USA

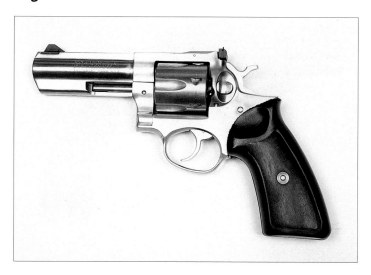

The GP 100 replaced the Security Six as the standard police revolver in 1987 and incorporated a number of improvements that experience had suggested, such as the full-length ejector shroud to give a slight degree of muzzle preponderance and the construction of the trigger guard and mechanism as a separate inserted subassembly. It is a robust revolver and will be around for many years to come.

SPECIFICATION:

CARTRIDGE:
0.357 Magnum

DIMENSIONS:
LENGTH O/A: 238 mm (9.4 in)
WEIGHT: 1.2 kg (2 lb 10 oz)
BARREL: 102 mm (4 in)
RIFLING: 5 grooves, rh
CHAMBERS: 6 rounds

IN PRODUCTION:
1987–

MARKINGS:
"STURM RUGER & CO INC SOUTHPORT CONN USA" on left side of barrel. "RUGER GP 100 .357 MAGNUM CAL [or .38 SPECIAL CAL]" on right side of barrel. Serial number on right side of frame.

SAFETY:
No applied safety device.

UNLOADING:
Push in recessed catch on left side of frame behind cylinder; allow cylinder to swing out to left of frame. Press in ejector rod to force out ejector plate and eject contents of chambers. Return cylinder to frame, ensuring catch locks.

Ruger Police Service Six USA

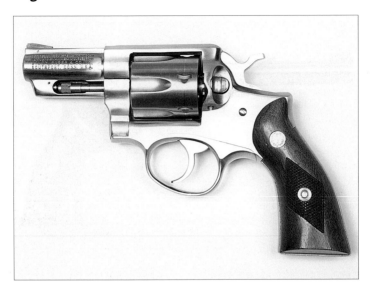

This is simply the Security Six with slightly modified grips and with a sighting groove in the backstrap instead of a separate rear sight, a modification intended to provide adequate sights for rapid combat firing at short range and to avoid the sights being deranged by careless insertion into the holster or other rough handling. A highly successful weapon, it was widely adopted by US police forces and sold for home defense.

SPECIFICATION:

CARTRIDGE:
0.357 Magnum

DIMENSIONS:
LENGTH O/A: 254 mm (10 in)
WEIGHT: 950 g (2 lb 1 oz)
BARREL: 102 mm (4 in)
RIFLING: 6 grooves, rh
CHAMBERS: 6 rounds

IN PRODUCTION:
1969–87

MARKINGS:
"STURM RUGER & CO INC SOUTHPORT CONN USA" on left side of barrel. ".38 SPECIAL CAL [or .357 MAGNUM CAL]" on right side of barrel. "RUGER POLICE SERVICE SIX" on right side of frame.

SAFETY:
No applied safety device.

UNLOADING:
Push in recessed catch on left side of frame behind the cylinder; allow cylinder to swing out to left of frame. Press in ejector rod to force out ejector plate and eject the contents of chambers. Return cylinder to frame, ensuring catch locks.

Ruger Security Six USA

Sturm, Ruger & Co. got into the revolver business in the early 1950s, making single-action Western guns for the "quick-draw" craze of the time. These were so popular that they persuaded Colt to restart making single-action guns, and many others joined in. Ruger then moved successfully to the police market with this extremely sound and reliable revolver. The Speed Six is the same pistol but with a rounded butt and is also offered in 0.385 Spl caliber.

SPECIFICATION:

CARTRIDGE:
0.357 Magnum

DIMENSIONS:
LENGTH O/A: 235 mm (9.3 in)
WEIGHT: 950 g (2 lb 1 oz)
BARREL: 102 mm (4 in)
RIFLING: 6 grooves, rh
CHAMBERS: 6 rounds

IN PRODUCTION:
1968–

MARKINGS:
"STURM RUGER & CO INC SOUTHPORT CONN USA" on left side of barrel. ".38 SPECIAL CAL [or .357 MAGNUM CAL]" on right side of barrel. "RUGER SECURITY SIX" on right side of frame.

SAFETY:
No applied safety device.

UNLOADING:
Press in recessed catch on left side of frame behind cylinder; allow cylinder to swing out to left of frame. Press in ejector rod to force out ejector plate and eject contents of chambers. Return cylinder to frame, ensuring catch locks.

Smith & Wesson .38/200 British Service USA

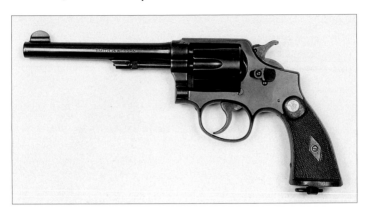

Like the M1917, this was another standard commercial model (the Military & Police) modified to meet a British World War II order. The only difference between it and the M&P is the sizing of the chamber for the British service 0.38 200-grain round; this dimension is such that the standard 0.38 S&W and 0.38 Colt New Police cartridges will also fit. About 890,000 were made, and early orders were filled with a mixture of 102, 127 and 152 mm (4, 5 and 6 in) barrel models. All were blued and polished, with checkered butts and S&W medallions. After April 1942 production was standardized on a 127 mm (5 in) barrel, sandblast blue finish, and plain walnut butt grips.

SPECIFICATION:

CARTRIDGE:
0.38 British Service, or 0.38 S&W, or similar

DIMENSIONS:
LENGTH O/A: 258 mm (10.2 in)
WEIGHT: 680 g (1 lb 8 oz)
BARREL: 127 mm (5 in)
RIFLING: 5 grooves, rh
CHAMBERS: 6 rounds

IN PRODUCTION:
1940–54

MARKINGS:
"SMITH & WESSON" on left side of barrel. "UNITED STATES PROPERTY" on left side of top strap above cylinder. Serial number on bottom of butt frame.

SAFETY:
None.

UNLOADING:
Press forward thumb catch on left side of frame behind cylinder. Cylinder can then be swung out to left side on its crane. Push back on ejector rod and a central ejector plate emerges from cylinder to remove cases from chambers. Release ejector rod, swing cylinder back into frame until it locks.

Smith & Wesson Model 36 "Chiefs Special" USA

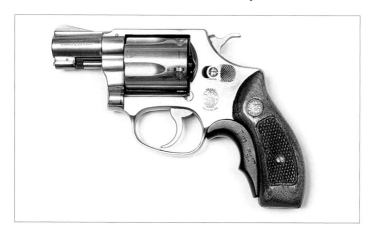

Smith & Wesson's steel-framed Model 36 Chiefs Special was the first of their small J-frame five-shot double-action revolvers. The name originated at a police officers' conference held in Colorado in 1950, where the revolver was first shown publicly. An ultra-lightweight version, known as the Chiefs Special Airweight, was introduced in 1952 with an aluminum frame and cylinder and an unloaded weight of 298 g. This was discontinued in 1954; an improved steel-cylinder derivative, the Model 37, was launched in 1957 using the same name. Other J-frame Chiefs Special derivatives are the shrouded-hammer Model 38 Bodyguard Airweight and Model 49 Bodyguard. In 1989, the J-frame range were repackaged as LadySmith revolvers and gained more barrel and grip options. The stainless steel version (shown) is known as the Model 60.

SPECIFICATION:

CARTRIDGE:
0.38 S&W Special

DIMENSIONS (WITH 76 MM/3 IN BARREL):
LENGTH O/A: 191 mm (7.5 in)
WEIGHT: 694 g (1 lb 8 oz)
BARREL: 76 mm (3 in); also available with 63 mm (2.5 in) barrel
RIFLING: 5 grooves, rh (Model 60, 6 grooves)
CHAMBERS: 5 rounds

IN PRODUCTION:
1950–

MARKINGS:
"SMITH & WESSON" on left side of barrel. "0.38 S&W SPL" on right side of barrel. Smith & Wesson motif on right side of frame behind recoil shield. "MADE IN USA, MARCAS REGISTRADAS SMITH & WESSON, SPRINGFIELD, MASS" on right side of frame below cylinder. Model number and serial number on frame under cylinder crane.

SAFETY:
Trigger-retracted hammer block.

UNLOADING:
Cylinder latch is on left of frame behind cylinder. Push cylinder latch forwards, swing out cylinder to left; eject any live or spent cartridges by pushing cylinder ejector rod to rear.

Smith & Wesson Model 586/686 USA

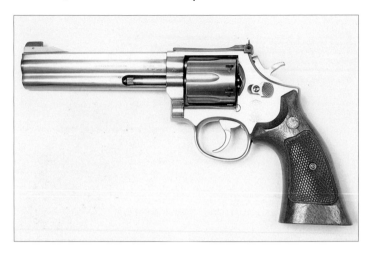

The L-frame Smith & Wesson 0.357 Magnums in blued carbon steel (Model 586) and stainless steel (Model 686) have been among S&W's fastest-selling revolvers since their introduction and are available in a wide range of barrel lengths. Their heavy medium frame with heavy barrel lug contributes to low recoil and good reliability.

SPECIFICATION:

CARTRIDGE:
0.357 Magnum (& 0.38 S&W Special)

DIMENSIONS (213 MM/8.375 IN BARREL):
LENGTH O/A: 351 mm (13.8 in)
WEIGHT: 1.4 kg (3 lb 1 oz)
BARREL: 213 mm (8.4 in); also available in 63 mm (2.5 in), 102 mm (4 in), and 152 mm (6 in)
RIFLING: 6 grooves, rh
CHAMBERS: 6 rounds

IN PRODUCTION:
1981–

MARKINGS:
"SMITH & WESSON" on left side of barrel. "S.&W. 357 MAGNUM" on right side of barrel. Smith & Wesson motif on left side of frame behind recoil shield. "MADE IN USA, MARCAS REGISTRADAS SMITH & WESSON, SPRINGFIELD, MASS" on right side of frame below cylinder. Model number and serial number on frame under cylinder crane.

SAFETY:
Trigger-retracted hammer block.

UNLOADING:
Cylinder latch is on left of frame behind cylinder. Push cylinder latch forwards, swing out cylinder to left; eject any live or spent cartridges by pushing cylinder ejector rod to rear.

Smith & Wesson Model 625 USA

The stainless steel N-frame Model 625 was introduced in 1987 as a limited edition of 5000 based on a carbon steel revolver, the Model 25, which fired the rimless 0.45 ACP pistol cartridge. The ammunition is secured in "half moon" three-round clips or "full moon" six-round clips before insertion into the cylinder. With a quantity of prepared full-moon clips, reloading is extremely swift. The success of the Model of 1987 limited edition as a moderately powerful and reliable double-action revolver prompted Smith & Wesson to change the 625 to a catalogued product known as the Model of 1988.

SPECIFICATION:

CARTRIDGE:
0.45 ACP

DIMENSIONS:
LENGTH O/A: 264 mm (10.4 in)
WEIGHT: 1.3 kg (2 lb 13 oz)
BARREL: 127 mm (5 in)
RIFLING: 6 grooves, rh
CHAMBERS: 6 rounds

IN PRODUCTION:
1987–

MARKINGS:
"SMITH & WESSON" on left side of barrel. "45 CAL MODEL OF 1988" on right side of the barrel. Smith & Wesson motif on right side of frame behind recoil shield. "MADE IN USA, MARCAS REGISTRADAS SMITH & WESSON, SPRINGFIELD, MASS" on right side of frame below cylinder. Model number and serial number on frame under cylinder crane.

SAFETY:
Trigger-retracted hammer block.

UNLOADING:
Cylinder latch is on left of frame behind cylinder. Push cylinder latch forwards, swing out cylinder to left; eject any live or spent cartridges by pushing cylinder ejector rod to rear.

Smith & Wesson Hand Ejector USA

The 0.32 Hand Ejector was the first Smith & Wesson revolver to employ the side-opening cylinder, and it went through three models, the second of which (shown here) adopted the innovations of the Military Police, such as the now-familiar push-catch for releasing the cylinder and the front anchorage for the ejector rod. The third model added the safety hammer block and a few refinements to the trigger mech-anism. It was a popular weapon, widely used by police forces and for home defense, over 300,000 of the three models being made.

SPECIFICATION:

CARTRIDGE:
0.32 S&W Long

DIMENSIONS:
LENGTH O/A: 190 mm (7.5 in)
WEIGHT: 505 g (1 lb 2 oz)
BARREL: 83 mm (3.3 in)
RIFLING: 5 grooves, rh
CHAMBERS: 5 rounds

IN PRODUCTION:
1896–1942

MARKINGS:
"SMITH & WESSON" on left side of barrel. ".32 S&W LONG CTG" on right side of barrel. Serial number on bottom of butt frame.

SAFETY:
None.

UNLOADING:
Press thumb catch on left side of frame behind cylinder forward. Cylinder can then be swung out to left side on its crane. Push back on ejector rod and a central ejector plate emerges from cylinder to remove cases from chambers. Release ejector rod. Swing cylinder back into frame until it locks.

Smith & Wesson Military & Police (Model 10) USA

This Model began production in 1899 and, with improvements and modifications, has continued to the present day. Prior to 1902, the ejector rod was unsupported at its front end; after that date, the familiar socket was used, supporting the ejector rod at the front end. Production stopped in 1942, about 800,000 having been made, and was resumed after the war as the Model 10. Various barrel lengths have been produced, from 51 to 165 mm (2 to 6.5 in), though 102 and 127 mm (4 and 5 in) appear to have been the most popular. An Airweight model, with alloy frame, appeared in 1952 (Model 12) and a stainless-steel model in 1970 (Model 64).

SPECIFICATION:

CARTRIDGE:
0.38 Special

DIMENSIONS:
LENGTH O/A: 235 mm (9.3 in)
WEIGHT: 865 g (1 lb 14 oz)
BARREL: 101 mm (4 in)
RIFLING: 5 grooves, rh
CHAMBERS: 6 rounds

IN PRODUCTION:
1899–

MARKINGS:
"MADE IN U.S.A./MARCA REGISTRADA/SMITH & WESSON/SPRINGFIELD MASS" on right side of frame. S&W monogram on right side of frame below hammer. "SMITH & WESSON" on right side of barrel. ".38 S&W SPECIAL CTG" on right side of barrel. Serial number on bottom of butt grip.

SAFETY:
None.

UNLOADING:
Press thumb catch on left side of frame behind the cylinder forward. Cylinder can then be swung out to left side on its crane. Push back on ejector rod and a central ejector plate emerges from cylinder to remove cases from chambers. Release ejector rod. Swing cylinder back into frame until it locks.

Smith & Wesson Model 29/629 USA

Smith & Wesson launched the carbon steel N-frame Model 29 as the first 0.44 Magnum revolver in 1955. In 1972, it won an awesome reputation as the "Most Powerful Handgun in the World" following its discovery by Hollywood. The stainless steel equivalent, the Model 629, was first produced in 1979. Both models have been made in a number of styles and barrel lengths, the early versions had only a shrouded ejector rod; recent production models designated the Model 629 Classic (shown) have the ejector rod shroud extended into a full-length barrel underlug. A lightweight-barrel model known as the Mountain Gun has a 102 mm (4 in) barrel.

SPECIFICATION:

CARTRIDGE:
0.44 Magnum (& 0.44 Special)

DIMENSIONS (WITH 213 MM/8.4 IN BARREL):
LENGTH O/A: 353 mm (13.9 in)
WEIGHT: 1.5 kg (3 lb 3 oz)
BARREL: 213 mm (8.4 in); also available in 102 mm (4 in), 152 mm (5 in), and 260 mm (10.6 in) barrels
RIFLING: 6 grooves, rh
CHAMBERS: 6 rounds

IN PRODUCTION:
1955– (Model 629, 1979–)

MARKINGS:
"SMITH & WESSON" on left side of barrel. "44 MAGNUM" on right side of barrel. Smith & Wesson motif on right side of frame behind recoil shield. "MADE IN USA, MARCAS REGISTRADAS SMITH & WESSON, SPRINGFIELD, MASS" on right side of frame below cylinder. Model number and serial number on frame under cylinder crane.

SAFETY:
Trigger-retracted hammer block.

UNLOADING:
Cylinder latch is on left of frame behind cylinder. Push cylinder latch forwards, swing out cylinder to left, eject any live or spent cartridges by pushing cylinder ejector rod to rear.

Smith & Wesson Model 60 USA

The J-frame Smith & Wesson Model 60 was the first stainless steel revolver produced anywhere in the world. Designed to combat the corrosion found on blued carbon steel firearms, which are carried close to the body, the Model 60 was based on the popular Model 36 Chiefs Special.

SPECIFICATION:

CARTRIDGE:
0.38 S&W Special

DIMENSIONS (WITH 76 MM/3 IN BARREL):
LENGTH O/A: 191 mm (7.5 in)
WEIGHT: 694 g (1 lb 8 oz)
BARREL: 76 mm (3 in); also available with 63 mm (2.5 in) barrel
RIFLING: 6 grooves, rh
CHAMBERS: 5 rounds

IN PRODUCTION:
1965–

MARKINGS:
"SMITH & WESSON" on left side of barrel. "0.38 S&W SPL" on right side of barrel. Smith & Wesson motif on right side of frame behind recoil shield. "MADE IN USA, MARCAS REGISTRADAS SMITH & WESSON, SPRINGFIELD, MASS" on right side of frame below cylinder. Model number and serial number on frame under cylinder crane.

SAFETY:
Trigger-retracted hammer block.

UNLOADING:
Cylinder latch is on left of frame behind cylinder. Push cylinder latch forwards, swing out cylinder to left, eject any live or spent cartridges by pushing cylinder ejector rod to rear.

Smith & Wesson New Century Hand Ejector USA

The flagship of the Smith & Wesson line in its day, this was also called the Triple Lock model, as it incorporated a third cylinder lock in the shroud beneath the barrel. About 20,000 were made in all, over 13,000 in 0.44 S&W caliber. Small numbers were also made in 0.45 Colt, 0.44 S&W Russian, 0.450 Eley, and 0.44–40 Winchester calibers, and 5000 were made in 0.455 Webley for the British Army in 1915–17.

SPECIFICATION:

CARTRIDGE:
0.44 S&W Special and others (see remarks)

DIMENSIONS:
LENGTH O/A: 298 mm (11.8 in)
WEIGHT: 1.1 kg (2 lb 6 oz)
BARREL: 165 mm (6.5 in)
RIFLING: 5 grooves, rh
CHAMBERS: 6 rounds

IN PRODUCTION:
1907–15

MARKINGS:
"SMITH & WESSON SPRINGFIELD MASS USA" and patent dates on top of barrel. "S&W DA 44" on left side of barrel. Serial number on bottom of butt frame.

SAFETY:
No safety device.

UNLOADING:
Press thumb catch on left side of frame behind cylinder forward. Cylinder can then be swung out to left side on its crane. Push back on ejector rod and a central ejector plate emerges from cylinder to remove cases from chambers. Release ejector rod. Swing cylinder back into frame until it locks.

Smith & Wesson Safety Hammerless USA

This is more or less the same revolver as the contemporary standard Double Action model, but with the hammer concealed under a rise in the frame and with a grip safety bar let into the rear edge of the butt. It is not actually hammerless. A popular weapon, it went through a number of minor changes during its life, though it was finalized in 1907 and remained unchanged until 1940. It is commonly called the "Lemon Squeezer," for obvious reasons.

SPECIFICATION:

CARTRIDGE:
0.38 S&W

DIMENSIONS:
LENGTH O/A: 190 mm (7.5 in)
WEIGHT: 510 g (1 lb 2 oz)
BARREL: 83 mm (3.3 in)
RIFLING: 5 grooves, rh
CHAMBERS: 6 rounds

IN PRODUCTION:
1887–1940

MARKINGS:
S&W monogram on right rear side of frame.
".38 S&W CTG" on left side of barrel.

SAFETY:
Grip safety must be depressed to unlock hammer mechanism.

UNLOADING:
Grasp two knurled buttons above standing breech; pull back and up. This will unlock frame latch and pivot barrel/cylinder assembly about on frame, so raising rear of cylinder. Cam forces out extractor plate to empty chambers. Once emptied, swing barrel up with sufficient force to engage frame latch.

Smith & Wesson US Model 1917 USA

The Model 1917, like the similar Colt, was a standard Smith & Wesson product (the 0.45 Hand Ejector) modified to accept the 0.45 automatic pistol cartridge for the sake of ammunition commonality. The cartridges were loaded into semicircular clips, three at a time, and two clips loaded into the cylinder. It is possible to load the cartridges without the clips, and they will chamber satisfactorily, being held at the correct point by a slight step in the chamber; however, they will not eject without the clip. The pistol was released to the commercial market in the 1920s, and a special cartridge with a thick rim, to reproduce the thickness of the clip and so fill the space between the cylinder and the standing breech, was made under the name ".45 Auto Rim," but this has been obsolete for many years.

SPECIFICATION:

CARTRIDGE:
0.45 ACP

DIMENSIONS:
LENGTH O/A: 274 mm (10.8 in)
WEIGHT: 1 kg (2 lb 4 oz)
BARREL: 140 mm (5.5 in)
RIFLING: 6 grooves, rh
CHAMBERS: 6 rounds

IN PRODUCTION:
1917–45

MARKINGS:
"SMITH & WESSON SPRINGFIELD MASS USA" and patent dates on top of barrel. "S&W DA 45" on left side of barrel. Serial number on bottom of butt frame.

SAFETY:
No safety device.

UNLOADING:
Press forward thumb catch on left side of frame behind cylinder. Cylinder can then be swung out to left side on its crane. Push back on ejector rod and central ejector plate emerges from cylinder to remove cases from chambers. Release ejector rod. Swing cylinder back into frame until it locks.

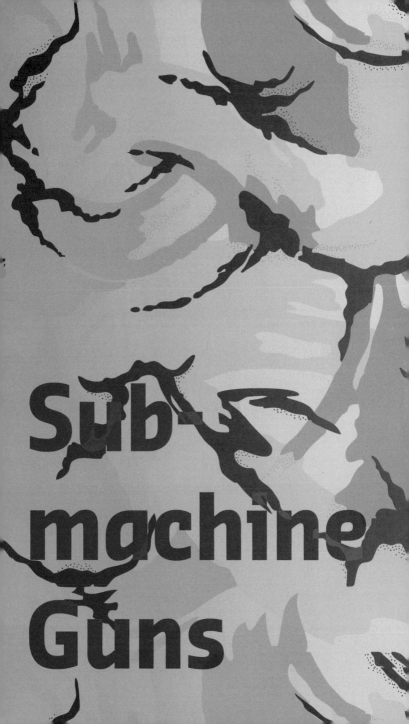

Sub-machine Guns

FMK Mod 2 ARGENTINA

An Argentine Army weapon, this was originally called the PA3(DM) for Pistola Ametralladora 3, Domingo Matheu factory. It replaced the earlier PA2(DM), which was simply a copy of the US M3A1 gun, in the early 1970s. There is also a version with a solid wooden butt. The FMK is reliable and well balanced; it can be fired single-handed quite easily.

SPECIFICATION:

CARTRIDGE:
9 x 19 mm Parabellum

DIMENSIONS:
LENGTH, STOCK EXTENDED: 693 mm (27.3 in)
LENGTH, STOCK RETRACTED: 523 mm (20.5 in)
WEIGHT: 3.4 kg (7 lb 8 oz)
BARREL: 290 mm (11.4 in)
RIFLING: 6 grooves, rh
MAGAZINE CAPACITY: 25 rounds
RATE OF FIRE: 650 rounds/min

IN PRODUCTION:
1974–

MARKINGS:
"FMK 2 CAL 9MM FABRICA MILITAR DE ARMAS PORTATILES ROSARIO ARGENTINA." Serial number on right of receiver. Serial number repeated on bolt.

SAFETY:
Grip safety with selector on left side of receiver: up for safe, midway for single shots, down for automatic fire.

UNLOADING:
Remove magazine. Squeeze in grip safety. Pull back cocking handle to eject any round in chamber. Inspect chamber through ejection port to ensure it is empty. Release bolt. Press trigger.

Although extremely popular with the troops, the Owen gun was somewhat out of date by the early 1960s and a new gun—the X3—was therefore designed and produced in 1962. The X3 could be described as an Australian version of the Sterling type. It has many features of the Sterling, particularly internally, though there are obvious differences in the trigger housing, and the bolt handle is on the left side. The rear sight is a special design and the top-mounted magazine of the Owen has been retained in response to the army's demands. An interesting feature is the way in which the small of the butt fits into the rear of the receiver, which is possible with the straight-line layout. It is a simple and effective gun that performed well in the jungle war in Vietnam and was then formally adopted as the 9 mm submachine gun F1. Manufacture ceased in the late 1980s with the advent of the AUG rifle.

SPECIFICATION:

CARTRIDGE:
9 x 19 mm Parabellum

DIMENSIONS:
LENGTH O/A: 715 mm (28.2 in)
WEIGHT: 3.3 kg (7 lb 3 oz)
BARREL: 203 mm (8 in)
RIFLING: 6 grooves, rh
MAGAZINE CAPACITY: 34 rounds
RATE OF FIRE: 600 rounds/min

IN PRODUCTION:
1963–87

MARKINGS:
"F1 LITHGOW" and serial number on right side of receiver.

SAFETY:
Combined safety and fire selector switch on left side of trigger mechanism housing: when applied, locks bolt if it is in forward position, preventing it from moving should weapon be dropped. If bolt is cocked, safety will move bolt away from sear and lock it.

UNLOADING:
Magazine catch at rear of magazine housing. Remove magazine. Pull back bolt until cocked. Inspect chamber through ejection port to ensure it is empty. Hold cocking handle and press trigger, allowing bolt to go forward under control.

Steyr AUG Para

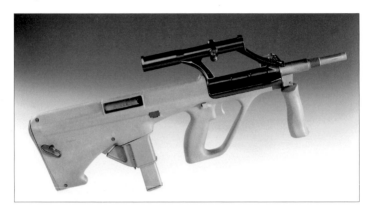

Although of similar appearance to the AUG assault rifle, the polymer stock or receiver is specific to this model. Ejection is to the right only and, unlike the rifle, cannot be altered for left-handed ejection. It has been converted to 9 x 19 mm Parabellum caliber by fitting a new barrel, a new bolt, and a magazine adapter to take the MPi69 magazines. The gas operating system of the rifle is disabled, and the AUG Para is a blowback weapon. The long barrel gives it excellent accuracy and a higher velocity than is usual from this cartridge. Steyr were one of the first to adapt an existing assault rifle design to the 9 mm cartridge, so producing a submachine gun requiring few new parts, and to date it is the most successful. For some time the company also sold a kit of parts from which any AUG rifle could be converted into the submachine gun version.

SPECIFICATION:

CARTRIDGE:
9 x 19 mm Parabellum

DIMENSIONS:
LENGTH O/A: 665 mm (26.2 in)
WEIGHT: 3.3 kg (7 lb 4 oz)
BARREL: 420 mm (16.5 in)
RIFLING: 6 grooves, rh
MAGAZINE CAPACITY: 25 or 32 rounds
RATE OF FIRE: 700 rounds/min

IN PRODUCTION:
1988–

MARKINGS:
"STEYR-DAIMLER-PUCH AG MADE IN AUSTRIA" and serial pressed into plastic stock.

SAFETY:
Cross-bolt safety catch above trigger: press in from left to right to make safe; press from right to left to fire. Fire selection performed by trigger; first pressure gives single shots, further pressure gives automatic fire.

UNLOADING:
Remove magazine. Pull back cocking handle. Inspect chamber to ensure it is empty. Release cocking handle and pull trigger.

Steyr MPi69 AUSTRIA

The MPi69 was adopted by the Austrian Army in 1969 and remains in wide use by several other armies and security forces. An excellent weapon, its only peculiarity is the attachment of the sling to the cocking system; some people do not like this, and for them the Steyr company makes the MPi81, which is the same weapon but with a conventional cocking handle and with the rate of fire increased to about 700 rounds/min. There is also a special long-barrel version of the MPi81, designed for firing out of the ports of an armored personnel carrier and known as the Loop-Hole model.

SPECIFICATION:

CARTRIDGE:
9 x 19 mm Parabellum

DIMENSIONS:
LENGTH, STOCK EXTENDED: 670 mm (26.4 in)
LENGTH, STOCK RETRACTED: 465 mm (18.3 in)
WEIGHT: 3.1 kg (6 lb 14 oz)
BARREL: 260 mm (10.2 in)
RIFLING: 6 grooves, rh
MAGAZINE CAPACITY: 25 or 32 rounds
RATE OF FIRE: 550 rounds/min

IN PRODUCTION:
1969–90

MARKINGS:
"STEYR-DAIMLER-PUCH AG MADE IN AUSTRIA" and serial number pressed into plastic stock.

SAFETY:
Cross-bolt passing through receiver: one end is marked "S" in white and protrudes when weapon is safe, the other is marked "F" in red and protrudes when weapon is set to fire. If button is pushed only halfway in either direction, the gun will fire single shots only.

UNLOADING:
Magazine release in heel of butt. Remove magazine. Cock weapon by holding pistol grip in one hand and grasping sling with the other. Hold sling out sideways, disengage cocking slide catch from front sight, then pull back bolt by pulling back on sling. Inspect chamber through ejection port, to ensure it is empty. Press trigger and allow sling and bolt to go forward.

Steyr-Solothurn MP34 AUSTRIA

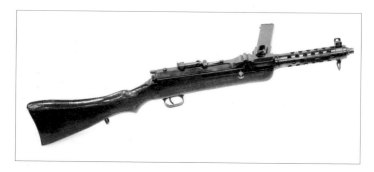

A solid and extremely well made weapon, designed in Germany, perfected by a German-owned company in Switzerland, and manufactured in Austria. It was used by the Austrian Army, taken into limited use by the German Army, and bought by the Portuguese in 1942, where it remained in use by their Fiscal Guards until the late 1970s. A number were also made in 9 x 19 mm Parabellum caliber for the Germany Army in 1938–39. An unusual feature is a magazine-loading device built into the magazine housing.

SPECIFICATION:

CARTRIDGE:
9 x 23 mm Steyr

DIMENSIONS:
LENGTH O/A: 808 mm (31.8 in)
WEIGHT: 4.4 kg (9 lb 10 oz)
BARREL: 200 mm (7.9 in)
RIFLING: 6 grooves, rh
MAGAZINE CAPACITY: 32 rounds
RATE OF FIRE: 500 rounds/min

IN PRODUCTION:
1934–39

MARKINGS:
Serial number and year over chamber. Steyr monogram (SSW) may also be above chamber.

SAFETY:
Sliding safety catch on top of receiver in front of rear sight: slide forward to make weapon safe by locking bolt whether in open or closed position.

UNLOADING:
Magazine catch on magazine housing. Remove magazine, pull back cocking handle to eject any round in chamber. Inspect chamber through ejection port to ensure it is empty. Release cocking handle. Press trigger.

Steyr TMP AUSTRIA

The TMP (Tactical Machine Pistol) replaced the MPi69 and MPi81 as the standard Steyr production sub-machine gun. The receiver is made almost entirely of synthetic material. A sound suppressor can be fitted. Plans to adopt a modular system of construction, similar to that of the AUG rifle, to permit changing a few parts to convert the TMP to other calibers such as 10 mm Auto, were not commercially successful. The same weapon, without the forward hand grip and firing single shots only, was marketed as the SPP (Special Purpose Pistol). In 2001, manufacturing rights to the TMP were purchased by Brüger & Thomet of Germany, who now manufacture an improved version as the MP9.

SPECIFICATION:

CARTRIDGE:
9 x 19mm Parabellum

DIMENSIONS:
LENGTH O/A: 270 mm (10.6 in)
WEIGHT: 1.3 kg (2 lb 14 oz)
BARREL: 150 mm (5.9 in)
RIFLING: 6 grooves, rh
MAGAZINE CAPACITY: 15, 20, or 25 rounds
RATE OF FIRE: 900 rounds/min

IN PRODUCTION:
1993–

MARKINGS:
"Steyr-Mannlicher" and serial number on left side of receiver.

SAFETY:
Cross-bolt safety catch lies in top of grip behind trigger: push from left to right to make weapon safe; push from right to left for automatic fire; push halfway for single shots.

UNLOADING:
Magazine catch is button in left front edge of butt, just behind trigger. Remove magazine. Grasp cocking handle (a pair of wings beneath the rear sight) and pull back to eject any round in chamber. Inspect chamber through the ejection port to ensure it is empty. Pull trigger and allow cocking handle and bolt to run forward.

FN HERSTAL P90 BELGIUM

The P90 was the first of a class of compact firearms firing a cartridge designed to defeat soft body armor at short combat ranges. It was intended for issue to military personnel who required a short, compact weapon more effective than a pistol or conventional submachine gun. Of unconventional appearance, the P90 uses the unlocked blowback system of operation. The magazine is unique in lying above the weapon with the cartridges at 90°. The penetrative power of the bullet is substantial, given its size. Fired cases are ejected downward through the hollow pistol grip. Subsequently, FN offered the FiveseveN self-loading pistol in this caliber.

SPECIFICATION:

CARTRIDGE:
5.7 x 28 mm

DIMENSIONS:
LENGTH O/A: 500 mm (19.7 in)
WEIGHT: 2.5 kg (5 lb 9 oz)
BARREL: 263 mm (10.4 in)
RIFLING: 6 grooves, rh
MAGAZINE CAPACITY: 50 rounds
RATE OF FIRE: 900 rounds/min

IN PRODUCTION:
1990–

MARKINGS:
"P90 Cal 5.7 X 28" and serial number on left side of sight mount. "FN HERSTAL SA BELGIUM" on left side of receiver.

SAFETY:
Manual serrated safety catch in rear edge of trigger guard: push back for safe, forward to fire.

UNLOADING:
Magazine catch at rear of magazine on top of receiver. Squeeze in, remove magazine by drawing rear end up and back. Pull back cocking lever to eject any round in chamber; repeat to be sure, as chamber cannot be inspected through ejection port. Release cocking handle. Press trigger.

Vigneron BELGIUM

A Belgian design, the Vigneron was issued to the Belgian Army in 1953 and then to the Belgian forces in the Belgian Congo. After the Congo became independent, these weapons were taken over by Congo troops, after which they were undoubtedly dispersed all over Central Africa. Numbers also appear to have been acquired by the Portuguese, who took it into service as the M/961, and these were probably left in Angola. As a result, the Vigneron can be expected to turn up anywhere in Africa for some years to come.

SPECIFICATION:

CARTRIDGE:
9 x 19 mm Parabellum

DIMENSIONS:
LENGTH, STOCK EXTENDED: 872 mm (34.3 in)
LENGTH, STOCK RETRACTED: 695 mm (27.3 6in)
WEIGHT: 3.3 kg (7 lb 4 oz)
BARREL: 300 mm (11.8 in)
RIFLING: 6 grooves, rh
MAGAZINE CAPACITY: 32 rounds
RATE OF FIRE: 600 rounds/min

IN PRODUCTION:
1952–62

MARKINGS:
"ABL52 VIG M1" and serial number on right side of magazine housing. "Licence Vigneron" cast into right side of receiver.

SAFETY:
Combined safety catch and fire selector lever on left side of receiver: turn to rear to make weapon safe; turn forward one notch for single shots; turn forward and down for automatic fire. Grip safety on pistol grip that must be squeezed in to unlock bolt.

UNLOADING:
Magazine catch on right side of magazine housing. Remove magazine. Pull back cocking handle to eject any round in chamber, inspect chamber through ejection port to ensure it is empty. Release cocking handle. Pull trigger.

Arsenal Shipka BULGARIA

While submachine guns continue to fall from favor among West European armies, several East European countries continue to develop and market this class of weapon. One is the Bulgarian Shipka, an Arsenal Corporation product that, although completely conventional in operation and basic construction, does introduce high-impact polymer moldings for the furniture. The blowback Shipka is available chambered for one of two cartridges: 9 x 18 mm Makarov or 9 x 19 mm Parabellum. The Makarov-cartridge variant (shown) has a 32-round box magazine.

SPECIFICATION:

CARTRIDGE:
9 x 18 mm Makarov (or 9 x 19 mm Parabellum)

DIMENSIONS:
LENGTH, STOCK EXTENDED: 625 mm (24.6 in)
LENGTH, STOCK FOLDED: 338 mm (13.3 in)
WEIGHT: 2.2 kg (4 lb 13 oz)
BARREL: 150 mm (5.9 in)
RIFLING: 4 grooves, rh
MAGAZINE CAPACITY: 32 rounds

IN PRODUCTION:
1999–

MARKINGS:
"ARSENAL" molded into top of magazine well on left side. "SMG SHIPKA," followed by caliber and serial number engraved in cocking slide housing.

SAFETY:
Trigger lock that is pressed into place behind trigger to prevent operation.

UNLOADING:
Magazine catch located just below and in front of trigger group: press to release magazine downwards, ready to have any rounds removed. Pull back cocking slide on left hand side to eject any round in chamber. Inspect chamber and feedway through ejection slot on right side of receiver to ensure it is empty. Press trigger and manually control forward movement of slide.

FAMAE SAF CHILE

This is the Chilean Army issue weapon; it is also exported. The weapon is based on the SIG 550 rifle design, which is made under license in Chile, and the designer's object was to utilize as many parts of the rifle as possible to save production costs. The standard model has a folding butt; there is also a fixed-butt model; a version with an integral silencer; and the Mini-SAF, a shortened version with no butt and a fixed forward grip. The 30-round magazine is of translucent plastic, enabling the ammunition to be visually checked, and there are studs and slots allowing two or more magazines to be connected together.

SPECIFICATION:

CARTRIDGE:
9 x 19 mm Parabellum

DIMENSIONS:
LENGTH, STOCK EXTENDED: 640 mm (25.2 in)
LENGTH, STOCK RETRACTED: 410 mm (16.2 in)
WEIGHT: 2.9 kg (6 lb 6 oz)
BARREL: 200 mm (7.9 in)
RIFLING: 6 grooves, rh
MAGAZINE CAPACITY: 20 or 30 rounds
RATE OF FIRE: 1200 rounds/min

IN PRODUCTION:
1990–

MARKINGS:
"FAMAE Mod SAF Cal 9mm [serial number]" on left side of receiver.

SAFETY:
Combined safety catch and fire selector on left side of receiver, above pistol grip: up for safe, down one notch for single shots, down two notches for three-round burst.

UNLOADING:
Magazine catch on front edge of trigger guard, behind magazine housing. Remove magazine. Pull back cocking handle to eject any round in chamber. Inspect chamber via ejection port to ensure it is empty. Release cocking handle. Pull trigger.

Type 64 CHINA

The Type 64 has an integral silencer and uses a special cartridge based on the 7.62 x 25 mm cartridge but with a pointed, heavy bullet fired at subsonic velocity. The mechanism combines the blowback action and bolt of the Soviet PPS-43 sub-machine gun; the trigger mechanism of the Czech ZB26 machine gun; and silencer of classical Maxim pattern, full of baffles and with a perforated barrel. With the special cartridge it is reasonably silent, but with standard full-charge pistol ammunition it is almost as noisy as an unsilenced weapon.

SPECIFICATION:

CARTRIDGE:
7.62 x 25 mm Type P Subsonic

DIMENSIONS:
LENGTH, STOCK EXTENDED: 843 mm (33.3 in)
LENGTH, STOCK RETRACTED: 635 mm (25 in)
WEIGHT: 3.4 kg (7 lb 8 oz)
BARREL: 244 mm (9.6 in)
RIFLING: 4 grooves, rh
MAGAZINE CAPACITY: 30 rounds
RATE OF FIRE: 1300 rounds/min

IN PRODUCTION:
1966–?

MARKINGS:
Factory identifier and serial number on top of receiver.

SAFETY:
Safety catch on right side of receiver: hinged plate moves up to block bolt.

UNLOADING:
Magazine catch behind magazine. Remove magazine. Press down safety plate. Pull back cocking handle to eject any round in chamber. Inspect chamber through ejection port to ensure it is empty. Release bolt. Press trigger.

Type 79 CHINA

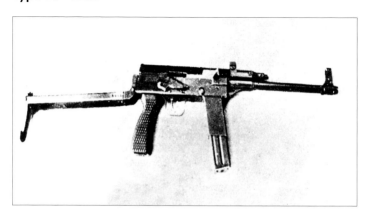

A somewhat unusual weapon, the Type 79 is gas operated, using a short-stroke tappet above the barrel that forces back an operating rod to drive a rotating bolt. The system is broadly that of the AK series of rifles, as are the outer controls such as the safety and pistol grip, making it easier to train soldiers already familiar with the AK. It is remarkably light and falls into the class of machine pistol, no doubt due to the rotating bolt system, which removes the need for the heavy bolt of a simple blowback weapon.

SPECIFICATION:

CARTRIDGE:
7.62 x 25 mm Soviet Pistol

DIMENSIONS:
LENGTH, STOCK EXTENDED: 740 mm (29.1 in)
LENGTH, STOCK RETRACTED: 470 mm (18.5 in)
WEIGHT: 1.9 kg (4 lb 3 oz)
BARREL: 225 mm (8.9 in)
RIFLING: unknown
MAGAZINE CAPACITY: 20 rounds
RATE OF FIRE: 650 rounds/min

IN PRODUCTION:
1980–?

MARKINGS:
Factory identifier and serial number on top of receiver.

SAFETY:
Manual safety catch/fire selector on right side of receiver: up for safe, center for automatic fire, down for single shots.

UNLOADING:
Magazine catch at front of magazine housing. Remove magazine. Pull back cocking lever to eject any round in chamber. Inspect chamber through ejection port to ensure it is empty. Release cocking lever. Press trigger.

The JS 9 is a bullpup design, with the magazine located behind the pistol grip to reduce the weapon's overall length. It is usually seen fitted with a sound suppressor. It has a blowback system of operation and is known to exist in two caliber variants. It is of modular construction with the lower section, comprising pistol grip and trigger assembly, and the forward grip and the butt constructed of polymer. A pistol-grip safety is fitted and must be pressed into the grip to fire. The top of the gun has a length of sight rail fitted for the mounting of optical or night-vision devices.

SPECIFICATION:

CARTRIDGE:
9 x 19 mm; 5.8 x 21 mm

DIMENSIONS:
LENGTH O/A: 500 mm (19.6 in)
WEIGHT: 2 kg (4.4 lbs)
MAGAZINE CAPACITY: 20 or 30 rounds
RATE OF FIRE: Not known

IN PRODUCTION:
2004–

MARKINGS:
None noted.

SAFETY:
Pistol-grip "squeeze" safety.

UNLOADING:
Magazine catch on left side behind magazine housing. Remove magazine. Pull back cocking handle to eject any round in chamber. Inspect chamber through ejection port to ensure it is empty. Point weapon in safe direction and pull trigger.

Agram 2000 CROATIA

The Agram 2000 is a locally manufactured weapon of the machine pistol class, constructed principally of metal stampings and plastic moldings. The muzzle is threaded and a protecting sleeve is screwed on; this can be removed and a silencer fitted. There is no provision for a shoulder stock, and the sights are a simple front blade and rear flip-over marked for 50 and 150 meters, so the practical accuracy of this weapon is questionable. An alternative model, the Agram 2002, lacks the forward "thumbhole" pistol grip.

SPECIFICATION:

CARTRIDGE:
9 x 19 mm Parabellum

DIMENSIONS:
LENGTH O/A: 350 mm (13.8 in); with suppressor, 472 mm (18.6 in)
WEIGHT: 1.9 kg (4 lb 3 oz)
BARREL: 152 mm (6 in)
RIFLING: 4 grooves, rh
MAGAZINE CAPACITY: 20 or 32 rounds
RATE OF FIRE: 750 rounds/min

IN PRODUCTION:
1997–2000

MARKINGS:
Not known; only specimen examined had all markings defaced by acid.

SAFETY:
Manual safety/selector switch on left side above trigger: "S" for safe, "R" for automatic, "1" for single shots.

UNLOADING:
Magazine catch at bottom rear of magazine housing. Remove magazine. Pull back cocking handle to eject any round in chamber. Inspect chamber to ensure it is empty. Release cocking handle.

The ERO is a direct copy of the folding-stock version of the Uzi submachine gun. It uses the same wrap-round bolt, grip safety, pistol grip magazine housing, top cocking handle, and every other Uzi feature; the end result is indistinguishable from the original Uzi. Taken into military and police service after the creation of an independent Croatia following the breakup of the former Federal Republic of Yugoslavia, it has also been offered for export. The Mini-ERO version (shown) is similar to the Mini Uzi, but is distinguished by a telescoping twin-strut metal stock.

SPECIFICATION:

CARTRIDGE:
9 x 19 mm Parabellum

DIMENSIONS (ERO):
LENGTH O/A: 650 mm (25.6 in)
WEIGHT: 3.7 kg (8 lb 4 oz)
BARREL: 260 mm (10.2 in)
RIFLING: 4 grooves, rh
MAGAZINE CAPACITY: 20 or 32 rounds

IN PRODUCTION:
1995–?

MARKINGS:
"ERO Zagreb" and serial number on left side of receiver.

SAFETY:
Three-position selector-lever on left side of receiver above grip: rear position (Z) for safe, center position (P) for single shot, and forward position (R) for automatic. Grip safety must be squeezed in before bolt can be cocked or released.

UNLOADING:
Magazine release catch on lower left side of pistol grip. Remove magazine. Hold grip firmly to squeeze in grip safety. Pull back bolt and inspect chamber through the ejection port to ensure it is empty. Push selector to a "fire" position, point weapon in a safe direction, pull trigger, and allow bolt to go forward under control.

ZAGI M91 CROATIA

This is a cheaply made weapon that shows signs of original thinking. The receiver and jacket are of the same diameter, and the jacket is perforated. The magazine housing is unusually deep and can act as a foregrip without putting strain on the magazine, which can otherwise cause stoppages. There is a knurled surface on the lower receiver that can be used as an alternate foregrip. The stock is of steel rod, which slides into sheaths alongside the receiver. It has a curiously short butt pad. There is a push-through safety catch but no provision for firing single shots.

SPECIFICATION:

CARTRIDGE:
9 x 19 mm Parabellum

DIMENSIONS:
LENGTH, BUTT EXTENDED: 850 mm (33.5 in)
LENGTH, BUTT FOLDED: 565 mm (22.3 in)
WEIGHT: 3.41 kg (7 lb 8 oz)
BARREL: 220 mm (8.7 in)
RIFLING: 4 grooves, rh
MAGAZINE CAPACITY: 32 rounds
RATE OF FIRE: Not known

IN PRODUCTION:
1991–95

MARKINGS:
"ZAGI M-91" on left side of receiver above trigger. "PHTO BS7 9mm PARA" on left side above magazine housing.

SAFETY:
Push-through button in front of and above trigger: push to left for safe.

UNLOADING:
Magazine catch on left side of magazine. Remove magazine and empty if necessary. Pull back cocking handle until sear engages and examine feedway and chamber through ejection port to ensure it is empty. Grasp cocking handle, draw back slightly, press trigger and allow bolt to go forward under control.

CZ Model 25 CZECH REPUBLIC

This is one of a family of four similar weapons: the Model 23 has a wooden stock and the Model 25 a folding stock; both fire the 9 x 19 mm Parabellum cartridge. The Model 24 has a wooden stock and the Model 26 a folding stock; both fire the 7.62 mm Soviet Pistol cartridge and will usually fire the 7.63 mm Mauser pistol cartridge. They were produced in large numbers and widely exported.

SPECIFICATION:

CARTRIDGE:
9 x 19 mm Parabellum

DIMENSIONS:
LENGTH, STOCK EXTENDED: 686 mm (27 in)
LENGTH, STOCK RETRACTED: 445 mm (17.5 in)
WEIGHT: 3.1 kg (6 lb 13 oz)
BARREL: 284 mm (11.2 in)
RIFLING: 6 grooves, rh
MAGAZINE CAPACITY: 24 or 40 rounds
RATE OF FIRE: 600 rounds/min

IN PRODUCTION:
1949–68

MARKINGS:
"ZB 1949 she" with serial number on left side of receiver behind pistol grip.

SAFETY:
Metal switch inside trigger guard behind trigger: push to right to lock bolt open or closed, push to left to fire. For single shots, press trigger to first resistance; for automatic fire press trigger as far as possible.

UNLOADING:
Press magazine catch in bottom of pistol grip and remove magazine. Pull back cocking handle in top of receiver to eject any round in chamber. Release bolt. Press trigger.

Skorpion CZECH REPUBLIC

The Skorpion was originally developed as a personal-defense weapon for armored vehicle crews. It may be regarded more as a machine pistol than a submachine gun. It is fitted with a wire-stock that sits over the top of the gun. A rate reducer in the pistol grip provides a cyclic rate of 850–900 rounds/min, which will soon empty a magazine. Box magazines can hold 10 or 20 rounds. The original version was the Model 61 chambered for 0.32 ACP and is the model most likely to be encountered. Series production of this model ceased during the mid-1970s, but it remains available for export sales. To boost such sales, the weapon is now available chambered for 9 x 18 mm Makarov (shown), 0.380 ACP, and 9 x 19 mm Parabellum, the latter model having slightly enlarged dimensions overall. Numerous tactical accessories, from reflex sights to tactical lights, are now available.

SPECIFICATION:

CARTRIDGE:
0.32 ACP/7.65 mm, 9 x 18 mm Makarov, 0.380 ACP, or 9 x 19 mm Parabellum

DIMENSIONS:
LENGTH, STOCK EXTENDED: 517 mm (20.4 in)
LENGTH, STOCK RETRACTED: 270 mm (10.6 in)
WEIGHT: 1.3 kg (2 lb 13 oz)
BARREL: 115 mm (4.5 in)
RIFLING: 6 grooves, rh
MAGAZINE CAPACITY (7.65 MM): 12 or 20 rounds
RATE OF FIRE: 850–900 rounds/min

IN PRODUCTION:
1960–

MARKINGS:
Serial number on left side of receiver. Otherwise, no markings.

SAFETY:
Manual safety catch and fire selector on left side above pistol grip. Move back, to notch marked "1," for single shots; move to center, to notch marked "0" for safe; move forward, to notch marked "20" for automatic.

UNLOADING:
Magazine catch on left side of frame just behind magazine housing. Remove magazine. Grasp cocking knobs on each side of upper receiver and pull back to eject any round in chamber. Inspect chamber through ejection port to ensure it is empty. Release cocking knobs. Press trigger.

Madsen Model 1946/1950 DENMARK

The Madsen design is unusual in having a "clamshell" receiver, which is made of two pressings hinged down the back; by removing the barrel retaining nut and barrel, it is possible to open the receiver up like a book, exposing all the parts inside. The cocking handle on this model is actually a plate on top of the receiver that has "wings" on the sides and can be grasped and pulled back. The Model 1946 was used by the Danish Army and also sold to some South American countries and to Thailand. The Model 1950 is similar but has the cocking handle in the form of a round knob on top of the receiver.

SPECIFICATION:

CARTRIDGE:
9 x 19 mm Parabellum

DIMENSIONS:
LENGTH, STOCK EXTENDED: 780 mm (30.7 in)
LENGTH, STOCK RETRACTED: 550 mm (21.7 in)
WEIGHT: 3.2 kg (6 lb 15 oz)
BARREL: 200 mm (7.9 in)
RIFLING: 4 grooves, rh
MAGAZINE CAPACITY: 32 rounds
RATE OF FIRE: 500 rounds/min

IN PRODUCTION:
1945–53

MARKINGS:
"MADSEN" on right side of receiver. Serial number on top of receiver.

SAFETY:
Manual safety sliding button on left side of receiver: push forward for safe, rearward to fire. Grip safety device behind magazine housing must be gripped and squeezed towards housing to permit bolt to close.

UNLOADING:
Magazine catch at rear of magazine housing. Remove magazine. Pull back cocking handle to eject any round in chamber. Inspect chamber through ejection port to ensure it is empty. Grip magazine housing and squeeze grip safety. Pull trigger.

Suomi M1931 FINLAND

One of the earliest non-German submachine guns, the Suomi was developed in Finland and saw use in Scandinavian armies, the Swiss Army, South America, and Poland, and was built under license in Denmark and Switzerland. It was generally considered to be among the best designs available in 1939 when the British Army tried to acquire some (without luck—the Russians attacked Finland and the Finns had no guns to spare). It remained in Finnish service until well after 1945, most guns being modified to accept the Carl Gustav magazine, on which the other Scandinavian countries had standardized.

SPECIFICATION:

CARTRIDGE:
9 x 19 mm Parabellum

DIMENSIONS:
LENGTH O/A: 870 mm (34.3 in)
WEIGHT: 4.6 kg (10 lb 2 oz)
BARREL: 314 mm (12.4 in)
RIFLING: 6 grooves, rh
MAGAZINE CAPACITY: 71-round drum, or 20- or 50-round box
RATE OF FIRE: 900 rounds/min

IN PRODUCTION:
1931–44

MARKINGS:
Serial number on end cap and on left side of receiver.

SAFETY:
Manual safety lever in front edge of trigger guard: push backwards, into guard, to make safe; this locks bolt in either forward or rearward position.

UNLOADING:
Magazine release behind magazine housing. Remove magazine. Pull back cocking lever to eject any round in chamber. Inspect chamber through ejection port to ensure it is empty. Release cocking lever. Press trigger.

MAT 49 FRANCE

This replaced the MAS 38 submachine gun and fires a far more practical cartridge. It is a very compact design and the magazine housing, complete with magazine, can be folded forward to lie under to barrel and make it more convenient to carry. It was more or less replaced in the French Army by the adoption of the 5.56 mm FAMAS rifle but is still in use by reserve forces and by police and other paramilitary forces. It will also be encountered in former French colonies.

SPECIFICATION:

CARTRIDGE:
9 x 19 mm Parabellum

DIMENSIONS:
LENGTH, STOCK EXTENDED: 660 mm (26 in)
LENGTH, STOCK RETRACTED: 404 mm (15.9 in)
WEIGHT: 3.6 kg (8 lb)
BARREL: 230 mm (9.1 in)
RIFLING: 4 grooves, lh
MAGAZINE CAPACITY: 32 rounds
RATE OF FIRE: 600 rounds/min

IN PRODUCTION:
1949–90

MARKINGS:
"M.A.T. Mle 49 9m/m [serial number]" on left side of receiver.

SAFETY:
Grip safety in rear edge of pistol grip must be squeezed in to allow bolt to move. No other safety device.

UNLOADING:
Magazine catch behind magazine housing. Remove magazine. Pull back cocking handle to eject any round in chamber. Inspect chamber through ejection port to ensure it is empty. Release cocking handle. Press trigger.

Heckler & Koch MP5 GERMANY

The Heckler & Koch MP5 is the most widely employed and distributed submachine gun of recent decades and is still in production in Germany and several other nations, including the USA, Greece, Pakistan, and Turkey. Unlike other submachine guns, the MP5 employs the Heckler & Koch roller-delayed blowback breech mechanism, as employed on the G3 automatic rifle. Numerous variants have been produced, with both fixed and telescopic butt stocks (shown). At least 20 subvariants have been produced, but they all have the same basic receiver and mechanism. Barrel lengths may vary. Some models have combined safety and selector switches that cater for burst-fire-limiting devices, while others fire semiautomatically only. Versions produced for the US market may be chambered for 10 mm Auto or 0.40 S&W, but most models fire 9 x 19 mm. Both straight and curved box magazines may be encountered.

SPECIFICATION:

CARTRIDGE:
9 x 19 mm Parabellum

DIMENSIONS (FIXED BUTT):
LENGTH O/A: 680 mm (26.8 in)
WEIGHT: 2.5 kg (5 lb 9 oz)
BARREL: 225 mm (8.9 in)
RIFLING: 6 grooves, rh
MAGAZINE CAPACITY: 15 or 30 rounds
RATE OF FIRE: 800 rounds/min

IN PRODUCTION:
1966–

MARKINGS:
"Kal 9mm x 19" on left side of magazine housing. Numerous other national markings likely to be encountered.

SAFETY:
Combined safety and fire selector switch on left side of receiver. As a general rule, top position is safe (S), with fire modes usually marked by representations of one, three or several bullets. Other markings used instead of bullets are "E" for single shots or "F" for fully automatic.

UNLOADING:
Magazine release behind and below magazine housing. Remove magazine. Pull back handle and cock weapon. Inspect breech to ensure chamber is empty. Grasp cocking handle and pull trigger, allowing cocking handle to go forward under control.

Heckler & Koch MP5K GERMANY

This is a special short version of the MP5 intended for use by police and antiterrorist squads who require very compact firepower. The weapon can be carried concealed under clothing or in the glove compartment of a car, and it can also be concealed in, and fired from, a specially fitted briefcase. Mechanically it is the same as the MP5 but with a shorter barrel and smaller magazines. Four versions are made; the MP5K is fitted with adjustable iron sights or a telescope; the MP5KAI has a smooth upper surface so that there is little to catch in clothing or a holster in a quick draw; the MP5KA4 is similar to the MP5K but has an additional three-round burst facility; and the MP5KA5 is similar to the AI, with the addition of the three-round burst unit. No butt is fitted, but there is a robust front grip that gives good control when firing. A close copy is manufactured in Pakistan.

SPECIFICATION:

CARTRIDGE:
9 x 19 mm Parabellum

DIMENSIONS:
LENGTH O/A: 325 mm (12.7 in)
WEIGHT: 2 kg (4 lb 6 oz)
BARREL: 115 mm (4.5 in)
RIFLING: 6 grooves, rh
MAGAZINE CAPACITY: 15 or 30 rounds
RATE OF FIRE: 900 rounds/min

IN PRODUCTION:
1972–

MARKINGS:
"Kal 9mm x 19" on left side of magazine housing.

SAFETY:
Combined safety and fire-selector switch on left side of receiver. In MP5K and KAI, this is a three-position switch: up for safe (S), down one notch for single shots (E), to bottom for automatic fire (F). In KA4 and KA5, it is a four-position switch: up for safe; down one notch for single shots, two notches for three-round bursts, and three notches for automatic fire, these positions being marked by representations of one, three, and several bullets. Post-1990 production will have switch duplicated on both sides of weapon.

UNLOADING:
Magazine release behind and below magazine housing. Remove magazine, pull back handle and cock weapon. Examine breech to ensure chamber is empty. Grasp cocking handle and pull trigger, allowing cocking handle to go forward under control.

Heckler & Koch MP5K-PDW Personal Defense Weapon GERMANY/USA

This was designed by the Heckler & Koch subsidiary in the USA as a weapon for aircrew or vehicle-borne troops who need something extremely compact. It is, in effect, the MP5K fitted with a folding butt and with the muzzle modified to accept a silencer. There is also provision for fitting a laser spot projector. Should the butt not be needed, it can be easily removed and a butt cap fitted on the end of the receiver. Selective fire is standard, but a two- or three-round burst unit can be fitted to the trigger mechanism if required.

SPECIFICATION:

CARTRIDGE:
9 x 19 mm Parabellum

DIMENSIONS:
LENGTH, WITH BUTT CAP: 349 mm (13.8 in)
LENGTH, WITH BUTT EXTENDED: 603 mm (23.8 in)
LENGTH, WITH BUTT FOLDED: 368 mm (14.5 in)
WEIGHT, WITH BUTT: 2.8 kg (6 lb 2 oz)
WEIGHT, WITH BUTT-CAP: 2.1 kg (4 lb 10 oz)
BARREL: 127 mm (5 in)
RIFLING: 6 grooves, rh
MAGAZINE CAPACITY: 30 rounds
RATE OF FIRE: 900 rounds/min

IN PRODUCTION:
1991–

MARKINGS:
"Made in Germany for HK Inc Chantilly Va" on right side of magazine housing. "Kal 9mm x 19" on left side of magazine housing.

SAFETY:
Combined safety and fire-selector switch on both left and right sides of receiver. Four-position switch: up for safe; down one notch for single shots, two notches for three-round bursts, and three notches for automatic fire, these positions being marked by representations of one, three, and several bullets.

UNLOADING:
Magazine release behind and below magazine housing. Remove magazine, pull back handle, and cock weapon. Examine breech to ensure chamber is empty. Grasp cocking handle and pull trigger, allowing cocking handle to go forward under control.

Heckler & Koch MP5SD GERMANY

This is the silenced member of the MP5 family; the mechanism is exactly the same as the standard MP5, but the short barrel is drilled with 30 holes and surrounded by a large silencer casing. This casing is divided into two chambers: the first surrounds the barrel and receives the propellant gas via the 30 holes, which serve also to reduce the bullet's velocity to below the speed of sound.

There are six versions of this weapon: the MP5SD1 has the end of the receiver closed by a cap and has no buttstock; the SD2 has a fixed plastic butt; the SD3 has a sliding retractable butt; all three can fire either single shots or automatic. The SD4 is the SD1 with a three-round burst facility; the SD5 is the SD2 with three-round burst; and the SD6 is the SD3 with three-round burst.

SPECIFICATION:

CARTRIDGE:
9 x 19 mm Parabellum

DIMENSIONS:
LENGTH O/A: SD1, 550 mm (1.7 in); SD2, 780 mm (30.7 in); SD3, butt extended, 780 mm (30.7 in), butt retracted, 610 mm (24 in)
BARREL: 146 mm (5.8 in)
WEIGHT: SD1, 2.9 kg (6 lb 6 oz); SD2, 3.2 kg (7 lb 1 oz); SD3, 3.5 kg (7 lb 11 oz)
RIFLING: 6 grooves, rh
MAGAZINE CAPACITY: 15 or 30 rounds
RATE OF FIRE: 800 rounds/min

IN PRODUCTION:
1970–

MARKINGS:
"Kal 9mm x 19" on left side of magazine housing.

SAFETY:
Combined safety and fire-selector switch on left side of receiver. In SD1, 2, and 3, this is a three-position switch: up for safe (S), down one notch for single shots (E), and to bottom for automatic fire (F). In SD4, 5, and 6, it is a four-position switch: up for safe, down one notch for single shots, down two notches for three-round bursts, and down three notches for automatic fire, these positions being marked by representations of one, three, and several bullets.

UNLOADING:
Magazine release behind and below magazine housing. Remove magazine, pull back handle. Cock weapon. Examine breech to ensure chamber is empty. Grasp cocking handle and pull trigger, allowing cocking handle to go forward under control.

Heckler & Koch MP7 GERMANY

The MP7 is another weapon that falls within the personal defense weapon category. It differs from other sub-machine guns in that it fires a special-to-type 4.6 x 30 mm cartridge, and it is a gas-operated weapon with a rotating locking bolt. The MP7 was designed primarily for personnel who need to be armed but who require a weapon more compact than a rifle. Realizing that something better than a pistol was needed, the personal-defense weapon concept emerged. The MP7 is therefore light, easy to carry, and, when needed, accurate up to about 200 m (656 ft). Magazines are inserted through the pistol grip, and the weapon is fired either using the telescopic buttstock or freehand, as with a pistol. In either firing mode, the folding forward grip may be used to control fire, either folded up as a forestock or lowered as a forward pistol grip. The special 4.6 mm cartridge was developed to defeat soft body armors at normal combat ranges.

SPECIFICATION:

CARTRIDGE:
4.6 x 30mm Special

DIMENSIONS:
LENGTH, STOCK EXTENDED: 540 mm (21.3 in)
LENGTH, STOCK RETRACTED: 340 mm (13.4 in)
WEIGHT, LESS MAGAZINE: 1.5 kg (3 lb 5 oz)
BARREL: 180 mm (7.1 in)
RIFLING: 6 grooves, rh
MAGAZINE CAPACITY: 20 or 40 rounds
RATE OF FIRE: Circa 950 rounds/min

IN PRODUCTION:
2002–

MARKINGS:
"H&K PDW Kal 4.6mm x 30" on left side of receiver. Serial number on right of receiver, just above pistol grip.

SAFETY:
Combined safety and fire-selector three-position switch on both sides of receiver: up for safe, down one notch for single shots, two notches for fully automatic fire. Fire rates are indicated by outlines of a single bullet and four bullets respectively.

UNLOADING:
Magazine release just above trigger. Remove magazine. Pull back cocking handle at rear of receiver to cock weapon. Examine chamber through ejection port. If empty, grasp cocking handle and pull trigger, allowing cocking handle to go forward under control.

Heckler & Koch UMP GERMANY

Originally developed and manufactured in the USA to fire the 0.45 ACP cartridge, the UMP (Universal Machine Pistol) is also manufactured in Germany chambered for the 9 x 19 mm Parabellum cartridge. The UMP is based around the receiver of the H&K G36 assault rifle and makes extensive use of high-impact polymers throughout its construction. A skeleton buttstock folds along the right side of the receiver. A length of Picatinny rail above the receiver can be used to mount various forms of reflex or optical sight, while another length of rail under the forestock can accommodate a foregrip (shown) or other tactical accessories. A sound suppressor can be screwed over the muzzle.

SPECIFICATION:

CARTRIDGE:
0.45 ACP or 9 x 19 mm Parabellum

DIMENSIONS:
LENGTH, STOCK EXTENDED: 690 mm (27.1 in)
LENGTH, STOCK RETRACTED: 450 mm (17.7 in)
WEIGHT, LESS MAGAZINE: 2.1 kg (4 lb 10 oz)
BARREL: 200 mm (7.2 in)
RIFLING: 6 grooves, rh, polygonal
MAGAZINE CAPACITY: 10 or 25 rounds
RATE OF FIRE: 580 (0.45) or 700 (9 mm) rounds/min

IN PRODUCTION:
2002–

MARKINGS:
"H&K UMP" and caliber on left side of receiver. Serial number on right side of receiver.

SAFETY:
Combined safety and fire-selector three-position switch on both sides of receiver: up for safe; down one notch for single shots, and two notches for fully automatic fire. Fire rates are indicated by outlines of a single bullet and four bullets respectively. Cocking handle can engage in holding slot when action is cocked.

UNLOADING:
Magazine release is just behind magazine well. Remove magazine. Pull back cocking handle over and to left of barrel to cock weapon. Examine chamber through ejection port. If empty, grasp cocking handle and pull trigger, allowing cocking handle to go forward under control.

MP38/40 GERMANY

This is the familiar German Army weapon generally, and wrongly, called the "Schmeisser." It was made by the Erma company and designed by Vollmer, and like all his designs has the characteristic telescoping casing around the recoil spring and bolt assembly. It was later replaced in production by the MP40, which simplified some features and made manufacture easier and quicker. The MP38 is distinguished by the corrugated surface of the machined steel receiver, the hole in the magazine housing, and the machined aluminum grip frame. Numbers of these weapons were converted by modifying the cocking handle so that it could be pushed in through the bolt to engage in a hole in the receiver and lock the bolt in the forward position. When so modified, the weapon became the MP38/40.

SPECIFICATION:

CARTRIDGE:
9 x 19 mm Parabellum

DIMENSIONS:
LENGTH, STOCK EXTENDED: 833 mm (32.8 in)
LENGTH, STOCK RETRACTED: 630 mm (24.8 in)
WEIGHT: 4.1 kg (9 lb)
BARREL: 251 mm (9.9 in)
RIFLING: 6 grooves, rh
MAGAZINE CAPACITY: 32 rounds
RATE OF FIRE: 500 rounds/min

IN PRODUCTION:
1938–45

MARKINGS:
"MP38 [year]" on rear receiver cap. Serial number on left side of rear cap. May have the factory code "27" stamped on the top of the receiver.

SAFETY:
Pull back cocking handle and turn it up into notch in receiver slot. No selector device; MP38 fires only in automatic mode.

UNLOADING:
Magazine catch on rear of magazine housing. Remove magazine. Pull back cocking handle to eject any round in chamber. Inspect chamber through ejection port. Release cocking handle. Press trigger.

Walther MPK/MPL GERMANY

The post–World War II MPK and MPL are simply the same weapon with either short (K) or long (L) barrels. The long model has a 260 mm barrel, which increases the overall length to 749 mm. In spite of its excellent quality and performance, it was never adopted by any army, but some German naval units and various European police forces took it into use in the 1960s. A silencer-equipped model was later developed, but this apparently attracted few customers.

SPECIFICATION:

CARTRIDGE:
9 x 19 mm Parabellum

DIMENSIONS (MPK)
LENGTH, STOCK EXTENDED: 659 mm (25.9 in)
LENGTH, STOCK RETRACTED: 373 mm (14.7 in)
WEIGHT: 2.8 kg (6 lb 3 oz)
BARREL: 173 mm (6.8 in)
RIFLING: 6 grooves, rh
MAGAZINE CAPACITY: 32 rounds
RATE OF FIRE: 550 rounds/min

IN PRODUCTION:
1963–85

MARKINGS:
Serial number on left side of receiver.

SAFETY:
Manual safety catch on both sides of receiver behind trigger. Turn up and to rear for safe, turn forward and down to fire. Original design had no provision for single shots; as an option, a different mechanism with third position on safety catch could be fitted to give single shots, but how many of these were actually made is not known.

UNLOADING:
Magazine release behind magazine housing below trigger guard. Remove magazine, pull back cocking handle to eject any round in chamber. Inspect chamber through ejection port. Release cocking handle. Pull trigger.

KGP-9 HUNGARY

This was first revealed in the latter 1980s and is the standard submachine gun of the Hungarian military and police forces. It is a conventional blowback weapon, principally assembled from pressed steel components stiffened with castings. It fires from an open bolt, but the bolt carries a floating firing pin, and the actual firing is done by a hammer mechanism. An unusual feature is that the standard barrel can be removed and replaced by a longer one, presumably to convert the weapon into a form of carbine with a longer range.

SPECIFICATION:

CARTRIDGE:
9 x 19 mm Parabellum

DIMENSIONS:
LENGTH, BUTT EXTENDED: 615 mm (24.2 in)
LENGTH, BUTT FOLDED: 355 mm (14 in)
WEIGHT: 2.8 kg (6 lb 1 oz)
BARREL: 190 mm (97.5 in)
RIFLING: 6 grooves, rh
MAGAZINE CAPACITY: 25 rounds
RATE OF FIRE: 900 rounds/min

IN PRODUCTION:
1987–95

MARKINGS:
"F.E.G. Hungary Cal 9mm P" and serial number on right side of receiver.

SAFETY:
Combined safety catch and fire-selector switch on left side above and in front of trigger: rear for safe, forward and down for single shots, fully forward for automatic fire.

UNLOADING:
Magazine release is behind magazine housing below trigger guard. Remove magazine. Pull back cocking handle and hold bolt open while verifying that chamber is empty. Release bolt. Pull trigger.

Uzi ISRAEL

Although no longer in production in its home nation, the Uzi remains one of the most widely used modern submachine gun and can be met almost anywhere, not always in official hands. It has been license-manufactured in Belgium and South Africa. It has been copied by Norinco of China and in Croatia, where it is known as the ERO. The Uzi uses the magazine feed through the pistol grip approach and also has the forward section of the bolt over-lapping the barrel to keep the overall form compact. Fixed and folding butts exist. Derivatives include the Mini-Uzi, with much-reduced dimensions, and the Micro-Uzi, an easily concealed subcompact variant. There is also a semiautomatic Uzi pistol with no buttstock. All Uzi derivatives remain much the same as the full-size Uzi and operate along much the same lines.

SPECIFICATION:

CARTRIDGE:
9 x 19 mm Parabellum

DIMENSIONS:
LENGTH, FIXED STOCK: 640 mm (25.2 in)
LENGTH, STOCK EXTENDED: 640 mm (25.2 in)
LENGTH, STOCK RETRACTED: 440 mm (17.3 in)
WEIGHT: 3.5 kg (7 lb 11 oz)
BARREL: 260 mm (10.2 in)
RIFLING: 4 grooves, rh
MAGAZINE CAPACITY: 20, 25, or 32 rounds
RATE OF FIRE: 600 rounds/min

IN PRODUCTION:
1953–98

MARKINGS:
Serial number on left rear side of receiver (Israeli models); may also have Hebrew markings. "M.P. UZI Kal 9mm [serial number]" on left rear side of receiver (German models).

SAFETY:
Combined safety catch and fire-selector fitted into top of pistol grip on left side: pull back to make safe, with bolt locked; central position for single shots; forward position for automatic fire. Grip safety on pistol grip must be squeezed in to release bolt.

UNLOADING:
Magazine catch at bottom left side of pistol grip. Remove magazine. Pull back the cocking handle to eject any round in chamber. Inspect chamber through the ejection port. Release cocking handle. Pull trigger.

Beretta Model 12 ITALY

The Model 12 is considerably different from earlier Beretta submachine guns, due to the retirement of the designer Marengoni in 1956 and the appearance of a new designer, Salza. It is primarily made of metal stampings and uses a "telescoping" or "overhung" bolt that wraps around the barrel and thus reduces the length of the weapon. It has a front hand grip, and the stock may be a hinged, tubular metal type folding around to the right side of the weapon or a detachable wooden type. The Model 12 was adopted by the Italian forces in 1961 and by various South American and African countries. It has also been made under license in Brazil and Indonesia.

SPECIFICATION:

CARTRIDGE:
9 x 19 mm Parabellum

DIMENSIONS:
LENGTH, STOCK EXTENDED: 645 mm (25.4 in)
LENGTH, STOCK RETRACTED: 418 mm (16.5 in)
WEIGHT: 3 kg (6 lb 10 oz)
BARREL: 200 mm (7.9 in)
RIFLING: 6 grooves, rh
MAGAZINE CAPACITY: 20, 30, or 40 rounds
RATE OF FIRE: 550 rounds/min

IN PRODUCTION:
1959–78

MARKINGS:
"P.M. BERETTA Mod 12 Cal 9mm Parabellum" and serial number on top of receiver.

SAFETY:
Grip safety let into rear of pistol grip must be pressed in to unlock bolt for either cocking or firing. Push-button safety catch above grip on left side, when pushed in, locks grip safety in safe position.

UNLOADING:
Magazine catch behind magazine housing. Remove magazine. Grasp grip and press in grip safety. Pull back bolt. Inspect chamber. Release bolt. Press trigger.

Beretta Model 38/44 ITALY

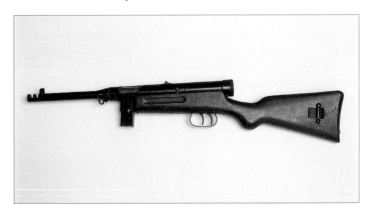

First produced in 1938 as the Model 1938A, this is a simplified version of the subsequent Model 38/42, differing in the size of the bolt and details of the mainspring. A visual distinction is the absence of the small spring housing, which projects from the rear of the receiver in earlier models. This weapon was entirely exported, users being Pakistan, Syria, Costa Rica, and Iraq, among many others.

SPECIFICATION:

CARTRIDGE:
9 x 19 mm Parabellum

DIMENSIONS:
LENGTH O/A: 798 mm (31.4 in)
WEIGHT: 4 kg (8 lb 12 oz)
BARREL: 210 mm (8.3 in)
RIFLING: 6 grooves, rh
MAGAZINE CAPACITY: 20 or 40 rounds
RATE OF FIRE: 550 rounds/min

IN PRODUCTION:
1945–55

MARKINGS:
"MOSCH. AUTOM. BERETTA MOD 38/A44 CAL 9" and serial number on top of receiver.

SAFETY:
Manual safety catch on left side of receiver: move to "S" (rearwards) to make safe, to "F" to fire. Two triggers: front trigger for single shots, rear trigger for automatic fire.

UNLOADING:
Magazine catch on magazine housing. Remove magazine. Pull back cocking handle to eject any round in chamber. Inspect chamber. Release cocking handle. Pull trigger.

MGP-84 PERU

When it first appeared, this small submachine gun, designed for issue to special forces, was known as the MGP-15. The name was changed to reflect some slight changes introduced during production, most noticeably the revision of the screwed-on muzzle cap to allow the installation of a sound suppressor. A folding buttstock is provided, so arranged that, with the butt folded along the right side of the receiver, the butt plate can act as a form of foregrip (as shown). The MGP-84 is a basic blowback weapon, with box magazines inserted through the pistol grip. The result is a very compact weapon that can be easily carried. An even more compact MGP-14 carbine version exists, as does a so-called assault pistol.

SPECIFICATION:

CARTRIDGE:
9 x 19 mm Parabellum

DIMENSIONS:
LENGTH, STOCK EXTENDED: 503 mm (19.8 in)
LENGTH, STOCK FOLDED: 284 mm (11.2 in)
WEIGHT: 2.3 kg (5 lb 1 oz)
BARREL: 166 mm (6.5 in)
RIFLING: 12 grooves, rh
MAGAZINE CAPACITY: 20 or 32 rounds
RATE OF FIRE: 650–750 rounds/min

IN PRODUCTION:
1990–

MARKINGS:
"SIMA-ELECTRONICA 9mm MGP-84" and serial number on left side of receiver.

SAFETY:
Manual safety catch/selector lever on left side of receiver above trigger guard: up for safe, to rear for automatic fire, forward for single shots.

UNLOADING:
Magazine catch at left bottom of pistol grip. Remove magazine. Pull back cocking handle to eject any round in chamber. Inspect chamber through ejection port. Release cocking handle. Press trigger.

PM-63 (Wz63) POLAND

This is an unusual weapon of the machine-pistol class intended for close-range defense. A folding pistol-grip forms part of the fore-end and a telescoping twin-strut metal stock is fitted. Instead of a bolt moving inside the receiver, it uses a moving slide, just like a pistol. The lower portion of the slide is extended beneath the muzzle to act as a compensator, deflecting the muzzle gases upwards to counteract the natural rise of the weapon when firing automatically. It is also possible in an emergency to cock the PM-63 single-handedly by pressing the extended muzzle compensator against a hard surface. Although the PM-63 is no longer in production in Poland, a copy remains available from Norinco of China.

SPECIFICATION:

CARTRIDGE:
9 x 18 mm Makarov

DIMENSIONS:
LENGTH, STOCK EXTENDED: 583 mm (23 in)
LENGTH, STOCK RETRACTED: 333 mm (13.1 in)
WEIGHT: 1.8 kg (3 lb 15 oz)
BARREL: 152 mm (6 in)
RIFLING: 6 grooves, rh
MAGAZINE CAPACITY: 25 or 40 rounds
RATE OF FIRE: 600 rounds/min

IN PRODUCTION:
1963–80

MARKINGS:
Serial number on right side of side and frame. Factory number "11" in oval.

SAFETY:
Manual safety catch on left side top of pistol grip: turn up to make safe, turn down to fire. Fire selection performed by trigger; short pull gives single shots, longer pull gives automatic fire.

UNLOADING:
Magazine catch at heel of butt. Remove magazine. Grasp serrated rear section of slide and pull it to rear to eject any round in chamber. Inspect chamber through ejection port. Release slide. Pull trigger.

PM-84/98 POLAND

The PM-84 (Glauberyt) is blowback operated and constructed of metal pressings. An ambidextrous cocking handle is located on top of the receiver, and a folding forward pistol grip is fitted to the handguard. It has an extending twin-strut metal stock, which lies alongside the receiver when not in use. Similar to the Uzi, the pistol grip also contains the magazine well; this combination is said to aid tactile loading in night conditions. Originally chambered for the 9 x 18 mm Makarov cartridge, it is now offered in the more common 9 x 19 mm caliber with the PM-98, which features a revised single-side cocking handle and monobloc front handguard, which has a fitting for a tactical light.

SPECIFICATION:

CARTRIDGE:
9 x 18 mm; 9 x 19 mm

DIMENSIONS:
LENGTH, BUTT EXTENDED: 605 mm (23.8 in)
LENGTH, BUTT FOLDED: 405 mm (15.9 in)
WEIGHT: 2.3 kg (5.1 lbs)
BARREL: 185 mm (7.3 in)
RATE OF FIRE: 640 rounds/min
MAGAZINE CAPACITY: 15 or 30 rounds

IN PRODUCTION:
1984–

MARKINGS:
Model designation on left side of receiver behind trigger. Manufacturer's logo on pistol grip.

SAFETY:
Two levers above pistol grip on left side: one permits "fire" or "safe," the other "single" or "automatic" fire.

UNLOADING:
Magazine catch on left side of magazine housing. Remove magazine. Pull cocking handle to rear until bolt is held by sear. Inspect chamber through ejection port. Grasp cocking handle, point weapon in safe direction, pull trigger, and allow bolt to go forward under control.

A Portuguese service weapon, developed in Portugal and based upon features of other designs, combining the stock and firing mechanism of the US M3 and the bolt and general construction of the German MP40. A reliable and robust weapon, like several of its contemporaries, it has a bayonet fitting. It was widely used in Africa, and many found their way into the hands of insurgents of one sort and another. It could also turn up in the Far East, due to its use in Portuguese Timor. A slightly improved version of this weapon will be found marked as the M63 pattern, and this was superseded by the M1973 model which has a perforated barrel jacket. All are mechanically almost identical.

SPECIFICATION:

CARTRIDGE:
9 x 19 mm Parabellum

DIMENSIONS:
LENGTH, STOCK EXTENDED: 813 mm (32.1 in)
LENGTH, STOCK RETRACTED: 625 mm (24.6 in)
WEIGHT: 3.8 kg (8 lb 5 oz)
BARREL: 250 mm (9.9 in)
RIFLING: 6 grooves, rh
MAGAZINE CAPACITY: 32 rounds
RATE OF FIRE: 500 rounds/min

IN PRODUCTION:
1948–55

MARKINGS:
"FBP M/48" and serial number on left side of magazine housing.

SAFETY:
Pull back cocking handle and turn up into cutout in receiver slot to lock it in rear position. When bolt is forward, pushing cocking handle in will lock inner end into cut in receiver wall and lock bolt forward.

UNLOADING:
Magazine catch on side of magazine housing. Remove magazine. Pull back cocking handle to eject any round in chamber. Release cocking handle. Press trigger.

Lusa A2

This weapon was developed by the Portuguese INDEP company to replace the earlier FBP models. A robust and compact design, it has an unusual double-cylinder receiver, with the bolt and barrel in the lower section and the overhung section of the bolt, together with its recoil spring, in the top. The fire selector gives the full choice of options, and sound suppressors and laser sighting aids are provided as accessories. It is thought to have had little commercial success.

SPECIFICATION:

CARTRIDGE:
9 x 19 mm Parabellum

DIMENSIONS:
LENGTH, STOCK EXTENDED: 585 mm (23 in)
LENGTH, STOCK RETRACTED: 458 mm (18 in)
WEIGHT: 2.9 kg (6 lb 5 oz)
BARREL: 160 mm (6.3 in)
RIFLING: 6 grooves, rh
MAGAZINE CAPACITY: 30 rounds
RATE OF FIRE: 900 rounds/min

IN PRODUCTION:
1992–

MARKINGS:
"INDEP LUSA A2 [year] [serial number]" on right side of receiver.

SAFETY:
Combined safety catch and fire-selector lever mounted on left side of receiver above pistol grip: "0" for safe, "1" for single shots, "3" for three-round bursts, "30" for automatic fire.

UNLOADING:
Magazine catch on left side of receiver behind magazine housing. Remove magazine. Pull back cocking handle to eject any round in chamber. Inspect chamber through ejection port. Release cocking handle. Press trigger.

Bison-2 RUSSIA

The Bison-2 is based on a much-modified AK-74. The receiver and side-folding metal stock are retained, but the double-column box magazine has been replaced with a high-capacity helical magazine. It is blowback operated and the selector lever provides for fire control in the same manner as the rifle: upper position locks the working parts, center position provides automatic fire, and lower position is for "self-loading" fire. The bird-cage flash hider can be replaced with a sound suppressor. The left side of the gun is fitted with a standard Russian sight bracket. The later Bison-2-01 has a revised stock arrangement with an "up and over" design. Two modes of fire are offered, either self-loading only or selective fire. Three caliber options are now available by model type, as listed. Data is for Bison-2.

SPECIFICATION:

CARTRIDGE:
9 x 18 mm (Bison-2); 9 x 19 mm (Bison-2-01); 9 x 17 mm/.380 ACP (Bison-2-02)

DIMENSIONS:
LENGTH, BUTT EXTENDED: 690 mm (27.2 in)
LENGTH, BUTT FOLDED: 460 mm (18.1 in)
WEIGHT: 2.8 kg (6 lb 3 oz)
BARREL: 230 mm (9.1 in)
RATE OF FIRE: 690 rounds/min
MAGAZINE CAPACITY: 64 rounds

IN PRODUCTION:
1996–

MARKINGS:
None on gun, other than serial number on left front side of body. Magazine marked with caliber.

SAFETY:
As described.

UNLOADING:
Magazine release catch forward of trigger guard. Remove magazine by rotating it down and forward. Move selector lever to a "fire" position and pull cocking handle to rear until bolt is held by sear. Inspect chamber through ejection port. Grasp cocking handle, point weapon in safe direction, pull trigger, and allow bolt to go forward under control.

PPS-43 RUSSIA

Probably the best of the three wartime Soviet submachine guns, the PPS-43 was initially designed and manufactured inside Leningrad during the 900-day siege; the weapon was designed so as to be made on existing machinery using existing materials, since nothing could be brought in from outside. The PPS-43 has been manufactured in China as the Type 53. Although of the same capacity, the PPS-43 magazine is not interchangeable with its equally common PPSh-41 SMG.

SPECIFICATION:

CARTRIDGE:
7.62 mm Soviet Pistol

DIMENSIONS:
LENGTH, STOCK EXTENDED: 808 mm (31.8 in)
LENGTH, STOCK RETRACTED: 606 mm (23.9 in)
WEIGHT: 3.3 kg (7 lb 6 oz)
BARREL: 254 mm (10 in)
RIFLING: 4 grooves, rh
MAGAZINE CAPACITY: 35 rounds
RATE OF FIRE: 700 rounds/min

IN PRODUCTION:
1943–45

MARKINGS:
Serial number and factory identifying mark on top or side of receiver.

SAFETY:
Manual safety catch in front edge of trigger guard: push forward to make safe; this locks bolt in either fully forward or fully rearward position. No fire selector lever; weapon fires only at full-automatic.

UNLOADING:
Magazine catch around rear of magazine housing. Remove magazine. Pull back cocking handle to eject any round in chamber. Inspect chamber through ejection port. Release cocking handle. Pull trigger.

PPSh-41 RUSSIA

The third wartime Soviet submachine gun and the most common, some 5 million having been made. They were widely distributed to Communist countries after 1947 and can be found all over the world. Conversions to 9 x 19 mm Parabellum chambering have been done, though they are unlikely to be encountered. This superseded the PPS-40 to provide a weapon capable of using box or drum magazines and simpler and quicker to manufacture. Early models have an adjustable tangent back sight; later models, the majority of production, have a simple two-position flip-over notch back sight.

SPECIFICATION:

CARTRIDGE:
7.62 mm Soviet Pistol

DIMENSIONS:
LENGTH O/A: 828 mm (32.6 in)
WEIGHT: 3.6 kg (7 lb 13 oz)
BARREL: 265 mm (10.4 in)
RIFLING: 4 grooves, rh
MAGAZINE CAPACITY: 71-round drum or 35-round box
RATE OF FIRE: 900 rounds/min

IN PRODUCTION:
1941–47

MARKINGS:
Serial number and factory identifying code on receiver.

SAFETY:
Manual safety latch on cocking handle can be pushed into notches cut into receiver wall when bolt is either fully forward or fully back, and locks bolt in that position. Fire-selector switch inside trigger guard in front of trigger: push forward for automatic fire, back for single shots.

UNLOADING:
Magazine release is behind magazine housing and folds up under stock. Fold down, press forward, and slide magazine out. Pull back cocking handle to eject any round in chamber. Inspect chamber through ejection port. Release cocking handle. Press trigger.

One of a series of radically new submachine-gun designs to emerge from the former Soviet design bureaus in the 1990s. Designed for special-forces use and firing a newly developed cartridge designed to defeat body armor and material up to 100 m (328 ft), it remains a compact weapon that has been improved to meet user needs. It is of pressed metal construction with a polymer fore-end and pistol grip that also serves as the magazine housing.

A folding twin-strut metal stock folds up and over to lie flat along the top of the receiver. Although provided with simple iron sights for emergency use, it is designed to be used with late-generation "red-dot" or night-vision sights.

SPECIFICATION:

CARTRIDGE:
9 x 21 mm

DIMENSIONS:
LENGTH, BUTT EXTENDED: 603 mm (23.7 in)
LENGTH, BUTT FOLDED: 367 mm (14.4 in)
WEIGHT: 1.7 kg (3 lb 10 oz)
RATE OF FIRE: Unknown
MAGAZINE CAPACITY: 20 or 30 rounds

IN PRODUCTION:
1999–

MARKINGS:
Model designation and serial number on lower left rear of receiver.

SAFETY:
Selector lever on right side of receiver: top position locks working parts, center position for automatic fire, lower position for self-loading mode.

UNLOADING:
Magazine release catch is behind trigger guard. Remove magazine. Move selector lever to a "fire" position and pull cocking handle to rear until bolt is fully to rear. Inspect chamber through ejection port, allow bolt to go forward under control. Point weapon in safe direction and pull trigger.

A South African design, used by their army and police, the BXP is a versatile weapon that can be fitted with a silencer, a grenade-launching attachment, or various types of muzzle compensator. It is made from steel pressings, and the bolt is hollowed out to wrap around the portion of the barrel that is inside the receiver, so that it has a full-length barrel even though only part of it is visible.

SPECIFICATION:

CARTRIDGE:
9 x 19mm Parabellum

DIMENSIONS:
LENGTH, STOCK EXTENDED: 607 mm (23.9 in)
LENGTH, STOCK RETRACTED: 387 mm (15.2 in)
WEIGHT: 2.5 kg (5 lb 8 oz)
BARREL: 208 mm (8.2 in)
RIFLING: 6 grooves, rh
MAGAZINE CAPACITY: 22 or 32 rounds
RATE OF FIRE: 1000 rounds/min

IN PRODUCTION:
1988–99

MARKINGS:
"G.D.P.S." and serial number on top of receiver.

SAFETY:
Manual safety catch on left and right sides of receiver above pistol grip: up (green dot) for safe, down (red dot) for fire. No fire selector; pulling trigger to first stop gives single shots, pulling it beyond this point produces automatic fire. Safety notch on bolt will catch sear should bolt be jarred back or hand slip during cocking.

UNLOADING:
Magazine catch in pistol grip. Remove magazine. Pull back cocking handle (top of receiver) to eject any round in chamber. Inspect chamber through ejection port. Release cocking handle. Pull trigger.

Sanna 77 SOUTH AFRICA

This weapon appeared in South Africa in the 1970s and is based upon the Czech CZ 25, though whether it was actually made in South Africa or whether the guns were refurbished CZ 75s bought from Czechoslovakia and modified to fire only in the semiautomatic mode is not certain. It was not a military weapon but was sold for self-defense to farmers and others who felt the need for it, and it can be assumed that some have passed into other hands by this time and are liable to appear anywhere in Africa. The side-folding stock also acts as a forward pistol grip.

SPECIFICATION:

CARTRIDGE:
9 x 19 mm Parabellum

DIMENSIONS:
LENGTH, STOCK EXTENDED: 650 mm (25.6 in)
LENGTH, STOCK RETRACTED: 450 mm (17.7 in)
WEIGHT: 2.8 kg (6 lb 3 oz)
BARREL: 290 mm (11.4 in)
RIFLING: 6 grooves, rh
MAGAZINE CAPACITY: 40 rounds
RATE OF FIRE: Single shots

IN PRODUCTION:
1977–80

MARKINGS:
Serial number on left side of receiver.

SAFETY:
Manual safety catch inside trigger guard behind trigger: push from left to right to lock bolt, rendering weapon safe.

UNLOADING:
Magazine catch at heel of pistol grip. Remove magazine. Pull back cocking handle to eject any round in chamber. Inspect chamber through ejection port. Release cocking handle. Press trigger.

The DS9A is of conventional design, being blowback operated, and fires from an open bolt. The receiver is derived from a modified M16 assault rifle, and weapon, control features have been retained in their usual place, except that the cocking handle has been moved to the left side of the handguard. A side-folding tubular stock is fitted, and the top of the upper receiver has a length of Mil Spec 1913 Picatinny sight rail for the mounting of optical or night-vision devices. The rifle-caliber magazine well has an insert to support a smaller-diameter pistol-caliber magazine. A compact version of the DS9A is available with a shortened barrel and single-strut folding stock.

SPECIFICATION:

CARTRIDGE:
9 x 19 mm

DIMENSIONS:
LENGTH, BUTT EXTENDED: 684 mm (26.9 in)
LENGTH, BUTT FOLDED: 430 mm (16.9 in)
WEIGHT: 2 kg (4 lb 6 oz)
BARREL: 220 mm (8.7 in)
RIFLING: 6 grooves, rh
RATE OF FIRE: 860 rounds/min
MAGAZINE CAPACITY: 30 rounds

IN PRODUCTION:
2003–

MARKINGS:
Manufacturer's markings on left side of magazine housing.

SAFETY:
Four-position selector lever on lower left side providing safe, single three-round burst, and automatic fire modes.

UNLOADING:
Magazine catch on left side of magazine housing. Remove magazine. Pull cocking-handle to rear, lock bolt in rear position using bolt catch, and inspect chamber through ejection port. Grasp cocking handle, point weapon in safe direction, release bolt catch and allow bolt to go forward under control.

Star Z-62 SPAIN

The Star Z-62 was developed for the Spanish Army, replacing the Z-45 in 1953 and remaining in service until 1971, when it was replaced by the Z-70B. The Z-62 looks the same as the Z-70B but has a conventional trigger and a selector lever above it to give single shots or automatic fire. Both weapons were offered on the export market and were also offered in 9 x 19 mm Parabellum chambering, but whether any were adopted by other countries is not known.

SPECIFICATION:

CARTRIDGE:
9 x 23 mm Largo (Bergmann-Bayard)

DIMENSIONS:
LENGTH, STOCK EXTENDED: 701 mm (27.6 in)
LENGTH, STOCK RETRACTED: 480 mm (18.9 in)
WEIGHT: 2.9 kg (6 lb 5 oz)
BARREL: 201 mm (7.9 in)
RIFLING: 6 grooves, rh
MAGAZINE CAPACITY: 20 or 30 rounds
RATE OF FIRE: 550 rounds/min

IN PRODUCTION:
1963–70

MARKINGS:
"STAR EIBAR ESPANA MODEL Z-62" and serial number on left side of magazine housing.

SAFETY:
Manual cross-bolt safety in upper part of pistol grip: when pushed from right to left, it blocks sear and weapon is safe. Fire selection is performed by trigger: pull upper part of trigger for single shots, pull lower part for automatic fire.

UNLOADING:
Magazine catch at rear of magazine housing. Remove magazine. Pull back cocking handle to eject any round in chamber. Inspect chamber through ejection port. Release cocking handle. Pull trigger.

Star Z-84 SPAIN

The Z-84 replaced the earlier Z-70B in Spanish service in the mid-1980s and is a thoroughly modern and compact design using pressed metal for lightness. The center of balance is above the pistol grip, so that it can be easily fired one-handed if necessary. As well as being used by Spain, numbers have been sold to security forces in several countries, though no details are forthcoming from the manufacturers.

SPECIFICATION:

CARTRIDGE:
9 x 19 mm Parabellum

DIMENSIONS:
LENGTH, STOCK EXTENDED: 615 mm (24.2 in)
LENGTH, STOCK RETRACTED: 410 mm (16.1 in)
WEIGHT: 3 kg (6 lb 10 oz)
BARREL: 215 mm (8.5 in)
RIFLING: 6 grooves, rh
MAGAZINE CAPACITY: 25 or 30 rounds
RATE OF FIRE: 600 rounds/min

IN PRODUCTION:
1985–95

MARKINGS:
"STAR EIBAR ESPANA MOD Z-84" and serial number on right side of receiver.

SAFETY:
Cross-bolt safety button inside trigger guard: push from right to left for safe; push from left to right to expose a red mark to indicate weapon is ready to fire. Sliding fire selector on left side of receiver is pushed forward for single shots, rearward for automatic fire.

UNLOADING:
Magazine release in heel of pistol grip. Remove magazine. Pull back cocking handle to eject any round in chamber. Inspect chamber through ejection port. Release cocking handle. Pull trigger.

Carl Gustav 45 SWEDEN

One of the oldest submachine guns still in service, the Carl Gustav is a robust weapon that is likely to last a long time. The original models had no magazine housing and used a drum magazine, but in 1948 a box magazine was developed, leading to a magazine housing being added to all guns. The Carl Gustav has been used by the Swedish, Irish, and Indonesian armies and was also made under license in Egypt as the Port Said. A highly modified version, with an integral silencer replacing the usual barrel, was used by US Special Forces in Vietnam.

SPECIFICATION:

CARTRIDGE:
9 x 19 mm Parabellum

DIMENSIONS:
LENGTH, STOCK EXTENDED: 808 mm (31.8 in)
LENGTH, STOCK RETRACTED: 552 mm (21.7 in)
WEIGHT: 3.9 kg (8 lb 9 oz)
BARREL: 213 mm (8.4 in)
RIFLING: 6 grooves, rh
MAGAZINE CAPACITY: 36 rounds
RATE OF FIRE: 600 rounds/min

IN PRODUCTION:
1945–

MARKINGS:
Serial number on top of receiver.

SAFETY:
Pull back cocking handle and turn it up into notch in cocking handle slot. When bolt is forward, it can be locked in place by pushing cocking handle into bolt so its other end passes through bolt and into hole in receiver.

UNLOADING:
Remove magazine. Pull back cocking handle. Inspect chamber. Release cocking handle. Press trigger.

Sten Mark I UK

This was the original Sten, designed at the Royal Small Arms Factory, Enfield, and made by BSA and various ordnance factories. It is recognisable by the spoonlike muzzle compensator and the wooden cover over the trigger mechanism, and also by the folding forward grip. A Mark I* version appeared late in 1941 with a metal cover for the trigger mechanism and without the grip or muzzle compensator. About 100,000 of these models were made, and most went to the regular forces. Various patterns of metal stock can be found.

SPECIFICATION:

CARTRIDGE:
9 x 19 mm Parabellum

DIMENSIONS:
LENGTH O/A: 896 mm (35.3 in)
WEIGHT: 3.3 kg (7 lb 3 oz)
BARREL: 198 mm (7.8 in)
RIFLING: 6 grooves, rh
MAGAZINE CAPACITY: 32 rounds
RATE OF FIRE: 550 rounds/min

IN PRODUCTION:
1941–42

MARKINGS:
"STEN Mk I" on top of magazine housing.

SAFETY:
Pull back cocking handle and turn down into notch in operating slot. Fire mode selected by crossbolt passing through trigger mechanism housing: push from left to right for single shots, push from right to left for automatic fire.

UNLOADING:
Magazine catch on top of magazine housing. Press down and remove magazine. Pull back cocking handle to eject any round in chamber. Inspect the chamber through ejection port. Release cocking handle. Press trigger.

Sten Mark II UK

This was the most common version of the Sten, over 2 million being made in the UK, Canada, and New Zealand. The mechanism is the same as the Mark I, but the barrel and stock are removable for easier packing and storage. The magazine housing can also be rotated to close the ejection port. Used by British forces in World War II, it was also dropped to resistance movements all over Europe and the Far East; it can thus be encountered anywhere in the world. It was also copied by the resistance (notably in Denmark) and by the Germans as the MP 3008.

SPECIFICATION:

CARTRIDGE:
9 x 19 mm Parabellum

DIMENSIONS:
LENGTH O/A: 952 mm (37.5 in)
WEIGHT: 3 kg (6 lb 10 oz)
BARREL: 197 mm (7.7 in)
RIFLING: 2 or 6 grooves, rh
MAGAZINE CAPACITY: 32 rounds
RATE OF FIRE: 550 rounds/min

IN PRODUCTION:
1942–44

MARKINGS:
"STEN MK II" on top of magazine housing. Weapons made in Canada may also have "LONG BRANCH" and year.

SAFETY:
Pull back cocking handle and turn up into notch in operating slot. Fire mode selected by crossbolt passing through trigger mechanism housing: push from left to right for single shots, push from right to left for automatic fire.

UNLOADING:
Magazine catch on top of magazine housing. Press down and remove magazine. Pull back cocking handle to eject any round in chamber. Inspect chamber through ejection port. Release cocking handle. Press trigger.

Sten Mark IIS UK

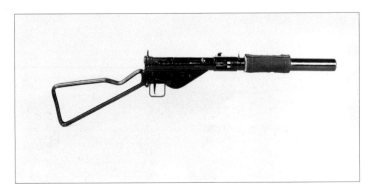

This is the "Silent Sten," originally produced for clandestine forces but then taken into use by the British Army for use by patrols and raiding parties. The mechanism is that of the Mark II weapon, though using a lighter bolt, and the barrel and silencer are a special integral unit that screws into the receiver in place of the normal barrel and retaining sleeve. The canvas sleeve around the silencer is to protect the user's hand from heat, and it was not recommended to fire this weapon at full automatic except in the gravest emergencies.

SPECIFICATION:

CARTRIDGE:
9 x 19 mm Parabellum

DIMENSIONS:
LENGTH O/A: 900 mm (35.4 in)
WEIGHT: 3.5 kg (7 lb 11 oz)
BARREL: 90 mm (3.5 in)
RIFLING: 6 grooves, rh
MAGAZINE CAPACITY: 32 rounds
RATE OF FIRE: 450 rounds/min

IN PRODUCTION:
1943–45

MARKINGS:
"STEN M.C. Mk IIS" on top of magazine housing.

SAFETY:
Pull back cocking handle and turn up into notch in operating slot. Fire mode selected by crossbolt passing through the trigger mechanism housing: push from left to right for single shots, push from right to left for automatic fire.

UNLOADING:
Magazine catch on top of magazine housing. Press down and remove magazine, pull back cocking handle to eject any round in chamber. Inspect chamber through ejection port. Release cocking handle. Press trigger.

Sten Mark V UK

The Sten Mark V was an attempt to improve the quality of the weapon and produce something that looked less cheap than the Mark II. The mechanism remained unchanged, but the gun now had a wooden stock, a wooden pistol grip, and a muzzle formed in the same manner as the service No. 4 rifle, so a standard spike bayonet could be fitted. The gun was finished in stove enamel, and the butt on early models had a brass buttplate with a trap for carrying cleaning equipment; later models have a steel buttplate without the trap. However, the greatest design defect of the Sten—the magazine—remained the same, so that the Mark V was little more reliable than the models that had gone before.

SPECIFICATION:

CARTRIDGE:
9 x 19 mm Parabellum

DIMENSIONS:
LENGTH O/A: 7.6 mm (30 in)
WEIGHT: 3.9 kg (8 lb 9 oz)
BARREL: 198 mm (7.8 in)
RIFLING: 6 grooves, rh
MAGAZINE CAPACITY: 32 rounds
RATE OF FIRE: 600 rounds/min

IN PRODUCTION:
1944–46

MARKINGS:
"STEN M.C. Mk V" on top of magazine housing.

SAFETY:
Pull back cocking handle and turn up into notch in operating slot to lock bolt in cocked position. Press in cocking handle when bolt is forward to lock it to receiver. Fire mode selected by crossbolt passing through trigger mechanism housing: push in from left to right for single shots, push from right to left for automatic fire.

UNLOADING:
Magazine catch on top of magazine housing. Press down and remove magazine. Pull back cocking handle to eject any round in chamber. Inspect chamber through ejection port. Release cocking handle. Press trigger.

Sterling UK

The Sterling has been used by some 50 or more countries; it is the Canadian C1, forms the basis of the Australian F1 submachine gun and, although Sterling collapsed in 1988, it is still made under license in India. There must be tens of thousands of them in existence, and they could appear anywhere. There is a silenced version, known as the L34 in British service, which bears the same relationship to the L2A3 as did the Sten IIS to the Mark II. There are also innumerable semiautomatic versions of the L2 pattern used by police and security forces around the world.

SPECIFICATION:

CARTRIDGE:
9 x 19 mm Parabellum

DIMENSIONS:
LENGTH, STOCK EXTENDED: 710 mm (28 in)
LENGTH, STOCK RETRACTED: 480 mm (18.9 in)
WEIGHT: 2.7 kg (5 lb 15 oz)
BARREL: 198 mm (7.8 in)
RIFLING: 6 grooves, rh
MAGAZINE CAPACITY: 34 rounds
RATE OF FIRE: 550 rounds/min

IN PRODUCTION:
1953–88

MARKINGS:
"STERLING SMG 9mm" and serial number on top of magazine housing on standard production. "Gun Submachine 9mm L2A3," serial number, and NATO Stock Number, on top of magazine housing on weapons produced for British Army.

SAFETY:
Combined safety catch and fire-selector lever on left side of frame above pistol grip. Rear for safe, center for single shots, forward for automatic fire.

UNLOADING:
Magazine catch at rear of magazine housing. Press down and remove magazine. Pull back cocking handle to eject any round in chamber. Inspect chamber through ejection port. Release cocking handle. Press trigger.

Sterling L34A1 UK

When the Sten was replaced by the Sterling, it became necessary to replace the Sten Mark 6 silenced version as well, and the L2 Sterling was therefore redesigned into this L34 model, using the silent Sten as a guide but improving the technology. The mechanism is similar to that of the L2 weapon, but the barrel has 72 radial holes to permit the escape of gas and thus reduce the emergent velocity of the bullet. This escaping gas is contained within an expanded metal wrapping around the barrel, and after seeping through this it expands into the cylindrical silencer casing. The front part of this contains a spiral diffuser, through the center of which the bullet passes, but which causes the gases to swirl and slow down further before escaping at a velocity too low to cause a loud report. The reduced gas pressure necessitates the use of a lighter bolt than standard.

SPECIFICATION:

CARTRIDGE:
9 x 19 mm Parabellum

DIMENSIONS:
LENGTH, BUTT EXTENDED: 864 mm (34 in)
LENGTH, BUTT FOLDED: 660 mm (26 in)
WEIGHT: 3.6 kg (7 lb 15 oz)
BARREL: 198 mm (7.8 in)
RIFLING: 6 grooves, rh
MAGAZINE CAPACITY: 34 rounds
RATE OF FIRE: 550 rounds/min

IN PRODUCTION:
1966–85

MARKINGS:
"Gun, Submachine, 9mm L34A1," serial number, and NATO Stock Number on top of magazine housing.

SAFETY:
Combined safety catch and fire-selector lever on left side of frame above pistol grip. Rear for safe, center for single shots, forward for automatic fire.

UNLOADING:
Magazine catch at rear of magazine housing. Remove magazine. Pull back cocking handle to eject any round in chamber. Inspect chamber through ejection port. Release cocking handle. Press trigger.

Colt USA

This is based on the well-known M16 rifle configuration, so that training time is greatly reduced when soldiers already familiar with the rifle are given this weapon. The buttstock is telescoping, and the only outward difference between this and various short M16-type rifles is the thin and long magazine. Note that purchasers had the option of full automatic fire or three-round bursts, and the fire-selector switch marking will indicate which mechanism is in place. It is also possible to have a purely semiautomatic model with no automatic or burst-fire capability.

SPECIFICATION:

CARTRIDGE:
9 x 19 mm Parabellum

DIMENSIONS:
LENGTH, STOCK EXTENDED: 730 mm (28.8 in)
LENGTH, STOCK RETRACTED: 650 mm (25.6 in)
WEIGHT: 2.6 kg (5 lb 11 oz)
BARREL: 260 mm (10.3 in)
RIFLING: 6 grooves, rh
MAGAZINE CAPACITY: 20 or 32 rounds
RATE OF FIRE: 900 rounds/min

IN PRODUCTION:
1990–

MARKINGS:
Rampant colt trademark, "COLT" in script form, "SMG," and serial number on left side of magazine housing.

SAFETY:
Selector switch on left side above pistol grip: switch is to rear and its associated pointer to front for safe, switch forward and pointer to rear for either automatic fire or three-round bursts. Switch down for single shots.

UNLOADING:
Magazine release on both sides of weapon, shrouded button on right and hinged tab on left. Press either to remove magazine. Pull back cocking handle ("wings" at the base of the carrying handle). Inspect chamber through ejection slot. Release bolt. Press trigger.

Ingram USA

The Ingram with its small compact size and high cyclic rate of fire, places it in the machine-pistol class of weapons. Designed by Gordon Ingram as a follow-on to his conventional sized Models 6, 7 and 8 SMGs, the Model 10 (shown) was intended as a compact weapon for urban use, offered in both .45 ACP and 9 mm Parabellum calibers. Most production models were also provided with a threaded muzzle for attachment of an add-on suppressor. A further version, produced in smaller numbers was the Model 11 which was designed from the outset to be used with a suppressor, and the caliber of .380 ACP (9 mm Short) was chosen for its subsonic velocity. Originally manufactured by the Military Armament Corporation, subsequent guns were made by RPB Industries Inc. of Atlanta.

SPECIFICATION:

CARTRIDGE:
9 x 9 mm, or .45 ACP, or .380 ACP (9 mm Short)

DIMENSIONS:
LENGTH, STOCK RETRACTED: 298 mm (11.8 in)
LENGTH, STOCK EXTENDED: 559 mm (22 in)
WEIGHT: 690 g (1 lb 8 oz)
BARREL: 146 mm (5.7 in)
RIFLING: 6 grooves, rh
MAGAZINE CAPACITY: .45 ACP, 30 rounds; 9 mm or .380 ACP, 32 rounds

IN PRODUCTION:
1970–80

MARKINGS:
"INGRAM M10 .45 AUTO MILITARY ARMAMENT CORP POWDER SPRINGS GA USA," or "RPB Industries Inc, Atlanta, GA, USA." Serial numbers all on right side of receiver.

SAFETY:
Applied safety on inside right of trigger guard. Cocking handle can also be rotated to lock bolt in forward position.

UNLOADING:
Magazine catch at rear of pistol grip. Remove magazine. Pull back cocking handle to eject any round in chamber. Inspect chamber and magazine well to ensure no cartridges are present. Point weapon in safe direction. Grasp cocking handle. Pull trigger.

Ruger MP-9 USA

This weapon was designed by Uzi Gal, designer of the Uzi submachine gun, in the early 1980s. It was originally to be manufactured in Canada, but this fell through and the design was sold to Sturm, Ruger, who made some minor changes and put it into production in 1994.

The frame and lower receiver are made of Zytel synthetic material; the upper portion of the receiver is steel. Internally, the operation is similar to that of the Uzi, using a telescoping bolt but firing from a closed bolt. The pistol grip is at the center of balance and acts as the magazine housing. Behind the grip is an openwork frame that runs back and up to the rear of the receiver. The butt is jointed to fold down and lie alongside this frame when not needed.

SPECIFICATION:

CARTRIDGE:
9 x 19 mm Parabellum

DIMENSIONS:
LENGTH, BUTT EXTENDED: 556 mm (21.9 in)
LENGTH, BUTT FOLDED: 376 mm (14.8 in)
WEIGHT: 3 kg (6 lb 10 oz)
BARREL: 173 mm (6.8 in)
RIFLING: 6 grooves, rh
MAGAZINE CAPACITY: 34 rounds
RATE OF FIRE: 600 rounds/min

IN PRODUCTION:
1994–

MARKINGS:
Variable

SAFETY:
Three-position sliding safety catch/selector switch on left side above pistol grip, as on Uzi submachine gun: rearward position for safe, middle position for single shots, forward for full automatic fire.

UNLOADING:
Magazine release at bottom of pistol grip. Remove magazine, pull back cocking handle and hold bolt on sear. Examine chamber through ejection port and verify that it is empty. Grasp cocking handle. Pull trigger and allow bolt to close under control.

Thompson M1928/M1 USA

It can be claimed that this is the first submachine gun, insofar as Thompson was the man who invented the word, though it was not the first such weapon to see service. It did not appear until 1921, well after the Bergmann and Beretta designs, and the 1928 version was much the same as the 1921 except for some minor changes to the bolt to reduce the rate of fire. The original Thompson, with its "Blish" locking system, was an overly complex and expensive gun to manufacture, and during World War II the redesigned and simplified MI and MIA versions were produced, although the gun remained excessively heavy for the cartridge it fired.

SPECIFICATION:

CARTRIDGE:
0.45 ACP

DIMENSIONS:
LENGTH O/A: 857 mm (33.7 in) with compensator
WEIGHT: 4.9 kg (10 lb 12 oz)
BARREL: 267 mm (10.5 in)
RIFLING: 6 grooves, rh
MAGAZINE CAPACITY: 20- or 30-rounds box,
50- or 100- round drum
RATE OF FIRE: 700 rounds/min

IN PRODUCTION:
1919–42

MARKINGS:
"THOMPSON SUBMACHINE GUN/CALIBER .45 COLT AUTOMATIC CARTRIDGE/ MANUFACTURED BY/ COLT'S PATENT FIREARMS MFG CO/HARTFORD, CONN, USA/ MODEL OF 1928/[serial number]" on left side of receiver.

SAFETY:
Manual safety catch above pistol grip on left side of receiver: back for safe, forward for fire. Weapon can only be set to safe when bolt is drawn back. Fire-selector switch is further forward on left side of receiver: move forward for automatic fire, back for single shots.

UNLOADING:
Magazine catch is a thumb-operated latch just behind trigger on left grip. Release magazine. Pull back cocking handle to eject any round in chamber. Inspect chamber through ejection port. Release cocking handle. Pull trigger.

This could be called America's answer to the Sten gun, since it was the US's examination of the Sten that prompted the demand for a cheap and simple weapon to replace the Thompson. George Hyde, assisted by a metal-pressing expert from General Motors, designed the M3 was designed so as to be capable of being altered to 9 mm caliber by changing the bolt, barrel, and magazine, though it seems very few such changes were ever made in the field. The original bolt-retracting lever used to cock the weapon proved unreliable and was replaced with a large cutout in the bolt that was used to "thumb-cock" the weapon.

SPECIFICATION:

CARTRIDGE:
0.45 ACP or 9 x 19 mm Parabellum

DIMENSIONS:
LENGTH, STOCK EXTENDED: 745 mm (29.3 in)
LENGTH, STOCK RETRACTED: 570 mm (22.4 in)
WEIGHT: 3.7 kg (8 lb 2 oz)
BARREL: 203 mm (8 in)
RIFLING: 4 grooves, rh
MAGAZINE CAPACITY: 30 rounds
RATE OF FIRE: 400 rounds/min

IN PRODUCTION:
1942–44

MARKINGS:
"UIDE LAMP DIV OF GENERAL MOTORS/ US MODEL M3/[serial number]" on top of receiver.

SAFETY:
Hinged cover over ejection port carries a lug that when cover is closed, engages with a recess in bolt if bolt is forward, or with front edge of bolt when bolt is to rear, locking bolt in either position.

UNLOADING:
Magazine catch on left side of magazine housing. Open ejection port cover; remove magazine. Pull back bolt-retracting lever on right side of receiver to cock bolt. Inspect chamber through ejection port. Press trigger. Close ejection port cover.

K-50M NORTH VIETNAM

In 1950, the Chinese produced a copy of the Soviet PPSh-41 submachine gun, calling it the Type 50. Numbers of these were supplied to North Vietnam, who then redesigned it and produced it as the K-50M. The major changes were removing the original fold-over butt, replacing it with a telescoping wire butt, shortening the barrel jacket and removing the muzzle compensator, and adding a pistol grip. The curved magazine is similar to the Chinese pattern. The result is a quite distinctive weapon, unlikely to be mistaken for anything else. With regards to the mechanism, though, it is still a Soviet PPSh.

SPECIFICATION:

CARTRIDGE:
7.62 mm Soviet Pistol

DIMENSIONS:
LENGTH, STOCK EXTENDED: 756 mm (29.8 in)
LENGTH, STOCK RETRACTED: 571 mm (22.5 in)
WEIGHT: 3.4 kg (7 lb 8 oz)
BARREL: 269 mm (10.6 in)
RIFLING: 4 grooves, rh
MAGAZINE CAPACITY: 25, 32, or 40 rounds
RATE OF FIRE: 600 rounds/min

IN PRODUCTION:
1958–65

MARKINGS:
Serial number on top of receiver.

SAFETY:
Manual safety latch on cocking handle can be pushed into notches cut into receiver wall when bolt is either fully forward or fully back, locking bolt in that position. Fire-selector switch inside trigger guard in front of trigger: push forward for automatic fire, back for single shots.

UNLOADING:
Magazine release is behind magazine housing and folds up under stock. Fold down, press forward and slide magazine out. Pull back cocking handle to eject any round in chamber. Inspect chamber through ejection port. Release cocking handle. Press trigger.

Model 56 YUGOSLAVIA

The Model 56 was a replacement for the elderly Model 49 and was a simpler design to manufacture. It was basically similar in outline to the German MP40 and followed some of the internal design layout. The folding butt was a direct copy of the MP40, as was the pistol grip. The bolt was simplified and the return spring was a single large coil. A bayonet was fitted, and the overall effect was of a modern well-designed weapon. In fact, it suffered from using the 7.62 mm Soviet Pistol round, and something with better stopping power would have made it a more effective weapon. As a result, a later version, known as the M65, was developed in 9 x 19 mm Parabellum caliber for export, but it is not thought that many were ever sold.

SPECIFICATION:

CARTRIDGE:
7.62 mm Soviet Pistol

DIMENSIONS:
LENGTH O/A: 870 mm (34.3 in)
WEIGHT: 3 kg (6 lb 9 oz)
BARREL: 250 mm (9.8 in)
RIFLING: 4 grooves, rh
MAGAZINE CAPACITY: 32 rounds
RATE OF FIRE: 600 rounds/min

IN PRODUCTION:
1957–90

MARKINGS:
"M56," factory identification number, and serial number on left side of receiver.

SAFETY:
Crossbolt safety catch in receiver above trigger: push to right for fire, to left for safe. In front of this catch, on left side, is a two-position selector for single shots or automatic fire.

UNLOADING:
Magazine catch on magazine housing. Depress and remove magazine. Pull back cocking handle until it catches on sear. Examine chamber through ejection port to ensure it is empty. Grasp cocking handle, press trigger, and allow bolt to go forward under control.

Bolt-
Action
Rifles

Bolt-Action Rifles

There have been only a handful of successful bolt actions; there have been a number of unsuccessful ones, and there are some that appear to be different simply to avoid patent litigation, but knowledge of the principal systems will probably be a sufficient guide to anything which may be encountered. Bolt systems are divided into two types—turn bolts and straight-pull bolts.

Turn bolts

So-called because, to open them, it is necessary to lift the handle and rotate the body of the bolt in order to unlock it from the chamber or action.

Mauser

The most widely used, because it is undoubtedly the strongest and generally considered to be the most reliable and accurate. The bolt carries lugs with which it locks firmly into the chamber so that the bolt cannot move during firing. The drawback is that the bolt must revolve sufficiently to disengage these lugs before it can move backwards, and on loading it must close completely before it can be rotated to lock. Together with this bolt came the charger-loading system, adopted by many other bolt actions, in which the ammunition is held in some form of spring clip. This clip is positioned above the magazine, and the cartridges are pushed from the clip into the magazine, after which the clip is discarded. The Mauser system (and Lee system and others) is called "charger loading," in contrast to the Mannlicher "clip loading" system.

Lee

The Lee turn bolt is theoretically weaker and less accurate than the Mauser, but it is undoubtedly the fastest and smoothest of all bolt actions; a trained soldier with a Lee-Enfield rifle can deliver aimed fire twice as fast as one with a Mauser. The fundamental difference is that the bolt lugs lock into recesses in the action body; these have curved surfaces so that, as soon as the bolt begins to turn, it begins to open and move backwards, and on closing it can begin rotation before it is completely closed. The theoretical disadvantage is that, since the bolt is not locked into the chamber, it can compress slightly under the pressure of the explosion and so affect the chamber pressure and ballistics. In practice, this is scarcely noticeable.

Krag-Jorgensen

The Krag system, from Norway, is less a bolt system than a magazine system: the bolt is of no great interest, but the magazine lies laterally beneath the bolt and feeds up and around the left side to deliver the cartridge to the boltway on the left side of the action. Loading is done by opening a hinged trap-door and pushing loose rounds in; on closing the door, a magazine spring bears on the rounds and forces them up to the feedway. It is a reliable-enough system, particularly with rimmed ammunition, but, as with so many other systems, one wonders whether avoiding existing patents was the major reason for its development.

Lebel

The French Lebel bolt system uses two forward locking lugs plus a large rectangular lug on the outside of the bolt body that locks into a recess in the action. A screw passes through this lug to retain the bolt head; the screw must be removed and the head detached in order to remove the bolt, as the head will not pass through the boltway and out the back of the action. It has a unique tubular magazine, lying beneath the barrel, from which rounds are lifted up to the breech by a linkage operated by the movement of the bolt.

Mannlicher

The essence of the Mannlicher system is not so much the bolt, which is comparable to that of the Mauser, but the magazine, since Mannlicher invented the clip-loading system. In this system, the cartridges are held in a clip, and clip and cartridges are dropped into the magazine as a unit. The clip is locked in place and a spring-loaded arm pushes the cartridges up as they are loaded. When the last shot is fired, the clip can be expelled; in some later designs, it expels itself.

Mosin-Nagant

Developed by Captain Mosin of the Russian Army, this bolt is a complex three-piece device that appears to have been designed primarily to avoid patent litigation.

Straight-pull bolts

So-called because, to open them, the user grasps the handle and pulls it straight back without lifting.

Mannlicher

Mannlicher developed two types of straight-pull system. The first used a wedge beneath the bolt, which was pushed down and lifted up by a sleeve attached to the bolt handle. The second also used a sleeve, with helical grooves inside, which connected with lugs on the bolt

body, carried inside the sleeve; as the handle was pulled back, the sleeve rode over and forced the lugs to turn the bolt and unlock it.

Schmidt

This resembles the Mannlicher second type but uses a bolt sleeve, which carries the bolt body. A rod is driven back and forth by the handle and engages in a cam track in the bolt sleeve to rotate the sleeve. The locking lugs are actually on the sleeve, and the bolt body does not rotate. It was later modified to become much shorter, but the principle remained the same. It has only ever been used on Swiss Army rifles and carbines.

Lee

The Lee straight pull is similar to the first Mannlicher system, using a wedge beneath the bolt, which is controlled by the bolt handle; as the handle is pulled back, it first lifts the wedge and then pulls on the bolt. It is unlikely to be encountered; almost all Lee straight-pull rifles are museum pieces.

Ross

The Ross resembles the second Mannlicher type but uses a screw-thread in the bolt sleeve that engages with a helical screw-thread on the bolt body, so reciprocal movement of the sleeve rotates the bolt and its locking lugs. Unfortunately it proved susceptible to dirt in active service, and the bolt could be assembled wrongly, leading to dangerous accidents. Not recommended.

Mannlicher straight-pull bolt rifles AUSTRIA

There are two varieties of straight-pull bolt used in Mannlicher rifles. The first has a wedge beneath the bolt that is forced down by movement of the handle, as found on the M1886 Austrian rifle. The second uses a bolt sleeve with helical grooves, inside which is a bolt body with lugs; as the bolt handle, attached to the sleeve, is pulled back, the grooves in the sleeve force the bolt body to turn and unlock. This was used on the Austrian M1895 service rifle. Both are designed so that, if the bolt is not securely locked, the firing pin cannot go forward.

SPECIFICATION:

CARTRIDGE:
8 x 50R Austrian Service

DIMENSIONS (AUSTRIAN M1895 RIFLE):
LENGTH O/A: 1272 mm (50 in)
WEIGHT: 3.8 kg (8 lb 6 oz)
BARREL: 765 mm (30.1 in)
RIFLING: 4 grooves, rh
MAGAZINE CAPACITY: 5 rounds

IN PRODUCTION:
1895–1918

MARKINGS:
"STEYR M.95" over chamber. Serial number on left side of chamber.

SAFETY:
Manual safety catch on the left rear side of the action. When turned up, it engages with bolt, locking it in place, and also partly withdraws striker; when turned down, to left, the rifle is ready to fire.

UNLOADING:
Place safety catch in "fire" position. Open the bolt to extract any round in chamber. Examine magazine aperture; if there is ammunition in magazine, press clip-release button in front edge of trigger guard to eject clip and any ammunition upwards through action. Check that chamber and magazine are both empty. Close bolt. Pull trigger.

Mannlicher turn bolt rifles AUSTRIA

The essential difference between the Mannlicher and other turn-bolt systems lies in Mannlicher's pioneering clip-loading system. The bolt is opened and a complete clip of ammunition is dropped into the magazine. An arm forces the cartridges up in the clip, to be collected by the bolt; when the last round is loaded, the clip drops out of the magazine through a hole in the bottom, or, in some designs, is ejected upwards when the bolt is opened after the last round is fired. The clip is an essential part of the magazine system: without a clip, the magazine is unusable and the rifle is rendered a single-shot weapon.

SPECIFICATION:

CARTRIDGE:
6.5 x 53 R (Dutch); 6.5 x 53 mm (Romanian)

DIMENSIONS (DUTCH M1895):
LENGTH O/A: 1295 mm (51 in)
WEIGHT: 4.3 kg (9 lb 8 oz)
BARREL: 790 mm (31.1 in)
RIFLING: 4 grooves, rh
MAGAZINE CAPACITY: 5 rounds

IN PRODUCTION:
1895–1940

MARKINGS:
Manufacturer ("STEYR" or "HEMBRUG"), year, and serial number above chamber.

SAFETY:
Thumb switch at top rear of bolt: turn to right for safe; turn to left to fire. Note: On the Romanian M1893, safety can only be applied when striker is cocked; on Dutch M1895, it can be applied in any condition of bolt.

UNLOADING:
Open bolt to extract any cartridge in chamber. Examine magazine aperture; if there are cartridges in magazine, press clip-release button on front edge of trigger guard to allow clip, with any remaining ammunition, to be ejected upwards through action. Check that chamber and magazine are both empty, close bolt, and press trigger.

Steyr-Mannlicher SSG-69 AUSTRIA

Developed as a sniping rifle for the Austrian Army in 1969, the SSG-69 was later put on the commercial market and was also adopted by numerous military and police forces. Minor changes have been made, such as a heavier and larger bolt knob, a short-barrelled version, and a special "Police Version" that will accept a silencer, but they all use the same basic turn-bolt mechanism with lugs on the bolt turning into recesses in the receiver behind the magazine. The magazine is now the Schoenauer type, though for some years a 10-round detachable box was offered as an alternative. The SSG-69 is license-manufactured in Greece by EBO with either wooden or synthetic furniture. The EBO model has the name Kefefs.

SPECIFICATION:

CARTRIDGE:
7.62 x 51 mm NATO

DIMENSIONS:
LENGTH O/A: 1140 mm (44.9 in)
WEIGHT: 3.9 kg (8 lb 9 oz)
BARREL: 650 mm (25.6 in)
RIFLING: 4 grooves, rh
MAGAZINE CAPACITY: 5 rounds

IN PRODUCTION:
1969–

MARKINGS:
"STEYR-MANNLICHER SSG69" and serial number on left side of receiver.

SAFETY:
Manual safety catch on right rear of receiver: push forward to fire, back for safe

UNLOADING:
Squeeze in two sides of magazine-release catch at bottom edge of stock and withdraw rotary magazine (rear end is transparent and reveals the contents). Empty out any ammunition by pushing top round out and allowing spool to turn and present next round. Open bolt to extract any round in chamber. Examine chamber and feedway, close bolt, and press trigger. Replace the empty magazine.

Steyr Scout AUSTRIA

The Steyr Scout was developed as a high-accuracy multipurpose rifle and has several novel features, including a three-position safety tang over the small of the butt. A spare 5- or 10-round box magazine can be stowed under the buttstock that, as with the rest of the weapon, is made from non-slip synthetic materials. The forestock is arranged so that what would normally be two handgrip panels can be lowered to form a bipod. A combat-accessory rail is located under the forestock, and a sound suppressor can be installed. Various optical or night sights can be installed. Butt pad spacers can be added to suit individual users. A Tactical Elite model with a heavier-than-standard barrel has been produced for police applications.

SPECIFICATION:

CARTRIDGE:
7.62 x 51 mm NATO

DIMENSIONS:
LENGTH O/A: 1005 mm (39.6 in)
WEIGHT: 3.2 kg (7 lb)
BARREL: 483 mm (19 in)
RIFLING: 4 grooves, rh
MAGAZINE CAPACITY: 5 or 10 rounds

IN PRODUCTION:
1998–

MARKINGS:
"STEYR SCOUT" and serial number on left side of receiver.

SAFETY:
The bolt mechanism has a three-position safety tang over the small of the butt: when a red dot is visible, the rifle is ready to fire; a white dot indicates the loading position, with the trigger mechanism locked; the third position locks both the trigger and bolt.

UNLOADING:
Squeeze both sides of box magazine below receiver to release box magazine downwards and empty manually. Open bolt to remove a round from chamber and ensure chamber is empty. Close bolt and press trigger. Place safety tang in either of the two safe positions.

FN 30-11 BELGIUM

Developed as a sniping rifle for police and military use, the FN 30-11 uses a standard Mauser bolt action and integral magazine in a heavy receiver and barrel. The butt has an adjustable check-piece and, unusually, a flash-hide fitted to the muzzle. Aperture sights are fitted but a telescope is the more usual sighting method. Accessories such as a firing sling and bipod were usually supplied with the rifle.

SPECIFICATION:

CARTRIDGE:
7.62 x 51 mm NATO

DIMENSIONS:
LENGTH O/A: 1117 mm (44 in)
WEIGHT: 4.9 kg (10 lb 10 oz)
BARREL: 502 mm (19.8 in)
RIFLING: 4 grooves, rh
MAGAZINE CAPACITY: 10 rounds

IN PRODUCTION:
1978–86

MARKINGS:
"FABRIQUE NATIONALE HERSTAL" on left side of barrel. Serial number on right side of action.

SAFETY:
Manual catch alongside the cocking piece of the bolt: press forward for fire, to rear for safe.

UNLOADING:
Move safety catch to "fire." Open bolt to eject any round in chamber. Inspect magazine aperture; if ammunition is in magazine, work bolt to load and unload cartridges until magazine is empty. Check both chamber and magazine, then depress magazine platform and close bolt. Press trigger.

Sako TRG

The TRG is a specialized sniping rifle. The receiver is of forged steel; the heavy barrel is also cold-forged and fitted with a combined flash hider and muzzle brake. The action and barrel are mounted to an aluminum skeleton frame, to which is attached the synthetic stock and fore-end. The muzzle brake can be removed and replaced with a silencer. The stock is fully adjustable in every direction and is also capable of adaptation to right- or left-handed users. The TRG21 is the 7.62 mm model. There is also a TRG41, which fires 0.338 Lapua Magnum; it has a 690 mm barrel and a 5-round magazine.

SPECIFICATION:

CARTRIDGE:
7.62 x 51mm NATO or 0.308 Lapua Magnum

DIMENSIONS (TRG21):
LENGTH O/A: 1150 mm (45.3 in)
WEIGHT: 4.7 kg (10 lb 6 oz)
BARREL: 660 mm (26 in)
RIFLING: 4 grooves, rh
MAGAZINE CAPACITY: 10 rounds

IN PRODUCTION:
1992–

MARKINGS:
"SAKO TRG21" and serial number on left side of receiver.

SAFETY:
Manual safety catch inside the trigger guard: press forward to fire; pull back to make safe, which locks the bolt, trigger, and firing pin.

UNLOADING:
Magazine release at rear of magazine. Remove magazine; empty out any ammunition. Open bolt to extract any cartridge left in chamber. Inspect chamber and feedway, close bolt, and press trigger. Replace empty magazine.

TIKKA M65-A308 FINLAND

The M65 was a popular sporting and hunting rifle for many years and can be found in a variety of chamberings and finishings from 6.5 mm to 7.62 mm. The model shown here, the A308, is so called because it is chambered for 0.308 Winchester, the commercial version of 7.62 mm NATO. A heavy-barrel rifle with bipod and pistol grip, it is designed for precision shooting, either big game or sniping. The depth of the wooden stock conceals and protects the 10-round magazine. Other M65s have a five-round magazine. Shown is a variant model fitted with a full-length suppressor.

SPECIFICATION:

CARTRIDGE:
7.62 x 51 mm NATO

DIMENSIONS:
LENGTH O/A: 1210 mm (47.6 in)
WEIGHT: 5.2 kg (11 lb 6 oz)
BARREL: 475 mm (18.7 in)
RIFLING: 6 grooves, rh
MAGAZINE CAPACITY: 10 rounds

IN PRODUCTION:
1965–89

MARKINGS:
"TIKKA M65" and serial number on left side of receiver.

SAFETY:
Mauser-type manual safety catch at rear of bolt.

UNLOADING:
Magazine release at base of magazine well in front of trigger. Remove magazine and empty if necessary. Open bolt. Inspect feedway and chamber. Close bolt. Press trigger.

GIAT FR-F1/FR-F2 FRANCE

This is a precision sniping rifle based on the action of the MAS36 service rifle; it was designed first as a target rifle, and then modified for the sniping role. The F1 was issued first in 7.5 mm caliber, and then changed to 7.62 mm caliber in the late 1970s. The FR-F2 model is an improved version; the fire-end is of plastic-covered metal instead of wood, the bipod is stronger, and there is a thermal insulating sleeve over the barrel to prevent warping due to heat and reduce the infrared signature.

SPECIFICATION:

CARTRIDGE:
7.5 x 54 mm or 7.62 x 51 mm

DIMENSIONS:
LENGTH O/A: 1138 mm (44.8 in)
WEIGHT: 5.2 kg (11 lb 7 oz)
BARREL: 552 mm (22.9 in)
RIFLING: 4 grooves. rh
MAGAZINE CAPACITY: 10 rounds

IN PRODUCTION:
1966–80 (F1); 1984– (F2).

MARKINGS:
"FR-F1 7.62 N M.A.S." and serial number on left side of receiver.

SAFETY:
Manual safety catch inside trigger guard behind trigger: press down to make safe, press up and to left to fire.

UNLOADING:
Magazine catch on right side of receiver above front end of magazine. Remove magazine. Place safety catch to "fire" and open bolt to eject any round in chamber. Inspect chamber, and close bolt. Pull trigger.

MAS Mle 1936 FRANCE

Ugly, roughly made, but immensely strong and reliable, this was the French Army's rifle to match the 7.5 mm cartridge introduced in 1929. A folding-butt model was also made for paratroops and Alpine troops, though this is rarely encountered. Late models (converted in the 1950s) have an extended barrel with concentric rings to permit the launch of rifle grenades. The finish varies from phosphated to browned to enameled, according to when it was made and for which arm of the service.

SPECIFICATION:

CARTRIDGE:
7.5 x 54 mm French Service

DIMENSIONS:
LENGTH O/A: 1022 mm (40.3 in)
WEIGHT: 3.8 kg (8 lb 4 oz)
BARREL: 575 mm (22.6 in)
RIFLING: 4 grooves, rh
MAGAZINE CAPACITY: 5 rounds

IN PRODUCTION:
1936–55

MARKINGS:
"ST ETIENNE" and year of manufacture on left side of action. Serial number on right side of action.

SAFETY:
No manual safety device. BE CAREFUL.

UNLOADING:
Open bolt to extract any cartridge in chamber. Press in magazine floor-plate release button on right side of action body, at front edge of magazine, and allow magazine contents to fall into hand. Check that magazine space and chamber are empty, close bolt, and press trigger. Replace magazine follower, spring, and floor plate.

PGM Hecate II FRANCE/BELGIUM

PGM Precision are well-known makers of sporting rifles, and in the late 1980s they developed a range of sniping rifles, largely adopted by French and other continental police forces. The Hecate is more or less a scaled-up version of their Intervention sniping rifle and is a conventional bolt-action repeating rifle. The wooden butt, with cheekpiece, can be removed for trans-portation and has a monopod beneath it; there is a bipod attached to the receiver fore-end, and a pistol grip. A large single-baffle muzzle brake reduces the recoil to a reasonable amount, and it can be removed and replaced with a silencer. The rifle has been taken into use by the French Army. It is now marketed in Belgium by FN HERSTAL.

SPECIFICATION:

CARTRIDGE:
0.50 Browning

DIMENSIONS:
LENGTH O/A: 1380 mm (54.3 in)
BARREL: 700 mm (27.6 in)
WEIGHT: 13.5 kg (29 lb 12 oz)
RIFLING: 8 grooves, rh
MAGAZINE CAPACITY: 7 rounds

IN PRODUCTION:
1988–

MARKINGS:
"FN HERSTAL"

SAFETY:
Manual safety catch on right side of receiver locks sear and trigger.

UNLOADING:
Remove magazine. Open bolt to extract any cartridge in chamber. Examine magazine aperture and chamber to ensure both are empty. Close bolt. Pull trigger.

Mauser Gewehr 98 GERMANY

Mauser made many military rifles for various nations, but most of them were variations of this, the perfected Mauser rifle that served the German Army for half a century; understand this model and you understand them all. Robust, well made, accurate, and reliable, these rifles will last for years to come and still be serviceable. The Gewehr 98 improved on the basic Mauser design by having a third locking lug beneath the bolt, locking into the receiver behind the magazine. The bolt sticks out at right angles, making it awkward to manipulate; a variation with a turned-down bolt was provided for cyclist troops in 1904 but is unlikely to be met.

SPECIFICATION:

CARTRIDGE:
7.92 x 57 mm Mauser

DIMENSIONS:
LENGTH O/A: 1250 mm (49.2 in)
WEIGHT: 4.1 kg (9 lb)
BARREL: 740 mm (29.1 in)
RIFLING: 4 grooves, rh
MAGAZINE CAPACITY: 5 rounds

IN PRODUCTION:
1898–1918

MARKINGS:
"Mod 98," manufacturer's name, and serial number on top of chamber.

SAFETY:
Manual safety catch on rear of bolt: turn to left to fire, turn to right for safe.

UNLOADING:
Place safety catch to "fire" and open bolt to extract any round in chamber. Examine magazine aperture. If there is ammunition in magazine, press magazine floor-plate catch in front edge of trigger guard, allowing magazine floor plate to hinge at its front end, open, and dump contents of magazine. Examine chamber and magazine aperture again, close bolt, press trigger, and then close magazine floor plate.

Mauser Karabiner 98k GERMANY

This is the "short rifle" version of the Gewehr 98, developed in time for World War II and immediately recognizable by its shorter length, turned-down bolt handle, and recess in the woodwork to allow the bolt to be grasped. Rifles made from 1942 to 1945 are often of lesser quality—using stamped metal for the barrel bands and trigger guard, for example, and laminated plywood for the furniture. They shot just as well, however, since there was no diminution in the quality of the bolt, barrel, and action. About 11.5 million 98ks were made in 10 years, so they will be around for a long time yet.

SPECIFICATION:

CARTRIDGE:
7.92 x 57 mm Mauser

DIMENSIONS:
LENGTH O/A: 1110 mm (43.7 in)
WEIGHT: 3.9 kg (8 lb 11 oz)
BARREL: 600 mm (23.6 in)
RIFLING: 4 grooves, rh
MAGAZINE CAPACITY: 5 rounds

IN PRODUCTION:
1935–45

MARKINGS:
"Kar 98k," manufacturer's code, and serial number on sides of chamber.

SAFETY:
Manual safety catch on rear of bolt: turn to left to fire, turn to right for safe.

UNLOADING:
Move safety catch to "fire" and open bolt to extract any round in chamber. Examine magazine aperture. If there is ammunition in magazine, press magazine floor-plate catch in front edge of trigger guard, allowing magazine floor plate to hinge at its front end, open, and dump contents of magazine. Examine chamber and magazine aperture again, close bolt, press trigger, and then close magazine floor plate.

Gepard M1/M1A1 HUNGARY

This is a single-shot anti-matériel rifle firing the Russian 12.7 mm cartridge. The barrel is carried in a tubular cradle, which also mounts the bipod, and a barrel extension carries the padded buttplate. The pistol grip acts as the bolt handle; to load, the grip is twisted up, unlocking the heavy, double-lug breech block, which can then be withdrawn from the rifle. A round is loaded into the chamber, the breech block is replaced, and the pistol grip turned down to lock. A hammer in the pistol-grip unit is now manually cocked and the trigger pressed to fire the rifle. Aiming is done by means of a 12x telescope, and the cartridge is sufficiently accurate to deliver a 300 mm (11.8 in) group at 600 m (1968.5 ft) range. The armor-piercing bullet will defeat 15 mm (0.6 in) of steel armor at the same range.

The M1A1 is the same weapon but mounted on a backpack frame that serves as a firing mount for use in soft ground or snow; the bipod is still attached to the cradle but folded up when the frame is used.

SPECIFICATION:

CARTRIDGE:
12.7 x 107 mm Soviet

DIMENSIONS:
LENGTH O/A: 1570 mm (61.8 in)
WEIGHT: 19 kg (41 lb 14 oz)
BARREL: 1100 mm (43.3 in)
RIFLING: 8 grooves, rh
MAGAZINE: None (single shot)

IN PRODUCTION:
1992–

MARKINGS:
A small flat surface on the top of the receiver is stamped "cal 12.7 GEPARD M1A 1011."

SAFETY:
Thumb-operated catch on pistol grip locks hammer.

UNLOADING:
Grasp pistol grip and twist anticlockwise until it unlocks, then remove breech unit, together with any roundheld by extractor. Remove cartridge, inspect chamber, replace breech piece and pull trigger.

Beretta Sniper

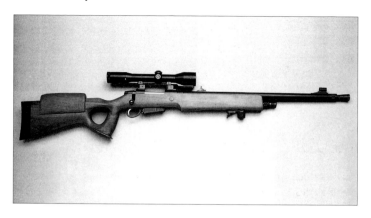

This is a conventional Mauser-type bolt action, with a heavy free-floating barrel and a harmonic balancer contained within a tube concealed by the wooden fore-end. This is vibrated when the shot is fired and is designed to damp out vibrations in the barrel, ensuring maximum accuracy. There is a flash hider on the muzzle, and the tube of the balance forms a point of attachment for a bipod. Fully adjustable iron sights are provided, but it also carries a NATO-standard mount for telescope and electro-optical sights.

SPECIFICATION:

CARTRIDGE:
7.62 x 51 mm NATO

DIMENSIONS:
LENGTH O/A: 1165 mm (45.9 in)
WEIGHT: 5.6 kg (12 lb 4 oz)
BARREL: 586 mm (23.1 in)
RIFLING: 4 grooves, rh
MAGAZINE CAPACITY: 5 rounds

IN PRODUCTION:
1985–

MARKINGS:
"P. BERETTA" above chamber. Serial number on right side of receiver.

SAFETY:
Thumb catch behind bolt handle.

UNLOADING:
Magazine catch behind magazine. Push safety catch to "fire." Remove magazine. Open bolt to eject any round in chamber. Inspect chamber, close bolt, and press trigger.

Mannlicher-Carcano M1938 ITALY

World War I experience suggested that the Italian 6.5 mm cartridge was insufficiently powerful, and experience in North Africa and Abyssinia reinforced this view, thus the Model 1938 rifle and carbine were built around a new 7.35 mm cartridge. However, when Italy entered the war in 1940, it was decided to withdraw these new weapons and give them to the militia so as to simplify ammunition supply in the field. A handful of the carbines were modified in 1944 to fire German 7.92 mm Mauser ammunition. These can be recognized by "7.92 S" stamped into the top of the chamber; it is unwise to fire these converted weapons.

SPECIFICATION:

CARTRIDGE:
7.35 x 51 mm Italian M38

DIMENSIONS:
LENGTH O/A: 1021 mm (40.2 in)
WEIGHT: 3.4 kg (7 lb 8 oz)
BARREL: 530 mm (29.9 in)
RIFLING: 4 grooves, rh
MAGAZINE CAPACITY: 6 rounds

IN PRODUCTION:
1937–40

MARKINGS:
Year of manufacture, "TERNI," and serial number on right side of chamber.

SAFETY:
Manual safety catch in the form of a collar with a knurled "flag" around end of bolt: turn down to right to fire, turned up so flag is visible in line of sight for safe.

UNLOADING:
Move safety catch to "fire" and open bolt, thus ejecting any round in chamber. Inspect chamber and magazine. If there is ammunition in magazine, press clip latch in front edge of trigger guard. Ammunition clip and any cartridges it contains will be ejected upwards through top of action. Check again, close bolt, and press trigger.

Mannlicher-Carcano TS Carbine M1891 ITALY

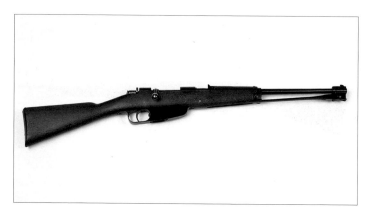

The Italian service was equipped with Mannlicher-Carcano weapons from 1891 to 1945. The TS (Truppo Special) carbine is one of the more common examples of the system; the other weapons—rifle M1891, cavalry carbine M1891, carbine M91/24, and rifle M91/38—are identical in their mechanism. The bolt is basically Mauser, the magazine with its associated clip is Mannlicher, and the Carcano part of the title comes from the Italian who designed the bolt safety system. They were mostly sold off after 1945 and spread throughout the world; President Kennedy was shot with a Mannlicher-Carcano carbine. A folding bayonet is permanently fitted. Shown is the M91/38 variant.

SPECIFICATION:

CARTRIDGE:
6.5 x 52 mm Mannlicher

DIMENSIONS:
LENGTH O/A: 920 mm (36.2 in)
WEIGHT: 3.1 kg (6 lb 14 oz)
BARREL: 450 mm (17.7 in)
RIFLING: 4 grooves, rh
MAGAZINE CAPACITY: 6 rounds

IN PRODUCTION:
1891–1918

MARKINGS:
Year of manufacture, "TERNI," and serial number on side of breech.

SAFETY:
Manual safety catch in the form of a collar with a knurled "flag" around end of bolt: turn down to right to fire, turn up so flag is visible in line of sight for safe.

UNLOADING:
Move safety catch to "fire" and open bolt, ejecting any round in chamber. Inspect chamber and magazine. If there is ammunition in magazine, press clip latch in front edge of trigger guard. Ammunition clip and any cartridges it contains will be ejected upwards through top of action. Check again, close bolt, and press trigger.

Arisaka 38th Year JAPAN

This Japanese service rifle, based on the Mauser system, was also supplied to the UK, Mexico, Russia, Indonesia, and Thailand at various times. It can be found with British and/or Russian markings, since both these countries purchased quantities during World War I. It was also supplied to Mexico in 7 mm Mauser caliber. Something like 3 million were made and they can be found almost anywhere. In Japanese nomenclature, "38th Year" refers to the reign of the emperor at the time of introduction; it equates to 1905. The system changed in the 1930s.

SPECIFICATION:

CARTRIDGE:
6.5 x 50 SR Japanese Service

DIMENSIONS:
LENGTH O/A: 1275 mm (50.2 in)
WEIGHT: 4.1 kg (9 lb 1 oz)
BARREL: 799 mm (31.5 in)
RIFLING: 4 or 6 grooves, rh
MAGAZINE CAPACITY: 5 rounds

IN PRODUCTION:
1907–44

MARKINGS:
Japanese ideographs for "38th Year" above chamber. Serial number and arsenal mark on left side of frame.

SAFETY:
Knurled cap at rear end of bolt. With rifle cocked, press in this cap with the palm of the hand and twist it to right to make safe, to left to fire. It only works with rifle cocked.

UNLOADING:
Set safety catch to "fire." Open bolt to extract any round left in chamber. Examine magazine aperture; if there is ammunition in magazine, place one hand underneath magazine plate under stock, and with other hand press magazine catch in front edge of trigger guard forward. This will release magazine floor plate and contents of magazine. Replace magazine spring and plate (front edge first), check there is no ammunition in magazine or chamber, close bolt, and press trigger.

Arisaka Type 99

This short rifle began as a conversion of the 38th Year rifle to a 7.7 mm cartridge. That proved unwieldy, and the design was changed to a short rifle, which did away with the need for carbines. Early models were excellent, but those made in the last year of World War II were crude; few have survived. The Paratroop version is similar but has either an interrupted thread or wedge joint between barrel and action, allowing it to be dismantled into two pieces. "Type 99" refers to the year in the Japanese calendar and equates to 1939 in Western chronology.

SPECIFICATION:

CARTRIDGE:
7.7 x 58 mm Japanese Service

DIMENSIONS:
LENGTH O/A: 1150 mm (45.3 in)
WEIGHT: 3.8 kg (8 lb 6 oz)
BARREL: 657 mm (25.9 in)
RIFLING: 4 grooves, rh
MAGAZINE CAPACITY: 5 rounds

IN PRODUCTION:
1940–45

MARKINGS:
Japanese ideographs for "Type 99" above chamber. Serial number and arsenal mark on left side of frame.

SAFETY:
Knurled cap at rear end of bolt. With rifle cocked, press in this cap with the palm of the hand and twist it to right to make safe, to left to fire. Only works with rifle cocked.

UNLOADING:
Set safety catch to "fire." Open bolt to extract any round left in chamber. Examine magazine aperture; if there is ammunition in magazine, place one hand underneath magazine plate under stock, and with other hand pull magazine catch inside trigger guard back. This will release magazine floor plate and contents of magazine. Replace magazine spring and plate (front edge first), check there is no ammunition in magazine or chamber, close bolt, and press trigger.

Krag-Jorgensen NORWAY

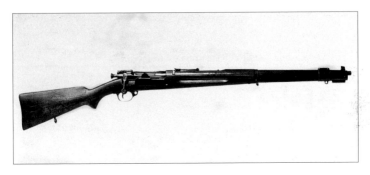

The Krag-Jorgensen was developed in Norway and is unusual because of its side-loading magazine. The magazine gate is opened, loose rounds placed inside, and the door closed, which puts pressure on the rounds and feeds them under and around the bolt to appear on the left side of the boltway. It was adopted by Denmark, then Norway, and then the USA, but only Norway stayed with it, developing their last version as late as 1930. Many thousands of these rifles and carbines were sold for hunting purposes in Scandinavia and the USA and are still in use in both areas.

SPECIFICATION:

CARTRIDGE:
6.5 x 55 mm (Norway); 0.30 Krag (USA); 8 x 56 R (Denmark)

DIMENSIONS (NORWAY, M1930):
LENGTH O/A: 1219 mm (48 in)
WEIGHT: 5.2 kg (11 lb 7 oz)
BARREL: 750 mm (29.5 in)
RIFLING: 4 grooves, lh
MAGAZINE CAPACITY: 5 rounds

IN PRODUCTION:
1888–1935

MARKINGS:
"MODEL 1894 SPRINGFIELD ARMORY" and serial number on left side of receiver (USA).

SAFETY:
Manual safety catch on end of bolt: turn to left for fire, to right to make safe.

UNLOADING:
Open magazine by hinging door forward (Danish weapons) or down (US and Norwegian), tipping rifle to right and allowing cartridges to fall out. Close magazine, set safety catch to "fire" and open bolt to eject any round in chamber. Inspect chamber and magazine aperture to left of boltway to ensure no ammunition remains in weapon. Close bolt. Press trigger.

Vapensmia NM149S NORWAY

This was developed as a sniper rifle for the Norwegian Army and police forces and is also available commercially as a target or hunting rifle. The action is that of the Mauser Gewehr 98, using the standard Mauser three-lug bolt. The barrel is exceptionally heavy, and it is normally issued with a 6 x 42 telescope sight; there are emergency iron sights fitted, but optical sights are virtually mandatory. The stock is of laminated beech and the butt is adjustable for length and may be fitted with a cheekpiece. A bipod and a sound suppressor are also available for this rifle.

SPECIFICATION:

CARTRIDGE:
7.62 x 51 mm NATO

DIMENSIONS:
LENGTH O/A: 1120 mm (44 in)
WEIGHT: 5.6 kg (12 lb 6 oz)
BARREL: 600 mm (23.6 in)
RIFLING: 4 grooves, rh
MAGAZINE CAPACITY: 5 rounds

IN PRODUCTION:
1990–

MARKINGS:
"NM149" on left side of action. Serial number on right side.

SAFETY:
Manual safety catch on rear end of bolt: turn to right to make safe, to left to fire.

UNLOADING:
Magazine catch behind magazine. Remove magazine and empty it of ammunition. Open bolt to extract any round in chamber. Examine chamber and feedway, close bolt, pull trigger. Replace empty magazine.

Mosin-Nagant RUSSIA

This design originated in 1891 with a long rifle that remained in service until World War II. It was generally superseded by the short 1938 carbine and the 1944 carbine (shown), which had an attached bayonet. Copies of the 1944 model were also made in China, Hungary, and Poland, and Mosin-Nagant rifles were converted to 8 mm in Austria and 7.92 mm in Germany and Poland during and after World War I. Large numbers of 1891 rifles were made in France and the USA on contract.

SPECIFICATION:

CARTRIDGE:
7.62 x 54 R Russian Service

DIMENSIONS (MODEL 1938 CARBINE):
LENGTH O/A: 1020 mm (40.2 in)
WEIGHT: 3.5 kg (7 lb 10 oz)
BARREL: 510 mm (20 in)
RIFLING: 4 grooves, rh
MAGAZINE CAPACITY: 5 rounds

IN PRODUCTION:
1892–1950

MARKINGS:
Arsenal mark, year, and serial number on top of chamber. Serial number on bolt.

SAFETY:
Manual safety by pulling back cocking-piece at rear of bolt and rotating it to left as far as it will go, then releasing it. This turns part of cocking-piece so that it rests on a solid part of receiver. Trigger still functions but striker cannot go forward.

UNLOADING:
Open bolt to extract any round remaining in chamber. Examine magazine aperture; if there is ammunition in magazine, release magazine floor plate by pressing catch behind plate in front of trigger guard. Plate will hinge forward, allowing contents of magazine to fall out. Close magazine floor plate, check that chamber and magazine are empty, close bolt, and pull trigger.

Schmidt-Rubin M1931 SWITZERLAND

Although called a carbine, this was really a short rifle. It was made for the Swiss Army, and numbers are still in use today. The Schmidt straight-pull bolt action was completely revised; what had been the bolt sleeve became the bolt, with lugs at the front end locking into the chamber, so that the action body was shortened by almost half from the 1889 pattern. Numbers of these carbines were adapted as sniper rifles in 1942–43, and in the 1930s 100 were supplied to the Papal Guard in Vatican City.

SPECIFICATION:

CARTRIDGE:
7.5 x 54 mm Swiss Service M1911

DIMENSIONS:
LENGTH O/A: 1105 mm (43.5 in)
WEIGHT: 4 kg (8 lb 13 oz)
BARREL: 652 mm (25.7 in)
RIFLING: 4 grooves, rh
MAGAZINE CAPACITY: 6 rounds

IN PRODUCTION:
1933–58

MARKINGS:
Serial number on left side of action body and on bolt. Swiss cross on top of chamber.

SAFETY:
Pull back on ring at rear of bolt, turn it to right, and release it. This withdraws firing pin and locks it, making rifle safe.

UNLOADING:
Magazine catch on right side at top of magazine. Press in and remove magazine. Open bolt, examine chamber and feedway, and close bolt. Press trigger.

SIG SAUER SSG-2000 SWITZERLAND

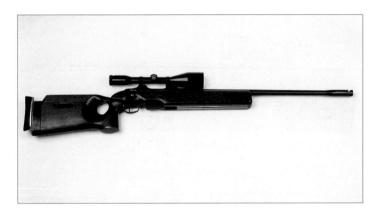

The SIG SSG-2000 uses an unusual bolt system: hinged wedges just in front of the bolt handle are forced outwards by cam action when the handle is turned down. These lock into recesses in the receiver; the bolt body does not revolve. Once cocked, the trigger is pushed forward to "set" it; thereafter, a slight touch is sufficient to fire. This weapon has been designed as a target rifle and as a law enforcement sniper. There are no iron sights; a telescope is mandatory. In addition to the 7.62 mm caliber, it is also chambered for the 5.56 x 45 mm and 7.5 x 55 mm military calibers and the 0.300 Weatherby Magnum caliber.

SPECIFICATION:

CARTRIDGE:
7.62 x 51 mm NATO and others

DIMENSIONS:
LENGTH O/A: 1210 mm (47.6 in)
WEIGHT: 6.6 kg (14 lb 9 oz) with sight
BARREL: 510 mm (20 in) without flash hider
RIFLING: 4 grooves, rh
MAGAZINE CAPACITY: 4 rounds

IN PRODUCTION:
1989–2002

MARKINGS:
"SIG-SAUER SSG 2000" on left side of action. Serial number alongside chamber on right side.

SAFETY:
Sliding manual safety catch behind bolt: when pushed forward to reveal red dot, weapon is ready to fire; pulled back, weapon is safe.

UNLOADING:
Magazine catch behind magazine. Remove magazine and empty it of ammunition. Open bolt to extract any round in chamber. Examine chamber and feedway, close bolt, and pull trigger. Replace empty magazine.

SIG SAUER SSG-3000 SWITZERLAND

This is a military and police sniping rifle derived from a successful target rifle. It is modular in form; the barrel and receiver are joined by screw clamps, and the trigger and magazine systems form a single unit that fits into the receiver. The stock is of laminated wood and ventilated to counter possible heat warping the heavy barrel. The bolt has six lugs and locks into the barrel. There is a rail under the fore-end to take a bipod or a firing sling. There are no iron sights; a mount for the standard Hensoldt telescope sight is normal, but a NATO STANAG sight mount can also be found.

SPECIFICATION:

CARTRIDGE:
7.62 x 51 mm NATO

DIMENSIONS:
LENGTH O/A: 1180 mm (45.5 in)
WEIGHT: 5.4 kg (11 lb 14 oz)
BARREL: 610 mm (24 in)
RIFLING: 4 grooves, rh
MAGAZINE CAPACITY: 5 rounds

IN PRODUCTION:
1991–2002

MARKINGS:
"SIG-SAUER SSG 3000" on left side of action. Serial number alongside chamber on right side.

SAFETY:
Sliding manual safety catch above trigger inside trigger guard: push forward to fire, pull back to make safe.

UNLOADING:
Magazine catch behind magazine. Remove magazine and empty it of ammunition. Open bolt to extract any round in chamber. Examine chamber and feedway, close bolt, and pull trigger. Replace empty magazine.

Accuracy International AW50F UK

The AW50F may be regarded as a L96A1 rifle scaled up to fire the 12.7 x 99 mm/0.50 Browning cartridge to operating ranges of up to 1500 m (4921.3 ft). It has been procured by several armed forces, including the British and Australian armies, as an anti-matériel rifle. Apart from its overall size and weight, the AW50F differs from its smaller-caliber counterpart by a prominent muzzle brake and extensive adjustment features on the folding buttstock, allowing it to be fitted to the physical measurements of individual users. The buttstock also includes an adjustable butt rest to enable the user to observe a target area for prolonged periods without fatigue. A rail over the receiver accepts both optical and night sights. A slightly lighter version, the AW50FT, makes use of titanium components where appropriate.

SPECIFICATION:

CARTRIDGE:
12.7 x 99 mm/0.50 Browning

DIMENSIONS:
LENGTH, BUTT EXTENDED: 1350 mm (53.1 in)
LENGTH, BUTT FOLDED: 1120 mm (44.1 in)
WEIGHT: 13.6 kg (30 lb)
BARREL: 686 mm (27 in)
RIFLING: 8 grooves, rh
MAGAZINE CAPACITY: 5 rounds

IN PRODUCTION:
1999–

MARKINGS:
"ACCURACY INTERNATIONAL ENGLAND" plus NATO stock number (if applicable) and serial number on left of action.

SAFETY:
Ambidextrous safety catch above trigger: back to make safe, forward to fire. When safe, bolt, trigger, and firing pin are all locked.

UNLOADING:
Magazine catch behind magazine. Remove magazine and empty out any rounds. Set safety catch to fire and open bolt to extract any round in chamber. Examine chamber and feedway, close bolt, and press trigger. Replace empty magazine.

Accuracy International L96A1 UK

The standard sniping rifle of the British Army, the L96A1 features an aluminum chassis to support the action and barrel, clothed in a plastic outer casing. It is also sold commercially in various models: the Long Range, chambered for 7 mm Remingtion Magnum or 0.300 Winchester Magnum; the Counter-Terrorist, in 7.62 mm; the Moderated, with an integral silencer; and the Infantry with a non-zoom telescope sight. The Long Range PM model is a single shot; the rest are magazine rifles.

SPECIFICATION:

CARTRIDGE:
7.62 x 51 mm NATO

DIMENSIONS:
LENGTH O/A: 1124 mm (44.3 in)
WEIGHT: 6.5 kg (14 lb 5 oz)
BARREL: 654 mm (25.8 in)
RIFLING: 4 grooves, rh
MAGAZINE CAPACITY: 10 rounds

IN PRODUCTION:
1985–

MARKINGS:
"CR 156 GA ACCURACY INTERNATIONAL ENGLAND," NATO stock number and serial number on left side of action.

SAFETY:
Manual safety catch on left rear of action: forward to fire, back to make safe. Safety catch locks bolt, trigger, and firing pin. Bolt cannot be closed when safety is applied, and safety cannot be applied unless striker is cocked.

UNLOADING:
Magazine catch behind magazine. Remove magazine. Empty out any ammunition. Set safety catch to "fire." Open bolt to extract any round remaining in chamber. Examine chamber and feedway, close bolt, and press trigger. Replace empty magazine.

De Lisle UK

This unusual silent carbine was designed around the standard Lee-Enfield bolt action but chambered for the US 0.45 pistol cartridge. Since this cartridge is subsonic, the De Lisle, with its integral silencer, is probably the most silent of all silenced weapons. Two versions were made, with a fixed butt and with a metal folding butt; the resemblance between the folding butt of the De Lisle and that of the Sterling submachine gun is because both weapons were made by Sterling. Various modern copies have been made; original production was in the low hundreds.

SPECIFICATION:

CARTRIDGE:
0.45 ACP

DIMENSIONS:
LENGTH O/A: 960 mm (37.8 in)
WEIGHT: 3.7 kg (8 lb 2 oz)
BARREL: 210 mm (8.3 in)
RIFLING: 4 grooves, lh
MAGAZINE CAPACITY: 8 rounds

IN PRODUCTION:
1942–45

MARKINGS:
Serial number on right side of receiver.

SAFETY:
Manual safety catch on left side of receiver: forward to fire, back to make safe.

UNLOADING:
Magazine catch inside trigger guard. Remove magazine. Set safety catch to "fire" and open bolt to extract any round in breech. Close bolt. Press trigger.

Enfield Enforcer UK

This was developed by the Royal Small Arms Factory, Enfield, as a result of requests from British police forces for a sniping rifle. It uses the basic Lee-Enfield action, allied with a heavy barrel and a shortened "sporter" fore-end. It is, in fact, the same rifle as the British Army's L42A1 sniping rifle; the difference is that when issued to the British Army, it had a plain sighting telescope, but when sold to the police, it was given a more modern zoom telescope sight. A very similar weapon was also sold without optical sight in the civil market as the Envoy target rifle.

SPECIFICATION:

CARTRIDGE:
7.62 x 51 mm NATO

DIMENSIONS:
LENGTH O/A: 1180 mm (46.5 in)
WEIGHT: 4.4 kg (9 lb 12 oz)
BARREL: 700 mm (27.6 in)
RIFLING: 4 grooves, rh
MAGAZINE CAPACITY: 10 rounds.

IN PRODUCTION:
1970–85

MARKINGS:
"ENFIELD" and year of manufacture on stock band beneath bolt. Serial number on right side of chamber.

SAFETY:
Manual safety catch on left side of action: forward to fire, back to make safe.

UNLOADING:
Magazine catch behind magazine. Remove magazine. Set safety catch to "fire" and open bolt to eject any round in chamber. Inspect chamber, and close bolt. Press trigger.

Enfield Rifle No. 2 (Pattern '14) UK

This was developed in 1912–14 as a potential replacement for the Lee-Enfield and uses a Mauser-type action. The design was in 0.276 caliber, substantially more efficient than the 0.303 it was intended to replace. Developmental problems prevented its introduction, and on the outbreak of war in 1914 the project was abandoned; to satisfy the enormous demand for rifles it was redesigned to fire the 0.303 cartridge and manufactured in the USA under contract by Remington and Winchester. The rifles remained in store during 1919–40 and were then brought out again and issued to the British Home Guard and some home defense units. Thousands were sold after 1945 for target rifles. It was later manufactured in 30-06 caliber and issued to the US Army as the M1917.

SPECIFICATION:

CARTRIDGE:
0.303 British Service

DIMENSIONS:
LENGTH O/A: 1176 mm (46.3 in)
WEIGHT: 4.1 kg (9 lb 2 oz)
BARREL: 660 mm (26 in)
RIFLING: 5 grooves, lh
MAGAZINE CAPACITY: 5 rounds

IN PRODUCTION:
1915–17

MARKINGS:
Maker's mark and serial number on top of chamber.

SAFETY:
Manual safety catch on right side of action behind bolt handle: forward to fire, rearward to make safe.

UNLOADING:
Set safety catch to "fire" position. Open bolt to extract any round in chamber. Inspect magazine; if it contains ammunition, continue working bolt until all rounds have been loaded and ejected. Depress magazine platform to allow bolt to go forward, close bolt, and pull trigger.

Lee-Enfield Rifle No. 4 UK

This was the replacement for the SMLE Mark III (see p.261); it was virtually the same rifle but simplified in order to make wartime mass production easier. The nosecap was changed, and a spike bayonet replaced the old sword. The sights were changed from a U-notch tangent halfway along the rifle to a tangent aperture pattern on the rear of the receiver.

It made teaching recruits easier, but expert shots felt they had better control with the older pattern. About 4 million were made in the UK, USA, Canada, India, and Australia; about 40,000 American-made rifles were also supplied to China.

SPECIFICATION:

CARTRIDGE:
0.303 British Service

DIMENSIONS:
LENGTH O/A: 1128 mm (44.4 in)
WEIGHT: 4.1 kg (9 lb 1 oz)
BARREL: 640 mm (25.2 in)
RIFLING: 5 grooves, lh
MAGAZINE CAPACITY: 10 rounds

IN PRODUCTION:
1940–45

MARKINGS:
Maker and year on right of stock band beneath bolt handle. Serial number on right side of chamber. Rifles manufactured in USA may have "UNITED STATES PROPERTY" on left side of receiver; those made in Canada may have "LONG BRANCH" in same place.

SAFETY:
Manual safety catch on left side of action: press forward to fire, rearward to make safe.

UNLOADING:
Press up on magazine catch inside trigger guard to release magazine. Remove magazine and contents and empty. Open bolt to extract any cartridge in chamber. Examine chamber and feedway, close bolt, and pull trigger. Replace empty magazine.

Lee-Enfield Rifle No. 5 UK

The No. 5 is a shortened and lightened version of the No. 4 Rifle intended for jungle warfare. A handsome weapon, it never lived up to its appearance; blast and recoil were unpleasant due to the short barrel and powerful cartridge, and the rifle suffered from a "wandering zero." Much time and energy was spent on trying to solve this problem but in the end the authorities gave up and the rifle was declared obsolete in 1947. A blade bayonet replaced the short-lived spike bayonet of the No. 4 rifle.

SPECIFICATION:

CARTRIDGE:
0.303 British Service

DIMENSIONS:
LENGTH: 875 mm (34.5 in)
WEIGHT: 2.9 kg (6 lb 6 oz)
BARREL: 300 mm (11.8 in)
RIFLING: 5 grooves, lh
MAGAZINE CAPACITY: 10 rounds

IN PRODUCTION:
1943–47

MARKINGS:
"No 5 Mk1" on left side of action. Serial number, year, and manufacturer's mark on left side of buttstrap behind trigger.

SAFETY:
Manual safety catch on left side of action: press forward to fire, rearward to make safe.

UNLOADING:
Magazine catch at rear of magazine. Remove magazine. Set safety catch to "fire." Open bolt to eject any round in chamber. Inspect chamber, close bolt, and press trigger.

Lee-Enfield Rifle, Short, Magazine (SMLE) Mark III UK

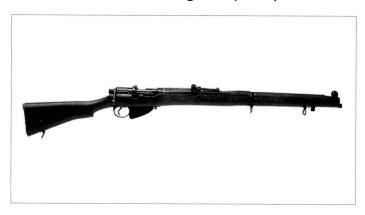

The SMLE comes in one or two sub-varieties, with minor differences, but the Mark III is the one that matters: over 3 million were made in the UK, India, and Australia, and it served in both world wars. Indeed, many British soldiers in 1939–45 went to great lengths to acquire one instead of the wartime replacement, the Rifle No. 4; there was nothing wrong with the No. 4, but the SMLE was a legend in its own time. Utterly reliable and with the smoothest bolt action ever made, the SMLE was sneered at by purists for not being a Mauser, but it silenced all its critics in 1914: German units on the receiving end thought they were under machine-gun fire. It remained in production in Australia until 1957.

SPECIFICATION:

CARTRIDGE:
0.303 British Service

DIMENSIONS:
LENGTH O/A: 1132 mm (44.6 in)
WEIGHT: 4 kg (8 lb 12 oz)
BARREL: 640 mm (25.2 in)
RIFLING: 5 grooves, lh
MAGAZINE CAPACITY: 10 rounds

IN PRODUCTION:
1907–57

MARKINGS:
Maker, date, and "SHT L.E." on right side of stock band beneath bolt. Serial number on right side of chamber.

SAFETY:
Manual safety catch on left side of action: press forward to fire, rearward to make safe.

UNLOADING:
Press up on magazine catch inside trigger guard to release magazine. Remove magazine and contents and empty. Open bolt to extract any cartridge in chamber. Pull out magazine cutoff by pressing down round catch on right side of action and pulling it out. Examine chamber and feedway, close bolt, and pull trigger. Replace empty magazine and push cutoff back in.

Parker-Hale M82 UK

This is a sniping rifle that employs a commercial Mauser 98 bolt action allied with a heavy cold-forged barrel. It was adopted as the military sniping rifle of the Australian, New Zealand, and Canadian armies. A version using a shorter butt and a shortened wooden fore-end was adopted by the British Army as the L81A1 Cadet Training Rifle in 1983. These rifles are still in service with the various forces, though Parker-Hale have given up rifle manufacture.

SPECIFICATION:

CARTRIDGE:
7.62 x 51 mm NATO

DIMENSIONS:
LENGTH O/A: 1162 mm (45.8 in)
WEIGHT: 4.8 kg (10 lb 9 oz)
BARREL: 660 mm (26 in)
RIFLING: 4 grooves, rh
MAGAZINE CAPACITY: 4 rounds

IN PRODUCTION:
1982–84

MARKINGS:
"PARKER-HALE LTD BIRMINGHAM ENGLAND 7.62 NATO" on top of barrel. Serial number on left side of chamber.

SAFETY:
Manual safety catch on right side of receiver tang, alongside bolt cocking piece: press forward to fire, to rear to make safe.

UNLOADING:
Press in magazine floorplate catch in front of trigger guard; floor plate will hinge forward and contents of magazine will fall out. Open bolt to extract any round remaining in chamber. Examine chamber and magazine space, close bolt, and pull trigger. Close magazine floor plate.

Barrett Model 95M USA

The Barrett Model 95M, developed from the earlier Barrett Model 90, is the bolt-action equivalent of the widely used Barrett Model 82 family and was at one time selected for service with the US Army. However, a change of policy resulted in the selection of the semiautomatic Barrett Model 82AM1 in its place. Even so, the Model 95M is understood to be in use with more than 15 countries. It is a bullpup rifle, with the five-round box magazine behind the trigger group to reduce the overall length for ease of carrying. The barrel may be removed, also for ease of carrying. A folding bipod is provided, as is a prominent multi-port muzzle brake. A rail mount over the receiver carries an optical or night sight. There are no iron sights. The Barrett Model 99 is a single-shot version of the Model 95M.

SPECIFICATION:

CARTRIDGE:
12.7 x 99 mm/0.50 Browning

DIMENSIONS:
LENGTH O/A: 1143 mm (56.4 in)
WEIGHT: 9 kg (19 lb 13 oz)
BARREL: 736 mm (29 in)
RIFLING: 8 grooves, rh
MAGAZINE CAPACITY: 5 rounds

IN PRODUCTION:
1995–

MARKINGS:
"BARRETT FIREARMS MANUFACTURING INC MURFREESBORO, TN, USA CAL .50" and serial number on left side of receiver.

SAFETY:
Thumb operated switch on left side above trigger: down to make safe, vertical to fire.

UNLOADING:
Magazine catch behind magazine. Remove magazine and any rounds. Raise and pull back bolt handle to remove any round in chamber and examine chamber via ejection slot. Close bolt, and press trigger. Replace magazine.

M40A1 Sniper USA

This is a militarized version of the commercial Remington 700 sporting rifle. The bolt is a Remington design, using two lugs locking into the receiver behind the chamber. There is a catch set into the front of the trigger guard that, when pressed, allows the bolt to be removed from the receiver. The barrel is particularly heavy and rigid, and no iron sights are fitted, as the rifle is issued with a 10x telescope sight. It is currently in service with the US Marine Corps, and the commercial original (the Model 700) has sold in large numbers.

SPECIFICATION:

CARTRIDGE:
7.62 x 51 mm NATO

DIMENSIONS:
LENGTH O/A: 1118 mm (44 in)
WEIGHT: 6.6 kg (14 lb 8 oz)
BARREL: 610 mm (24 in)
RIFLING: 4 grooves, rh
MAGAZINE CAPACITY: 5 rounds

IN PRODUCTION:
1962–

MARKINGS:
"US RIFLE M40A1" and serial number over chamber.

SAFETY:
Manual safety catch at right rear of receiver: forward to fire, back to make safe.

UNLOADING:
Press release catch at front edge of magazine floor plate. Remove plate, spring and magazine contents. Open bolt to eject any round in chamber. Examine chamber and feedway, close bolt, and press trigger. Replace magazine spring and floor plate.

Ruger Model 77 USA

The Model 77 has been manufactured in a range of styles and calibers and is widely distributed. The bolt action is adapted from the Mauser 98 pattern. The Model 77V is a "varmint" rifle, intended for small game, and has a heavy barrel and no iron sights, and is invariably used with a telescope sight. As such, it has been used by some police forces as a sniping rifle.

SPECIFICATION:

CARTRIDGE:
0.308 Winchester

DIMENSIONS (M77V):
LENGTH O/A: 1118 mm (44 in)
WEIGHT: 4.1 kg (9 lb)
BARREL: 610 mm (24 in)
RIFLING: 4 grooves, rh
MAGAZINE CAPACITY: 5 rounds

IN PRODUCTION:
1968–

MARKINGS:
"STURM, RUGER INC SOUTHPORT CONN USA" and serial number on receiver.

SAFETY:
Manual safety catch on rear of bolt: turn to left to fire, turn to right to make safe.

UNLOADING:
Press in magazine floorplate release catch in front edge of trigger guard and allow floor plate to hinge forward and dump contents of magazine. Open bolt to remove any cartridge remaining in chamber. Examine chamber and feedway. Close bolt, press trigger and close magazine floor plate.

Springfield US M1903 USA

The M1903 was the standard US service rifle from 1903 to the mid-1940s, though it remained in service until the early 1960s as a sniping rifle. The M1903 had a straight stock, the 1903A1 a pistol-grip stock; both had the rear sight ahead of the chamber. The 1903A3 had a straight stock, and the sight was just in front of the bolt handle; the 1903A4 is the sniper version of the A3, with no iron sights and the bolt handle cut away to avoid striking the sighting telescope when opening.

SPECIFICATION:

CARTRIDGE:
0.30-06 (7.62 x 63 mm)

DIMENSIONS:
LENGTH O/A: 1097 mm (43.2 in)
WEIGHT: 3.9 kg (8 lb 11 oz)
BARREL: 610 mm (24 in)
RIFLING: 4 grooves rh; WWII make may have 2 grooves
MAGAZINE CAPACITY: 5 rounds

IN PRODUCTION:
1903–65

MARKINGS:
"SPRINGFIELD ARSENAL" above the chamber. "UNITED STATES PROPERTY" on left side of receiver. Serial number on right side of receiver, bolt handle, and magazine cover.

SAFETY:
Manual safety catch on rear end of bolt: turn to right to make safe (word "Safe" will be seen), turn to Left to fire (word "Fire" will be seen).

UNLOADING:
Magazine cutoff prevents rounds feeding from magazine to breech; control for this is on left side of receiver. Press down and the word "Off" can be seen, meaning that magazine contents will NOT load. Lift up until the word "On" is visible and magazine can be loaded and contents fed to breech. Lift and pull back bolt handle to eject cartridge in breech. Close bolt and repeat until magazine is empty. When cutoff is set to "Off," bolt cannot move back far enough to collect a cartridge from magazine, but rifle can be used as single-shot weapon, loading each round individually.

Automatic
Rifles

FARA 83   ARGENTINA

The FARA 83 was developed in the early 1980s for the Argentine Army, but financial problems led to slow production and it is probable that only a part of the army received this weapon. It is of local design and uses the usual gas piston, bolt carrier, and rotating-bolt method of operation. Note that the cocking handle lies on top of the gas cylinder, well forward of the receiver, and actually operates on the gas piston, which has the bolt carrier machined as an integral part. The rifle may be encountered with a bipod attached below the gas block, in which case it has a special fore-end with a recess to accept the folded bipod legs. Note also that the twist of rifling allows M193 or NATO ammunition to be fired with equal facility.

SPECIFICATION:

CARTRIDGE:
5.56 x 45 mm NATO or M193

DIMENSIONS:
LENGTH, STOCK EXTENDED: 1000 mm (39.4 in)
LENGTH, STOCK FOLDED: 745 mm (29.3 in)
WEIGHT: 4 kg (8 lb 11 oz)
BARREL: 452 mm (17.8 in)
RIFLING: 6 grooves, rh
MAGAZINE CAPACITY: 30 rounds
RATE OF FIRE: 750 rounds/min

IN PRODUCTION:
1984–90

MARKINGS:
"FMAP DOMINGO MATHEU," year, and serial number on top of receiver.

SAFETY:
Manual safety catch inside trigger guard: push to rear for safe, forward to fire. Fire selector for either single shots or automatic fire on right side of receiver above trigger.

UNLOADING:
Magazine catch behind magazine housing. Remove magazine. Pull back cocking handle to eject any round remaining in chamber. Inspect chamber and feedway through ejection slot. Release cocking handle. Press trigger.

Steyr-Mannlicher AUG

The AUG was designed to an Austrian Army specification and adopted in 1979. It has since been adopted by Ireland, Australia, several Middle Eastern countries, the US Customs service, and the Falkland Islands Defence Force. It is made under license in Australia as the F88. Modular in design, the barrel can be quickly removed and changed for a longer or shorter one, and the firing mechanism can be removed and changed for one giving three-round bursts or semiautomatic fire only, allowing a number of different combinations. The receiver can be changed so that the built-in telescope can be replaced with a mounting platform to which other types of sight can be fitted. It was the first rifle to make extensive use of plastics, not only for the furniture but also for the firing mechanism.

SPECIFICATION:

CARTRIDGE:
5.56 x 45 mm M198 or NATO

DIMENSIONS:
LENGTH O/A: 790 mm (31.1 in)
WEIGHT: 3.9 kg (8 lb 8 oz)
BARREL: 508 mm (20 in)
RIFLING: 6 grooves, rh
MAGAZINE CAPACITY: 30 or 42 rounds
RATE OF FIRE: 650 rounds/min

IN PRODUCTION:
1978–

MARKINGS:
"STEYR-DAIMLER-PUCH AG AUSTRIA" or "STEYR-MANNLICHER GmbH AUSTRIA," and "AUG/A1" molded into stock on right side. Serial number on right side of barrel.

SAFETY:
Push-through safety is fitted into stock behind trigger: when pushed from left to right, rifle is safe; pushed from right to left, rifle is ready to fire. Fire selectionis performed by trigger: a light pull gives single shots, a heavier pull gives automatic fire.

UNLOADING:
Magazine catch is behind magazine. Remove magazine. Pull back cocking handle to eject any round remaining in chamber. Inspect chamber and feedway through ejection slot. Release cocking handle. Pull trigger.

FN 1949 BELGIUM

Development of this rifle actually started in the 1930s, but the war caused a halt in the proceedings and it was not until 1949 that it was completed. It was adopted in various calibers by Belgium, Egypt, Argentina, Luxembourg, Venezuela, Brazil, and Colombia and was reliable, if somewhat expensive. The locking system used a tilting gas-operated bolt and generally formed the prototype for the later and better-known FAL model. The magazine was loaded by chargers, through the top of the open action. The designer, Dieudonne Saive, worked with the British in Enfield during World War II, and the earliest version of this rifle was tested by the British in 7.92 mm caliber in 1946/47.

SPECIFICATION:

CARTRIDGE:
7.92 x 57 mm Mauser and others

DIMENSIONS:
LENGTH O/A: 1116 mm (43.5 in)
WEIGHT: 4.3 kg (9 lb 8 oz)
BARREL: 590 mm (23.2 in)
RIFLING: 4 grooves, rh
MAGAZINE CAPACITY: 10 rounds

IN PRODUCTION:
1950–58

MARKINGS:
"FABRIQUE NATIONALE D'ARMES DE GUERRE HERSTAL BELGIQUE" on right of action. Serial number on side of chamber and on bolt.

SAFETY:
Manual safety catch on right side of trigger guard: press Down for safe. This also causes catch to interfere with finger if attempt is made to press trigger. No fire selector—fires only single shots.

UNLOADING:
Magazine catch in front of magazine needs to be pressed in with a bullet or similar pointed tool. Remove magazine and pull back cocking handle to eject any round remaining in chamber. Inspect chamber and feedway through ejection port. Release cocking handle. Press trigger.

FN 2000 BELGIUM

A modular-design assault rifle of bullpup configuration. The large wraparound polymer body contains the gas-operated rotating-bolt mechanism, but it is also designed to be adapted for any mission-specific task. The lower forward hand-guard can be detached to mount an under-barrel 40 mm grenade launcher. The upper sighting unit is also detachable and provides a base for the mounting of additional thermal or night-vision sighting devices. Provision is also made for the mounting of a bayonet. An unusual feature is the forward ejection of cart-ridge cases through a tube that runs along the right side of the receiver, making this rifle fully ambidextrous in use. A flap at the rear of the sighting unit can be lifted to check whether the weapon is loaded or unloaded. NATO standard M16 magazines are used.

SPECIFICATION:

CARTRIDGE:
5.56 x 45 mm NATO

DIMENSIONS:
LENGTH O/A: 694 mm (27.3 in)
WEIGHT: 3.6 kg (7.8 lbs)
BARREL: 400 mm (15.8 in)
RATE OF FIRE: 850 rounds/min
MAGAZINE CAPACITY: 30 rounds

IN PRODUCTION:
2001–

MARKINGS:
Manufacturer's logo on right side of trigger housing.

SAFETY:
Fire and safety selector lever in lower trigger guard, allowing control/selection with index finger.

UNLOADING:
Magazine release catch is located next to selector lever in lower trigger guard. Remove magazine. Cock weapon. Retain working parts to rear using bolt hold-open device. Lift flap and check chamber and ejection tube are clear. When clear, allow working parts to go forward. Point weapon in a safe direction and pull trigger.

The FN FAL is one of the most widely used rifles in history, adopted by over 90 countries. Many of these demanded minor modifications; many countries have manufactured under license and have incorporated their own modifications. The FN factory recognizes four standard models: the fixed-butt rifle 50-00; the folding-butt rifle 50-64; a folding-butt carbine 50-63; and a fixed-butt heavy-barrel model with bipod 50-41. Moreover, most models were available in either semiautomatic-only or selective-fire versions.

Commercial semiautomatic models are also available. With a huge number of minor-variant models possible, absolute identification of some models is difficult. All one can do is identify the rifle as an FN FAL, decide the nationality from its markings, and leave it at that.

SPECIFICATION:

CARTRIDGE:
7.62 x 51 mm NATO

DIMENSIONS:
LENGTH O/A: 1090 mm (42.9 in)
WEIGHT: 4.5 kg (9 lb 13 oz)
BARREL: 533 mm (21 in)
RIFLING: 4 grooves, rh
MAGAZINE CAPACITY: 20 rounds
RATE OF FIRE: 650 rounds/min

IN PRODUCTION:
1953–

MARKINGS:
"FABRIQUE NATIONALE HERSTAL" on Belgian-made weapons. Since this rifle has appeared in numerous variations, has been employed by 90 countries, and made under license or copied in many of them, the variety of possible markings is infinite and a full list cannot be given. Origin of weapon will usually be evident from markings.

SAFETY:
Manual safety catch and fire-selector lever on left side of receiver over trigger. In semiautomatics, weapon is safe with catch pressed up, ready to fire when pressed down. Same applies to automatic weapons, but they also have a third position: push down and forward past single-shot position for full automatic fire.

UNLOADING:
Magazine catch behind magazine housing. Remove magazine. Pull back cocking handle to eject any round left in chamber. Examine chamber and feedway through ejection port. Release cocking handle. Press trigger.

FN FNC BELGIUM

This succeeded the CAL at a time when potential customers were taking note of NATO's adoption of a 5.56 mm cartridge, and consequently it met with a better reception; it was also cheaper and more reliable than the CAL. Steel, alloy, and plastic feature in the construction, and much use has been made of pressings and stampings. The mechanism is similar to that of the CAL, gas operated with a rotating bolt, and the magazine interface is NATO standard and will thus accept M16 and similar types of magazine. A variant model is used by Sweden as the AK5, and it is also made under license in Indonesia.

SPECIFICATION:

CARTRIDGE:
5.56 x 45 mm NATO

DIMENSIONS:
LENGTH, STOCK EXTENDED: 997 mm (39.3 in)
LENGTH, STOCK FOLDED: 766 mm (30.2 in)
WEIGHT: 3.8 kg (8 lb 6 oz)
BARREL: 450 mm (17.7 in)
RIFLING: 6 grooves, rh
MAGAZINE CAPACITY: 30 rounds
RATE OF FIRE: 700 rounds/min

IN PRODUCTION:
1979–

MARKINGS:
"FN" monogram and "FNC 5.56 [serial number]" on left side of receiver.

SAFETY:
Combined safety catch and fire-selector lever on left side of receiver above trigger: rotate to rear for safe, down one notch for single shots, forward to next notch for three-round bursts, and fully forward for automatic fire.

UNLOADING:
Magazine catch at left rear of magazine housing. Remove magazine. Pull back cocking handle to eject any round remaining in chamber. Examine chamber and feedway through ejection slot. Release cocking handle. Press trigger.

Type 56 CHINA

The Type 56 assault rifle is a Chinese copy of the AK-47/AKM. No distinction is made in type number between the solid-steel receiver of the AK-47 and the pressed-metal receiver of the later AKM: both are Type 56. There are three variants: the Type 56 has a fixed butt and folding bayonet, the 56-1 has a folding stock that passes over the receiver, and the 56-2 has a folding stock that folds sideways to lie along the right side of the receiver. Neither the 56-1 nor the 56-2 have folding bayonets. All these models are commercially available in semiautomatic form.

SPECIFICATION:

CARTRIDGE:
7.62 x 39 mm Soviet M1943

DIMENSIONS:
LENGTH O/A: 874 mm (34.4 in)
WEIGHT: 3.8 kg (8 lb 6 oz)
BARREL: 414 mm (16.3 in)
RIFLING: 4 grooves, rh
MAGAZINE CAPACITY: 30 rounds
RATE OF FIRE: 600 rounds/min

IN PRODUCTION:
1958–

MARKINGS:
Chinese markings for factory, year, and serial number on left side of receiver. There may also be Chinese symbols on safety lever on early production models.

SAFETY:
Combined safety catch and fire-selector lever on right rear side of receiver: press all the way up for safe (obstructs movement of cocking handle and bolt), move down one notch to first mark or letter "L" for full automatic fire, and move to bottom or letter "D" for single shots.

UNLOADING:
Magazine catch at rear of magazine housing. Remove magazine. Pull back cocking handle to extract any round which may be in chamber. Inspect chamber through ejection port. Release cocking handle. Pull trigger.

Type 63 CHINA

This is a purely Chinese design that has adapted the best features of various rifles with which the Chinese have had experience. Although it resembles the Type 58 carbine, the mechanism is based on that of the AK-47 Kalashnikov rifles. It has the usual type of folding bayonet beneath the fore-end. The standard magazine is a 20-round box. The Type 63 saw limited use with the Chinese armed forces; it is also available for export.

SPECIFICATION:

CARTRIDGE:
7.62 x 39 mm Soviet M1943

DIMENSIONS:
LENGTH O/A: 1029 mm (40.5 in)
WEIGHT: 3.5 kg (7 lb 11 oz)
BARREL: 521 mm (20.5 in)
RIFLING: 4 grooves, rh
MAGAZINE CAPACITY: 20 rounds
RATE OF FIRE: 750 rounds/min

IN PRODUCTION:
1970–

MARKINGS:
Chinese symbols for factory identification, year, and serial number on left side of receiver.

SAFETY:
Combined safety catch and selector lever in front of trigger on right side: pull to rear, to mark "0" for safe (trigger is locked but bolt can be opened); move to vertical position, to mark "1" for single shots; move fully forward, to mark "2" for automatic fire.

UNLOADING:
Magazine catch beneath receiver, behind magazine. Remove magazine. Pull back cocking handle to eject any round left in chamber. Inspect chamber and feedway through ejection port. Release cocking handle. Pull trigger.

Type 95 CHINA

The Type 95 was first seen in public at the Hong Kong hand-over ceremony in 1998. This rifle is another bullpup configuration, a design intended to permit the maximum length of barrel in a weapon of reduced overall length. It is constructed of largely of polymer, only the barrel and operating mechanism being of metal, apart from small components such as springs. Ejection of fired cartridge cases in this design, as in many other similar weapons, is to the right and parallel to the user's cheek; it cannot therefore be fired safely from the left shoulder. It fires a new cartridge of 5.8 mm caliber, the equivalent of the 5.56 mm NATO cartridge. An export version in 5.56 mm NATO is known as the Type 97.

SPECIFICATION:

CARTRIDGE:
5.8 x 42 mm

DIMENSIONS:
LENGTH O/A: 743 mm (29.2 in)
WEIGHT: 3.3 kg (7.3 lbs)
BARREL: 490 mm (19.3 in)
RATE OF FIRE: 650 rounds/min
MAGAZINE CAPACITY: 30 rounds

IN PRODUCTION:
1995–

MARKINGS:
Manufacturer's logo on right side of trigger housing with serial number.

SAFETY:
Fire-selector lever in front of the butt on left rear.

UNLOADING:
Magazine release catch is located on right rear of magazine housing. Remove magazine. Pull working parts to rear. Inspect chamber and magazine well through ejection port. When clear, allow working parts to go forward. Point weapon in a safe direction and pull trigger.

VZ52 CZECH REPUBLIC

The VZ52 was developed in Czechoslovakia in the short time between the end of World War II and the country's absorption into the Communist Bloc. It was an unusual design, gas operated with a gas piston in the form of a sleeve surrounding part of the barrel and acting on the bolt carrier, and it fired a unique cartridge. When the country came under Soviet domination, it was required to conform to Soviet standards, and the rifle was therefore redesigned to fire the 7.62 x 39 Soviet cartridge. Such models are known as the vz.52/57 and are so marked. They are not as accurate or reliable as the original 7.62 x 45 mm models. Note that there is a permanently attached folding sword bayonet on both models of this rifle.

SPECIFICATION:

CARTRIDGE:
7.62 x 45 mm M52 or 7.62 x 39 mm Soviet M1943

DIMENSIONS:
LENGTH O/A: 1003 mm (39.5 in)
WEIGHT: 4.1 kg (9 lb 1 oz)
BARREL: 523 mm (20.6 in)
RIFLING: 4 grooves, rh
MAGAZINE CAPACITY: 10 rounds

IN PRODUCTION:
1952–59

MARKINGS:
Factory identifier and serial number on right side of receiver. Later model 52/57 will be so marked at right front of receiver.

SAFETY:
Manual safety catch fitted in forward edge of trigger guard: pull back, so catch protrudes into trigger-guard space, for safe; push forward to fire.

UNLOADING:
Magazine catch behind magazine. Remove magazine. Pull back cocking handle to extract any round remaining in chamber. Examine chamber and feedway through ejection port. Release cocking handle. Pull trigger.

VZ58

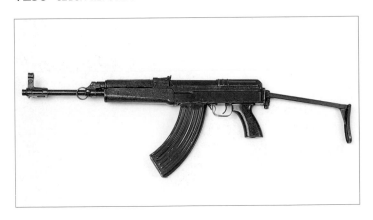

Although this may resemble the Kalashnikov, it is an entirely different weapon of Czech design; due to Warsaw Pact standardization, however, it is chambered for the standard Soviet cartridge. It is gas operated, and the bolt is locked to the receiver by a vertically moving block similar to that of the Walther P38 pistol. Gas pressure on a piston drives a bolt carrier back; this lifts the lock, and the bolt then opens. Two model types were produced: the VZ58p with fixed stock and the VZ58v with a folding metal stock. Either may be fitted with a flash hider on the muzzle and a bipod attached to the barrel.

SPECIFICATION:

CARTRIDGE:
7.62 x 39 mm Soviet M1943

DIMENSIONS:
LENGTH, STOCK EXTENDED: 820 mm (32.3 in)
LENGTH, STOCK FOLDED: 635 mm (25 in)
WEIGHT: 3.1 kg (6 lb 15 oz)
BARREL: 401 mm (15.8 in)
RIFLING: 4 grooves, rh
MAGAZINE CAPACITY: 30 rounds
RATE OF FIRE: 800 rounds/min

IN PRODUCTION:
1959–80

MARKINGS:
Factory identifier and serial number on rear top of receiver.

SAFETY:
Combined manual safety catch and fire selector on right side of receiver above trigger: rotate to vertical position for safe (this locks trigger but permits bolt to be opened); turn forward for automatic fire, rearward for single shots.

UNLOADING:
Magazine catch between magazine and trigger guard. Remove magazine. Pull back cocking handle to extract any round remaining in chamber. Inspect chamber and feedway through ejection port. Release cocking handle. Press trigger.

Sako M90 FINLAND

The Sako M90 is the successor to the Valmet M62/M76 series of Finnish service rifles, Sako having absorbed Valmet in the late 1980s. The original Valmet designs were based upon Kalashnikov AK-47s obtained from Russia in the 1950s; they followed the Kalashnikov pattern but had a few small changes due to Finnish preferences. There was no wood, the fore-end and pistol grip both made from steel with a plastic coating; the butt was a large-diameter tube with a cross-member welded on at the end; and there was a prominent pronged flash hider. The M90 merely streamlined and improved the design, adopting a new side-folding butt, new sights with night-firing aids, and a new flash hider that also functioned as a grenade launcher. It is probably the best Kalashnikov clone ever made.

SPECIFICATION:

CARTRIDGE:
7.62 x 39 mm Soviet M1943 or 5.56 x 45 mm NATO

DIMENSIONS (7.62 MM VERSION):
LENGTH, STOCK EXTENDED: 930 mm (36.6 in)
LENGTH, STOCK FOLDED: 675 mm (26.6 in)
WEIGHT: 3.9 kg (8 lb 8 oz)
BARREL: 416 mm (16.4 in)
RIFLING: 4 grooves, rh
MAGAZINE CAPACITY: 30 rounds
RATE OF FIRE: 700 rounds/min

IN PRODUCTION:
1991–99

MARKINGS:
"M90" and serial number on left side of receiver.

SAFETY:
Combined safety catch and fire-selector lever on right rear side of receiver: press all the way up for safe (obstructs movement of cocking handle and bolt); move down one notch to first mark for full automatic fire; move to bottom position for single shots.

UNLOADING:
Magazine catch at rear of magazine housing. Remove magazine. Pull back cocking handle to extract any round in chamber. Inspect the chamber through ejection port. Release cocking handle. Pull trigger.

Valmet M76 FINLAND

This is the Finnish version of the Kalashnikov AK rifle, and the differences are largely those that the Finns regard as being necessary to withstand their permanently Arctic conditions. The first model was the M60, which had a plastic fore-end and tubular-steel butt; some models were without trigger-guards for use with Arctic mittens. Then came the M62, with a machined-steel receiver and some changes to the sights and furniture. The M71 adopted a stamped-steel receiver, but this proved less strong and was dropped for a return to the M62, with a new folding butt. Finally came the M76, with a stronger sheet-steel receiver and a variety of fixed or folding steel, plastic, or wooden butts. As well as being used by the Finns, these rifles have also been bought by Qatar and Indonesia and have also been sold in semiautomatic form on the commercial market.

SPECIFICATION:

CARTRIDGE:
7.62 x 39 mm Soviet M1943

DIMENSIONS:
LENGTH, STOCK EXTENDED: 950 mm (37.4 in)
LENGTH, STOCK FOLDED: 710 mm (29.1 in)
WEIGHT: 3.6 kg (7 lb 15 oz)
BARREL: 418 mm (16.5 in)
RIFLING: 4 grooves, rh
MAGAZINE CAPACITY: 15, 20, or 30 rounds
RATE OF FIRE: 700 rounds/min

IN PRODUCTION:
1976–86

MARKINGS:
"VALMET Jyvaskyla" and serial number on right side of receiver.

SAFETY:
Combined safety catch and fire-selector lever on right rear side of receiver: press all the way up for safe (obstructs movement of cocking handle and bolt); move down one notch to first mark (three dots) for full automatic fire; move to bottom position (a single dot) for single shots.

UNLOADING:
Magazine catch at rear of magazine housing. Remove magazine. Pull back cocking handle to extract any round in chamber. Inspect chamber through ejection port. Release cocking handle. Pull trigger.

FAMAS FRANCE

This odd-looking weapon is the standard French Army rifle and was the first bullpup design to enter military service. It uses a two-part bolt in a delayed-blowback system and has the chamber fluted to avoid difficult extraction; cartridges from this weapon are easily recognized by their longitudinal marks. It handles well and shoots accurately, and can also launch grenades. There is also a 0.22 rimfire training version that looks exactly like the service weapon. In 1994 a new model, the F2, appeared with a full-sized hand-guard instead of a small trigger guard and a NATO-standard magazine housing to accept M16 type magazines (as shown). Note that all 5.56 mm ammunition will chamber in this weapon, but optimum performance is only achieved with the French service ammunition.

SPECIFICATION:

CARTRIDGE:
5.56 x 45 mm Type France

DIMENSIONS:
LENGTH O/A: 757 mm (29.8 in)
WEIGHT: 3.6 kg (7 lb 15 oz)
BARREL: 488 mm (19.2 in)
RIFLING: 6 grooves, rh
MAGAZINE CAPACITY: 25 rounds
RATE OF FIRE: 950 rounds/min

IN PRODUCTION:
1975–

MARKINGS:
"FA MAS 5.56 F1" and serial number on right side of magazine housing. Serial number repeated on bolt.

SAFETY:
Rotary switch inside front of trigger guard acts as safety catch and fire selector. When parallel with bore, it is safe; when switched to right, it gives single shots; and when switched to left, it gives automatic fire. With switch in automatic position, operation of a burst-limiting button, beneath buttstock and behind magazine, activates three-round burst limiter.

UNLOADING:
Magazine catch in front of magazine. Remove magazine. Pull back cocking handle (between receiver and carrying handle) to eject any round left in chamber. Inspect chamber through ejection port. Release cocking handle. Pull trigger.

MAS-49 FRANCE

This model was adopted somewhat hurriedly in 1949 when the French Army was anxious to equip with a modern rifle instead of the collection of oddments that had survived the war.

Gas operated, the MAS-49 uses direct gas impingement to move the bolt carrier backwards, instead of the more usual piston. It remained the standard French rifle until the arrival of the FAMAS in 1980, and large numbers were handed over to former colonies, who later disposed of them. A very small number were converted to 7.62 x 51 mm caliber for use by French gendarmeries, which suggests that such conversions could also be done by others, since the French 7.5 mm ammunition is not now in common supply.

SPECIFICATION:

CARTRIDGE:
7.5 x 54 mm French Service

DIMENSIONS:
LENGTH O/A: 1100 mm (43.3 in)
WEIGHT: 4.7 kg (10 lb 6 oz)
BARREL: 580 mm (22.8 in)
RIFLING: 4 grooves, lh
MAGAZINE CAPACITY: 10 rounds

IN PRODUCTION:
1951–65

MARKINGS:
"MAS 49," year and serial number on left side of receiver. May have script "St Etienne" marking in same area.

SAFETY:
Manual safety catch on right side of receiver, above front end of trigger guard. Turn down for safe, up to fire.

UNLOADING:
Magazine catch on right side of magazine housing; press in lower end with thumb to remove magazine. Pull back cocking handle to eject any round remaining in chamber. Examine chamber and feedway. Release cocking handle. Pull trigger.

Heckler & Koch G3 GERMANY

The heart of the G3, as with almost every other Heckler & Koch weapon, is the roller-delayed blowback breech system, which has a long and curious history. It was designed by Mauser in 1944–45, taken to Spain and developed further by CETME, taken to Holland to manufacture, and then given to Heckler & Koch to perfect, which they did to very good effect. The G3 equipped the German Army for many years and is made under license in Mexico, Portugal, Greece, Turkey, Pakistan, Norway, and Saudi Arabia as well as being employed by some 60 armies. There are variant models with short barrels and fixed or folding butts, and there are also variations in the license-produced models of some countries, but these are generally minor.

SPECIFICATION:

CARTRIDGE:
7.62 x 51 mm NATO

DIMENSIONS:
LENGTH, FIXED BUTT: 1025 mm (40.4 in)
WEIGHT: 4.4 kg (9 lb 11 oz)
BARREL: 450 mm (17.7 in)
RIFLING: 4 grooves, rh
MAGAZINE CAPACITY: 20 rounds
RATE OF FIRE: 550 rounds/min

IN PRODUCTION:
1964–

MARKINGS:
"G3 HK," serial number, and month/year of manufacture on left side of magazine housing. Refurbished weapons will have "HK" and month/year of manufacture stamped into right side of magazine housing.

SAFETY:
Combined safety catch and fire selector on left side above trigger. In topmost position (marked "0" or "S"), weapon is safe; fully down ("F" or "20") gives full automatic fire; middle position ("E" or "1") gives single shots.

UNLOADING:
Magazine catch at rear of magazine housing. Remove magazine. Pull back cocking handle to eject any round remaining in chamber. Examine chamber and feedway through ejection slot. Release cocking handle. Press trigger.

Heckler & Koch G36 GERMANY

When the G11 program collapsed, the German Army was left without a 5.56 mm rifle to conform to NATO standard; after a rapid comparative trial, they selected this as their new standard rifle. In this design, H&K abandoned their well-tried roller-locked delayed-blowback system and adopted a gas-operated rotating-bolt solution. The layout is conventional, with the gas cylinder beneath the barrel, a pistol grip, a box magazine, and a folding tubular butt. A raised sight block at the rear of the receiver carries a 3x optical sight, and the integral carrying handle runs from this block to the front end of the receiver, with an aperture for the line of sight. The cocking handle is underneath the carrying handle and also acts as a bolt-closing assist if needed.

The G36 was adopted by the German Army in 1996. An export version, the G36E, is also available; this differs only in the optical sight, the G36E having a 1.5x telescope. Two short-barrelled versions of the G36 exist.

SPECIFICATION:

CARTRIDGE:
5.56 x 45 mm NATO

DIMENSIONS (G36):
LENGTH, BUTT EXTENDED: 998 mm (39.3 in)
LENGTH, BUTT FOLDED: 758 mm (29.8 in)
WEIGHT: 3.6 kg (8 lb)
BARREL: 480 mm (18.9 in)
RIFLING: 6 grooves, rh
MAGAZINE CAPACITY: 30 rounds
RATE OF FIRE: 750 rounds/min

DIMENSIONS (G36K):
LENGTH, BUTT EXTENDED: 860 mm (33.9 in)
LENGTH, BUTT FOLDED: 615 mm (24.2 in)
WEIGHT: 3.3 kg (7 lb 6 oz)
BARREL: 318 mm (12.5 in)
RIFLING: 6 grooves, rh
MAGAZINE CAPACITY: 30 rounds
RATE OF FIRE: 750 rounds/min

IN PRODUCTION:
1995–

MARKINGS:
Left side of gun above trigger marked "HK G36 Cal 5.56 x 45 mm Serial number block."

SAFETY:
Combined safety catch and fire-selector switch on both sides of receiver, behind and above trigger.

UNLOADING:
Magazine catch on magazine housing. Remove magazine. Pull back cocking handle (beneath carrying handle) and examine feedway and chamber through ejection port, ensuring both are empty. Return cocking handle and bolt to forward position. Pull trigger.

Heckler & Koch G41 GERMANY

This was designed as an improved HK33 specifically for the NATO-standard 5.56 mm cartridge. It incorporates the low-noise bolt-closing device first used on the PSG1 sniping rifle. It has a dustcover on the ejection port and a hold-open device that keeps the bolt open when the magazine is emptied. It uses the NATO-standard magazine interface, accepting M16 and similar magazines, and has a NATO-standard sight mount for day or night optical sights, and may be fitted with a bipod. There is also a folding-butt model. It was not adopted by any military force.

SPECIFICATION:

CARTRIDGE:
5.56 x 45 mm NATO

DIMENSIONS:
LENGTH O/A: 997 mm (39.3 in)
WEIGHT: 4.1 kg (9 lb 1 oz)
BARREL: 450 mm (17.7 in)
RIFLING: 6 grooves, rh
MAGAZINE CAPACITY: 30 rounds
RATE OF FIRE: 850 rounds/min

IN PRODUCTION:
1983–

MARKINGS:
"HK G41 5.56mm [serial number]" on left side of magazine housing.

SAFETY:
Combined safety catch and fire selector on left side above trigger. Topmost position (marked by a white bullet and cross) is safe, one notch down (single red bullet) gives single shots, two notches down (three red bullets) gives three-round burst, fully down (seven red bullets) gives full automatic fire.

UNLOADING:
Magazine catch at rear of magazine housing. Remove magazine. Pull back cocking handle to eject any round remaining in chamber. Examine chamber and feedway through ejection slot. Release cocking handle. Press trigger.

Heckler & Koch HK33E GERMANY

This is more or less the standard G3 reduced to 5.56 mm caliber; its mechanical operation is exactly the same, as is its outline. Several parts are common, but interchanging is not recommended; some parts are not common, though they may look the same and appear to fit both weapons. There is a fixed-butt model and also a short-barreled carbine version known as the HK33KE. There was also an HK33SG1 sniper version, with a special sight mount and telescope sight, and the fixed-butt model can be found with a bipod. It has been used by Chile, Brazil, Malaysia, and Thailand and various other forces in Southeast Asia and South America.

SPECIFICATION:

CARTRIDGE:
5.56 x 45 mm NATO or M193

DIMENSIONS:
LENGTH, STOCK EXTENDED: 940 mm (37 in)
LENGTH, STOCK FOLDED: 735 mm (28.9 in)
WEIGHT: 3.7 kg (8 lb 1 oz)
BARREL: 390 mm (15.4 in)
RIFLING: 6 grooves, rh
MAGAZINE CAPACITY: 25 rounds
RATE OF FIRE: 750 rounds/min

IN PRODUCTION:
1968–

MARKINGS:
"HK 33E 5.56mm [serial number]" on left side of magazine housing.

SAFETY:
Combined safety catch and fire selector on left side above trigger. Topmost position (marked "0" or "S") is safe, fully down ("F" or "20") gives full automatic fire, middle position ("E" or "1") gives single shots.

UNLOADING:
Magazine catch at rear of magazine housing. Remove magazine. Pull back cocking handle to eject any round remaining in chamber. Examine chamber and feedway through ejection slot. Release cocking handle. Press trigger.

Heckler & Koch HK53 GERMANY

The HK53 is often described as a submachine gun but, as it fires a rifle-power cartridge, it is better categorized as a short assault rifle. It crams the firepower of a 5.56 x 45 mm cartridge into as compact a package as can be realistically managed, and to this end the HK53 features, in addition to the usual Heckler & Koch roller-delay locking mechanism, a telescopic buttstock and a barrel only 211 mm (8.3 in) long that has to have a very efficient flash suppressor. This weapon has been widely procured by numerous special military and police units all around the world.

SPECIFICATION:

CARTRIDGE:
5.56 x 45 mm NATO

DIMENSIONS:
LENGTH, BUTT EXTENDED: 780 mm (30.7 in)
LENGTH, BUTT RETRACTED: 590 mm (23.2 in)
WEIGHT: 3 kg (6 lb 10 oz)
RIFLING: 6 grooves, rh
MAGAZINE CAPACITY: 25 or 30 rounds
RATE OF FIRE: 700 rounds/min

IN PRODUCTION:
1975–

MARKINGS:
"MP53 Kal 5.56mm x 45 [serial number/month/year]" along top rib of receiver. "Kal 5.56mm x 45" on left side of magazine housing.

SAFETY:
Manual safety catch/fire selector on left side of receiver above trigger: up for safe, center for single shots, down for automatic fire.

UNLOADING:
Magazine catch behind magazine housing. Remove magazine, pull back cocking handle to clear any round from breech, inspect chamber through ejection port. Release cocking handle. Pull trigger.

Heckler & Koch HK 416 GERMANY

The HK 416 was developed to provide enhanced performance over the long-serving M16 assault rifle. The HK 416 uses a short-stroke, gas-piston system of operation, rather than the direct gas-impingement system of the generic M16 series. The basic design of the M16 has been substantially modified, with the substitution of the two-piece polymer fore-end, with an alloy monobloc, modular-rail fore-end, and free-floating barrel. Folding iron sights are fitted, as it is intended that optical and night-vision devices will be fitted as standard. A companion model, the HK 417, in 7.62 mm NATO is also under development.

SPECIFICATION:

CARTRIDGE:
5.56 x 45 mm NATO

DIMENSIONS:
LENGTH O/A: 886 mm (34.9 in)
WEIGHT: 3.5 kg (7 lbs 11 oz)
BARREL LENGTH: 368 mm (14.5 in)
RATE OF FIRE: 7–900 rounds/min
MAGAZINE CAPACITY: 30 rounds

IN PRODUCTION:
2005–

MARKINGS:
Manufacturer's logo on right side of magazine housing. Serial number on left side of lower receiver.

SAFETY:
Fire-selector lever is located on left side of lower receiver. Mode of fire is shown by pictogram.

UNLOADING:
Magazine release catch on upper right rear of magazine housing. Remove magazine. Pull working parts to rear, and lock in rear position with bolt-retaining catch. Inspect chamber and magazine well through ejection port. When clear, allow working parts to go forward. Point weapon in a safe direction and pull trigger.

Heckler & Koch MSG90 GERMANY

This is intended as a military sniping rifle and is really a lighter and less-expensive version of the PSG1. The barrel is lighter, cold forged, and tempered; the trigger mechanism is preadjusted to a 1.5 kg (3.3 lb) pull, and the trigger has an adjustable shoe that gives better control. There is usually a bipod fitted to a rail in the fore-end, and the standard sight is a 10x telescope with range settings to 1200 m (3937 ft). The sight mount is to NATO standard and, thus, any compatible day or night sight can be fitted. The butt can be adjusted in most directions for an individual fit.

SPECIFICATION:

CARTRIDGE:
7.62 x 51 mm NATO

DIMENSIONS:
LENGTH O/A: 1165 mm (45.9 in)
WEIGHT: 6.4 kg (14 lb 2 oz)
BARREL: 600 mm (23.6 in)
RIFLING: 4 grooves, rh
MAGAZINE CAPACITY: 5 or 20 rounds

IN PRODUCTION:
1987–

MARKINGS:
"HK MSG90 7.62 x 51 [serial number]" on left side of magazine housing.

SAFETY:
Manual safety catch on left side of receiver above trigger: up for safe, down to fire.

UNLOADING:
Magazine catch at rear of magazine housing. Remove magazine. Pull back cocking handle to eject any round remaining in chamber. Examine chamber and feedway through ejection slot. Release cocking handle. Press trigger.

Heckler & Koch PSG1 GERMANY

The PSG1 is a high-precision sniping rifle using the standard H&K roller-locked delayed-blowback breech system with a special long and heavy barrel. The trigger unit can be removed from the pistol grip and adjusted for pull. The stock is fully adjustable in all directions to fit every individual stance. No iron sights are fitted; a NATO-standard mounting is built into the receiver top, and the rifle is always issued with a 6 x 42 telescope with illuminated graticule. The PSG's accuracy is outstanding: it will put 50 rounds of match-grade ammunition inside an 80 mm (3.1 in) circle at 300 m (984.3 ft) range.

SPECIFICATION:

CARTRIDGE:
7.62 x 51 mm NATO

DIMENSIONS:
LENGTH O/A: 1208 mm (47.6 in)
WEIGHT: 8.1 kg (17 lb 13 oz)
BARREL: 650 mm (25.6 in)
RIFLING: 4 grooves, rh
MAGAZINE CAPACITY: 5 or 20 rounds

IN PRODUCTION:
1975–

MARKINGS:
"PSG1 HK Kal 7.62x51 [serial number]" on left side of magazine housing.

SAFETY:
Manual safety catch on left side of receiver above trigger: up for safe, down to fire.

UNLOADING:
Magazine catch on right side behind magazine housing. Remove magazine. Pull back cocking handle to eject any round remaining in chamber. Examine chamber and feedway through ejection slot. Holding cocking handle, press trigger and allow cocking handle to go forward under control. Push on bolt-closing catch on right side of receiver to close bolt firmly.

MP 44 GERMANY

This is the father of all assault rifles, developed in Germany in 1941–42 and using a new short cartridge. Originally known as the MP 43 (Machine Pistol—for Nazi political reasons), it was renamed the Sturmgewehr 44 after its successful introduction into battle on the eastern front. It introduced the concept of using a short cartridge with limited range in order to permit controllable automatic fire and a compact weapon, and because experience showed that most rifle fire was conducted at ranges under 400 m (1312.3 ft). After the war, it was examined and dissected by almost every major gunmaking nation and led, in one way or another, to the present-day 5.56 mm assault rifles. In postwar years it was used by East German Border Guards, and many found their way into central Africa.

SPECIFICATION:

CARTRIDGE:
7.92 x 33 mm "Kurz"

DIMENSIONS:
LENGTH O/A: 940 mm (37 in)
WEIGHT: 5.2 kg (11 lb 8 oz)
BARREL: 419 mm (16.5 in)
RIFLING: 4 grooves, rh
MAGAZINE CAPACITY: 30 rounds
RATE OF FIRE: 500 rounds/min

IN PRODUCTION:
1943–45

MARKINGS:
"MP44," factory mark "fxo" (Haenel & Co) or "ayf" (Ermawerke), year, and serial number on top of receiver. Serial number often repeated on left side of magazine housing.

SAFETY:
Manual safety catch on left of receiver above pistol grip. Press up for safe, down to fire. Push-button just behind and above safety catch selects single shots or automatic fire.

UNLOADING:
Magazine release push-button on left side of magazine housing. Remove magazine. Pull back cocking handle to eject any round left in chamber. Inspect chamber and feedway through ejection port. Release cocking handle. Pull trigger.

Gepard M2/M2A1 HUNGARY

The Gepard M2 is a similar to the M1 but is a semiautomatic rifle operating on the long-recoil system. The barrel recoils inside a cylindrical jacket and receiver, and uses a rotating bolt to lock the breech. On firing, the barrel and bolt recoil for about six in; the bolt is then unlocked and held, while the barrel runs forward again. During this movement, the cartridge case is extracted. As the barrel stops, it trips a catch to release the bolt, which then runs forward, chambering a cartridge. The magazine is oddly placed on the left side of the pistol grip, making it impossible to fire left-handed. A bipod is attached to the barrel jacket, and a telescope sight is standard.

The M2A1 is a short-barreled version of the M2 intended for use by airborne and special forces who require a more compact weapon.

SPECIFICATION:

CARTRIDGE:
12.7 x 107 mm Soviet

DIMENSIONS (M2):
LENGTH O/A: 1530 mm (60.2 in)
WEIGHT: 12 kg (26 lb 7 oz)
BARREL: 1100 mm (43.3 in)
RIFLING: 8 grooves, rh
MAGAZINE: 5 or 10 rounds

DIMENSIONS (M2A1):
LENGTH O/A: 1260 mm (49.6 in)
WEIGHT: 10 kg (22 lb 1 oz)
BARREL: 830 mm (32.7 in)
RIFLING: 8 grooves, rh
MAGAZINE: 5 or 10 rounds

IN PRODUCTION:
1994–

MARKINGS:
None.

SAFETY:
Manual safety catch on left side of receiver.

UNLOADING:
Magazine release on magazine housing, left of pistol grip. Remove magazine. Pull back cocking handle and examine feedway and chamber through ejection port. Release cocking handle. Pull trigger.

Gepard M3 HUNGARY

This is more or less an enlarged version of the Gepard M2, with the addition of a hydropneumatic recoil system and a more-effective muzzle brake to absorb some of the firing shock. Firing the powerful 14.5 mm AP bullet, with a muzzle velocity of 1000 m/sec (3280 ft/sec), it can penetrate 25 mm (1 in) of homogenous armor plate at a range of 600 m (1968.5 ft) and has a maximum range well in excess of 914 m (3000 ft).

SPECIFICATION:

CARTRIDGE:
14.5 x 114 mm Soviet

DIMENSIONS:
LENGTH O/A: 1880 mm (74 in)
WEIGHT: 20 kg (44 lb 1 oz)
BARREL: 1480 mm (58.3 in)
RIFLING: 8 grooves, rh
MAGAZINE: 5 or 10 rounds

IN PRODUCTION:
1995–

MARKINGS:
None.

SAFETY:
Manual safety catch on left side of receiver.

UNLOADING:
Magazine release on magazine housing, left of pistol grip. Remove magazine. Pull back cocking handle and examine feedway and chamber through ejection port. Release cocking handle.
Pull trigger.

INSAS INDIA

Developed in the mid-1980s, this gas-operated selective-fire assault rifle, part of the INSAS (Indian Small Arms System) family, is an interesting mixture of features taken from other designs. The receiver and pistol grip show Kalashnikov influence, the fore-end resembles that of the M16, and the forward cocking handle is based on the Heckler & Koch rifles. An unusual feature is the use of the old Lee-Enfield buttplate to provide a trap for the cleaning material and oil bottle. The rifle uses the well-tried operating system of a gas piston driving a bolt carrier and rotating bolt, and the magazine housing has been standardized on the M16 dimensions. The fire selector permits single shots or three-round bursts, but there is no provision for automatic fire. The assault rifle is made in fixed- and folding-butt versions, and there is also a heavy-barreled version for use in the squad automatic role.

SPECIFICATION:

CARTRIDGE:
5.56 x 45 mm

DIMENSIONS:
LENGTH FIXED BUTT: 945 mm (37.2 in)
LENGTH, BUTT FOLDED: 750 mm (29.5 in)
LENGTH, BUTT EXTENDED: 960 mm (37.8 in)
WEIGHT: 3.2 kg (7 lb 1 oz)
BARREL: 464 mm (18.3 in)
RIFLING: 6 grooves, rh
MAGAZINE CAPACITY: 22 rounds
CYCLIC RATE: 650 rounds/min

IN PRODUCTION:
1999–

SAFETY:
Large thumb-operated safety catch and fire-selector lever on left side of receiver above pistol grip: up for safe, down for single shots, and down again for automatic fire.

UNLOADING:
Magazine release behind magazine housing in front of trigger guard. Remove magazine. Pull back cocking handle to open bolt and remove any round from chamber. Examine chamber and feedway, ensuring both are empty. Release cocking handle. Pull trigger.

Galil ISRAEL

The Galil was the result of careful Israeli examination of practically every rifle they could find. In the end, they settled for a modified version of the Kalashnikov rotating bolt system; indeed, the first models were built up from Finnish M62 rifle bodies, themselves AK-47 clones. It was originally developed in 5.56 mm caliber, but later a 7.62 x 51 mm model was also produced, though this was never as popular as the 5.56 mm version. The Galil is used by the Israeli Defense Force and has also been adopted by several Central and South American and African armies.

SPECIFICATION:

CARTRIDGE:
5.56 x 45 mm M193 or 7.62 x 51 mm NATO

DIMENSIONS:
LENGTH, STOCK EXTENDED: 979 mm (38.5 in)
LENGTH, STOCK FOLDED: 742 mm (29.2 in)
WEIGHT: 4 kg (8 lb 11 oz)
BARREL: 460 mm (18.1 in)
RIFLING: 6 grooves, rh
MAGAZINE CAPACITY: 35 or 50 rounds
RATE OF FIRE: 550 rounds/min

IN PRODUCTION:
1971–

MARKINGS:
Hebrew markings on left side of receiver, including serial number.

SAFETY:
Combined safety catch and fire selector on left side at top of pistol grip. Forward for safe, fully rearward for single shots, center for automatic fire.

UNLOADING:
Magazine catch at rear of magazine housing. Remove magazine. Pull back cocking handle to eject any round remaining in chamber. Examine chamber and feedway through ejection slot. Release cocking handle. Press trigger.

Magal ISRAEL

The Magal 0.30 carbine is a semiautomatic law-enforcement weapon based on the Galil assault rifle, firing a special high-stopping-power soft-point-bullet 0.30 M1 Carbine round, sufficient for most internal-security tasks. The weapon generally resembles a Galil but is much more compact and features a strap in front of the pistol group. The weapon can be provided with a tactical light (shown) and laser target designators, a reflex or other optical sight, and a riot-control rubber-ball launcher. If required, a 40 mm M203 grenade launcher can be installed to launch tear gas grenades.

SPECIFICATION:

CARTRIDGE:
0.30 Carbine

DIMENSIONS:
LENGTH, STOCK EXTENDED: 735 mm (28.9 in)
LENGTH, STOCK FOLDED: 485 mm (19 in)
WEIGHT: 3.1 kg (6 lb 13 oz)
BARREL: 230 mm (9 in)
RIFLING: 4 grooves, rh
MAGAZINE CAPACITY: 20 rounds

IN PRODUCTION:
1998–

MARKINGS:
None yet seen. Serial number on left side at front of receiver.

SAFETY:
Safety catch is behind trigger: back for safe, forward to fire.

UNLOADING:
Magazine catch just in front of trigger group. Press catch to release magazine. Pull back cocking handle to eject any round in chamber and inspect chamber and feedway through ejection slot. Release cocking handle. Pull trigger.

SR-99 ISRAEL

While a semiautomatic and highly tuned variant of the standard Galil assault rifle has been used as a dedicated marksman's weapon for many years, a higher-precision weapon was also desired. Once again, Israel Military Industries (IMI) turned to the basic Galil gas-operated mechanism, but everything except the original receiver and bolt carrier has been reengineered and constructed for the sniper role. The most visually noticeable items are the long cold-forged barrel with a muzzle brake and the fully adjustable side-folding butt with its molded outlines. Fire is semiautomatic only and cocking is silent. There are no iron sights, just a telescopic or night sight, and a bipod, for aiming stability, is provided attached to a rail under the forestock. Standard Galil rifle magazines continue to be used but, as a general rule, only match-grade ammunition is fired to obtain optimum accuracy.

SPECIFICATION:

CARTRIDGE:
7.62 x 51 mm NATO Match Grade

DIMENSIONS:
LENGTH, STOCK EXTENDED: 1120 mm (47.8 in)
LENGTH, STOCK FOLDED: 845 mm (33.3 in)
WEIGHT: 5.1 kg (11 lb 2 oz)
BARREL: 508 mm (20 in)
RIFLING: 4 grooves, rh
MAGAZINE CAPACITY: 10 or 25 rounds

IN PRODUCTION:
1999–

MARKINGS:
Hebrew markings, including "SR-99" and serial number on left side of receiver.

SAFETY:
Two-position safety catch located on left side just above pistol grip: forward for safe, back to fire.

UNLOADING:
Magazine catch at rear of magazine housing. Remove magazine and pull back cocking handle to eject any round remaining in chamber. Inspect chamber and feedway through ejector slot. Release cocking handle. Pull trigger.

Tavor ISRAEL

The Tavor is not just one weapon but a family of bullpup weapons, all based around a common receiver and rotary bolt. All models in the Tavor family have passed extensive field and other trials and are stated to be reliable, easy to operate, and sturdy. All controls are ambidextrous. The general-service base model is an assault rifle with a reflex sight and a M16-pattern 30-round magazine. A Commando model (shown) for armored vehicle crews and commanders is exactly the same, but the length of barrel protruding from the front handguard is reduced. This model can accommodate a sound suppressor. The Micro Tavor is an ultrashort (480 mm/18.9 in) model for special forces, while the Sharp-shooter model has an optical sight and a folding bipod. There is also a 9 mm submachine-gun version. A number have been sold to India for use by their special forces.

SPECIFICATION:

CARTRIDGE:
5.56 x 45 mm NATO

DIMENSIONS:
LENGTH O/A: 720 mm (28.3 in)
WEIGHT: 2.8 kg (6 lb 3 oz)
BARREL: 460 mm (18.1 in)
RIFLING: 6 grooves, rh
MAGAZINE CAPACITY: 30 rounds
RATE OF FIRE: 750–900 rounds/min

IN PRODUCTION:
2004–

MARKINGS:
None yet seen. Serial number on left side of receiver above trigger group.

SAFETY:
Ambidextrous combined safety switch located just above pistol grip: forward for safe, vertical for single shot, and fully back for automatic.

UNLOADING:
Ambidextrous magazine catch in magazine housing. Press catch to release magazine. Pull back cocking handle on each side of receiver to eject any round in chamber. Inspect chamber and feedway through ejection slot normally on right side of receiver although it may be on left. Ease cocking handle forward. Pull trigger.

Beretta AR 70/.223 ITALY

This was Beretta's first 5.56 mm rifle, gas-operated with a two-lug bolt. It was adopted by Italian special forces and sold to some other countries, but it failed to attract much of a market and experience showed it to have a few minor defects, notably a lack of rigidity in the receiver. It appeared with some variations: a solid-butt model was standard, but there was also a folding-butt model with long and short barrels. The muzzle is adapted for grenade firing, and a hinged tap on the gas block has to be raised to allow a grenade to be loaded; this also shuts off the gas supply to the cylinder, ensuring that all the gas from the launching cartridge goes to propel the grenade.

SPECIFICATION:

CARTRIDGE:
5.56 x 45 mm NATO

DIMENSIONS:
LENGTH O/A: 955 mm (37.6 in)
WEIGHT: 3.8 kg (8 lb 6 oz)
BARREL: 450 mm (17.7 in)
RIFLING: 4 grooves, rh
MAGAZINE CAPACITY: 30 rounds
RATE OF FIRE: 650 rounds/min

IN PRODUCTION:
1972–80

MARKINGS:
"P BERETTA AR 70/223 MADE IN ITALY [serial number]" on left side of receiver.

SAFETY:
Manual safety catch and fire selector on left side of receiver above pistol grip: turn down for safe, up for automatic fire, midway for single shots.

UNLOADING:
Magazine catch behind magazine. Remove magazine. Pull back cocking handle to eject any round left in chamber. Inspect chamber through ejection port. Release cocking handle. Pull trigger.

Beretta BM59 ITALY

In the late 1940s, the Beretta company began making the US M1 rifle under license for the Italian Army, and they later made more for Denmark and Indonesia. In 1959, Beretta set about redesigning the Garand, giving it automatic-fire capability, fitting it with a larger magazine, and adapting the barrel to grenade launching. Apart from these points, the BM59 is much the same as any US M1 Garand. Various models were produced, with bipods, folding butts, folding bayonets, removable grenade-launching adapters, or shorter barrels, but the mechanism remained the same. If a weapon looks like a Garand but has a removable magazine, it is either a US M14 or an Italian BM59.

SPECIFICATION:

CARTRIDGE:
7.62 x 51 mm NATO

DIMENSIONS:
LENGTH O/A: 1095 mm (43.1 in)
WEIGHT: 4.6 kg (10 lb 2 oz)
BARREL: 490 mm (19.3 in)
RIFLING: 4 grooves, rh
MAGAZINE CAPACITY: 20 rounds
RATE OF FIRE: 750 rounds/min

IN PRODUCTION:
1961–66

MARKINGS:
"P BERETTA BM59 [serial number]" on top rear end of receiver.

SAFETY:
Manual safety catch in front edge of trigger guard: push forward to fire, rearward for safe. Fire selector mounted on left side of receiver alongside chamber, marked "A" for automatic fire and "S" for single shots. May be permanently locked in single-shot position in some rifles.

UNLOADING:
Magazine catch behind magazine. Remove magazine. Pull back cocking handle to open bolt and extract any round left in chamber. Inspect chamber and feedway, release bolt. Press trigger.

Type 64 JAPAN

This rifle was developed in Japan and made by the Howa Machinery Company. It uses a gas-piston operating system driving a tilting bolt. The principal concern was to provide a rifle suited to the smaller stature of Japanese soldiers; the weapon fires a special reduced-load cartridge as standard and uses a muzzle brake to further reduce the recoil force. The gas regulator is adjustable and can be set to permit the use of full-power NATO cartridges, if required. The rifle can also launch grenades.

SPECIFICATION:

CARTRIDGE:
7.62 x 51 mm Japanese Service

DIMENSIONS:
LENGTH O/A: 990 mm (39 in)
WEIGHT: 4.4 kg (9 lb 11 oz)
BARREL: 450 mm (17.7 in)
RIFLING: 4 grooves, rh
MAGAZINE CAPACITY: 20 rounds
RATE OF FIRE: 500 rounds/min

IN PRODUCTION:
1964–90

MARKINGS:
Japanese ideographs for "64" and "7.62mm," serial number and year in Western form, and arsenal mark on left side of receiver.

SAFETY:
Manual safety catch and fire selector on right side of receiver above trigger: rearward for safe, forward for single shots, fully upward for automatic.

UNLOADING:
Magazine catch behind magazine housing. Remove magazine. Pull back cocking handle to remove any round in chamber. Inspect chamber and feedway through ejection port. Release cocking handle. Press trigger.

Type 89 JAPAN

This rifle was designed by the Japanese Defense Agency and is replacing the Type 64 as the standard Japanese service rifle. Gas operated, with a rotating bolt, it uses a somewhat unusual gas system that ensures a lower initial impulse on the gas piston, so giving a lower felt recoil and prolonging the life of the weapon. There is a fixed-butt version as well as the folding-butt type, and both models are equipped with a bipod. Another unusual feature is the entirely separate three-round burst mechanism; if anything should go wrong with it, the single-shot and automatic functions are not impaired.

SPECIFICATION:

CARTRIDGE:
5.56 x 45 mm NATO

DIMENSIONS:
LENGTH, STOCK EXTENDED: 916 mm (36 in)
LENGTH, STOCK FOLDED: 570 mm (22.4 in)
WEIGHT: 3.5 kg (7 lb 12 oz)
BARREL: 420 mm (16.5 in)
RIFLING: 6 grooves, rh
MAGAZINE CAPACITY: 20 or 30 rounds
RATE OF FIRE: 750 rounds/min

IN PRODUCTION:
1990–

MARKINGS:
Japanese ideographs for "89" and "5.56mm", serial number and year in Western form, and arsenal mark on left side of receiver.

SAFETY:
Manual safety catch and fire selector on right side of receiver above trigger: up for safe, down one notch for single shots, down and fully forward for automatic fire. When set at automatic, operate other catch behind trigger for three-round burst.

UNLOADING:
Magazine catch in right side of magazine housing. Remove magazine. Pull back cocking handle to eject any round remaining in chamber. Inspect chamber and feedway. Release cocking handle. Pull trigger.

Beryl POLAND

During 1998, the arms manufacturer ZM Lucnik SA of Radom commenced production of a 5.45 mm Tantal, a design closely following that of the Russian AK-74 assault rifle. The Tantal fired 5.45 x 39 mm ammunition, but by 1996, with Poland about to join NATO, it was decided to modify the Tantal to fire 5.56 x 45 mm NATO ammunition. The result is the Beryl, still basically an AK-74 variant but with numerous modifications to make the weapon attractive for potential export sales. As with the Tantal, the Beryl makes much use of molded plastic furniture, and the top of the receiver has been reconfigured with a length of Picatinny rail to accept various sights. The fire-selector mechanism has been altered to include a three-round-burst mode in addition to single shot and automatic. Optional extras such as a clip-on bipod and an under-barrel grenade launcher can be added. There is also a 5.56 mm Mini-Beryl similar to the AK-74SU.

SPECIFICATION:

CARTRIDGE:
5.56 x 45 mm NATO

DIMENSIONS:
LENGTH, STOCK EXTENDED: 943 mm (37.1 in)
LENGTH, STOCK FOLDED: 742 mm (29.2 in)
WEIGHT: 3.4 kg (7 lb 6 oz)
BARREL: 457 mm (18 in)
RIFLING: 6 grooves, rh
MAGAZINE CAPACITY: 20 or 30 rounds
RATE OF FIRE: 690 rounds/min

IN PRODUCTION:
1998–

MARKINGS:
May vary but are usually on left side of receiver. Typical is "Zaklady Metalowe LUZNIK SA" plus "5.56 x 45mm."

SAFETY:
Combined safety catch and fire-selector lever on right rear side of receiver: fully up for safe, first position for single shot, then three-round burst, with fully automatic at bottom.

UNLOADING:
Press magazine catch at rear of magazine housing to remove magazine. Pull back cocking handle to extra any round in chamber and inspect chamber through ejection port. Release cocking handle. Pull trigger.

AK-47/AKM/variants

It has been estimated that well over 50 million AK-47-pattern rifles have been manufactured worldwide. The base AK-47 was first issued during 1947, and it has since been manufactured or copied in Albania, Bulgaria, China, Egypt, Finland, the former East Germany, Hungary, Iraq, Kazakhstan, North Korea, Poland, Romania, and the former Yugoslavia. The original AK-47 had a solid-metal receiver, while the more prevalent AKM makes extensive use of steel stampings and can be recognized by the small dimple in the receiver, above the magazine well; the AK-47 has an elongated depression. The AKMS has a folding metal butt stock. Only the markings will indicate the country of origin, and on some examples only a serial number is provided. Romanian AKMs typically sport a forward pistol grip, while other nations have also made small local modifications and dimensional changes. Finishes can vary from poor to excellent, but, in whatever form, the AK-47/AKM is tough and reliable.

SPECIFICATION:

CARTRIDGE:
7.62 x 39 mm Soviet M1943

DIMENSIONS:
LENGTH, FIXED BUTT: 870 mm (34.3 in)
WEIGHT: 4 kg (8 lb 14 oz)
BARREL: 415 mm (16.3 in)
RIFLING: 4 grooves, rh
MAGAZINE CAPACITY: 30 rounds
RATE OF FIRE: 600 rounds/min

IN PRODUCTION:
1947– (AK47); 1959– (AKM)

MARKINGS:
Model number, factory identifier, and serial number on top of rear end of receiver.

SAFETY:
Combined safety catch and fire-selector lever on right rear side of receiver: press all the way up for safe (obstructs movement of cocking handle and bolt), move down one notch to first mark or letters "AB" for full automatic fire, and move to bottom position, or letter "O," for single shots.

UNLOADING:
Magazine catch at rear of magazine housing. Remove magazine. Pull back cocking handle to extract any round which may be in chamber. Inspect chamber through ejection port. Release cocking handle. Pull trigger.

The variants of the Kalashnikov family are now so numerous that it is not possible to list them all. Illustrated is a Romanian version of the AKMS. It should be noted that the distinctive forward pistol-grip can be fitted to any standard AK/AKMS, so any single component should not be used as a country-identifier without additional data.

The most significant difference is the solid steel receiver of the AK-47 series and the pressed or stamped metal receiver of the AKM series.

Kalashnikov 1974 (AK-74) RUSSIA

The AK-74 is a small-caliber version of the AKM, and it uses the same receiver, furniture, and system of operation. The 5.45 mm round is almost the same length as the 7.62 x 39 mm round but of smaller diameter; 7.62 mm x 5.45 mm magazines are NOT interchangeable. A noticeable feature of this rifle is the laminated plastic and the steel magazine, the design of which has subtly changed since its introduction as stiffening fillets have been added. Another feature is the muzzle brake and compensator, designed to reduce the recoil and compensate for the upward climb always present in automatic weapons. It is highly efficient, reducing the felt recoil to a low level and keeping the weapon steady during automatic fire. The AKS-74 version has a folding steel butt that swings to lie along the left side of the receiver. Late-production AK-74s have black high-impact plastic furniture; this variant is known as the AK-74M.

SPECIFICATION:

CARTRIDGE:
5.45 x 39.5 mm

DIMENSIONS:
LENGTH: 928 mm (36.5 in); AKS stock folded: 690 mm (27.2 in)
WEIGHT: 3.9 kg (8 lb 8 oz)
BARREL: 400 mm (15.8 in)
RIFLING: 4 grooves, rh
MAGAZINE: 30-round detachable plastic box
CYCLIC RATE: 650 rounds/min
MUZZLE VELOCITY: 900 m/sec (2952 ft/sec)

IN PRODUCTION:
1975–

MARKINGS:
Model number, factory identifier, and serial number on top of receiver.

SAFETY:
Standard Kalashnikov combined safety and selector lever on left side of receiver: press all the way up for safe (obstructs movement of cocking handle and bolt), down one notch for automatic fire, move all the way down for single shots.

UNLOADING:
Magazine catch at rear of magazine housing. Remove magazine. Pull back cocking handle to extract any round in chamber. Inspect chamber through ejection port to ensure it is empty. Release cocking handle. Pull trigger.

Kalashnikov AKS-74U RUSSIA

The AKS-74U is another short assault rifle that manages to pack rifle-ammunition firepower into a package normally associated with submachine guns. Consequently, the weapon is often referred to as a submachine and is just as often deployed in a similar manner. Overall, the AKS-74U is a much-shortened variant of the AK-74. Since the barrel length has been reduced to 206.5 mm (8.1 in), a prominent housing has been added to the muzzle to damp down firing flash. Examples have been manufactured in Bulgaria, Poland, and the former Yugoslavia, often with local modifications such as a side-folding steel buttstock of minimal form from Poland. Export versions have been offered chambered for 5.56 x 45 mm NATO ammunition.

SPECIFICATION:

CARTRIDGE:
5.45 x 39.5 mm Soviet

DIMENSIONS:
LENGTH, STOCK EXTENDED: 730 mm (28.8 in)
LENGTH, STOCK RETRACTED: 490 mm (19.3 in)
WEIGHT: 2.7 kg (5 lb 15 oz)
BARREL: 206.5 mm (8.1 in)
RIFLING: 4 grooves, rh
MAGAZINE CAPACITY: 30 rounds
RATE OF FIRE: 700 rounds/min

IN PRODUCTION:
1979–

MARKINGS:
Factory identification, serial number, and year of manufacture on left side of receiver.

SAFETY:
Manual safety catch/fire selector on right side of receiver: up for safe, center for automatic fire, down for single shots.

UNLOADING:
Magazine catch in front of trigger guard. Remove magazine. Pull back cocking lever on right side of receiver to eject any round in chamber. Inspect chamber through ejection port. Release cocking lever. Pull trigger.

The 5.66 mm APS underwater assault rifle is a companion weapon to the SPP-1 underwater pistol. It uses the same dartlike projectile, although of slightly larger caliber and greater length. It is a selective-fire, gas-operated weapon and has a large capacity interchangeable magazine. A telescoping metal wire-stock is provided, and the sights are simple nonadjustable iron sights, reflecting the short ranges at which this rifle is used. Effective range is dependent on water depth, with a range of 30 m (98.4 ft) at 5 m (16.4 ft) depth and 11 m (36 ft) at 40 m (131.2 ft) depth.

SPECIFICATION:

CARTRIDGE:
5.66 x 39 mm

DIMENSIONS:
LENGTH, STOCK EXTENDED: 823 mm (32.4 in)
LENGTH, STOCK TELESCOPED: 614 mm (24.2 in)
WEIGHT: 3.4 kg (7 lb 8 oz)
BARREL: Unknown
RATE OF FIRE: 350 rounds/min
MAGAZINE CAPACITY: 26 rounds

IN PRODUCTION:
1970?–

MARKINGS:
Model type and serial number on left side of receiver.

SAFETY:
Fire-control devices on left rear of receiver.

UNLOADING:
Magazine release catch at rear of magazine housing. Remove magazine. Pull working parts to rear, inspect chamber and magazine well through ejection port. When clear allow working parts to go forward. Point weapon in safe direction and pull trigger.

There are two models of silent sniper rifle produced in Russia: the AS and the VSS. Of the two, the AS is the most likely to be encountered as it was developed as a silent sniper rifle for special forces. The generally similar VSS is intended for use by undercover military and police units and can therefore be stripped into subassemblies that are carried inside an innocuous-looking briefcase. Both rifles fire a special 9 x 39 mm cartridge that, although subsonic, can penetrate body armor at ranges up to 400 m (1312.3 ft) and both have a fully automatic fire mode when necessary. The AS is often known as the Val (Rampart) and makes use of an integral sound-suppression system that virtually eliminates the firing signature, both sound and flash.

SPECIFICATION:

CARTRIDGE:
9 x 39 mm Special

DIMENSIONS:
LENGTH, STOCK EXTENDED: 875 mm (34.5 in)
LENGTH, STOCK FOLDED: 650 mm (25.6 in)
WEIGHT: 2.5 kg (5 lb 8 oz)
BARREL: 200 mm (7.9 in)
RIFLING: not known
MAGAZINE CAPACITY: 20 rounds
RATE OF FIRE: 800–900 rounds/min

IN PRODUCTION:
1993–

MARKINGS:
Factory identifier and serial number on right side of receiver.

SAFETY:
Manual safety catch behind trigger. Press upper portion in for safe; press lower portion in to fire.

UNLOADING:
Magazine catch behind magazine on front end of trigger guard. Remove magazine. Pull back cocking handle to eject any round in chamber. Inspect chamber and feedway through ejection slot. Release cocking handle. Press trigger.

Dragunov SVD RUSSIA

Although similar to the Kalashnikov in principle, this rifle differs in using a short-stroke piston to operate the bolt carrier; the AK series uses a long-stroke piston, which would be inappropriate in this case, since the SVD is a sniping rifle and the shift of balance during a long-stroke piston's movement can degrade the accuracy. The rifle is normally provided with the PSO-1 telescope sight, though the image-intensifying night sight NSPU-3 is claimed to have an effective range of 1000 m (3280 ft), which is also issued with this rifle. The SVD is also fitted with a big flash-hider and bayonet lug. SVD rifles are produced in China as the Type 79 or 85 and Russia has offered the SVD chambered for 7.62 x 51 mm NATO ammunition. A later folding-stock variant is known as the SVDS.

SPECIFICATION:

CARTRIDGE:
7.62 x 54 R Soviet

DIMENSIONS:
LENGTH O/A: 1225 mm (48.2 in)
WEIGHT: 4.3 kg (9 lb 8 oz)
BARREL: 610 mm (24 in)
RIFLING: 4 grooves, rh
MAGAZINE CAPACITY: 10 rounds

IN PRODUCTION:
1963–

MARKINGS:
Factory identification, year, and serial number on left side of receiver.

SAFETY:
Safety lever similar to Kalashnikov rifles, mounted on left rear of receiver: press up for safe; press down for single shots.

UNLOADING:
Magazine catch behind magazine. Remove magazine. Pull back cocking handle to extract any cartridge remaining in chamber. Inspect chamber and feedway through ejection port. Release cocking handle. Press trigger.

OSV-96 RUSSIA

A large-caliber self-loading rifle intended for use in an anti-matériel role or for long-range sniping using special match-grade ammunition. A large multibaffle muzzle brake is fitted to reduce the level of recoil on firing. To reduce the overall length for transit, the receiver and body are hinged at the junction of breech and receiver, with the latter lying along the right side of the barrel when folded. With the bipod folded, the carrying handle is at the center of gravity. Iron sights are fitted for emergency use, but the rifle is intended to be fired using long-range optical sights or night-vision devices. The original model of the OSV-96 carried the designation V-94.

SPECIFICATION:

CARTRIDGE:
12.7 x 107 mm

DIMENSIONS:
LENGTH O/A: 1746 mm (68.7 in)
LENGTH, FOLDED FOR TRANSIT: 1154 mm (45.4 in)
WEIGHT: 12.9 kg (28 lb 6 oz)
BARREL LENGTH: 1000 mm (39.4 in)
MAGAZINE CAPACITY: 5 rounds

IN PRODUCTION:
1996–

MARKINGS:
None recorded.

SAFETY:
Dependent on model type.

UNLOADING:
Magazine release catch at rear of magazine housing. Remove magazine. Pull working parts to rear. Inspect chamber and magazine well through ejection port. When clear, allow working parts to go forward. Point weapon in safe direction and pull trigger.

OTs-14 (Groza) RUSSIA

Developed for the Russian special forces in the period following the collapse of the Soviet Union, the OTs-14 Groza (Thunderstorm) is a compact bullpup assault rifle. Of modular design, it can mount an under-barrel grenade launcher (UBGL) or suppressor and has interchangeable barrels of different lengths to suit the tactical situation. A full range of optical or night-vision devices can be fitted to either the carrying handle/iron sight on top of the gun or the standard Russian sight bracket on the left of the receiver. Originally offered in four different calibers, only the 7.62 mm and 9 mm options are thought to have been taken into service.

SPECIFICATION:

CARTRIDGE:
5.45 x 39mm; 5.56 x 45 mm NATO; 7.62 x 39 mm; M43 9 x 39 mm

DIMENSIONS (7.62 MM CONFIGURATION):
LENGTH: 700 mm (27.5 in)
WEIGHT, RIFLE: 3.1 kg (6 lb 13 oz)
WEIGHT, WITH UBGL: 4.1 kg (9 lbs)
BARREL: 455 mm (17.9 in)
RATE OF FIRE: 750 rounds/min
MAGAZINE CAPACITY: 30 rounds

IN PRODUCTION:
1994–

MARKINGS:
Model type on right side of receiver. Serial number on left side.

SAFETY:
Selector lever on right side of receiver: upper position locks working parts, center position for automatic, lower position for self-loading.

UNLOADING:
Magazine release catch is located at rear of magazine housing. Remove magazine. Pull working parts to rear. Inspect chamber and magazine well through ejection port. When clear, allow working parts to go forward. Point weapon in safe direction and pull trigger.

Simonov SKS RUSSIA

The SKS was the first Soviet small arm to use the 7.62 x 39 mm M1943 cartridge (predating its use in the AK-47). Experimental models were in the hands of combat troops in 1944, modifications were made, and mass production began in 1946. The SKS is charger loaded from a 10-round clip and is fitted with a blade bayonet. It was widely issued after 1946 and also supplied to several Communist bloc countries, being copied in China, North Korea, East Germany, Romania, and Yugoslavia. The Chinese variant, the Type 56, is identified by its cruciform bayonet. It is estimated that perhaps 15 million in total have been made.

SPECIFICATION:

CARTRIDGE:
7.62 x 39 mm Soviet M1943

DIMENSIONS:
LENGTH O/A: 1122 mm (44.2 in)
WEIGHT: 3.9 kg (8 lb 8 oz)
BARREL: 620 mm (24.4 in)
RIFLING: 4 grooves, rh
MAGAZINE CAPACITY: 10 rounds

IN PRODUCTION:
1946–

MARKINGS:
Serial number on left side receiver and bolt.

SAFETY:
Manual safety catch on rear of trigger guard: push forward and up for safe, obstructing trigger finger and trigger movement.

UNLOADING:
Magazine catch at rear of magazine, under receiver. Press in and magazine swings open, allowing contents to be removed. Pull back cocking handle. Inspect chamber and feedway. Release cocking handle. Press trigger. Close empty magazine.

SR88 SINGAPORE

Chartered Industries of Singapore began by making the M16 under license from Colt. They then had Sterling Armaments of England design an automatic rifle for them, which they produced as the SAR-80. The SR88 is an improved version and became the standard rifle of the Singapore armed forces. It has also been sold elsewhere in the Far East. The mechanism is different from that of the M16, using a gas piston to drive the bolt carrier back and operate a rotating bolt. The gas cylinder is chromed to reduce fouling and corrosion; the butt, fore-end, and pistol grip are of glass-reinforced nylon; and the US M203 grenade launcher can be fitted beneath the barrel.

SPECIFICATION:

CARTRIDGE:
5.56 x 45 mm M198

DIMENSIONS:
LENGTH O/A: 912 mm (35.9 in)
WEIGHT: 3.7 kg (8 lb 1 oz)
BARREL: 460 mm (18.1 in)
RIFLING: 6 grooves, rh
MAGAZINE CAPACITY: 20 or 30 rounds
RATE OF FIRE: 750 rounds/min

IN PRODUCTION:
1988–95

MARKINGS:
Serial number and "CAL 5.56 SR 88" on right side of magazine housing.

SAFETY:
Manual safety catch and fire selector on left side of receiver over trigger: rearward for safe, forward one notch for single shots, forward two notches for automatic fire.

UNLOADING:
Magazine catch is a push-button on right rear side of magazine housing. Remove magazine. Pull back cocking handle to eject any round left in chamber. Inspect chamber and feedway through ejection port. Release cocking handle. Pull trigger.

SR88A SINGAPORE

An improved version of the SR88; mechanically it is the same, but there are significant differences in construction. The lower receiver is now an aluminum-alloy casting and the upper receiver a steel pressing. Stock, fore-end, and pistol grip are of fiber glass-reinforced nylon, and the fixed-stock model has part of the stock cut away for lightness and strength. The barrel is fitted to the receiver by a locknut and locating-lug system, which considerably simplifies barrel replacement in the field. The barrel is hammer forged and has a chromed chamber. There is also a carbine version with a shorter barrel, intended for use by paratroops or others requiring a compact rifle.

SPECIFICATION:

CARTRIDGE:
5.56 x 45 mm NATO

DIMENSIONS:
LENGTH, STOCK EXTENDED: 960 mm (37.8 in)
LENGTH, STOCK FOLDED: 810 mm (31.9 in)
WEIGHT: 3.7 kg (8 lb 2 oz)
BARREL: 460 mm (18.1 in)
RIFLING: 6 grooves, rh
MAGAZINE CAPACITY: 30 rounds
RATE OF FIRE: 800 rounds/min

IN PRODUCTION:
1990–2000

MARKINGS:
Serial number and "SR88A CAL 5.56" on right side of magazine housing.

SAFETY:
Manual safety catch and fire selector on left side of receiver over trigger: rearward for safe, forward one notch for single shots, forward two notches for automatic fire.

UNLOADING:
Magazine catch is a push-button on right rear side of magazine housing. Remove magazine. Pull back cocking handle to eject any round left in chamber. Inspect chamber and feedway through ejection port. Release cocking handle. Pull trigger.

ST Kinetics SAR 21 SINGAPORE

Singapore Technologies Kinetics (ST Kinetics, formerly Chartered Industries of Singapore) started to develop their SAR 21 5.56 mm assault rifle during 1995, and by 2002 it was in production for the local defense forces and has been widely marketed for export sales. It is basically the usual Stoner rotary bolt action configured into a compact bullpup configuration with the magazine behind the trigger group to reduce overall length. Almost the entire rifle is shrouded by smooth contoured high-strength plastics. The base assault rifle has a 30-round M16-pattern box magazine, and sighting involves a permanently attached 1.5x optical sight. In addition, the forward handguard also houses a red-dot laser aiming device. A P-Rail variant has a length of Picatinny rail over the receiver to accept various other forms of sight. There is also a Sharp Shooter variant with a 3x optical sight and a SAR 21 Light Machine Gun with a heavier barrel and a light bipod.

SPECIFICATION:

CARTRIDGE:
5.56 x 45 mm NATO

DIMENSIONS:
LENGTH O/A: 805 mm (31.7 in)
WEIGHT: 3.8 kg (8 lb 7 oz)
BARREL: 508 mm (20 in)
RIFLING: 6 grooves, rh
MAGAZINE CAPACITY: 30 rounds
RATE OF FIRE: 450–650 rounds/min

IN PRODUCTION:
2002–

MARKINGS:
None yet seen, other than "SINGAPORE TECHNOLOGIES KINETICS."

SAFETY:
Ambidextrous safety plunger just in front of trigger locks trigger and bolt mechanisms.

UNLOADING:
Recessed magazine catch button behind magazine housing. Press to remove magazine. Pull back cocking handle over receiver to eject any round in chamber. Inspect chamber and feedway through ejection port on right side above receiver. Release bolt. Pull trigger.

NTW 20/14.5 SOUTH AFRICA

Quite apart from its size, the NTW 20/14.5 anti-matériel rifle is unusual in several respects, not the least being that it may be configured to fire two different calibers. The largest caliber is 20 x 82 mm, normally regarded as a cannon round, and the other is 14.5 x 114 mm, an Eastern Bloc heavy machine-gun cartridge. This latter cartridge is effective for up to 1800 m (5905.5 ft) when fired from the NTW.

Changing from one caliber to the other involves the barrel, bolt, magazine, and sighting equipment and can be accomplished in the field without special tools. The three-round box magazine protrudes to the left of the receiver which contains a buffered slide to absorb some of the recoil forces when fired. Due to its weight, the NTW is normally broken down into two back-pack loads for transport in the field.

SPECIFICATION:

CARTRIDGE:
20 x 82 mm MG 151 or 14.5 x 114 mm

DIMENSIONS:
LENGTH O/A: 20 mm, 1.8 m (70.7 in); 14.5 mm, 2 m (79.3 in)
WEIGHT: 20 mm, 26 kg (57 lb 5 oz); 14.5 mm, 29 kg (63 lb 15 oz)
BARREL: 20 mm, 1 m (39.4 in); 14.5 mm, 1.2 m (48 in)
RIFLING: 6 grooves, rh
MAGAZINE CAPACITY: 3 rounds

IN PRODUCTION:
1995–

MARKINGS:
May vary. Can be either "PRETORIA METAL PRESSINGS NTW" or "MECHEM," together with "MADE IN RSA," usually on top of receiver together with serial number.

SAFETY:
Manual safety catch on right side of receiver, just in front of trigger. Forward to make safe, to rear to fire.

UNLOADING:
Magazine release catch is to rear of magazine housing. Remove magazine, pull back bolt handle to eject any round in chamber. Examine chamber and feedway. If clear, close bolt and press trigger.

Vektor R4

This is the South African standard rifle and is a slightly modified Israeli Galil; the modifications consisted of changing the butt and fore-end to synthetic materials rather than steel, in consideration of the high temperatures common in Africa, and lengthening the butt, since the average South African was rather larger than the average Israeli. Other components were strengthened, and a bipod with wire-cutting ability was provided. There is also a carbine version, the R5, with a 332 mm barrel, and a compact version, the R6, with a 280 mm barrel. Semi-automatic versions of all three weapons are produced for use by police and paramilitary forces and for export.

SPECIFICATION:

CARTRIDGE:
5.56 x 45 mm M193

DIMENSIONS:
LENGTH, STOCK EXTENDED: 1005 mm (39.6 in)
LENGTH, STOCK FOLDED: 740 mm (29.1 in)
WEIGHT: 4.3 kg (9 lb 8 oz)
BARREL: 460 mm (18.1 in)
RIFLING: 6 grooves, rh
MAGAZINE CAPACITY: 35 rounds
RATE OF FIRE: 700 rounds/min

IN PRODUCTION:
1982–

MARKINGS:
Vektor badge (V in circle) on right of receiver in front of ejection port. Serial number on left.

SAFETY:
Combined safety catch and fire-selector lever on right rear side of receiver: press all the way up (letter "S") for safe position (obstructs movement of cocking handle and bolt); move down one notch to first mark (or the letter "A") for full automatic fire; move to bottom position (or the letter "R"), for single shots.

UNLOADING:
Remove the magazine. Pull back cocking handle to extract any round which may be in chamber. Inspect chamber through ejection port. Release cocking handle. Pull trigger.

Daewoo K2 SOUTH KOREA

A gas-operated selective-fire rifle with a folding plastic butt, the K2 can fire single shots, three-round bursts, or fully automatically. The barrel is fitted with a muzzle brake and compensator that also doubles as a grenade launcher. The three-round-burst mechanism is unusual in that it does not reset to zero if a part-burst is fired; thus, if only two shots of a burst are fired, the next pull of the trigger will fire a single shot.

Virtually identical to the K2, other than in dimensions, is the short-barreled (263 mm/10.4 in) Daewoo K1A. The K1A is often referred to as a submachine gun but is really a short assault rifle.

SPECIFICATION:

CARTRIDGE:
5.56 x 45 mm NATO or M193

DIMENSIONS:
LENGTH, BUTT EXTENDED: 990 mm (40 in)
LENGTH, BUTT FOLDED: 730 mm (28.7 in)
WEIGHT: 3.3 kg (7 lb 3 oz)
BARREL: 465 mm (18.3 in)
RIFLING: 6 grooves, rh
MAGAZINE: 30-round detachable box
CYCLIC RATE: 650 rounds/min
MUZZLE VELOCITY: 920m/s (3018 ft/sec)

IN PRODUCTION:
1987–

MARKINGS:
"DAEWOO PRECISION INDUSTRIES LTD" on receiver top. "5.56MM K2" and serial number on left side of magazine housing.

SAFETY:
Three-position switch on left side of receiver: turn pointer forward for safe; vertical for single shots; to rear for automatic or three-round burst.

UNLOADING:
Magazine catch on left side of magazine housing. Remove magazine. Pull back cocking handle and inspect chamber to ensure it is empty. Release cocking handle. Press trigger.

Santa Barbara CETME Model L SPAIN

CETME (Centro de Estudios Técnicos de Materiales Especiales) is a Spanish design agency; the weapons are actually made by the Empresa Nacional de Industrial Militares Santa Barbara at Oviedo arsenal. CETME began designing rifles shortly after World War II and were responsible for the design that eventually became the German G3. The CETME rifles all use the same roller-locked delayed-blowback system that is used by the G3; they began with a 7.92 mm weapon, then 7.62 mm NATO, and moved into the 5.56 mm field with the Model L. There is also a short-barrel carbine with folding butt known as the Model LC.

SPECIFICATION:

CARTRIDGE:
5.56 x 45 mm NATO

DIMENSIONS:
LENGTH, STOCK EXTENDED: 930 mm (36.6 in)
LENGTH, STOCK FOLDED: 675 mm (26.6 in)
WEIGHT: 3.9 kg (8 lb 8 oz)
BARREL: 416 mm (16.4 in)
RIFLING: 6 grooves, rh
MAGAZINE CAPACITY: 10 or 30 rounds
RATE OF FIRE: 650 rounds/min

IN PRODUCTION:
1984–2001

MARKINGS:
"CETME 5.56 (.223)" on left side of magazine housing. Serial number on left side of receiver above trigger.

SAFETY:
Manual safety catch and fire-selector lever on left side of receiver above pistol grip: push catch up to letter "S" for safe, one notch down to "T" for single shots, two notches down to "R" for automatic fire. Some weapons will have a fourth notch, though lever will not move into it; this is because design originally had a three-round burst setting, but this was not adopted by Spanish Army. However, receivers are made with notch as three-round burst mechanism can be fitted as an option for other customers.

UNLOADING:
Magazine catch behind magazine housing on right side. Press in and remove magazine. Pull back cocking handle to eject any round left in chamber. Inspect chamber and feedway through ejection port. Release cocking handle. Press trigger.

This is actually a variant of the Belgian FN FNC rifle, extensively modified to meet Swedish requirements after a comprehensive series of trials in the mid-1980s. Changes were made to the butt, sights, cocking handle, bolt, selector switch, trigger guard, and sling swivels, largely in order to better withstand extremely cold conditions and be more easily operated by gloved hands. The three-round-burst option was removed. The metal is finished in a deep green enamel, making the rifle very easily recognizable.

SPECIFICATION:

CARTRIDGE:
5.56 x 45 mm NATO

DIMENSIONS:
LENGTH, STOCK EXTENDED: 1008 mm (39.7 in)
LENGTH, STOCK FOLDED: 753 mm (29.7 in)
WEIGHT: 3.9 kg (8 lb 10 oz)
BARREL: 450 mm (17.7 in)
RIFLING: 6 grooves, rh
MAGAZINE CAPACITY: 30 rounds
RATE OF FIRE: 650 rounds/min

IN PRODUCTION:
1984–

MARKINGS:
Month/year of manufacture at bottom right of receiver. Serial number and month/year of manufacture on left side.

SAFETY:
Manual safety catch and selector lever on left side of receiver above trigger: turn to letter "S" for safe, "1" for single shots, and "30" for full automatic fire.

UNLOADING:
Remove magazine. Pull back cocking handle. Inspect chamber through ejection port. Release cocking handle. Press trigger.

Ljungman AG42 SWEDEN

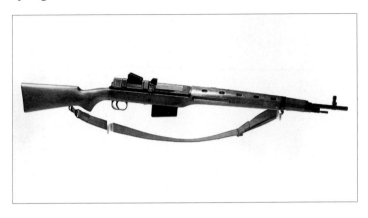

This appeared in Sweden in 1942 and uses a direct-gas-impingement system acting on the bolt carrier. Used by the Swedish Army until the 1970s, it was also used by the Danish Army in 7.92 mm Mauser caliber from 1945 to the 1960s. In 1954, the Swedish tooling was bought by Egypt and the rifle produced there as the Hakim, also in 7.92 mm Mauser caliber. In 1959–60, a somewhat modified design, chambered for the 7.62 x 39 mm Soviet cartridge, was produced in small numbers in Egypt as the Rashid.

SPECIFICATION:

CARTRIDGE:
6.5 x 55 mm Swedish Service

DIMENSIONS:
LENGTH O/A: 1214 mm (47.8 in)
WEIGHT: 4.7 kg (10 lb 6 oz)
BARREL: 622 mm (24.5 in)
RIFLING: 6 grooves, rh
MAGAZINE CAPACITY: 10 rounds

IN PRODUCTION:
1942–62

MARKINGS:
"MADSEN" and serial number on left side of chamber.

SAFETY:
Lever at end of receiver: move right for safe.

UNLOADING:
Two types of rifle, one with magazine fixed and the other removable. To unload fixed model, operate cocking handle back and forth until magazine is empty. Then check chamber and feedway, release cocking handle and pull trigger. Where there is a magazine catch behind magazine, remove magazine, pull back cocking handle to eject any round in chamber, inspect chamber and feedway, release cocking handle and pull trigger.

SIG SG 540/542/543 SWITZERLAND

This family—the SG 540 in 5.56 mm with long barrel, SG 542 in 7.62 mm with long barrel, and SG 543 in 5.56 mm with short barrel—was designed by SIG of Switzerland and licensed to Manurhin of France for manufactured as Swiss arms-export laws made it impossible for SIG to supply weapons to most countries. Manurhin made about 20,000 for the French Army, who used them while FAMAS rifle production got up to speed, and supplied them to Chile, Bolivia, Paraguay, Ecuador, and Nicaragua. In 1988, the license was relinquished and passed to INDEP of Portugal, who reassigned it to Chile, who currently make the 540 and 542.

SPECIFICATION:

CARTRIDGE:
5.56 x 4 5mm or 7.62 x 51 mm

DIMENSIONS (SG 542):
LENGTH O/A: 1000 mm (39.4 in)
WEIGHT: 3.6 kg (7 lb 13 oz)
BARREL: 465 mm (18.3 in)
RIFLING: 4 grooves, rh
MAGAZINE CAPACITY: 20 or 30 rounds
RATE OF FIRE: 800 rounds/min

IN PRODUCTION:
1977–2002

MARKINGS:
"MANURHIN FRANCE SG54X" and serial number on right side of receiver. May also have national army markings e.g. "EJERCITO DE CHILE."

SAFETY:
Four-position safety catch and fire selector on left side of receiver above pistol grip: up for safe; rotate down and forward for single shots, three-round burst, and full automatic fire.

UNLOADING:
Magazine catch in rear of magazine housing. Remove magazine. Pull back cocking handle to eject any round left in chamber. Inspect chamber and feedway through ejection port. Release cocking handle. Press trigger.

SIG SG 550/551 (Stgw 90) SWITZERLAND

This is an improved SG 540 developed in competition to meet a Swiss Army requirement in 1984. The SIG design was selected and became the Stgw (Sturmgewehr) 90 and will eventually replace the Stgw 57 as the official Swiss rifle. It is also made in a civilian version, without automatic fire. An interesting feature of this rifle is the provision of studs and slots on the plastic magazines so that two or three magazines can be clipped together side by side; one can then be inserted into the magazine housing, and, when the last shot is fired, reloading can be done by pulling the assembly out, shifting it sideways, and pushing in one of the loaded magazines.

The SIG SG 551 SWAT, introduced in 2001, is a short-barreled (328 mm/12.9 in) version intended for special law-enforcement marksmen. There is also an even shorter military model known as the SG 552 Commando and intended for use by special forces.

SPECIFICATION:

CARTRIDGE:
5.56 x 45 mm NATO

DIMENSIONS (SG 550):
LENGTH, STOCK EXTENDED: 998 mm (39.3 in)
LENGTH, STOCK FOLDED: 772 mm (30.4 in)
WEIGHT: 4.1 kg (9 lb 1 oz)
RIFLING: 6 grooves, rh
MAGAZINE CAPACITY: 20 or 30 rounds
RATE OF FIRE: 700 rounds/min

IN PRODUCTION:
1986–2002

MARKINGS:
"SG 550" and serial number on left side of receiver.

SAFETY:
Four-position safety catch and fire selector on left side of receiver above pistol grip: rear position for safe; rotate up and forward for single shots, three-round burst, and full automatic fire.

UNLOADING:
Magazine catch in rear of magazine housing. Remove magazine. Pull back cocking handle to eject any round left in chamber. Inspect chamber and feedway through ejection port. Release cocking handle. Press trigger.

SSG 550 Sniper SWITZERLAND

The SSG 550 was developed from the standard SG 550 rifle by fitting it with a heavy hammer-forged barrel and altering the mechanism for semiautomatic fire only. The trigger is a two-stage type, adjustable to the user's personal preference, and the butt is adjustable for length and has an adjustable cheekpiece. The pistol grip is also adjustable for rake and carries a handrest that can be positioned as required. A bipod is fitted, and the telescope can be adjusted to fit naturally to the eye when the user's face is against the cheekpiece. An antireflective screen can be drawn over the top of the rifle, which also prevents air disturbance due to barrel heat interfering with the sight line. Altogether, the sniper's convenience has been considered and catered for in every aspect of this rifle.

SPECIFICATION:

CARTRIDGE:
5.56 x 45 mm

DIMENSIONS:
LENGTH, BUTT EXTENDED: 1130 mm (44.5 in)
LENGTH, BUTT FOLDED: 905 mm (35.6 in)
BARREL: 650 mm (25.6 in)
WEIGHT: 7.3 kg (16 lb 1 oz)
RIFLING: 6 grooves, rh
MAGAZINE CAPACITY: 20 or 30 rounds

IN PRODUCTION:
1995–2002

MARKINGS:
"SSG 550" and serial number on left side of receiver.

SAFETY:
Two-position safety catch on right and left sides of receiver above pistol grip: with thumbpiece up and to rear, weapon is safe; press thumbpiece down and forward to fire.

UNLOADING:
Magazine release is behind magazine housing and in front of trigger guard. Remove magazine. Pull back cocking handle. Open breech and withdraw any round from chamber. Inspect chamber and feedway through ejection port, ensuring both are empty. Release bolt. Press trigger.

Stgw 57

This Swiss service rifle is distantly related to the German G3 and Spanish CETME Model L rifles, insofar as they are all based on the roller-locked delayed-blowback system first designed by Mauser in Germany for the abortive Stgw (Sturmgewehr) 45. Somewhat heavy, it is a superbly accurate and comfortable-to-shoot rifle and is noted for its reliability in harsh climatic conditions. A later version, the SIG 510-4, is chambered for the 7.62 mm cartridge; the two can be best told apart by the Stgw 57's rubber-covered butt, which is virtually straight behind the receiver, while the 510-4 has a wooden butt with a distinct drop.

SPECIFICATION:

CARTRIDGE:
7.5 x 55 mm Swiss Service or 7.62 x 51 mm NATO

DIMENSIONS:
LENGTH O/A: 1016 mm (40 in)
WEIGHT: 4.3 kg (9 lb 6 oz)
BARREL: 505 mm (19.9 in)
RIFLING: 4 grooves, rh
MAGAZINE CAPACITY: 24 rounds
RATE OF FIRE: 600 rounds/min

IN PRODUCTION:
1957–83

MARKINGS:
Serial number on left rear of receiver.

SAFETY:
Combined safety catch and fire selector on left side of receiver above trigger: vertical for safe, slanting forward for single shots, horizontal for automatic fire.

UNLOADING:
Magazine catch in rear of magazine housing. Remove magazine. Pull back cocking handle to eject any round left in chamber. Inspect chamber and feedway through ejection port. Release cocking handle. Press trigger.

Type 65 TAIWAN

This rifle was developed and manufactured by the Taiwanese Hsing Hua arsenal and is broadly based on the M16. The general shape of the receiver is similar to that of the M16, though only prototypes were made with the carrying handle, the production rifle having a flat top. The fore-end is longer than that used with the M16, and a bipod may be fitted, though it is not a standard fitment. A later model of this rifle has a three-round-burst facility in addition to full automatic fire.

SPECIFICATION:

CARTRIDGE:
5.56 x 45 mm M193 or NATO

DIMENSIONS:
LENGTH O/A: 990 mm (39 in)
WEIGHT: 3.2 kg (7 lb)
BARREL: 508 mm (20 in)
RIFLING: 4 grooves, rh
MAGAZINE CAPACITY: 20 or 30 rounds
RATE OF FIRE: 750 rounds/min

IN PRODUCTION:
1976–

MARKINGS:
"5.56m Type 65" on left side of magazine housing.

SAFETY:
Combined safety catch and fire selector on left side of receiver above trigger: pull catch back so pointer is directed to "Safe" for safe; press catch down and forward to vertical for single shots; press catch forward so pointer is to rear against "Auto" for automatic fire.

UNLOADING:
Magazine catch is a push-button on right side of receiver above trigger. Remove magazine. Pull back cocking handle (T-shaped "wings" behind carrying handle) to eject any round remaining in chamber. Inspect chamber and feedway through ejection port. Release cocking handle. Pull trigger.

Type 86 TAIWAN

Following on from the Type 65 assault rifle, the next Taiwanese rifle was the Type 75, little more than a M16-series clone, produced in both assault rifle and carbine forms. The follow-on Type 86 is really a US M16 in a modified package much reduced in size overall and with the barrel shortened. The Type 86 has a telescopic buttstock almost identical to that of the M16/M4 Carbine, but the forward handguard has been reconfigured slightly. A quick-release bipod can be attached, as shown, as can a 40 mm grenade launcher. Ammunition is normally fed from M16-pattern box magazines, although a 100-round C-Mag (also shown) is optional.

SPECIFICATION:

CARTRIDGE:
5.56 x 45 mm

DIMENSIONS:
LENGTH, STOCK EXTENDED: 880 mm (34.7 in)
LENGTH, STOCK RETRACTED: 800 mm (31.5 in)
WEIGHT: 3.2 kg (7 lb)
BARREL: 375 mm (14.8 in)
RIFLING: 6 grooves, rh
MAGAZINE CAPACITY: 20, 30 or 100 rounds
RATE OF FIRE: 600–900 rounds/min

IN PRODUCTION:
1986–

MARKINGS:
"5.56mm Type 86" on left side of magazine housing.

SAFETY:
Combined safety catch and fire selector lever on left side of receiver above trigger: back for safe, upright for single shot, and forward for automatic.

UNLOADING:
Magazine catch is a push-button on right side of receiver. Remove magazine. Pull back T-shaped cocking handle on top rear of receiver to eject any round in chamber. Inspect chamber and feedway and, if clear, release cocking handle and pull trigger.

L85A1/L85A2 Individual Weapon UK

Sometimes known as the SA80, the L85A1 Individual Weapon (IW) has had a somewhat protracted and troublesome service career, mainly due to the transition from development to mass production. It was 1988 before the type was finally accepted for service, even though production commenced during 1985. From 1988, numerous minor modifications were introduced, none of them making much difference to overall reliability, so in 2001 it was decided that a major rebuild was necessary, resulting in the L85A2 (shown). Most of the modifications were internal, the only external change being the comma-shaped cocking handle; on the L85A1, it was a post. The bullpup L85A2 is now a thoroughly efficient and reliable weapon. Sights may be of two types, the optical SUSAT or iron sights on a carrying handle, the latter being intended for non-infantry soldiers. A carbine version of the L22AZ has been ordered for armored combat-vehicle crewmen.

SPECIFICATION:

CARTRIDGE:
5.56 x 45 mm NATO

DIMENSIONS:
LENGTH O/A: 785 mm (30.9 in)
WEIGHT: 3.8 kg (8 lb 6 oz)
BARREL: 518 mm (20.4 in)
RIFLING: 6 grooves, rh
MAGAZINE CAPACITY: 30 rounds
RATE OF FIRE: 700 rounds/min

IN PRODUCTION:
1985–94

MARKINGS:
"RIFLE 5.56MM L85A1" and NATO stock number impressed into right side of handguard.

SAFETY:
Push-through bolt above trigger, pushed from left to right for safe. Fire selector on left side of stock: up for single shots, down for fully automatic.

UNLOADING:
Magazine catch on left side of receiver above magazine housing. Remove magazine. Pull back cocking handle to eject any round remaining in chamber. Inspect chamber and feedway through ejection port. Release cocking handle. Pull trigger.

ArmaLite AR-18 USA/UK

The AR-18 was intended to be the poor man's M16, a simplified weapon capable of being made in countries with limited manufacturing capability. But it was still cheaper to buy M16s than to set up a factory to make AR-18s. ArmaLite sold the rights to Howa Machinery of Japan in the early 1960s, but the Japanese government forbade them to make war weapons, effectively preventing military export sales. Sterling Armaments of England bought the rights in 1974 and began manufacturing, but they found few takers before they went out of business in the 1980s.

SPECIFICATION:

CARTRIDGE:
5.56 x 45 mm M109

DIMENSIONS:
LENGTH, STOCK EXTENDED: 940 mm (37 in)
LENGTH, STOCK FOLDED: 738 mm (29 in)
WEIGHT: 3.2 kg (7 lb)
BARREL: 464 mm (18.3 in)
RIFLING: 6 grooves, rh
MAGAZINE CAPACITY: 20, 30, or 40 rounds
RATE OF FIRE: 800 rounds/min

IN PRODUCTION:
Circa 1966–79

MARKINGS:
"AR 18 ARMALITE" molded into pistol grips. "ARMALITE AR-18 PATENTS PENDING" on left side of magazine housing. Serial number on top rear of receiver, on left of receiver, or on magazine housing. May be found with "MADE BY STERLING ARMAMENTS" on left side of receiver.

SAFETY:
Combined manual safety catch and fire selector switch on left side above pistol grip: turn switch to rear, so pointer points forward, for safe; turn switch to vertical for single shots; turn switch forward, and pointer to rear, for full automatic.

UNLOADING:
Magazine catch on right side of magazine housing. Remove magazine. Pull back cocking handle on right side, inspect chamber through ejection port. Release cocking handle. Pull trigger.

Barrett "Light Fifty" M82A1 USA

One of the first heavy sniping rifles to achieve success, the Barrett has been adopted by many military and police forces as an anti-matériel sniping weapon and also for detonating explosive devices at a safe distance. Originally, there was little danger of confusing the Barrett with anything else, but in the late 1980s a number of competing designs appeared, and the Barrett is no longer quite so individual.

SPECIFICATION:

CARTRIDGE:
12.7 x 99 mm (0.50 Browning)

DIMENSIONS:
LENGTH O/A: 1549 mm (61 in)
WEIGHT: 13.4 kg (25 lb 9 oz)
BARREL: 737 mm (29 in)
RIFLING: 12 grooves, rh
MAGAZINE CAPACITY: 10 rounds
RATE OF FIRE: Semiautomatic only

IN PRODUCTION:
1983–

MARKINGS:
"BARRETT FIREARMS MANUFACTURING INC MURFREESBORO, TN, USA. CAL .50" and serial number on left side of receiver.

SAFETY:
Thumb-operated manual safety on left side of receiver above pistol grip: turn to horizontal position for safe, to vertical position to fire.

UNLOADING:
Magazine catch behind magazine. Remove magazine and empty out any ammunition. Pull back cocking handle, examine chamber through ejection slot. Release cocking handle. Press trigger. Replace empty magazine.

Colt M16A2 USA

The M16A2 is an improved M16A1. It has a heavier barrel and an adjustable rear sight. The US Army–issued version has semiautomatic or three-round-burst fire capability only. Two further M16 models have been manufactured, the M16A3 and M16A4. Both have a length of Picatinny sight-mounting rail over the receiver while the M16A4 has a forestock configured for mounting combat accessories.

SPECIFICATION:

CARTRIDGE:
5.56 x 45 mm NATO

DIMENSIONS:
LENGTH: 1000 mm (39.4 in)
WEIGHT: 5.8 kg (12 lb 12 oz)
BARREL: 510 mm (20 in)
RIFLING: 6 grooves, rh
MAGAZINE CAPACITY: 30 rounds
CYCLIC RATE: 700 rounds/min

IN PRODUCTION:
1991–

MARKINGS:
"COLT M16A2 PROPERTY OF U.S.GOVT CAL 5.56MM" and serial number on left side of magazine housing. "COLT FIREARMS DIVISION COLT INDUSTRIES HARTFORD CONN USA" on left side of receiver. In place of Colt markings large numbers will be found marked "FN MANUFACTURING INC, COLUMBUS SC" on left side of receiver.

SAFETY:
M16-type three-position safety catch and fire-selector switch on left side of receiver above pistol grip: thumb-piece to rear for safe, vertical for single shots, to front for automatic fire.

UNLOADING:
Magazine catch on side of receiver above magazine housing. Remove magazine. Pull back cocking handle until bolt is held by sear. Inspect chamber and feedway through ejection port, ensuring both are empty. Grasp cocking handle, press trigger, and allow bolt to go forward under control.

FN SCAR USA

The FN SCAR (Special Forces Combat Assault Rifle) is produced in two model types: the SCAR-L (Light) in 5.56 mm NATO and the SCAR-H (Heavy) in 7.62 mm NATO, classified as the MK 16 MOD 0 and MK 17 MOD 0 respectively. Of ergonomic design and with many component parts, the SCAR series is intended to reduce training requirements and the maintenance burden. Both variants are designed to be used with the MK 13 MOD 0 Enhanced Grenade Launcher Module fitted to a rail on the lower fore-end. Both models have a side-folding and extendable stock and folding iron sights. Multiple integrated Mil-Std 1913 (Picatinny) rails are fitted to all sides, and the free-floating barrel enhances accuracy.

SPECIFICATION:

CARTRIDGE:
5.56 x 45 mm NATO (SCAR-L); 7.62 x 51 mm NATO (SCAR-H)

DIMENSIONS:
LENGTH O/A: SCAR-L, 851 mm (33.5 in); SCAR-H, 922 mm (36.3 in)
WEIGHT: SCAR-L, 3.2 kg (7 lb); SCAR-H, 3.2 kg (7 lb 2 oz)
BARREL: SCAR-L, 351 mm (13.8 in); SCAR-H, 400 mm (15.8 in)
MAGAZINE CAPACITY: SCAR-L, 30 rounds; SCAR-H, 20 rounds
RATE OF FIRE: 600 rounds/min

IN PRODUCTION:
2007–

MARKINGS:
Manufacturer's logo and serial number on right side of trigger housing.

SAFETY:
Fire-selector lever in front of butt on left-side rear.

UNLOADING:
Ambidextrous magazine release catch on upper rear of magazine housing. Remove magazine, pull working parts to rear, and inspect chamber and magazine well through ejection port. When clear, allow working parts to go forward. Point weapon in safe direction and pull trigger.

M14 Rifle USA

When the US needed a new 7.62 mm rifle to meet NATO standardization requirements, it seemed good sense to give the Garand a few simple tweaks: give it a detachable magazine instead of a clip feed and rebarrel it. The decision to make the rifle automatic caused problems, however. Provision of automatic fire with a cartridge as heavy as the 7.62 mm meant strengthening everything, and the result was a long and bulky weapon that did not meet the original requirement for a light, compact weapon of the assault-rifle class. Most were converted by locking the system at semiautomatic, and with some modifi-cations the weapon was reasonably serviceable. Early models had wooden furniture, were then produced with a glass-fiber handguard, and finally, were constructed with all-synthetic furniture.

SPECIFICATION:

CARTRIDGE:
7.62 x 51 mm NATO

DIMENSIONS:
LENGTH O/A: 1120 mm (44.1 in)
WEIGHT: 5.1 kg (11 lb 4 oz)
BARREL: 559 mm (22 in)
RIFLING: 4 grooves, rh
MAGAZINE CAPACITY: 20 rounds
RATE OF FIRE: 750 rounds/min

IN PRODUCTION:
1957–63

MARKINGS:
"US RIFLE 7.62MM M14," maker's name (e.g. "WINCHESTER," "SPRINGFIELD ARMORY"), and serial number on top rear of receiver.

SAFETY:
Manual safety catch in front of trigger guard: pull back toward trigger for safe; push forward to fire. Fire selection is by a rotary catch in right side of receiver above trigger. Press in and turn to point down for single shots, up for automatic fire.

UNLOADING:
Magazine catch behind magazine housing beneath receiver. Remove magazine. Pull back cocking handle to eject any round remaining in chamber. Inspect chamber and feedway. Release cocking handle. Pull trigger.

Ruger Mini-14 USA

The Mini-14 is based on the same gas piston and rotating-bolt mechanism used by the US M1 and M14 rifles, but the use of modern high-tensile alloy steels has allowed considerable weight and bulk to be saved, making this a light and handy weapon firing a now-common cartridge. Although intended as a hunting rifle, it was adopted by many paramilitary and police forces throughout the world. A militarized version, the K Mini/14-20GB has a bayonet lug, flash suppressor, and heat-resistant glass-fiber handguard and is also available with a folding stock. The AC-556 is also militarized and provided with selective fire, giving automatic fire at about 750 rounds/minute; a folding-stock version is also available. A variant model in 7.62 x 39 mm caliber is known as the Mini Thirty.

SPECIFICATION:

CARTRIDGE:
5.56 x 45 mm M193 or NATO

DIMENSIONS:
LENGTH O/A: 946 mm (37.3 in)
WEIGHT: 2.9 kg (6 lb 6 oz)
BARREL: 470 mm (18.5 in)
RIFLING: 6 grooves, rh
MAGAZINE CAPACITY: 5, 20, or 30 rounds

IN PRODUCTION:
1973–

MARKINGS:
"STURM, RUGER & Co Inc SOUTHPORT CONN USA" on left rear of receiver. Serial number on left side of receiver alongside chamber. "RUGER MINI-14 Cal .223" on rear top of receiver.

SAFETY:
Manual safety catch in front edge of trigger-guard: push back into guard for safe, forward for fire.

UNLOADING:
Magazine catch beneath receiver. Remove magazine. Pull back cocking handle to eject any round left in chamber. Inspect chamber and feedway. Release cocking handle. Pull trigger.

M1 Rifle (Garand) USA

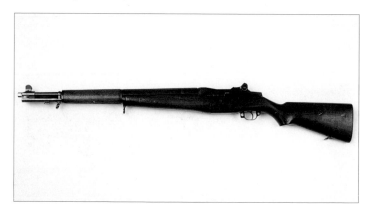

The first self-loading rifle to achieve the status of regulation sidearm for a major army, the Garand served well and was popular for its reliability and power. If it had a defect, it was the clip-loading system, which prevented "topping up" the magazine during a lull in the firing; it was a full clip or nothing. There was also the embarrassment of the empty clip ejecting after the last round and advertising the fact if it fell on a hard surface. But these were minor faults, and with over 6 million rifles made and distributed to many countries after 1945, they will continue to appear for many years to come.

SPECIFICATION:

CARTRIDGE:
7.62 x 63 mm (US 0.30-06)

DIMENSIONS:
LENGTH O/A: 1106 mm (43.6 in)
WEIGHT: 4.3 kg (9 lb 8 oz)
BARREL: 610 mm (24 in)
RIFLING: 4 grooves, rh
MAGAZINE CAPACITY: 8 rounds (en-bloc clip)

IN PRODUCTION:
1936–59

MARKINGS:
"U.S RIFLE .30 M1 SPRINGFIELD ARSENAL" and serial number on upper rear of receiver. Other manufacturer's names are: "WINCHESTER," "INTERNATIONAL HARVESTER," and "HARRINGTON & RICHARDSON." May also be found with "BERETTA" and with Indonesian markings.

SAFETY:
Manual safety catch in front of trigger guard: pull back toward trigger for safe, push forward to fire.

UNLOADING:
Ensure safety catch is forward. Pull back cocking handle to eject any round in chamber, and hold it to rear. Inspect chamber and magazine. If there is ammunition in magazine, grasp rifle with left hand in front of trigger guard and, without releasing cocking handle, reach across action with right thumb and press clip latch on left side of receiver. Clip, with any remaining ammunition, will be ejected from magazine into right hand. Remove clip and ammunition, check chamber and magazine area again, release cocking handle, press trigger.

M1/M2 Carbine USA

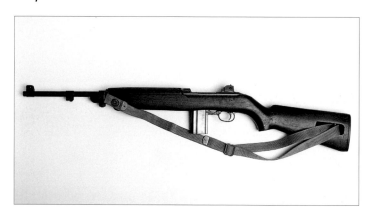

One of the most appealing of weapons, light, handy, and easy to shoot, the M1 Carbine lacks effectiveness at longer rifle ranges as it fires a pistol bullet. It was intended simply to replace the pistol and submachine gun with something having more range, but it found itself being used as a light rifle more often than not. Over 6 million were made in various forms; the M1 was the original semiautomatic; the M1A1 had a folding steel butt, for use by paratroops; the M2 added automatic fire; and the M3 was an M2 with special fittings for mounting infrared sights. After World War II, several companies began making them for the commercial market and continue to do so.

SPECIFICATION:

CARTRIDGE:
7.62 x 33 mm (0.30 Carbine)

DIMENSIONS (M1):
LENGTH O/A: 904 mm (35.6 in)
WEIGHT: 2.4 kg (5 lb 3 oz)
BARREL: 458 mm (18 in)
RIFLING: 4 grooves, rh
MAGAZINE CAPACITY: 15 or 30 rounds
RATE OF FIRE: (M2/M3) 750 rounds/min

IN PRODUCTION:
1942–

MARKINGS:
"U.S.CARBINE CAL .30 M1" across top of chamber. Serial number and maker's mark on rear of receiver. Various maker's marks and initials may be found on receiver and barrel.

SAFETY:
Manual safety catch on right front edge of trigger guard: push down to fire, up for safe. Original models had push-through crossbolt, but this was later changed and almost all were modified. M2 and M3 models have a selector switch on front left side of receiver, alongside chamber: push forward for automatic fire, rearward for single shots.

UNLOADING:
Magazine release push-button on right side of receiver behind magazine. Remove magazine. Pull back cocking handle to eject any round remaining in chamber. Inspect chamber and feedway. Release cocking handle. Pull trigger.

M4 Carbine USA

This is a true carbine, being simply a short-barreled version of the M16A2 rifle with a telescoping stock; it can be thought of as an inter-mediate between the full-sized rifle and the ultrashort Commando. Many mechanical components are interchangeable with those of the M16A2, and the M4 will accept any M16 or NATO STANAG 4179 magazines. As well as being used by US forces, it is in service with the Canadian Army as their C8 carbine and with a number of Central and South American forces. Shown is the M4 version with the Rail Adaptor System (RAS).

SPECIFICATION:

CARTRIDGE:
5.56 x 45 mm NATO

DIMENSIONS:
LENGTH, STOCK EXTENDED: 840 mm (33.1 in)
LENGTH, STOCK FOLDED: 760 mm (29.9 in)
WEIGHT: 2.5 kg (5 lb 10 oz)
BARREL: 368 mm (14.5 in)
RIFLING: 6 grooves, rh
MAGAZINE CAPACITY: 20 or 30 rounds
RATE OF FIRE: 700–1000 rounds/min

IN PRODUCTION:
1984–

MARKINGS:
"COLT FIREARMS DIVISION COLT INDUSTRIES HARTFORD CONN USA" on left side of receiver. "COLT M4 CAL 5.56mm [serial number]" on left side of magazine housing. In place of Colt markings, large numbers will be found marked "FN MANUFACTURING INC, COLUMBUS SC" on left side of receiver.

SAFETY:
Combined safety catch and fire selector on left side of receiver above trigger: pull catch back so pointer is at "Safe" for safe; press catch down and forward to vertical for single shots; press catch forward so pointer is to rear against "Auto" for automatic fire.

UNLOADING:
Magazine catch is push-button on right side of receiver above trigger. Remove magazine. Pull back cocking handle (T-shaped "wings" behind carrying handle) to eject any round remaining in chamber. Inspect chamber and feedway through ejection port. Release cocking handle. Pull trigger.

Zastava M59/66

Yugoslavia adopted the Simonov SKS in the 1950s as their M59 but, after some experience, decided to modify it to suit their requirements. The barrel was lengthened and provided with a 22 mm grenade-launching spigot; the gas cylinder connection to the barrel was altered; and a new foresight unit, including a night sight and a grenade sight, was attached to the extended barrel. The fore-end was shortened, but the hinged sword bayonet was retained. This model was known as the M59/66. They were widely exported before the breakup of Yugoslavia.

SPECIFICATION:

CARTRIDGE:
7.62 x 39 mm Soviet M1943

DIMENSIONS:
LENGTH O/A: 1120 mm (44.1 in)
WEIGHT: 4.1 kg (9 lb 1 oz)
BARREL: 620 mm (24.4 in)
RIFLING: 4 grooves, rh
MAGAZINE CAPACITY: 10 rounds

IN PRODUCTION:
1966–72

MARKINGS:
Factory identifier and serial number on right side of receiver.

SAFETY:
Thumb-operated safety catch at right rear of receiver: forward to fire, back to safe.

UNLOADING:
Magazine catch behind magazine beneath receiver. Remove magazine. Pull back cocking handle to eject any round remaining in chamber. Inspect chamber and feedway. Release cocking handle. Pull trigger.

Zastava M70B1 YUGOSLAVIA

The M70B1 is based on the AK-47 Kalashnikov, which the Yugoslavs obtained from the USSR and adopted as their M64. As with the Simonov, they felt that a few alterations were needed, and the M70 series is the result. While the general layout remains the same, there is a folding grenade sight attached to the gas-piston block that, when raised, shuts off the gas supply to the gas-actuating cylinder. A detachable, muzzle-mounted grenade-launcher spigot was carried in the issue ammunition pouch. Both fixed- and folding-stock models were made, and the M70B1 remained the standard Yugoslavian service rifle until the introduction of the 5.56 mm M21 assault rifle.

SPECIFICATION:

CARTRIDGE:
7.62 x 39 mm Soviet M1943

DIMENSIONS:
LENGTH, STOCK EXTENDED: 900 mm (35.4 in)
LENGTH, STOCK FOLDED: 640 mm (25.2 in)
WEIGHT: 3.7 kg (8 lb 3 oz)
RIFLING: 4 grooves, rh
MAGAZINE CAPACITY: 30 rounds
RATE OF FIRE: 650 rounds/min

IN PRODUCTION:
1974–

MARKINGS:
Model number, factory identifier, and serial number on top of rear end of receiver.

SAFETY:
Combined safety catch and fire-selector lever on right rear side of receiver: press all the way up for safe (obstructs movement of cocking handle and bolt); move down one notch to first mark ("R") for full automatic fire; move to bottom position ("J") for single shots.

UNLOADING:
Magazine catch at rear of magazine housing. Remove magazine. Pull back cocking handle to extract any round which may be in chamber. Inspect the chamber through ejection port. Release cocking handle. Pull trigger.

Zastava M76 YUGOSLAVIA

The M76 is based on the milled-steel action of the AK-47 rifle, but it is chambered for a much more powerful cartridge and has a longer and heavier barrel, as befits a sniping rifle. The sight bracket can be adapted to almost any type of optical or electro-optical sight. The rifle was taken into service by Yugoslavian forces and was also offered for export chambered for the 7.62 x 51 mm NATO cartridge. The long flash-hider also includes an interrupted thread at the rear end of the fitting of a suppressor. A bayonet of the Kalashnikov type is also issued.

SPECIFICATION:

CARTRIDGE:
7.92 x 57 mm Mauser

DIMENSIONS:
LENGTH O/A: 1135 mm (44.7 in)
WEIGHT: 4.2 kg (9 lb 4 oz)
BARREL: 550 mm (21.7 in)
RIFLING: 4 grooves, rh
MAGAZINE CAPACITY: 10 rounds

IN PRODUCTION:
1975–

MARKINGS:
Model number, factory identifier, and serial number on top of rear end of receiver.

SAFETY:
Manual safety catch on right rear side of receiver: press all the way up for safe position (obstructs movement of cocking handle and bolt); move down to lower notch to fire.

UNLOADING:
Magazine catch at rear of magazine housing. Remove magazine. Pull back cocking handle to extract any round which may be in chamber. Inspect chamber through ejection port. Release cocking handle. Pull trigger.

Zastava M80 YUGOSLAVIA

This rifle, along with its folding-stock companion the M80A, was designed to provide the export market with a Kalashnikov-pattern rifle in 5.56 mm caliber. The gas regulator has been redesigned in order to cope with the different energy levels of various makes of 5.56 mm ammunition, and every rifle has a grenade-launching spigot and sight provided which can be attached when required. Marketed for a number of years, it has been replaced by the M21 assault rifle, a further development of the Serbian-produced Kalashnikov series.

SPECIFICATION:

CARTRIDGE:
5.56 x 45 mm M193 or NATO

DIMENSIONS:
LENGTH O/A: 990 mm (39 in)
WEIGHT: 3.5 kg (7 lb 11 oz)
BARREL: 460 mm (18.1 in)
RIFLING: 6 grooves, rh
MAGAZINE CAPACITY: 30 rounds
RATE OF FIRE: 750 rounds/min

IN PRODUCTION:
1985–

MARKINGS:
Model number, factory identifier, and serial number on top of rear end of receiver.

SAFETY:
Combined safety catch and fire-selector lever on right rear side of receiver: press all the way up for safe (obstructs movement of cocking handle and bolt); move down one notch to first mark for full automatic fire; move to bottom position for single shots.

UNLOADING:
Magazine catch at rear of magazine housing. Remove magazine. Pull back cocking handle to extract any round which may be in chamber. Inspect chamber through ejection port. Release cocking handle. Pull trigger.

Shotguns

FN Police BELGIUM

The FN Police shotgun is a manual slide-action, or pump, shotgun primarily intended for employment by law-enforcement organizations but with many alternative military applications due to its rapid manual action involving a rotary locking bolt. For general use, the usual barrel length is 457 mm (18 in) although 356 mm (14 in) barrels are available. The usual tubular magazine capacity is seven rounds plus one in the chamber, while the short-barrel model contains four rounds plus one in the chamber. Various chokes to suit different ammunition can be installed. Iron sights are provided, and there is provision for mounting optical or reflex sights over the receiver. A Tactical Police variant has been developed for the US market, with a telescopic M16-pattern buttstock and pistol grip, a length of Picatinny rail over the receiver, and reducing ports over the muzzle area to reduce recoil.

SPECIFICATION:

CARTRIDGE:
12 gauge

DIMENSIONS:
LENGTH O/A: 984 mm (38.8 in)
WEIGHT: 2.9 kg (6 lb 8 oz)
BARREL: 457 mm (18 in)
MAGAZINE CAPACITY: 7 + 1 rounds

IN PRODUCTION:
1995–

MARKINGS:
"FN HERSTAL [or "FNH USA" in USA] POLICE 12ga" on left side of receiver.

SAFETY:
None

UNLOADING:
With fingers well clear of trigger, manually operate slide action until cartridges cease to be ejected. Pull back bolt and examine chamber and magazine.

Model 68 (Rachot) CZECH REPUBLIC

The Model 68 is a general-purpose machine gun. First seen as the Model 59 in 7.62 x 54 mm Rimmed in Czech Army service, it was rechambered for the 7.62 mm NATO for export sales. Widely sold overseas, the Model 59 uses a special nondisintegrating link; the later Model 68 uses NATO standard M13 disintegrating link. Light and heavy barrels are available, the latter intended for sustained fire off the tripod. Variant models designed for turret mountings are designated Rachot-T. Conversion kits to change the caliber from 7.62 mm Russian to 7.62 mm NATO and to change the Rachot-T back to a ground variant, are available.

SPECIFICATION:

CARTRIDGE:
7.62 x 54 mm Rimmed; 7.62 x 51 mm NATO

DIMENSIONS:
LENGTH O/A: 1115 mm (43.9 in)
WEIGHT: 8.7 kg (19 lb 2 oz)
BARREL: 593 mm (23.3 in)
RIFLING: 4 grooves rh
FEED SYSTEM: Belt
RATE OF FIRE: 7–800 rounds/min

IN PRODUCTION:
1959–

MARKINGS:
Manufacturer's logo on feed-cover with serial number.

SAFETY:
Combination safety and cocking mechanism operated through manipulation of pistol/trigger-group unit.

UNLOADING:
Lift feed-cover. Remove ammunition belt. Withdraw working parts to rear, inspect feedway and chamber area. Point weapon in safe direction and pull trigger, allowing working parts to go forward under control.

Benelli M1 Tactical/Tactical M ITALY

The Benelli M1 series of recoil-operated semiautomatic shotguns were developed specifically for military and police use. Thanks to their aluminum-alloy receivers, they are very light but rugged shotguns, with their actions locked by a rotating bolt. The two models employ the same basic operating system, the M1 Tactical (top) having a rifle-type buttstock, while the Tactical M (bottom) features a pistol grip and a smooth stock outline. The Tactical M also has a different, large-aperture rear sight. There is also a M1 Entry with a shorter 356 mm (14 in) barrel.

SPECIFICATION:

CARTRIDGE:
12 gauge

DIMENSIONS:
LENGTH O/A: 1009 mm (39.7 in)
WEIGHT: 3.2 kg (7 lb)
BARREL: 470 mm (18.5 in)
MAGAZINE CAPACITY: 5 + 1 rounds

IN PRODUCTION:
1995–

MARKINGS:
"BENELLI ARMI – URBINO – ITALY" on right side of receiver above trigger. "*BENELLI ARMI SYSTEM" visible on bolt.

SAFETY:
None.

UNLOADING:
With fingers well clear of trigger, manually operate bolt action until cartridges cease to be ejected. Pull back bolt and examine chamber and magazine.

Benelli M3 Convertible/M3T ITALY

The Benelli M3 Convertible tactical shotgun has two operating modes. When firing conventional-power ammunition, the action is semiautomatic; turning a spring-loaded ring changes the action to manual slide. This slide-action mode is employed when the gun is firing low-power less-than-lethal rounds. While the M3 Convertible has a fixed buttstock, the M3T's is of the "up and over" folding type to reduce carrying length. In addition, the M3T has a higher capacity magazine, holding six or seven rounds plus one in the chamber. By contrast, the M3 Convertible magazine holds five rounds plus one in the chamber.

SPECIFICATION:

CARTRIDGE:
12 gauge

DIMENSIONS (M3 CONVERTIBLE):
LENGTH O/A: 1041 mm (41 in)
WEIGHT: 3.3 kg (7 lb 4 oz)
BARREL: 502 mm (19.8 in)
MAGAZINE CAPACITY: 5 + 1 rounds

IN PRODUCTION:
1994–

MARKINGS:
"BENELLI ARMI – URBINO – ITALY" on right side of receiver above trigger. "12 GA – 3* - FOR 23/4" OR 3" SHELLS. *BENELLI ARMI SYSTEM" visible on bolt on right side of barrel.

SAFETY:
None.

UNLOADING:
With fingers well clear of trigger, manually operate bolt action until cartridges cease to be ejected. Pull back bolt and examine chamber and magazine.

Benelli M4 Super 90 ITALY

Notable for having been selected as the US armed forces Joint Services Combat Shotgun (M1014), the Benelli Super 90 is a militarized version of a commercial semi-automatic shotgun. In its purely military form, the Super 90 has a choice of three buttstocks (rifle, pistol grip, or collapsible), a length of Picatinny rail for mounting optical or reflex (red dot) sights over the receiver, and is generally a robust weapon. The US M1014 (shown bottom) has the collapsible-buttstock configuration; in place of the usual Benelli markings, it displays those for Heckler & Koch but is still marked as made in Italy because Heckler & Koch acted as main contractor for the M1014 program.

SPECIFICATION:

CARTRIDGE:
12 gauge

DIMENSIONS:
LENGTH O/A: 1011 mm (39.8 in)
LENGTH, STOCK RETRACTED: M1014, 886.4 mm (34.9 in)
WEIGHT: 3.8 kg (8 lb 7 oz)
BARREL: 470 mm (18.5 in)
MAGAZINE CAPACITY: 6 + 1 rounds

IN PRODUCTION:
1998–

MARKINGS:
"BENELLI ARMI – URBINO – MADE IN ITALY" on right side of receiver above trigger. "12 GA – 3* - FOR 23/4" OR 3" SHELLS. *BENELLI ARMI SYSTEM" visible on bolt on right side of barrel. "HECKLER & KOCH INC. STERLING. VA. - MADE IN ITALY" on right side of receiver above trigger; "12 GA – 3* - FOR 23/4" OR 3" SHELLS. *BENELLI ARMI SYSTEM" visible on bolt on right side of barrel (USA).

SAFETY:
None.

UNLOADING:
With fingers well clear of trigger, manually operate bolt action until cartridges cease to be ejected. Pull back bolt and examine chamber and magazine.

Franchi Model PA7/PA8E/PA8I ITALY

These three slide- (pump-) action tactical shotguns are all basically the same weapon, differing only in the form of the buttstock. The Model PA7, the base model, has a black varnished wooden stock of the rifle type; the Model PA8E has a hard plastic pistol grip and a simpler buttstock outline; while the Model PA8I (shown) has an "up and over" folding metal stock. The usual magazine capacity is five rounds, although this can be reduced to three for commercial-sales purposes by inserting a plug into the tubular magazine. One option is an extended magazine holding seven rounds. Barrels, capable of accommodating a wide array of muzzle chokes held in position by a sleeve, may be 610 mm (24 in) or 475 mm (18.7) in long.

SPECIFICATION:

CARTRIDGE:
12 gauge

DIMENSIONS:
LENGTH O/A: 1020 mm (40.2 in)
WEIGHT: 3.1 kg (6 lb 14 oz)
BARREL: 610 mm (24 in) or 475 mm (18.7 in)
MAGAZINE CAPACITY: 5 + 1 rounds

IN PRODUCTION:
1990–

MARKINGS:
"FRANCHI SPA – BRESCIA MADE IN ITALY" on right side of receiver with serial number below, both just above trigger.

SAFETY:
None.

UNLOADING:
With fingers well clear of trigger, manually operate slide action until cartridges cease to be ejected. Pull back bolt and examine chamber and magazine.

Franchi Special-Purpose Automatic Shotgun 12 ITALY

The Franchi Special-Purpose Automatic Shotgun 12 (SPAS 12) is one of the most widely used law-enforcement shotguns and has found many applications in many hands. Depending on the selected position of the forward slide, the gun can operate in either semiautomatic or slide (pump) mode to accommodate a variety of ammunition. Construction is extremely rugged, and much use is made of tough (usually gray) high-impact molded polymers and hard-wearing finishes. One odd feature of this gun is the optional folding buttstock which can have a folding insert that wraps around the wrist to allow the gun to be fired one-handed from car windows—with questionable accuracy. The SPAS 12 may also have a solid plastic buttstock.

SPECIFICATION:

CARTRIDGE:
12 gauge

DIMENSIONS:
LENGTH, STOCK EXTENDED: 980 mm (38.6 in)
LENGTH, STOCK FOLDED: 787 mm (31 in)
WEIGHT: 4.1 kg (8 lb 15 oz)
BARREL: 550mm (21.7 in)
MAGAZINE CAPACITY: 3 or 6 + 1 rounds

IN PRODUCTION:
1982–

MARKINGS:
"FRANCHI SPA – BRESCIA MADE IN ITALY" on right side of receiver with serial number below, both just above trigger. Markings may be engraved or etched.

SAFETY:
Safety catch located on left side of te receiver over trigger.

UNLOADING:
With fingers well clear of trigger, manually operate slide action until cartridges cease to be ejected. Pull back bolt and examine chamber and magazine.

Franchi Special-Purpose Automatic Shotgun 15 ITALY

The Franchi Special-Purpose Automatic Shotgun 15 (SPAS 15) is a heavy-duty tactical shotgun that has been procured by the Italian Army, among others. It can operate in two modes: in the usual Auto mode, it is gas operated, with the rotating bolt moving on a carrier; when using low-power less-than-lethal or riot-control cartridges, the forestock is locked in the forward position. Pressing a button under the fore-stock and pulling it slightly to the rear converts the gun's action to a manually operated slide (pump). The cocking handle is over the receiver, under a carrying handle that also carriers the iron sights. Ammunition is fed from a box magazine holding three or six rounds, and two separate safeties are provided. The bolt stays open when the last round is fired, and inserting a fresh magazine will automatically reload the chamber, considerably increasing the speed of firing in an emergency.

SPECIFICATION:

CARTRIDGE:
12 gauge

DIMENSIONS:
LENGTH O/A: 1000 mm (39.4 in)
WEIGHT: 4.1 kg (8 lb 15 oz)
BARREL: 450 mm (17.7 in)
MAGAZINE CAPACITY: 3 or 6 + 1 rounds

IN PRODUCTION:
1985–

MARKINGS:
"FRANCHI SPA – BRESCIA MADE IN ITALY" on right side of receiver with serial number below, both just above trigger. Markings may be engraved or etched.

SAFETY:
Safety catch on left side of receiver over trigger. Grip safety must be firmly gripped to allow gun to be fired.

UNLOADING:
Remove magazine using catch just in front of trigger group. Pull back bolt handle over receiver to eject any round in chamber. Examine chamber to ensure it is empty. Note: Replacing magazine, loaded or empty, will cause bolt assembly to close.

KS-23/KS-23M Special Carbine RUSSIA

Although categorized as a Special
Carbine the slide- (pump-) action
KS-23 and its military counterpart,
the KS-23M, is a shotgun intended
for the most difficult of heavy
targets. It has a caliber that approx-
imates to 4 gauge and can fire
cartridges loaded with heavy
buckshot, baton rounds, or a special
solid slug. The KS-23 visually
resembles a conventional shotgun,
although everything is scaled up and
a multilug locking bolt is necessary.
The militarized KS-23M (shown) is
very much a special-forces weapon
as it lacks a solid buttstock, sometimes featuring a removable skeleton
buttstock secured to the pistol grip.
Most examples seen lack the stock
altogether, having just the pistol
grip. The KS-23M can have a
grenade-launcher cup over the
muzzle, while a similar attachment
can project a scaling cable and
grapnel. The tubular magazine holds
three rounds. The KS-23 and
KS-23M are still rare in the West,
and for this reason it has not been
possible to describe the markings.

SPECIFICATION:

CARTRIDGE:
4 gauge

DIMENSIONS:
LENGTH O/A: 650 mm (25.6 in)
WEIGHT: 3.5 kg (7 lb 12 oz)
BARREL: 350mm (13.8 in)
MAGAZINE CAPACITY: 3 rounds

IN PRODUCTION:
1998(?)–

SAFETY:
None apparent.

MARKINGS:
Not yet known.

UNLOADING:
With fingers well clear of trigger, manually operate
slide action until cartridges cease to be ejected. Pull
back bolt and examine chamber and magazine.

SAIGA-410 RUSSIA

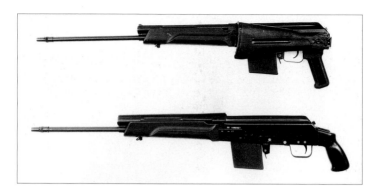

The 0.410 shotgun cartridge is normally considered a hunting cartridge, but within Eastern Europe and Russia it is often employed for security purposes. When firing slugs, the effective range is up to 100 m (328.1 ft). By combining the basic Kalashnikov gas operation with the 0.410 cartridge, the Russian IZMASH Joint Stock Company devised the semiautomatic SAIGA-410 for security and commercial sales. Three models may be encountered: SAIGA-410 Standard, with a 518 mm (20.4 in) barrel; SAIGA-410C Medium, with a 570 mm (22.44 in) barrel; and SAIGA-410K Short, with a 330 mm (13 in) barrel. The SAIGA-410 Standard has a fixed buttstock, the SAIGA-410C Medium can have a retractable stock or just a pistol grip (as shown), and the SAIGA-410K Short has a folding stock and a pistol grip. On the latter, a safety blocks the trigger when the buttstock is folded.

SPECIFICATION:

CARTRIDGE:
0.410 70 mm (2.76 in) or 78 mm (3.07 in) Magnum

DIMENSIONS:
LENGTH, STOCK EXTENDED: 1080 mm (42.5 in)
LENGTH, STOCK FOLDED: 835 mm (32.9 in)
WEIGHT: 3.4 kg (7 lb 8 oz)
BARREL: 570 mm (22.4 in)
MAGAZINE CAPACITY: 4 or 10 rounds

IN PRODUCTION:
1995–

MARKINGS:
In Cyrillic, with "410" added on right of receiver above magazine well. Serial number on left of receiver and bolt assembly.

SAFETY:
Two-position lever switch on right side above trigger group: up for safe, down to fire. On SAIGA-410K, safety blocks trigger when buttstock is folded.

UNLOADING:
Magazine catch just behind magazine well and in front of trigger group. Depress catch to remove magazine and draw back bolt handle on right of receiver to extract any round still in chamber. Examine chamber to ensure it is empty. Replace empty magazine.

Neostead

The Neostead was designed as an uncompromising slide- (pump-) action combat shotgun. It is much shorter, more compact, and more streamlined than any other shotgun. The all-in-line Neostead has an unusual action, in that the slide is pushed forward rather than rearward for loading. Two magazine tubes over and each side of the barrel each contain six cartridges, so that feeding can be from either side, or alternate between tubes, according to the position of a selector switch. A cartridge in the chamber therefore means that 13 rounds are ready to fire. The magazine-selector switch, the safety catch, and a slide lock can be operated by either hand. Spent cases are ejected downwards. High-strength polymers are used for the smooth outlines. Loading and unloading is easy and rapid, as each magazine tube is readily accessible once the weapon has been hinged open in the usual manner. Slots over the magazine tubes allow the user to see how many cartridges remain after firing.

SPECIFICATION:

CARTRIDGE:
12 gauge

DIMENSIONS:
LENGTH O/A: 690 mm (27.1 in)
WEIGHT: 3.9 kg (8 lb 10 oz)
BARREL: 570 mm (22.4 in)
MAGAZINE CAPACITY: 12 + 1 rounds

IN PRODUCTION:
2001–

MARKINGS:
No markings on early examples. "TRUVELO MANUFACTURERS" logo molded somewhere on body.

SAFETY:
Main safety catch is ambidextrous and located just behind trigger. Slide lock button located under slide.

UNLOADING:
Press slide lock under slide and push slide forward to raise magazine and expose magazine interiors. Cartridges can then be removed manually or shaken free. Pull back slide to maximum extent to eject any cartridge in chamber and eject it downwards through ejection slot under buttstock.

The Protecta 12-gauge compact shotgun was essentially an oversize double-action revolver, as its rotary magazine is really 12 chambers indexed by a firm pull on the trigger. Rounds are introduced into the rotary-chamber assembly through a loading guide on the right side of the receiver, and spent cases are automatically ejected. Once loaded, the gun is cocked by pulling back the cocking handle on the right-hand side of the shrouded barrel. The Protecta is well provided with safeties, as it was originally developed as a home-protection weapon. It has a hammer lock that eliminates "trigger snagging" as the user releases the manual safety catch, and the gun will not fire unless the trigger is deliberately pulled. An "up and over" folding buttstock is provided, something lacking on the similar Protecta Bulldog with its much shorter 171 mm (6.73 in) barrel.

SPECIFICATION:

CARTRIDGE:
12 gauge

DIMENSIONS:
LENGTH, STOCK EXTENDED: 800 mm (31.5 in)
LENGTH, STOCK FOLDED: 500 mm (19.7 in)
WEIGHT: 4.2 kg (9 lb 4 oz)
BARREL: 300mm (11.8 in)
MAGAZINE CAPACITY: 12 rounds

IN PRODUCTION:
Circa 1980–1990

MARKINGS:
"ASERMA MANUFACTURING PROTECTA" on left side of receiver above trigger.

SAFETY:
Safety catch above trigger on left of receiver.

UNLOADING:
Apply safety catch. Pull back cocking handle to right of barrel to empty each chamber.

C-MORE Lightweight Shotgun System USA

While the rifle/clip-on shotgun combination may be effective, it is cumbersome to handle, so in the C-MORE Lightweight Shotgun System (LSS), the shotgun component has been designed to be much simpler and lighter. As well as being mounted under an M16-series rifle (as above), the LSS can also be configured as a light and handy stand-alone weapon following the installation of standard components such as an M16-series telescopic buttstock and trigger group. In either form, the LSS employs a bolt action and a box magazine holding two or three rounds, although larger magazines are available. Due to the short barrel length, a sizeable flash suppressor is necessary.

The C-MORE LSS is only one example of this special category of shotgun. Colt, among others, produces a similar system.

SPECIFICATION:

CARTRIDGE:
12 gauge

DIMENSIONS:
LENGTH O/A: 559 mm (22 in)
WEIGHT: 1.4 kg (3 lb)
BARREL: Circa 374 mm (9.5 in)
MAGAZINE CAPACITY: 2 or 3 rounds

IN PRODUCTION:
2002–

MARKINGS:
On left side of receiver. Manufacturer may vary. Also marked "MANASSAS VA" on left side of magazine well. Serial number below.

SAFETY:
Safety catch just above LSS trigger on both sides. Down for safe, up to fire.

UNLOADING:
Magazine catch is behind magazine well, accessible from either side. Press catch forward to release magazine. Pull back bolt on left side of receiver to eject any round in chamber. Examine chamber to ensure it is empty. Replace empty magazine, then grasp bolt. Pull trigger to close bolt under manual control.

Ceiner Ultimate USA

The Ceiner Ultimate is one example of the over/under concept of combining a conventional military-pattern rifle with a shotgun capability, the latter usually firing less-than-lethal loads in riot or similar situations, reserving the rifle for when it is really needed. The shotgun component also forms a valuable means of close-range defense. The Ceiner Ultimate combination is designed for use with M16-series rifles: it is essentially the receiver and barrel of a Remington Model 870P shotgun secured under the M16 barrel with a bayonet lug under the muzzle. The shotgun component is loaded and fired in exactly the same way as the Remington from which it was taken. Numerous combinations have been produced; as so many variants are likely to be found, this entry is only a basic guide to all the others.

SPECIFICATION:

CARTRIDGE:
12 gauge

DIMENSIONS:
Highly variable.

IN PRODUCTION:
1989–

MARKINGS:
As on original guns used in combination.

SAFETY:
None.

UNLOADING:
Shotgun component: With fingers well clear of trigger, manually operate slide action until cartridges cease to be ejected. Pull back bolt and examine chamber and magazine. Rifle component: According to type.

Mossberg M9200A1 USA

The Mossberg M9200A1 is a gas-operated semiautomatic shotgun with a unique operating mechanism that has proved to be so successful that it was adopted for use by US Special Forces in drug-interdiction operations in Central America. Hence its widely adopted name "Jungle Gun." The M9200A1 is a militarized version of a commercial model (the M9200), with the mechanism modified to allow the use of a variety of cartridges, from the heaviest loads down to non-lethal loads, all without having to adjust the mechanism. The M9200A1 may be encountered with fixed or folding buttstocks; some have just a pistol grip and no stock at all.

SPECIFICATION:

CARTRIDGE:
12 gauge

DIMENSIONS:
LENGTH O/A: 1000 mm (33.4 in)
WEIGHT: 3.1 kg (6 lb 13 oz)
BARREL: 470 mm (18.5 in)
MAGAZINE CAPACITY: 5 + 1 rounds

IN PRODUCTION:
1982–2002

MARKINGS:
"O F MOSSBERG & SONS – NORTH HAVEN - CONN" on either side of receiver with serial number below, both just above trigger.

SAFETY:
None.

UNLOADING:
With fingers well clear of trigger, manually operate slide action until cartridges cease to be ejected. Pull back bolt and examine chamber and magazine.

Remington Model 870P USA

The Remington Model 870P is probably the most prolific and widely used of all US shotguns, having been in constant production since the early 1950s to meet demand from both sporting and law-enforcement fraternities. Due to the huge numbers manufactured, the Model 1870P can be encountered in numerous shapes and barrel lengths, as the basic slide action has proved to be highly adaptable and versatile. Even bayonet mounts may be encountered. The slide (pump) action is entirely conventional but very well made and reliable. Many different buttstocks and pistol grips have been manufactured over the years. Attempts have been made to introduce box magazines, but to little avail. The dimensions given here should be regarded as typical but do not reflect the full range of weapons manufactured under this model name. Many commercial shotguns from around the world are direct copies of the Model 870P.

SPECIFICATION:

CARTRIDGE:
12 gauge

DIMENSIONS:
LENGTH O/A: 972 mm (38.3 in)
WEIGHT: 3.6 kg (7 lb 15 oz)
BARREL: 457 mm (18 in)
MAGAZINE CAPACITY: 5 + 1 up to 8 + 1 rounds

IN PRODUCTION:
1950–

MARKINGS:
"REMINGTON ARMS COMPANY – MADISON – NC" on either side of receiver with serial number below, both just above trigger. Numerous variations may be found, some involving military markings.

SAFETY:
None

UNLOADING:
With fingers well clear of trigger, manually operate slide action until cartridges cease to be ejected. Pull back bolt and examine chamber and magazine.

Winchester Model 1300 Defender   USA

The Winchester Model 1300
Defender was based on the highly
successful Model 1200 riot gun that
had its origins as far back as World
War I. Due to the wide array of
potential customers for this gun, it
may be seen in many forms and
with different barrel lengths, with
magazine capacities to match. It may
also be encountered as a 20-gauge
shotgun, reflecting the need for a
less-stressful gun for use by lighter-
stature users, including women. The
conventional slide action dates back
to a John Browning design first
introduced during the 1890s. Many
examples in Europe will be found
with Fabrique Nationale (FN) marks
as they have been made in Belgium
under license.

SPECIFICATION:

CARTRIDGE:
12 or 20 gauge

DIMENSIONS:
LENGTH O/A: 1003 mm (39.5 in)
WEIGHT: 3.3 kg (7 lb 4 oz)
BARREL: 457 mm (18 in); many other barrel lengths
produced
MAGAZINE CAPACITY: 4 + 1 rounds up to 7 + 1
rounds

IN PRODUCTION:
1975–

MARKINGS:
"WINCHESTER ARMS – NEW HAVEN – CONN" on
either side of receiver with serial number below,
both usually just above trigger. Numerous other
locations and variations exist.

SAFETY:
None.

UNLOADING:
With fingers well clear of trigger, manually operate
slide action until cartridges cease to be ejected. Pull
back bolt and examine chamber and magazine.

Machine
Guns

Steyr AUG/HB AUSTRIA

This is basically the Steyr Mannlicher AUG automatic rifle but fitted with a heavy barrel and a bipod to act in the light-automatic role. The barrel is supplied in either 178 mm, 228 mm, or 305 mm pitch of rifling, and a muzzle attachment acts as a flash hider and reduces recoil and muzzle climb during automatic firing. There are two different versions, the HBAR and HBAR/T: the former has the carrying handle with built-in optical sight as on the AUG rifle; the latter has a mounting bar on which any sighting telescope or night-vision sight can be fitted. Both the HBAR and the HBAR/T can, if required, be further modified to fire from an open bolt; a new hammer assembly is inserted into the butt and a new cocking piece is fitted to the bolt assembly. This modification can be made retrospectively to weapons already issued. Changing to open-bolt firing does not change any of the firing characteristics.

362

SPECIFICATION:

CARTRIDGE:
5.56 x 45 mm NATO or M193

DIMENSIONS:
LENGTH O/A: 900 mm (35.4 in)
WEIGHT: 4.9 kg (10 lb 12 oz)
BARREL: 621 mm (24.5 in),
RIFLING: 6 grooves, rh
MAGAZINE CAPACITY: 30 or 42 rounds
RATE OF FIRE: 680 rounds/min

IN PRODUCTION:
1980–

MARKINGS:
"STEYR-DAIMLER-PUCH AG AUSTRIA" or "STEYR-MANNLICHER GmbH AUSTRIA" and "AUG/HB" molded into left rear of buttstock. Serial number on right side of barrel.

SAFETY:
Push-through crossbolt safety catch above trigger: push to right for safe, to left to fire. Selecting of single shots or automatic fire is done by trigger. Light pull for single shot, heavier pull for automatic fire.

UNLOADING:
Magazine release catch is behind magazine, under butt. Remove magazine. Pull back cocking handle to eject any round in chamber. Inspect chamber, release cocking handle. Pull trigger.

FN BAR Type D   BELGIUM

This is the Browning Automatic Rifle as improved by Fabrique Nationale of Belgium. As with most of Browning's designs, FN held a license to manufacture and modify it as they saw fit; in line with European thought of the 1920s, they soon did so, fitting a quick-change barrel, adding a pistol grip, making the dismantling system easier, and redesigning the gas regulator. The resulting weapon was adopted by Belgium, Poland, Egypt, and various other countries in the pre-1939 production period in 6.5 mm Swedish Mauser, 7 mm Spanish Mauser, 7.5 mm Belgian Mauser, or 7.92 x 57 mm Mauser caliber.

SPECIFICATION:

CARTRIDGE:
Various.

DIMENSIONS:
LENGTH O/A: 1145 mm (45 in)
WEIGHT: 9.2 kg (20 lb 5 oz)
BARREL: 500 mm (19.7 in)
RIFLING: 4 grooves, rh
FEED SYSTEM: 20-round magazine
RATE OF FIRE: 450 or 650 rounds/min

IN PRODUCTION:
1923–39 and 1945–67

MARKINGS:
FN monogram, "BROWNING PATENTED [year]," and serial number on top of receiver above magazine. "FABRIQUE NATIONALE D'ARMES DE GUERRE HERSTAL-BELGIQUE" on left above magazine.

SAFETY:
Combined safety catch and rate regulator on left side above trigger. Set to 'S' for safe, to 'F' for slow-rate automatic fire, and to 'M' for fast-rate automatic fire.

UNLOADING:
Magazine release below trigger guard. Remove magazine. Pull back cocking handle to eject any round remaining in chamber. Inspect chamber and feedway. Release cocking handle. Pull trigger.

FN MAG BELGIUM

This was the Belgian entry into the general-purpose machine-gun stakes, and it became extremely popular, being adopted by at least 80 countries and license-made in the USA, the UK, Argentina, Egypt, India, and Singapore. Well-made and reliable, it uses a similar gas system to that of the Browning Automatic Rifle, but inverted so that the bolt locks into the bottom of the receiver. This allows the top of the bolt to carry a lug that drives the feed system, which is adapted from that of the German MG42. There are a number of minor variations of the MAG available, suited to firing from vehicles or helicopters.

SPECIFICATION:

CARTRIDGE:
7.62 x 51 mm NATO

DIMENSIONS:
LENGTH O/A: 1250 mm (49.2 in)
WEIGHT: 10.2 kg (22 lb 6 oz)
BARREL: 546 mm (21.5 in)
RIFLING: 4 grooves, rh
FEED SYSTEM: belt
RATE OF FIRE: 850 rounds/min

IN PRODUCTION:
1955–to date

MARKINGS:
"Fabrique Nationale d'Armes de Guerre Herstal Belgium" on right side of receiver. Weapons produced by other countries will have their own markings: e.g., "L7A2" (UK).

SAFETY:
Safety catch is push-button above trigger. Push from left side to right to make safe, from right side to left to fire.

UNLOADING:
Press cover catch in front of rear sight and open cover. Lift out belt if present, inspect feedway, close cover. Pull cocking handle back to eject any round in chamber. While holding handle back, press trigger then ease handle forward.

FN Minimi BELGIUM

The Minimi was designed to extract the utmost performance from the 5.56 mm cartridge and has acquired a reputation for reliability. It is gas operated, using a simple rotating-bolt system, but is unusual in being able to fire from an M16-type magazine or a belt without any modification having to be made. A special cover plate closes the belt aperture when a magazine is loaded, or closes the magazine aperture when a belt is in place, so that there is no danger of trying to double-feed. There is a light, short-barreled paratroop version with a collapsible butt, and a slightly modified version of the standard model is produced for the US Army as the M249 machine gun. The Minimi is also used by the British Army.

SPECIFICATION:

CARTRIDGE:
5.56 x 45 mm NATO

DIMENSIONS:
LENGTH O/A: 1040 mm (41 in)
WEIGHT: 6.9 kg (15 lb 2 oz)
BARREL: 466 mm (18.4 in)
RIFLING: 6 grooves, rh
FEED SYSTEM: 30-round magazine or 200-round belt
RATE OF FIRE: 700–1000 rounds/min

IN PRODUCTION:
1982–

MARKINGS:
"FN MINIMI 5.56" on left side of receiver.

SAFETY:
Push-through safety catch on left side of receiver: push from right to left to fire, from left to right for safe.

UNLOADING:
Press in two spring catches at top rear of receiver and lift cover. Remove belt or magazine. Pull back cocking handle. Examine chamber and feedway. Release cocking handle. Press trigger.

Type 77 CHINA

This first appeared in the late 1980s and was designed primarily for air-defense purposes, though it is also capable of operating as a ground gun. It uses a direct-gas system, which is most unusual for a weapon of this caliber; a gas tube runs from the barrel take-off and regulator at the front of the receiver, and delivering the gas directly to the lower portion of the bolt carrier. The breech lock is a modified form of the Kjellman flap: the two flaps, operated by the bolt carrier, move outwards and lock into recesses in the receiver walls. The weapon is fed by belt, from a box carried on the left side. An optical antiaircraft sight is standard, and there is also a somewhat complex tripod air-defense mount.

SPECIFICATION:

CARTRIDGE:
12.7 x 107 mm Soviet

DIMENSIONS:
LENGTH: 2150 mm (84.7 in)
WEIGHT: 56.1 kg (123 lb 11 oz) with tripod
BARREL: 1016 mm (40 in)
RIFLING: 8 grooves, rh
MAGAZINE: 60-round metal belt
CYCLIC RATE: 700 rounds/min
MUZZLE VELOCITY: 800 m/sec (2625 ft/sec)

IN PRODUCTION:
1980–

MARKINGS:
Unknown.

SAFETY:
Unknown.

UNLOADING:
Unknown.

Model 52/57/59/68 CZECH REPUBLIC

This machine gun can be found in many forms. The original Model 52 fired a Czech 7.62 x 45 mm cartridge, but this changed to the Soviet 7.62 x 39 mm round with the Model 52/57. The Model 59 introduced the Soviet/Russian 7.62 x 54 Rimmed cartridge and remained in production until the appearance of the much-modified Model 68. The Model 68 faded from production during the 1980s, only to be relaunched as the Model 68 Rachot in 2000, this time firing either 7.62 x 54 R or 7.62 x 51 mm NATO, according to customer choice. The Model 68, shown, is a true general-purpose machine gun, capable of using box magazines or a belt feed, and may be bipod or tripod mounted. Quick-change barrels are provided for both roles, the light-machine-gun barrel being shorter and lighter.

SPECIFICATION:

CARTRIDGE:
7.62 x 45 mm Czech; 7.62 x 39 mm Soviet; 7.62 x 54 R Soviet; 7.62 x 51 mm NATO

DIMENSIONS:
LENGTH O/A: 1041 mm (41 in)
WEIGHT: 8 kg (17 lb 9 oz)
BARREL: 686 mm (27 in)
RIFLING: 4 grooves, rh
FEED SYSTEM: 25-round box or 100-round belt
RATE OF FIRE: 900 rounds/min (magazine) or 1150 rounds/min (belt)

IN PRODUCTION:
1952–85 and 2000–

MARKINGS:
Serial number on top behind magazine housing, with "egf" or "tgf" factory mark.

SAFETY:
Manual safety catch above pistol grip on left side: press up for safe, down to fire. Fire selection done by trigger. Press upper portion ("1") for single shots, lower portion ("D") for automatic fire.

UNLOADING:
Magazine catch in rear of magazine housing. Press in and remove magazine, if weapon is being magazine fed; if it is being belt fed, press in so magazine feed cover swings open, then lift side feed cover lever (on right side, alongside magazine housing) up and forward until side feed cover opens. Lift and remove belt if one is present. Inspect feedways to ensure no ammunition remains, close all covers. Grasp pistol grip, press push button in left side of grip and allow grip to run forward under control. Then push safety catch up to lock weapon.

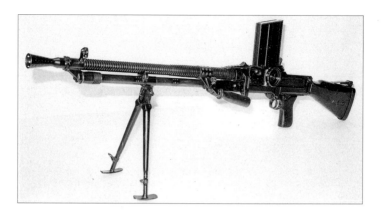

The vz26 ("vz" is short for "vzor," meaning "model") was designed by the Zbrojovka Brno (Brno Arms Factory) in Czechoslovakia in the early 1920s. It was an immediate success and was adopted by over 25 countries around the world. The design was slightly modified to make the ZGB33, suited to the British 0.303 cartridge, and this, in turn, became the famous Bren light machine gun. The German Army used the vz26, so that the same gun was being used on both sides in World War II. Brno continued to offer the gun in their catalogues after 1946, but none were ever made after the war. The vz26 can be distinguished from the Bren or Vickers-Berthier by the finned barrel and by the long gas cylinder, extending almost to the muzzle, beneath the barrel.

SPECIFICATION:

CARTRIDGE:
7.92 x 57 mm Mauser and others

DIMENSIONS:
LENGTH O/A: 1161 mm (45.7 in)
WEIGHT: 9.6 kg (21 lb 3 oz)
BARREL: 672 mm (26.5 in)
RIFLING: 4 grooves, rh
FEED SYSTEM: 30-round box magazine
RATE OF FIRE: 500 rounds/min

IN PRODUCTION:
1928–45

MARKINGS:
"VZ 26" and serial number on top of rear receiver. "BRNO" and factory marks on left side of receiver. "LEHKY KULOMET ZB VZ 26" on right side of receiver.

SAFETY:
Combined safety catch and fire selector on right side above trigger. Turn forward for automatic fire, to middle for safe, rearward for single shots.

UNLOADING:
Magazine catch behind magazine. Remove magazine. Pull back cocking handle. Inspect chamber and feedway through magazine opening. Release cocking handle. Pull trigger.

The vz37 was another Zbrojovka Brno product from Czechoslovakia, intended as a heavy-support accompaniment to the vz26. It was belt fed and could be adjusted to two rates of fire. An odd feature, repeated in some other Czech designs, is the use of the pistol grip and trigger unit as the cocking handle. To cock the gun, push the pistol grip forward until it engages with the bolt system, then pull back. Another oddity is that the gun is recoil operated, and the cartridge is fired while the barrel and bolt are still moving forwards on the return stroke; this means that the recoil force must first stop the moving parts before driving them back, and this additional load soaks up much of the recoil energy. The gun was widely adopted in Europe in 1938/9 and was licensed by the British, who used it as the Besa gun on armored vehicles.

SPECIFICATION:

CARTRIDGE:
7.92 x 57 mm Mauser

DIMENSIONS:
LENGTH O/A: 1104 mm (43.5 in)
WEIGHT: 18.6 kg (41 lb)
BARREL: 635 mm (25 in)
RIFLING: 4 grooves, rh
FEED SYSTEM: 100-round belt
RATE OF FIRE: 500 or 700 rounds/min

IN PRODUCTION:
1937–45

MARKINGS:
"VZ37" and serial number on top rear of receiver. "BRNO" on left side of receiver.

SAFETY:
Combined safety catch and fire selector on right side of receiver behind grips: central position is safe, turn left for single shots, turn right for automatic fire. Rate-of-fire selector on left side of receiver just in front of grip. Turn up and forward for slow rate, down and back for fast rate.

UNLOADING:
Set safety catch to safe. Pull out cover pin at right rear corner of receiver, press and hold back cover catch on left side of cover, and lift cover open as far as it will go. Inspect to see that no rounds remain in feedway. Close cover, pressing cover catch until it closes and then inserting pin. Hold grips and press up trigger-mechanism catch at rear bottom of receiver. Ease grips, bolt and trigger unit forward. Pull out on grips and swing them up against receiver.

Madsen DENMARK

It has been said that the remarkable thing about the Madsen is not that it works well, but that it works at all. The mechanism is practically a mechanized version of the Martini breech block, swinging up and down by the action of a cam driven by the barrel recoil. Since there is no bolt to push the cartridge into the chamber, it has a separate rammer. The cartridge actually travels in a curve during loading, which is theoretically almost impossible. However, it was certainly the first practical light machine gun, pioneering the overhead magazine among other things. It was adopted by the Danish Marines in the 1890s and first saw action with Russia in the Russo-Japanese War in 1904. After that, the same model, with only very minor modifications, stayed in production for 50 years. It was used all over the world in tanks and aircraft, as well as on the ground, yet it never became the official weapon of any major army.

SPECIFICATION:

CARTRIDGE:
Various, from 6.5 to 8 mm

DIMENSIONS:
LENGTH O/A: 1143 mm (45 in)
WEIGHT: 9.1 kg (20 lb)
BARREL: 584 mm (23 in)
RIFLING: 4 grooves, rh
FEED SYSTEM: 25-, 30- or 40-round box magazine
RATE OF FIRE: 450 rounds/min

IN PRODUCTION:
1897–1955

MARKINGS:
"Madsen Model [year]" and serial number on right side of receiver.

SAFETY:
Safety catch on left above trigger: move up for safe when gun is cocked.

UNLOADING:
Press in catch behind magazine and remove magazine. Pull back operating handle, inspect chamber, and release. Pull trigger.

AAT-F1 FRANCE

Known variously as the AAT-52, MAS-52, or F1, this is the standard French Army general-purpose machine gun. Operation is by delayed blowback, using a two-piece bolt similar to that of the FA-MAS rifle, in which the light forward part of the bolt has to overcome the inertia of the heavy rear section before the breech can be opened. The chamber is fluted so as to float the case on a layer of gas to ease extraction, but the result is somewhat on the borders of absolute safety, and the extraction is violent. Nevertheless, the gun is reliable and efficient and has been put into service by several former French colonies. The butt telescopes into the receiver, and, surprisingly, there is no handguard, making it difficult to adjust the gun's position when the barrel is hot.

SPECIFICATION:

CARTRIDGE:
7.5 x 54 French Service; 7.62 x 51 mm NATO

DIMENSIONS:
LENGTH O/A: 990 mm (38.9 in)
WEIGHT: 9.9 kg (21 lb 13 oz)
BARREL: 488 mm (19.2 in)
RIFLING: 4 grooves, rh
FEED SYSTEM: 50-round belt
RATE OF FIRE: 700 rounds/min

IN PRODUCTION:
1952–78

MARKINGS:
"AA F1 MAT [AAT-52]" and serial number on left side of receiver.

SAFETY:
Cross-bolt safety catch in top of pistol grip: push through from right to left to make safe, from left to right to fire.

UNLOADING:
Pull cocking handle back and then push it fully forward and press safety catch to left. Press cover latch (on top of receiver) and open feed cover. Lift out belt, if present. Inspect feedway. Close cover. Push safety catch to right. Pull cocking handle back and, while holding it, press trigger and ease handle forward.

Chatellerault M1924/29 FRANCE

Having had some unsatisfactory weapons during World War I, the French considered a new machine gun to be imperative, and wisely began by developing a new rimless cartridge in 7.5 mm caliber. After some modifications, the combination worked successfully, and as the M1924/29 light machine gun became standard in the French Army and remained in use until the 1950s. Numbers were also seized by the Germans in 1940 and used by them, so examples with German markings appear from time to time. Numbers were handed over to the armies of former French colonies when they became independent. Shown is a cut-away training version.

SPECIFICATION:

CARTRIDGE:
7.5 x 54 mm French Service

DIMENSIONS:
LENGTH O/A: 1082 mm (42.6 in)
WEIGHT: 9.2 kg (20 lb 6 oz)
BARREL: 500 mm (19.7 in)
RIFLING: 4 grooves, rh
FEED SYSTEM: 25-round box magazine
RATE OF FIRE: 500 rounds/min

IN PRODUCTION:
1930–40

MARKINGS:
"Mle 1924M29" and serial number on right side of receiver.

SAFETY:
Manual safety catch behind rear trigger: turn down for safe, up to fire.

UNLOADING:
Magazine catch behind magazine housing. Push safety catch down, remove magazine. Pull cocking handle to rear. Inspect feedway and chamber through magazine opening. Push safety catch up and, holding cocking handle, press one of the triggers and ease cocking handle forward. Close magazine dust cover and ejection port dust cover. Press safety catch down and pull back magazine catch until it locks.

Maxim '08/15

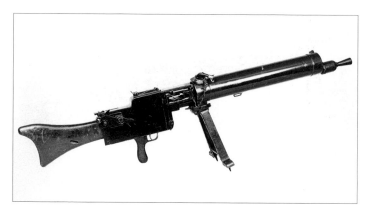

The '08/15 was an attempt to provide the German infantry with something more portable than the standard '08 on its sledge mount. It was given a small bipod, a shoulder stock, and a pistol grip, and the receiver was redesigned in order to try to save weight. Feed was still by a cloth belt, but a special short belt which could be coiled on a reel and carried in a container clamped to the side of the gun was used. In fixed positions, the standard 250-round belt could be used. There was also an aircraft version with a perforated barrel jacket instead of the water jacket, relying upon the airstream to cool the barrel.

SPECIFICATION:

CARTRIDGE:
7.92 x 57 mm Mauser

DIMENSIONS:
LENGTH O/A: 1448 mm (57 in)
WEIGHT: 14.1 kg (31 lb)
BARREL: 719 mm (23.3 in)
RIFLING: 4 grooves, rh
FEED SYSTEM: 50-round cloth belt
RATE OF FIRE: 500 rounds/min

IN PRODUCTION:
1915–18

MARKINGS:
"LMG 08/15 SPANDAU [year]" on top of receiver, or "MG 08/15 SPANDAU [year] GEWEHRFABRIK" on lock spring cover at left rear side of receiver. Serial number on left side of receiver.

SAFETY:
Safety latch between spade grips: must be lifted by the fingers to allow trigger to be pressed.

UNLOADING:
Press pawl depressor on right of feedway to remove belt. Pull back and release cocking handle twice. With a pencil or similar tool, check ejection hole under barrel for possible live cartridge. Press trigger.

Maxim MG '08 GERMANY

This is the classic Maxim recoil-operated machine gun and is essentially the same as every other Maxim of the period: heavy; water-cooled; and, in the case of the '08 model, mounted on a unique four-legged sledge which folded up to allow a crew to drag the gun across the ground. The gun uses a toggle system of breech locking: barrel and toggle recoil together until a spur on the toggle strikes a lug on the receiver wall, causing the toggle to fold and withdraw the breech block; a spring then folds the toggle forward again to load a fresh cartridge and fire. A very reliable weapon, the MG '08 proved able, during World War I, to fire for hours on end provided cooling water and ammunition were available. The MG '08 remained the standard German heavy machine gun until the mid-1930s, with many still in service in 1945.

SPECIFICATION:

CARTRIDGE:
7.92 x 57 mm Mauser

DIMENSIONS:
LENGTH O/A: 1175 mm (46.3 in)
WEIGHT: 26.4 kg (58 lb 5 oz); 62 kg (137 lb) with sledge
BARREL: 719 mm (28.3 in)
RIFLING: 4 grooves, rh
FEED SYSTEM: 250-round cloth belt
RATE OF FIRE: 450 rounds/min

IN PRODUCTION:
1908–18

MARKINGS:
"Deutsche Waffen und Munitionsfabriken BERLIN [year]" on left receiver. "8mm MASCH GEWEHR 1908" and serial number top rear of receiver.

SAFETY:
Safety latch between spade grips: must be lifted by the fingers to allow trigger to be pressed.

UNLOADING:
Press pawl depressor on right of feedway to remove belt. Pull back and release cocking handle twice. With a pencil or similar tool, check ejection hole under barrel for possible live cartridge. Press trigger.

MG34 GERMANY

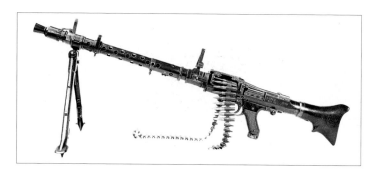

This began as the Solothurn Model 30, developed in Switzerland in the 1920s. The company was then bought by Rheinmetall; Solothurn became their development, engineering, and production plant, as this work was outlawed in Germany by the Versailles Treaty. Rheinmetall then went to work on the MG30 and modified it into the MG34, which was introduced into the German Army in 1936 and became their standard weapon until superseded by the MG42, although it continued in production until the end of World War II. The notable features of this design include the method of stripping, performed by pressing a release catch at the front end of the receiver and simply twisting the butt; the straight-line layout, which reduced the muzzle lift during firing; and the ability to use it on a bipod, as a rifle squad automatic weapon, or on a tripod for sustained support fire. It was the original general-purpose machine gun.

SPECIFICATION:

CARTRIDGE:
7.92 x 57 mm Mauser

DIMENSIONS:
LENGTH O/A: 1219 mm (48 in)
WEIGHT: 12.1 kg (26 lb 11 oz)
BARREL: 627 mm (24.7 in)
RIFLING: 4 grooves, rh
FEED SYSTEM: 50-round belt or 75-round saddle drum
RATE OF FIRE: 900 rounds/min

IN PRODUCTION:
1934–45

MARKINGS:
"MG34" and serial number on top rear of receiver.

SAFETY:
Manual safety catch on left side above trigger: press in and up to fire, press in and down for safe.

UNLOADING:
Cover latch at rear of receiver. Press in and allow cover to open. Remove belt, if one is present, check that no cartridge remains in feed tray. Pull cocking handle to rear and inspect chamber and feedway. Push feed slide to left and close cover. Press trigger.

MG42 GERMANY

Good as the MG34 was, it suffered from being complex and expensive to make, and in 1941 the German Army asked for something that retained all the advantages of the MG34 but was easier to mass-produce. Experts in metal stamping were called in to assist the Mauser company in the redesign, and the result was the MG42. It used a new system of breech-locking, and a highly efficient method of changing the barrel, and it was highly resistant to dust and dirt. In the 1950s, the German Army put the MG42 back into production, as they could see no other weapon that was as good as the MG1, and later MG3; it is still in use. As the MG42/59, it is used by the Austrian and Italian armies, and it was manufactured in Yugoslavia as the Sarac. At various times, the MG3 and its derivatives have been license-produced in Iran, Italy, and Spain. It remains in licensed production in Greece, Pakistan, and Turkey.

SPECIFICATION:

CARTRIDGE:
7.92 x 57 mm Mauser

DIMENSIONS:
LENGTH O/A: 1219 mm (48 in)
WEIGHT: 11.5 kg (25 lb 6 oz)
BARREL: 533 mm (21 in)
RIFLING: 4 grooves, rh
FEED SYSTEM: 50-round belt
RATE OF FIRE: 1200 rounds/min

IN PRODUCTION:
1942–5 and 1959–

MARKINGS:
"MG42," serial number, and factory identifier on left side of receiver.

SAFETY:
Push-button safety catch in top of pistol grip: push through from right to left for safe, from left to right to fire.

UNLOADING:
Pull cocking handle to rear, push safety catch to left. Press cover latch at rear of receiver and lift cover. Lift belt from feed tray. Push barrel-cover lock (on right side of receiver) forward until barrel swings out and chamber can be inspected. Pull back on lock and replace barrel. Check that no cartridge is in feed tray or receiver and close cover. Press safety catch to right, grasp cocking handle, press trigger and ease cocking handle forward.

Heckler & Koch HK13 GERMANY

This was developed to accompany the HK33 5.56 mm rifle and was among the earliest 5.56 mm caliber machine guns; it is generally similar to the rifle but has a heavier barrel that can quickly be removed and exchanged during sustained fire. The action is that of the rifle, a delayed blowback using a roller-locked delay system, and the magazines are interchangeable with those of the HK33 rifle. The HK13 was some-what early in the 5.56 mm era, and consequently its initial sales were largely to Southeast Asian countries. It has since been improved and released as the HK33E, which incorporates a three-round-burst setting in the selector lever and can be changed to belt feed by replacing the magazine housing and bolt.

SPECIFICATION:

CARTRIDGE:
5.56 x 45 mm M193 or NATO

DIMENSIONS:
LENGTH O/A: 980 mm (38.6 in)
WEIGHT: 6 kg (13 lb 5 oz)
BARREL: 450 mm (17.7 in)
RIFLING: 6 grooves, rh
FEED SYSTEM: 20 or 40 round magazine
RATE OF FIRE: 750 rounds/min

IN PRODUCTION:
1972–90

MARKINGS:
"HK 13 5.56 x 45" and serial number on left side of magazine housing.

SAFETY:
Combined safety catch and fire selector on left side of receiver above pistol grip: up for safe, midway for single shots ("E") and fully down for automatic fire ("A").

UNLOADING:
Magazine catch behind magazine housing, beneath receiver. Remove magazine. Pull back cocking handle to eject any round in chamber. Inspect chamber and feedway via ejection port. Release cocking handle. Press trigger.

Heckler & Koch HK21 GERMANY

The HK21 was designed as a general-purpose machine gun, capable of being used on a bipod or tripod, to accompany the G3 rifle. It is much the same as the rifle but has a heavier barrel, which can quickly be changed, and is belt fed. However, it is possible to remove the belt-feed mechanism and replace it with a magazine adapter, using the G3 rifle magazine. It can also be converted to 5.56 x 45 mm or 7.62 x 39 mm calibers by changing the barrel, belt-feed plate, and bolt, making it a very versatile design. It was adopted by Portugal and some African and Southeast Asian countries in the 1970s, and many are still in use. It was replaced in production by the HK21A1, an improved model, and then by the present HK21E, which has a three-round-burst facility and various other improvements.

SPECIFICATION:

CARTRIDGE:
7.62 x 51 mm NATO

DIMENSIONS:
LENGTH O/A: 1021 mm (40.2 in)
WEIGHT: 7.9 kg (17 lb 7 oz)
BARREL: 450 mm (17.7 in)
RIFLING: 4 grooves, rh
FEED SYSTEM: belt
RATE OF FIRE: 900 rounds/min

IN PRODUCTION:
1970–

MARKINGS:
Serial number on rib of receiver top.

SAFETY:
Combined safety catch and fire selector on left side of receiver above pistol grip: up for safe, midway for single shots ("E") and fully down for automatic fire ("A").

UNLOADING:
Press serrated catch beneath rear end of belt slot and allow belt feed to hinge down and forward. Pull back cocking handle to eject any round in chamber. Inspect chamber and feedway through ejection port. Release cocking handle. Press trigger. Close belt feed assembly by hinging it up until catch engages.

Heckler & Koch MG4 GERMANY

Originally designated the MG43, presumably a follow-on from the MG42 of World War II, it was re-designated MG4 on its adoption by the Bundeswehr. It is a belt fed, gas-operated light machine gun, with a quick-change barrel facility. Hot barrel changing is achieved by using the carrying handle attached to the barrel and folding buttstock. Unlike some it its contemporaries in this class, the MG4 has no facility for a box magazine. The feed cover is fitted with a length of Picatinny sight rail, to which an adjustable 1000 m mechanical sight is fitted as standard. However, the mechanical sight can be removed and a full range of optical sights or night-vision devices fitted. The front iron-sight post folded down when using the former.

SPECIFICATION:

CARTRIDGE:
5.56 x 45 mm NATO

DIMENSIONS:
LENGTH, STOCK EXTENDED: 1050 mm (41 in)
LENGTH, STOCK FOLDED: 810 mm (32 in)
WEIGHT: 6.4 kg (14 lb 5 oz)
BARREL: 480 mm (17 in)
RIFLING: 6 grooves, rh
FEED SYSTEM: belt
RATE OF FIRE: 750 rounds/min

IN PRODUCTION:
2001–

MARKINGS:
Model designation on left side with serial number.

SAFETY:
Ambidextrous selector lever above pistol grip, providing "safe" and "fire" modes.

UNLOADING:
Lift feed-cover. Remove ammunition belt. Withdraw working parts to rear, inspect feedway and chamber area. Point weapon in safe direction and pull trigger. Allow working parts to go forward under control.

This is the heavy-barreled light-machine-gun version of the INSAS (Indian Small Arms System) assault rifle. It is gas operated, uses a rotating bolt, and can deliver single shots or automatic fire. The barrel is heavier than that of the rifle, is chromed internally, and has a different rifling contour for better long-range ballistic performance. The weapon is sighted up to 1000 m. The muzzle is of NATO-standard 22 mm diameter for grenade launching, and a bayonet can be fitted. The bipod is instantly recognizable as that produced in Indian factories for the Bren and Vickers-Berthier machine guns during World War II. The INSAS light machine gun was approved for service with the Indian Army.

SPECIFICATION:

CARTRIDGE:
5.56 x 45 mm

DIMENSIONS:
LENGTH: 1050 mm (41.34 in)
WEIGHT: 6.2 kg (13 lb 11 oz)
BARREL: 535 mm (21.1 in)
RIFLING: 4 grooves, rh
MAGAZINE CAPACITY: 30 rounds
RATE OF FIRE: 650 rounds/min

IN PRODUCTION:
2000–

MARKINGS:
Unknown.

SAFETY:
Large thumb-operated safety catch and fire selector lever on left side of receiver above pistol grip: up for safe, down one notch for single shots, down two notches for automatic fire.

UNLOADING:
Magazine release behind magazine housing in front of trigger guard. Remove magazine. Pull back cocking handle to open bolt and remove any round from chamber. Examine chamber and feedway, ensuring both are empty. Release cocking handle. Pull trigger.

Negev ISRAEL

The Negev is a multipurpose weapon that can feed from standard belts, drums, or box magazines and can be fired from a bipod, tripod, or vehicle mounts. The standard barrel is rifled for SS109 ammunition; an alternative barrel is rifled for US M193 ammunition. The weapon is gas operated, with a rotating bolt that locks into the barrel extension, and fires from an open bolt. The gas regulator has three positions, allowing the rate of fire to be changed from 650–800 rounds/min to 800–950 rounds/min or the gas supply to be cut off to permit launching grenades from the muzzle. The weapon will fire in semi- or full-automatic modes, and, by removing the bipod and attaching a normal fore-end and short barrel, it can be used as an assault rifle. The Negev was introduced in 1988 and has been adopted by the Israel Defense Forces.

SPECIFICATION:

CARTRIDGE:
5.56 x 45mm NATO or M193

DIMENSIONS:
LENGTH, BUTT EXTENDED: 1020 mm (40.2 in)
LENGTH, BUTT FOLDED: 780 mm (30.7 in)
WEIGHT: 7.5 kg (16 lb 8 oz)
BARREL: 460 mm (18.1 in)
RIFLING: 6 grooves, rh
FEED SYSTEM: 30- or 35-round box, link belt or drum
CYCLIC RATE: 800 rounds/min

IN PRODUCTION:
1988–

MARKINGS:
Current Negev marked on left rear of receiver:
"LMG Negev Cal 5.56 mm."

SAFETY:
Manual safety and fire selector switch at top of left side of pistol grip. Button moves in an arc: extreme rear position for automatic fire, central position (bottom of arc) for safe, forward position for single shots.

UNLOADING:
Magazine release catch is at rear of magazine housing, in front of trigger guard. Remove magazine if fitted. Press in catch at rear of feed cover and lift cover to remove any belt. Leaving cover open, pull back bolt until feedway and chamber can be inspected. When satisfied that both are clear, close cover, release bolt and pull trigger.

Breda Model 30 ITALY

This was another of the idiosyncratic machine guns that the Italians were so expert at constructing in the 1930s. In this case, the oddity lay in the feed system: the magazine is a box on the right side of the receiver that can be unlatched and hinged forward; in this position, the gunner's mate loaded it from rifle chargers; he then swung the box back and latched it, whereupon the moving bolt could feed the rounds one by one. The advantage is that the whole magazine can be very well made, and the lips carefully machined, so that there is less likelihood of a stoppage than there is with sheet-steel magazines, which get knocked about. However, if anything goes wrong with the one magazine, the gun is useless, and the slow method of loading greatly reduces the effective rate of fire. Another oddity is that, although the barrel can be quickly changed, there is no handle; getting the hot barrel off must have been an interesting exercise.

SPECIFICATION:

CARTRIDGE:
6.5 x 52 mm Carcano

DIMENSIONS:
LENGTH O/A: 1230 mm (48.4 in)
WEIGHT: 10.2 kg (22 lb 7 oz)
BARREL: 520 mm (20.5 in)
RIFLING: 4 grooves, rh
FEED SYSTEM: 20-round box magazine
RATE OF FIRE: 475 rounds/min

IN PRODUCTION:
1930–37

MARKINGS:
"Mtr Legg Mod 30 [serial number] BREDA ROMA" on top of receiver.

SAFETY:
Spring-loaded catch alongside cocking handle: pull cocking handle to rear, press catch to lock in cocked position. To release, pull back slightly on cocking handle.

UNLOADING:
Press magazine release catch behind magazine and hinge magazine forward. Pull back cocking handle. Inspect chamber and feedway. Release handle and pull trigger.

Breda Model 37 ITALY

The standard heavy machine gun of the Italian Army from 1937 to 1945, the Model 37 had some peculiarities. The ammunition had to be oiled before it was loaded, to prevent the cases sticking in the chamber after firing, which was a feature of some other machine guns, but the Breda was fed by metallic strips into which cartridges were clipped. The gun took the cartridge from the strip, fired it, and then put the empty case neatly back into the strip before loading the next round. No reasonable explanation for this has ever appeared; it sounded good, but the fact remained that the overworked gunner had to remove all the empties from the strip before he could reload it. In spite of this, the gun was well liked, principally for its reliability.

SPECIFICATION:

CARTRIDGE:
8 x 59 mm Breda

DIMENSIONS:
LENGTH O/A: 1270 mm (50 in)
WEIGHT: 19.5 kg (43 lb)
BARREL: 679 mm (26.8 in)
RIFLING: 4 grooves, rh
FEED SYSTEM: 20-round strip
RATE OF FIRE: 450 rounds/min

IN PRODUCTION:
1936–43

MARKINGS:
"MITRAGLIATRICE BREDA MOD 37 [serial number] ROMA" and year on left side of receiver.

SAFETY:
Manual safety between grips: push right to lock trigger.

UNLOADING:
Push in pawl depressor on left side under feedway and remove feed strip. Pull back cocking handle to eject any round in chamber. Release cocking handle, pull back a second time. Examine feedway and chamber. Release cocking handle and pull trigger.

Type 99 JAPAN

When the Japanese Army decided to adopt a 7.7 mm rimless cartridge instead of the 6.5 mm round, this gun was developed to fire it. To save development time, the Type 96 was taken as the basis, but the 99 was a considerable improvement. The 7.7 mm cartridge did not need to be oiled; the extraction system was designed to give a slow unseating movement before a more rapid extraction, so curing all ruptured-case problems; the quick-change barrel was far easier to use; and manufacturing tolerances were held to a fine limit. There was more than one item of the design that suggested a good look had been taken at the Czech vz26 gun, several of which had been captured from the Chinese in the mid-1930s.

SPECIFICATION:

CARTRIDGE:
7.7 x 58 mm Arisaka

DIMENSIONS:
LENGTH O/A: 1181 mm (46.5 in)
WEIGHT: 10.4 kg (23 lb)
BARREL: 545 mm (21.5 in)
RIFLING: 4 grooves, rh
FEED SYSTEM: 30-round box magazine
RATE OF FIRE: 850 rounds/min

IN PRODUCTION:
1939–45

MARKINGS:
Model and serial number on top of receiver.

SAFETY:
Safety catch in front of trigger guard on right side: push down and forward to fire, up and back for safe.

UNLOADING:
Magazine catch behind magazine. Remove magazine and pull back cocking handle. Inspect chamber and feedway. Release cocking handle and pull trigger.

Mendoza RM2 MEXICO

Mendoza has been producing machine guns for the Mexican Army since 1933, and all have been noted for their lightness and cheap construction without sacrificing reliability. They use a gas-cylinder system that delivers a short impulse to the piston, and the bolt is similar to that of the Lewis gun, rotating and driven by two cams engaged with the piston rod. The RM2 is the most recent model and adds a simplified method of stripping: by simply removing a lock pin, the stock and rear of the receiver can be folded down to allow the bolt and piston to be withdrawn backwards.

SPECIFICATION:

CARTRIDGE:
0.30-06 US Service

DIMENSIONS:
LENGTH O/A: 1092 mm (43 in)
WEIGHT: 6.3 kg (13 lb 14 oz)
BARREL: 609 mm (24 in)
RIFLING: 4 grooves, rh
FEED SYSTEM: 20-round box magazine
RATE OF FIRE: 600 rounds/min

IN PRODUCTION:
Circa 1965–80

MARKINGS:
"Fusil Ametrallador Mendoza/Hecho en Mexico/ Caliber 30-06/Modeleo RM2 [year]" on left side of receiver.

SAFETY:
Left side above trigger: forward for safe, up for single shot, and to rear for automatic fire.

UNLOADING:
Magazine catch behind magazine. Remove magazine. Pull back cocking handle. Inspect chamber. Release cocking handle and pull trigger.

Degtyarev DP RUSSIA

Adopted by the Red Army in 1928 after two years of trials, the DP became the standard infantry squad machine gun. It remained in service until the Warsaw Pact of the 1950s and was widely distributed to sympathizers around the world. It fires only at automatic and uses the old rimmed 7.62 mm round. The thin, flat pan magazine is somewhat susceptible to damage, and the piston-return spring, beneath the barrel, tends to lose its elasticity after being subjected to barrel heat for long periods. The bipod was too weak for its job and frequently bent. All these defects came to light during 1941, when the gun was first put to the test of war, which led to the development of the DPM.

SPECIFICATION:

CARTRIDGE:
7.62 x 54 R Soviet

DIMENSIONS:
LENGTH O/A: 1290 mm (50.8 in)
WEIGHT: 9.1 kg (20 lb 1 oz)
BARREL: 605 mm (23.8 in)
RIFLING: 4 grooves, rh
FEED SYSTEM: 47-round drum
RATE OF FIRE: 550 rounds/min

IN PRODUCTION:
1928–41

MARKINGS:
Factory identifier and serial number on top of receiver.

SAFETY:
Automatic grip safety device behind trigger guard: when butt is gripped in order to position hand on trigger, safety is pressed in and weapon can be fired. As soon as butt is released, weapon is safe.

UNLOADING:
Magazine release is also rear sight guard. Pull back, and lift drum magazine upwards off receiver. Pull back cocking handle. Inspect feedway and chamber to ensure no cartridge is present. Release cocking handle. Pull trigger.

Degtyarev DPM RUSSIA

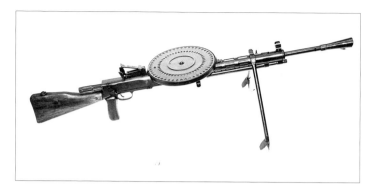

The DPM appeared in 1942 and was a modification of the DP to resolve two principal defects. The return spring was removed from around the gas piston and put behind the bolt, necessitating a tubular extension behind the receiver; this meant that it could no longer be gripped around the butt, and a pistol grip had to be added. The bipod was strengthened and attached to the barrel casing, raising the roll center and making the weapon easier to hold upright. It almost completely replaced the DP and was widely distributed to various Communist-backed forces after World War II.

SPECIFICATION:

CARTRIDGE:
7.62 x 54 R Soviet

DIMENSIONS:
LENGTH O/A: 1265 mm (49.8 in)
WEIGHT: 12.2 kg (26 lb 14 oz)
BARREL: 605 mm (23.8 in)
RIFLING: 4 grooves, rh
FEED SYSTEM: 47-round drum
RATE OF FIRE: 550 rounds/min

IN PRODUCTION:
1941–50

MARKINGS:
Factory identifier and serial number on top of receiver.

SAFETY:
Manual safety catch above right side of trigger: turn forward for safe, down and to rear to fire.

UNLOADING:
Magazine release is also rear sight guard. Pull back, and lift drum magazine upwards off receiver. Pull back cocking handle. Inspect feedway and chamber to ensure no cartridge is present. Release cocking handle. Pull trigger.

Degtyarev DT/DTM RUSSIA

The DT was more or less the same weapon as the DP but intended for fitting into tanks and other armored vehicles. It had a heavier barrel and a two-layer magazine, and was fitted with a telescoping metal butt and pistol grip. To allow it to be used outside the vehicle, a bipod and front sight were carried, to be fitted when required. Like the DP, it suffered from weakening of the return spring beneath the barrel due to heat. Also like the DP, it was modified into the DTM in 1942, the same solution being applied: the return spring was put into a tubular receiver extension behind the bolt. After the DT ceased to be used in tanks, many were given to other countries as infantry light machine guns.

SPECIFICATION:

CARTRIDGE:
7.62 x 54 R Soviet

DIMENSIONS (DTM):
LENGTH O/A: 1181 mm (46.5 in)
WEIGHT: 12.9 kg (28 lb 7 oz)
BARREL: 597 mm (23.5 in)
RIFLING: 4 grooves, rh
FEED SYSTEM: 60-round drum
RATE OF FIRE: 600 rounds/min

IN PRODUCTION:
1929–45

MARKINGS:
Factory identifier and serial number on top of receiver.

SAFETY:
Manual safety catch above right side of trigger: turn forward for safe, down and to rear to fire.

UNLOADING:
Magazine release may be in front of, or behind, rear sight. Press it to side or to rear and remove drum magazine. Pull back cocking handle. Inspect chamber and feedway. Release cocking handle. Press trigger.

Degtyarev RPD RUSSIA

The belt-fed RPD was for some years the standard light machine gun of the Soviet Army, having been introduced in the 1950s as the complementary squad weapon to the AK rifle. It was the logical development of the earlier DP and DPM, and it was progressively improved during its life. It was a gas-operated weapon and the modifications were principally to the gas-piston system to improve stability and provide sufficient power to lift the belt under adverse conditions. The replaceable barrel of the DP was abandoned in this fresh design, and gunners had to be trained to avoid firing more than 100 rounds/min to prevent the barrel over-heating. The remainder of the mechanism was similar to that of the DP, suitably scaled down for the smaller ammunition; like its predecessor the DP, the RPD was capable of automatic fire only.

SPECIFICATION:

CARTRIDGE:
7.62 x 39 mm Soviet M1943

DIMENSIONS:
LENGTH: 1041 mm (41 in)
WEIGHT: 7 kg (15 lb 7 oz)
BARREL: 520 mm (20.5 in)
RIFLING: 4 grooves, rh
MAGAZINE: 100-round belt
CYCLIC RATE: 700 rounds/min
MUZZLE VELOCITY: Ca. 734 m/sec (2410 ft/sec)

IN PRODUCTION:
1962–

MARKINGS:
Model number, factory identifier, and serial number on top of receiver.

SAFETY:
Thumb switch on right side of receiver above trigger: rotate forward for safe, to rear to fire.

UNLOADING:
Pull back cocking handle and rotate safety catch to front, push cover latch forward and lift receiver cover. Draw belt to left and feed it back into drum. Check to see that feedway and chamber are empty. Close cover. Turn drum lock (rear of drum, beneath receiver body) and slide drum off to rear. Rotate safety to rear. Grasp bolt handle. Pull trigger and allow bolt to go forward under control.

DShK RUSSIA

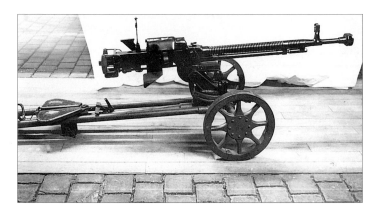

This was the premier heavy machine gun of the Soviet and Warsaw Pact armies since 1946 and is still in wide use, though now being replaced by the NSV. It has also been distributed to Communist sympathizers around the world and will undoubtedly be used for many more years. It was originally produced in 1934 in limited numbers. The gun was revised in 1938 (DShK-38), used during World War II and then revised once more in 1946 (DShK38/46). The 1938 revision gave it a rotary feed and a characteristic rounded cover to the receiver. The 1946 model reverted to a form of flat shuttle feed, so that the receiver cover became flat once more. Copies of these models have been made at various times in China, Pakistan, and Romania and can be identified by their national markings. Mounted on a high tripod, the DShK has been widely used in an antiaircraft role.

SPECIFICATION:

CARTRIDGE:
12.7 x 107 mm Soviet

DIMENSIONS:
LENGTH O/A: 1588 mm (62.5 in)
WEIGHT: 35.7 kg (78 lb 12 oz)
BARREL: 1070 mm (42.1 in)
RIFLING: 4 grooves, rh
FEED SYSTEM: 50-round belt
RATE OF FIRE: 550 rounds/min

IN PRODUCTION:
1938–80

MARKINGS:
Factory mark (arrow), year, and serial number on top rear of receiver, above grips.

SAFETY:
Manual safety catch on lower left edge of receiver: turn forward for safe, backward to fire.

UNLOADING:
Cover latch in front of rear sight. Press in and lift cover. Remove any belt, lift feed drum and check that no cartridges remain in it. Inspect feedway and chamber to ensure that no rounds remain. Close all covers. Turn safety catch to rear. Pull back cocking handle. Press trigger.

Goryunov SG43 RUSSIA

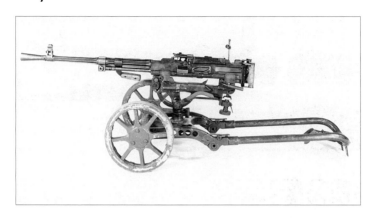

The SG43 became the standard Soviet medium machine gun during World War II, replacing the Maxim 1910 as it was lost in action or wore out. Gas operated, the SG43's mechanism is rather complex; the feed has to pull the cartridge out of the belt backwards, lower it into the feedway, and then chamber it. The locking system is similar to that of the Bren machine gun, but instead of tilting the bolt, it is swung sideways to lock into one wall of the receiver. Original models were smooth barreled; later versions have a grooved barrel to aid cooling. The design was copied in Hungary and China: the Chinese version is almost identical; the Hungarian KGK version sometimes has a pistol grip, butt, and bipod and was intended for use as a light machine gun.

SPECIFICATION:

CARTRIDGE:
7.62 x 54 R Soviet

DIMENSIONS:
LENGTH O/A: 1120 mm (44.1 in)
WEIGHT: 13.6 kg (30 lb)
BARREL: 720 mm (28.4 in)
RIFLING: 4 grooves, rh
FEED SYSTEM: 250-round cloth belt
RATE OF FIRE: 650 rounds/min

IN PRODUCTION:
1943–55

MARKINGS:
Factory identifier and serial number on top of receiver.

SAFETY:
Safety device on firing button between spade grips prevents button being pushed in: safety flap must be lifted with thumb to permit firing button to be pressed.

UNLOADING:
Cover latch is on left rear side of cover. Press forward and open cover. Lift belt off feed pawls and remove it. Lift lower feed cover and remove any cartridge in feed. Pull cocking handle to rear, examine interior of receiver, press trigger and ease cocking handle forward. Close both covers.

Maxim 1910 RUSSIA

This is much the same weapon as the German Maxim '08, since they were both built by the same licensee. The Russians adopted the Maxim in 1905, using a bronze water jacket; they changed this in 1910 to the cheaper and easier-to-manufacture corrugated type of jacket as used by the British Vickers gun, after which no change was made until 1942, when the jacket was fitted with an oversized water filler that allowed handfuls of snow to be dumped into it quickly when necessary. The usual mount is the wheeled Sokolov with the gun on a turntable with a small steel shield, though this was usually removed as it was too small to be of much use. The gun remained in use until the 1960s, after which it was given away freely to various other countries. Numbers can be expected to be available, particularly in the Far East, for some years to come.

SPECIFICATION:

CARTRIDGE:
7.62 x 54 R Soviet

DIMENSIONS:
LENGTH O/A: 1107 mm (43.6 in)
WEIGHT: 23.8 kg (52 lb 8 oz)
BARREL: 721 mm (28.4 in)
RIFLING: 4 grooves, rh
FEED SYSTEM: 250-round cloth belt
RATE OF FIRE: 550 rounds/min

IN PRODUCTION:
1910–50

MARKINGS:
Factory identifier, year, and serial number on spring cover, on left or top of receiver.

SAFETY:
Latch between spade grips. Lift to fire.

UNLOADING:
Press pawl depressor on right of feedway to remove belt. Pull back and release cocking handle twice. With a pencil or similar tool, check ejection hole under barrel for possible live cartridge. Press trigger.

This weapon appeared in the late 1970s on tank turrets as a commander's machine gun; it was later seen on a tripod for heavy-support use by infantry, and then on an air-defense mounting. The gun is gas operated, using a piston to drive a bolt carrier, and can be set up during manufacture to feed from the left or the right, as required. In addition to being made in Russia, it has been licensed to Poland, Bulgaria, and Yugoslavia, all of whom have offered it on the export market for some years. It is also produced as an armored vehicle gun in India. In all its forms, the NSV has proved to be a remarkably effective and reliable heavy machine gun.

SPECIFICATION:

CARTRIDGE:
12.7 x 107 mm Soviet

DIMENSIONS:
LENGTH O/A: 1560 mm (61.4 in)
WEIGHT: 25 kg (55 lb 2 oz)
BARREL: 1070 mm (42.1 in)
RIFLING: 8 grooves, rh
FEED SYSTEM: Belt
RATE OF FIRE: 750 rounds/min

IN PRODUCTION:
Circa 1980–

MARKINGS:
Serial number on top of receiver.

SAFETY:
None.

UNLOADING:
Press catch in front of sight and lift cover. Remove belt. Pull back cocking handle, examine chamber and feedway. Release cocking handle. Press trigger and close cover.

The PK was the first general-purpose machine gun to go into Soviet service, replacing the RP46. The design is a combination of Kalashnikov breech mechanism and a new feed system; it is light in weight and the quality of manufacture is high. There are a number of variant models: the PK is a basic company gun; the PKS is a tripod-mounted battalion-support weapon; the PKT is for use in tanks, with no pistol grip or butt. A later lightened version, the PKM series, was developed and is now offered in 7.62 mm NATO caliber by Poland and Bulgaria. Shown is the Serbian M84. As with other Soviet designs, the PK family can be found in all the former Warsaw Pact countries. Apart from Russia, the PK is license-manufactured in Bulgaria, China (Type 80), Kazakhstan, Poland, Serbia, and Romania, with the source reflected in the markings.

SPECIFICATION:

CARTRIDGE:
7.62 x 54 R Soviet; 7.62 x 51 mm

DIMENSIONS:
LENGTH O/A: 1193 mm (47 in)
WEIGHT: 8.9 kg (19 lb 10 oz)
BARREL: 660 mm (26 in)
RIFLING: 4 grooves, rh
FEED SYSTEM: Belt
RATE OF FIRE: 650 rounds/min

IN PRODUCTION:
1964–

MARKINGS:
Serial number and year on top of feed cover.

SAFETY:
Manual safety catch above trigger: turn forward to fire, rearward for safe.

UNLOADING:
Cover latch at rear of receiver. Press in and allow cover to open. Lift out belt, if one is present, and check that no cartridge remains in cartridge gripper. Pull back cocking handle. Inspect chamber and feedway. Close cover. Press trigger.

RP-46 RUSSIA

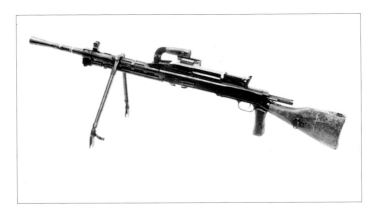

The RP-46 was a modernization of the DPM, intended for use as a company-support gun. The basic layout of the DPM was retained, the principal addition being a belt-feed attachment so that sustained fire could be delivered. However, the original 47-round DP drum can still be used if required, so the RP-46 could still be used in the squad automatic role. The barrel has been made heavier, again something demanded by the sustained-fire role. It was replaced in Soviet service by the RPD, which was a further modification of the original DP design, and almost all RP-46s were shipped off to Communist sympathizers overseas; they turn up in Africa and the Middle East quite regularly.

SPECIFICATION:

CARTRIDGE:
7.62 x 54 R Soviet

DIMENSIONS:
LENGTH O/A: 1283 mm (50.5 in)
WEIGHT: 13 kg (28 lb 11 oz)
BARREL: 607 mm (23.9 in)
RIFLING: 4 grooves, rh
FEED SYSTEM: 250-round cloth belt
RATE OF FIRE: 600 rounds/min

IN PRODUCTION:
1946–54

MARKINGS:
Factory identifier and serial number on top rear of receiver.

SAFETY:
Manual safety catch above trigger on right side: turn forward for safe, rearward to fire.

UNLOADING:
Belt cover catch is behind rear sight. Press catch backwards and cover will open. Lift out belt, if one is present. Pull cocking handle to rear. Inspect chamber and feedway. Press trigger and ease operating handle forward. Close cover.

The RPK replaced the RPD as the standard squad automatic for Soviet infantry and then went on to arm the Warsaw Pact armies and was distributed to sympathizers across the world. It is simply a heavy-barreled version of the standard AKM assault rifle with stiffening ribs around the breech extension; it will accept AK magazines, which makes resupply in the field relatively easy. Like the rifle, the barrel is fixed, so that sustained fire is limited compared with belt-feed guns, though the bore and chamber are chromium plated in an effort to keep the wear rate down as far as possible.

SPECIFICATION:

CARTRIDGE:
7.62 x 39 mm Soviet M1943

DIMENSIONS:
LENGTH O/A: 1035 mm (40.8 in)
WEIGHT: 4.8 kg (10 lb 8 oz)
BARREL: 590 mm (23.2 in)
RIFLING: 4 grooves, rh
FEED SYSTEM: 30- or 40-round box or 75-round drum magazine
RATE OF FIRE: 660 rounds/min

IN PRODUCTION:
1955–

MARKINGS:
Serial and factory mark on left of receiver.

SAFETY:
Combined safety catch and fire selector on left side of receiver: upper position is safe, one notch down for single shots, all the way down for automatic fire.

UNLOADING:
Magazine catch behind magazine housing. Remove magazine. Pull back cocking handle to eject any round in chamber. Inspect chamber through ejection slot. Release cocking handle and pull trigger.

RPK-74

The RPK-74 bears the same relationship to the AK-74 rifle as the RPK does to the AKM rifle; in other words, it is the heavy-barrel squad automatic in 5.45 mm caliber. Once the Soviets adopted the 5.45 mm cartridge, it was simply a matter of time before they produced the light automatic weapon to go with it, but it was not until 1980 that the first details reached the Western world. It seems likely that the Soviets, too, had found problems in developing a small-caliber machine gun that didn't shoot the rifling out of its barrel within 5000 rounds. There are four variant models: the RPK-74 is the basic weapon; the RPKS-74 has a folding butt; the RPK-N3 is the standard weapon with a special mount on the left side of the receiver for an electronic night sight; and the RPKS-N3 is the folding-stock model with night-sight mount.

SPECIFICATION:

CARTRIDGE:
5.45 x 39 mm Soviet

DIMENSIONS:
LENGTH O/A: 1060 mm (41.8 in)
WEIGHT: 4.6 kg (10 lb 2 oz)
BARREL: 616 mm (24.3 in)
RIFLING: 4 grooves, rh
FEED SYSTEM: 30-, 40-, or 45-round magazines
RATE OF FIRE: 650 rounds/min

IN PRODUCTION:
1977–

MARKINGS:
Factory identifier and serial number on top rear of receiver.

SAFETY:
Combined safety catch and fire-selector lever on right rear side of receiver: press all the way up for safe (obstructs movement of cocking handle and bolt); down one notch to first mark ("AB") for full automatic fire; move to bottom position ("O") for single shots.

UNLOADING:
Magazine catch at front end of trigger guard. Remove magazine. Pull back cocking handle. Inspect chamber and feedway through ejection port. Release cocking handle. Pull trigger.

The CIS .50 is modular in construction, with five basic groups. It is gas operated and fires from the open-bolt position. The locking system is the now-familiar bolt carrier and rotating bolt, the firing pin being part of the carrier assembly and driven onto the cap by the final forward movement of the gas piston; there are actually two gas pistons and cylinders, positioned below the barrel to prevent any torque twisting. The barrel is a quick-change pattern and is fitted with an efficient muzzle brake. Feed is by two belts, one on each side of the receiver, and the gunner can select either belt as required. The gun can be provided with either a tripod mount or a pintle mount for fitting into APCs. Chartered Industries of Singapore (CIS) is now known as Singapore Technologies Kinetics (ST Kinetics), and machine guns manufactured by them will be marked accordingly.

SPECIFICATION:

CARTRIDGE:
0.50 Browning MG

DIMENSIONS:
LENGTH: 1778 mm (70 in)
WEIGHT: 30 kg (66 lb 2 oz)
BARREL: 1143 mm (45 in)
RIFLING: 8 grooves, rh
MAGAZINE: Dual disintegrating link belt
CYCLIC RATE: 600 rounds/min
MUZZLE VELOCITY: Ca. 890 m/sec (2920 ft/sec)

IN PRODUCTION:
1988–

MARKINGS:
"CIS 50 MFG BY CHARTERED INDUSTRIES OF SINGAPORE PTE LTD" on left side of receiver.

SAFETY:
Two-position switch above trigger: safe and automatic fire.

UNLOADING:
Release catch and lift feed cover. Remove belt (note that weapon can be adjusted to feed belt from either side). Pull back bolt until it locks. Examine chamber and feedway to ensure they are empty. Holding cocking handle, press trigger and ease bolt forward. Close cover.

Ultimax SINGAPORE

The Ultimax was developed by Chartered Industries of Singapore as the partner to their SAR 80 5.56 mm rifle. Unfortunately CIS's timing was out, and the Ultimax appeared some time after the FN Minimi, with the result that several armed forces that would probably have chosen the Ultimax had already committed themselves to the Minimi. The Ultimax is an excellent weapon and is particularly comfortable to fire, using a long-stroke bolt and buffer system that keeps the recoil impulse to a very low level. It can be fed from a drum or a box magazine and uses the now-common bolt carrier and rotating bolt driven by a gas piston. It is currently used by the Singapore armed forces and has been favorably evaluated by several armies. It was also seen during the civil war in Bosnia in the early 1990s.

SPECIFICATION:

CARTRIDGE:
5.56 x 45 mm M193 or NATO

DIMENSIONS:
LENGTH O/A: 1030 mm (40.6 in)
WEIGHT: 4.8 kg (10 lb 9 oz)
BARREL: 506 mm (19.9 in)
RIFLING: 6 grooves, rh
FEED SYSTEM: 30-round box or 100-round drum
RATE OF FIRE: 550 rounds/min

IN PRODUCTION:
1982–

MARKINGS:
"ULTIMAX Mk III Mfd by Singapore Chartered Industries 5.56" and serial number on left side of receiver.

SAFETY:
Manual safety catch on left side above trigger: forward for automatic fire, rearward for safe.

UNLOADING:
Remove magazine. Pull back cocking handle to eject any round in chamber. Inspect chamber and feedway through ejection port. Release cocking handle. Pull trigger.

Vektor SS77 SOUTH AFRICA

After firing the SS77, gas drives the piston back and a post on the piston extension rides in a cam groove in the block and swings it out of engagement, then withdraws it to extract the empty case. During this movement, a post on top of the block engages with a belt-feed arm in the top cover, and this moves the ammunition belt a half-step inwards. The belt is then moved a further half-step, and the block strips out the fresh cartridge and chambers it. The final movement of the piston forces the block back into engagement with the receiver recess; the piston post then strikes the firing pin to fire the next round. The barrel has a quick-change facility and is externally fluted to save weight and also to increase the cooling surface. A kit of parts was developed to modify the SS77 to fire 5.56 x 45 mm ammunition. Late-production guns have been manufactured in 5.56 mm caliber and named Mini SS.

SPECIFICATION:

CARTRIDGE:
7.62 x 51 mm or 5.56 x 45 mm

DIMENSIONS:
LENGTH, STOCK EXTENDED: 1120 mm (45.5 in)
LENGTH, STOCK FOLDED: 940 mm (37 in)
WEIGHT: 9.6 kg (21 lb 3 oz)
BARREL: 550 mm (21.7 in)
RIFLING: 4 grooves, rh
RATE OF FIRE: 600–900 rounds/min

IN PRODUCTION:
1986–

MARKINGS:
Model number, serial number, and factory identifier on top of receiver.

UNLOADING:
Press release catch and lift feed cover. Remove belt. Pull back cocking handle. Inspect chamber to ensure it is empty. Release cocking handle. Press trigger. Close cover.

Daewoo K3 SOUTH KOREA

The K3 is a lightweight, gas-operated, full-automatic machine gun that appears to have drawn a good deal of its inspiration from the FN Minimi. It uses a similar system of belt or magazine feed and is fitted with a bipod as a squad automatic rifle, though it can also be tripod mounted for use in a sustained fire-support role. The rear sight is adjustable for elevation and windage, and the foresight can be adjusted in elevation for zeroing. The barrel is fitted with a carrying handle and can be quickly changed in action to permit sustained fire; as the barrel also carries the foresight, each can be individually zeroed. The action is gas-piston driven, using a rotating bolt in a bolt carrier.

SPECIFICATION:

CARTRIDGE:
5.56 x 45 mm NATO or M193

DIMENSIONS:
LENGTH: 1030 mm (40.6 in)
WEIGHT, UNLOADED: 6.9 kg (15 lb 21 oz)
BARREL: 533 mm (21 in)
RIFLING: 6 grooves, rh
FEED SYSTEM: 30 round box or 250-round metal belt
CYCLIC RATE: 700 rounds/min (belt),
1000 rounds/min (magazine)

IN PRODUCTION:
1987–

MARKINGS:
"5.56mm K3 [serial number]" on left side of magazine housing. "DAEWOO PRECISION INDUSTRIES LTD" on right side of upper receiver housing.

SAFETY:
M16-pattern three-position safety catch and selector switch on left side of receiver above pistol grip: turn fully clockwise for safe, turn to vertical for single shots, turn fully anticlockwise for automatic fire.

UNLOADING:
Magazine catch on left side of receiver behind magazine housing. Remove magazine, if fitted. Press in two spring buttons at top rear of receiver and lift top cover to remove any belt in feedway. Leaving top cover open, pull back cocking handle and hold to rear while examining chamber and feedway. When satisfied that both are clear, close top cover, let bolt move forward and press trigger.

CETME AMELI SPAIN

AMELI resembles a miniature German MG42, though the delayed-blowback mechanism is actually derived from the Santa Bárbara CETME rifle and is much the same as that used in the Heckler & Koch rifles. Firing the NATO-standard 5.56 x 45 mm cartridge, it is officially termed an assault machine gun, as it is light and compact enough to be carried and used while advancing in the final assault phase of an attack. Early guns used a T-shaped cocking handle similar to that of the MG42, but production models adopted a simpler pattern. AMELI was developed by a design team of the Centro de Estudios Técnicos de Materiales Especiales (CETME) and manufactured by the Spanish state armaments organization, Empresa Nacional de Industrias Militares Santa Bárbara. It was first announced in 1982 and has been in service with the Spanish Army since the late 1980s.

SPECIFICATION:

CARTRIDGE:
5.56 x 45 mm, all types

DIMENSIONS:
LENGTH O/A: 980 mm (38.6 in)
WEIGHT: 6.4 kg (14 lbs)
BARREL: 470 mm (18.5 in)
RIFLING: 6 grooves, rh
FEED SYSTEM: 200-round disintegrating link belt
RATE OF FIRE: 900–1250 rounds/min

IN PRODUCTION:
1982–

MARKINGS:
"CETME AMELI 5.56" and serial number on left side of body above trigger.

SAFETY:
Manual safety catch at top of right pistol grip: "F" for fire, "S" for safe.

UNLOADING:
Press latch at top rear of receiver forward. Open feed cover and remove belt. Pull back cocking lever. Inspect feedway and chamber to ensure that no ammunition remains. Close cover. Pull trigger and allow working parts to go forward under control.

Bren UK

Britain adopted this from Czechoslovakia, where it was known as the vz26. The vz26 was designed around the 7.92 mm Mauser, a rimless round, while the Bren version fires the British 0.303 rimmed cartridge. This is the reason for the characteristic curved magazine and some less-visible minor internal changes. Very reliable, accurate, and slow firing, the Bren was probably the best light machine gun of the World War II period and, changed to 7.62 mm NATO caliber, is still in use today in India. There are a number of variant models, differing in the sights, barrel length, bipod, and general degree of refinement, but all operate in the same way. Shown is an example of L4 series Bren in 7.62 mm.

SPECIFICATION:

CARTRIDGE:
0.303 British Service; 7.62 x 51 mm NATO

DIMENSIONS:
LENGTH O/A: 1150 mm (45.3 in)
WEIGHT: 10.2 kg (22 lb 6 oz)
BARREL: 635 mm (25 in)
RIFLING: 6 grooves, rh
FEED SYSTEM: 30-round box magazine
RATE OF FIRE: 500 rounds/min

IN PRODUCTION:
1936–

MARKINGS:
"BREN Mk [model number]" on right side.

SAFETY:
Combined safety catch and selector lever on left side above trigger: forward position for automatic fire, central for safe, rearward for single shots.

UNLOADING:
Magazine catch behind magazine housing. Press in and remove magazine. Pull cocking handle to rear. Inspect chamber through magazine opening. Hold cocking handle and press trigger, easing cocking handle forward. Close magazine cover by sliding it back. Close ejection port cover (beneath gun) by sliding it back.

L86A1/L86A2 LSW UK

This gun is the British 5.56 mm squad automatic weapon or "Light Support Weapon". It uses some 80% of the components of the L85 rifle and has a heavier and longer barrel. The LSW has undergone the same major modification program as the L85 Individual Weapon. The result is the L86A2 (shown), but not all weapons are scheduled to be modified. The limited magazine capacity has reduced the tactical usefulness of the L86A1/A2, which in operational theaters has been replaced with the FN Minimi.

SPECIFICATION:

CARTRIDGE:
5.56 x 45 mm NATO

DIMENSIONS:
LENGTH O/A: 900 mm (35.4 in)
WEIGHT: 5.4 kg (11 lb 14 oz)
BARREL: 646 mm (25.4 in)
RIFLING: 6 grooves, rh
FEED SYSTEM: 30-round box magazine
RATE OF FIRE: 700 rounds/min

IN PRODUCTION:
1985–94

MARKINGS:
"MG 5.56mm LIGHT SUPPORT L86 ENFIELD" on right of receiver. Serial above magazine housing.

SAFETY:
Push-through bolt above trigger: push from left to right for safe. Selector on left: up for single shots, down for automatic.

UNLOADING:
Remove magazine. Pull back cocking handle to eject any round in chamber. Inspect chamber and feedway through ejection port. Release cocking handle and pull trigger.

Vickers UK

Like many others, the British started with the Maxim gun and then sought something lighter. Vickers developed their answer, reducing weight by using high-quality steel and aluminum and better stress analysis, and inverting the Maxim toggle system for compactness. The resulting Mark 1 Vickers gun entered service in 1912 and remained unchanged until made obsolete in 1968. Utterly reliable, it set world records for non-stop firing during World War I, was adopted as the standard synchronized aircraft gun, armed the earliest armored cars and tanks, and was adopted by the various armies of the British Empire and Commonwealth, some of whom continued using it into the 1970s. It was also made in 0.50 caliber for aircraft and tank use, and a number were made by Colt in the USA in 0.30 caliber for the US Army in 1915. Vickers also sold the gun commercially between 1920 and 1938, principally to South American countries.

SPECIFICATION:

CARTRIDGE:
0.303 British Service and others

DIMENSIONS:
LENGTH O/A: 1155 mm (45.5 in)
WEIGHT: 18.1 kg (39 lb 14 oz)
BARREL: 723 mm (28.5 in)
RIFLING: 4 grooves, rh
FEED SYSTEM: 250-round cloth belt
RATE OF FIRE: 450 rounds/min

IN PRODUCTION:
1912–45

MARKINGS:
Serial number on top rear of water jacket.

SAFETY:
Safety catch above trigger, between spade grips: lift with the fingers to allow trigger to be pressed.

UNLOADING:
Pawl depressor on right side under feedway. Press in and remove belt. Pull back cocking handle. Inspect feedway and chamber. Release cocking handle and press trigger.

Browning Automatic Rifle USA

This is a gas-operated magazine-fed weapon, entirely different from other Browning machine guns. Designed as a light machine gun for World War I, the Browning Automatic Rifle (BAR) became the US Army's squad automatic weapon (SAW), remaining in service until the Korean War. It was finally replaced by the M249 SAW in the 1980s. Numbers were also issued to the British Home Guard in 1940–45. With a fixed barrel and a limited-capacity magazine, the BAR was never really a serious light machine gun; too much sustained fire and the fore-end burst into smoke and flames. It was too heavy to be a serious automatic rifle either, but since there was nothing better, it survived. It was also sold commercially by Colt as the semiautomatic Monitor for police use. Later models featured a bipod and carrying handle.

SPECIFICATION:

CARTRIDGE:
0.30-06 US Service

DIMENSIONS:
LENGTH O/A: 1219 mm (48 in)
WEIGHT: 7.3 kg (16 lb 1 oz)
BARREL: 610 mm (24 in)
RIFLING: 4 grooves, rh
FEED SYSTEM: 20-round box magazine
RATE OF FIRE: 500 rounds/min

IN PRODUCTION:
1917–45

MARKINGS:
"BROWNING BAR M1918 CAL 30 MFD BY [manufacturer's name]" on top of receiver.

SAFETY:
Combined safety catch and fire selector lever above trigger on left side: rear for safe, push forward to central position for slow automatic rate, push fully forward for fast automatic rate.

UNLOADING:
Press in magazine release button in front of trigger guard and remove magazine. Pull back cocking handle on left side of receiver to eject any round in chamber. Inspect chamber through ejection port. Push cocking handle back to its forward position. Pull trigger.

Browning M1917 USA

The M1917 was Browning's original recoil-operated military machine gun, upon which all later models (except the BAR) were based. As was the accepted form in the early twentieth century, it was a heavy water-cooled gun mounted on a tripod, reliable and long wearing. It survived through World War II in the same form and well into the 1950s, still working well, before it was finally ousted by the air-cooled models.

SPECIFICATION:

CARTRIDGE:
0.30-06 US Service

DIMENSIONS:
LENGTH O/A: 978 mm (38.5 in)
WEIGHT: 15 kg (32 lb)
BARREL: 610 mm (24 in)
RIFLING: 4 grooves, rh
FEED SYSTEM: 250-round cloth belt
RATE OF FIRE: 500 rounds/min

IN PRODUCTION:
1917–45

MARKINGS:
"US INSP BROWNING MACHINE GUN US CAL 30 MODEL OF 1917 MFD BY [manufacturer's name]."

SAFETY:
None.

UNLOADING:
Pull back milled knob on top cover (behind rear sight) to release cover; lift it open. Remove any belt. Pull back operating handle and inspect front face of bolt, pushing out any cartridge that may have been extracted. Inspect chamber. Close cover. Release cocking handle. Pull trigger.

Browning M1919A4 USA

This is an air-cooled version of the M1917, developed in 1918–19 to arm American tanks. The barrel was shortened to 457 mm and placed in a perforated jacket, and a small tripod was provided so that the gun could be used outside the tank. This proved that air-cooled guns could work as well as water-cooled guns. Various modifications were made, and eventually the M1919A4 appeared, having reverted to the same barrel length as the M1917. The M1919A4 was adopted by the US Cavalry in the early 1920s and as the standard ground gun for all US armed forces in the late 1930s and remained so until replaced by the M60 in the 1960s. Many remained in use in various parts of the world as reserve weapons when replaced by newer guns such as the MAG 58, with some modified to 7.62 mm NATO.

SPECIFICATION:

CARTRIDGE:
0.30-06 US Service

DIMENSIONS:
LENGTH O/A: 1041 mm (41 in)
WEIGHT: 14 kg (31 lb
BARREL: 610 mm (24 in)
RIFLING: 4 grooves, rh
FEED SYSTEM: 250-round cloth belt
RATE OF FIRE: 500 rounds/min

IN PRODUCTION:
1934–

MARKINGS:
"BROWNING M1919A4 US Cal .30 [maker's name, year, serial number]" on left side of receiver.

SAFETY:
None.

UNLOADING:
Pull back milled knob on top cover (in front of rear sight) to release cover; lift it open. Remove any belt. Pull back operating handle and inspect front face of bolt, pushing out any cartridge that may have been extracted. Inspect chamber. Close cover. Release cocking handle. Pull trigger.

Browning M1919A6 USA

The M1919A6 was developed during World War II and adopted in 1943 as the squad light machine gun in place of the Browning Automatic Rifle. It was far from light, however, as it was no more than the M1919A4 with the addition of a shoulder stock, muzzle flash hider, and bipod. It was heavy, cumbersome, and heartily disliked by all who encountered it; most users appear to have had the shoulder stock and bipod removed, bringing it back to M1919A4 standard, and then had tripods attached, the BAR being retained as long as possible as the squad automatic. With the arrival of the M60 machine gun, the remaining A6s were got rid of; some were unloaded onto other, unsuspecting, armies and may turn up from time to time, particularly in Central America.

SPECIFICATION:

CARTRIDGE:
0.30-06 US Service

DIMENSIONS:
LENGTH O/A: 1346 mm (53 in)
WEIGHT: 14.7 kg (32 lb 8 oz)
BARREL: 610 mm (24 in)
RIFLING: 4 grooves, rh
FEED SYSTEM: 250-round cloth belt
RATE OF FIRE: 500 rounds/min

IN PRODUCTION:
1943–54

MARKINGS:
"US INSP BROWNING MACHINE GUN US CAL 30 MFD BY [manufacturer's name]."

SAFETY:
None.

UNLOADING:
Pull back milled knob on top cover (in front of rear sight) to release cover; lift it open. Remove any belt. Pull back operating handle and inspect front face of bolt, pushing out any cartridge that may have been extracted. Inspect chamber. Close cover. Release cocking handle. Pull trigger.

Browning M2HB .50 USA

In 1918, the Germans developed a 13 mm antitank machine gun; the US Army in France demanded something similar. The Winchester company developed a 0.50 in cartridge, and Browning scaled up his M1917 machine gun to fire it. The M2 originally appeared as a water-cooled antiaircraft machine gun, but in the 1930s the air-cooled version was developed for use on tanks. Since it used a very thick barrel to dissipate the heat generated by firing, it became the HB for "Heavy Barrel." Some 3 million have been made by different companies; they have been used by virtually every armed force outside the former Communist bloc. In the 1980s, quick-change-barrel versions became common; these do away with the need for a ticklish adjustment when changing barrels or reassembling the weapon after cleaning.

SPECIFICATION:

CARTRIDGE:
12.7 x 99 mm (0.50 Browning)

DIMENSIONS:
LENGTH O/A: 1653 mm (65 in)
WEIGHT: 38.2 kg (84 lb 4 oz)
BARREL: 1143 mm (45 in)
RIFLING: 8 grooves, rh
FEED SYSTEM: Belt
RATE OF FIRE: 500 rounds/min

IN PRODUCTION:
1933–

MARKINGS:
"US [serial number] BROWNING MACHINE GUN CAL 50 M2 MFD BY [manufacturer's name]."

SAFETY:
No safety catch as such, but bolt latch release in centre of thumb trigger will lock bolt to rear. This must be pressed down before pressing trigger.

UNLOADING:
Press down bolt-latch release. Turn catch on top cover and open cover. Remove any belt in gun. Pull back operating handle on right side of gun until bolt locks back. Inspect front of bolt, knocking free any cartridge that may have been extracted from chamber, and check that chamber is empty. Press down extractor at front of bolt. Close cover. Press bolt latch release and allow bolt to go forward. Press trigger.

Colt Automatic Rifle USA

Over the years, numerous attempts have been made to produce a squad fire support weapon, usually little more than a standard M15 rifle series action coupled with a heavier barrel and a bipod. The aptly named Colt Automatic Rifle (CAR), or Colt 750, is one of the latest examples of this approach. The base M16-series mechanism and operation techniques are carried over but there is no single-shot mode, only fully automatic. The heavy barrel is protected inside a prominent square-section handguard and a M60-pattern or similar folding bipod is secured under the muzzle. M16-compatible 30-round box magazines can be used, as well as the 100-round C-Mag drum (as shown).

SPECIFICATION:

CARTRIDGE:
5.56 x 45 mm NATO

DIMENSIONS:
LENGTH O/A: 1000 mm (39.4 in)
WEIGHT: 5.8 kg (12 lb 12 oz)
BARREL: 510 mm (20 in)
RIFLING: 6 grooves, rh
MAGAZINE CAPACITY: 30 or 100 rounds
RATE OF FIRE: 600–750 rounds/min

IN PRODUCTION:
2001–

MARKINGS:
"COLT FIREARMS DIVISION COLT INDUSTRIES HARTFORD CONN USA" on left side of receiver. "COLT 750 cal 5.56mm" and serial number on left side of magazine well.

SAFETY:
Safety catch on left side of receiver above trigger: up for safe, down to fire.

UNLOADING:
Magazine catch is push-button just above trigger on right side. Push button to remove magazine and then pull back T-shaped cocking handle above receiver to eject any round in chamber. Inspect chamber and feedway through ejection port. Release cocking handle and pull trigger.

GAU 19/A USA

This was originally developed by General Electric and called the GECAL 50, gaining its formal nomenclature after adoption by the US Army. It is a three-barrelled Gatling-type weapon requiring an external source of power, such as vehicle batteries. Although it produces a much higher volume of fire than a standard Browning M2HB gun, it is only slightly heavier and delivers lesser recoil force to its mounting. It can be adjusted to give two rates of fire. The mechanism is based upon the Gatling-gun system, with the three barrels rotating in front of a receiver unit in which cam tracks control the movement of the three bolts. The gun will fire any type of 0.50 Browning ammunition, including SLAP discarding rounds. A delinking feed system accepts standard machine-gun belts and removes the rounds from the belt before feeding into the linkless supply chutes.

SPECIFICATION:

CARTRIDGE:
0.50 Browning

DIMENSIONS:
LENGTH O/A: 1181 mm (46.5 in)
WEIGHT: 33.6 kg (74 lb 1 oz)
BARRESL: 914 mm (36 in)
RIFLING: 8 grooves, rh
FEED SYSTEM: Linkless feed
CYCLIC RATE: Selectable 1000 or 2000 rounds/min

IN PRODUCTION:
1986–93

MARKINGS:
Usually found with am identification plate riveted to the receiver, bearing the serial number, stock number, designation, and "ROCK ISLAND ARSENAL."

SAFETY:
Safety is controlled by simply cutting off power supply to breech rotor, and is a function on control box rather than a mechanism on gun.

UNLOADING:
Unloading should not be necessary as operating system will stop ammunition supply and empty gun when trigger or firing button is released. Gun is therefore always unloaded except when actually firing.

Hughes Chain Gun EX34 USA

The Chain Gun's chain is driven by an electric motor. Cams rotate the bolt head to lock into the barrel and also actuate the firing pin as the bolt locks. A dynamic brake on the motor ensures that, when the trigger is released, the bolt stops in the open position, so that there is no danger of cook off. The belt feed is also driven by the motor, independently of the bolt mechanism, so that there is ample power to handle long belts, particularly in a vehicle bounding over rough country. The Chain Gun is particularly well suited to tank installation since case ejection is forward, under control, and the relatively long bolt-closure dwell time reduces the amount of fumes released into the vehicle. The Hughes Chain Gun is built on one of the few new operating principles that have appeared in recent years, and is in use in 25 mm caliber in the US M2 Bradley MICV and in 7.62 mm caliber on the British Warrior MICV, being manufactured under license in Britain as the L94A1.

SPECIFICATION:

CARTRIDGE:
7.62 x 51 mm NATO

DIMENSIONS:
LENGTH O/A: 1250 mm (49.2 in)
WEIGHT: 17.9 kg (39 lb 6 oz)
BARREL: 703 mm (27.7 in)
RIFLING: 6 grooves, rh
FEED SYSTEM: Disintegrating link belt
RATE OF FIRE: 520 rounds/min

IN PRODUCTION:
1980–

SAFETY:
Two independent safety devices: a mechanical safety knob on right front of receiver, with "safe" and "fire" markings, and an electrical master switch on control panel. Mechanical safety locks sear and prevents striker from reaching firing pin. The master switch controls supply of power to gun. Note: If master switch is on and mechanical safety is at safe, it is possible to operate gun and cycle unfired rounds through it.

UNLOADING:
Dynamic brake ensures gun always stops in unloaded position with chamber empty. Ammunition belt can be removed from feed rotor by opening feed cover.

M134 Minigun USA

The M134 Minigun is a six-barrel weapon of the Gatling type, and all operations are driven by an electric motor on the gun itself. As the barrels revolve around a central axis, each is loaded and fired, and the spent case extracted, all at a fire rate of up to 6000 rounds/min. The M134 Minigun was originally manufactured by General Electric back in 1963, and their production ceased some years ago. Manufacturing and design responsibility has now passed to Dillon Aero who have extensively modified the overall design, the main changes being access to the interior, numerous internal changes, and a reduction in fire rate to 3000 rounds/min to enhance reliability. Dillon Aero either modify existing guns or manufacture them from scratch, with the markings altered accordingly. As the M134 Minigun needs a power supply to operate, its use is normally confined to vehicles or aircraft platforms.

SPECIFICATION:

CARTRIDGE:
7.62 x 51mm NATO

DIMENSIONS:
LENGTH: 800 mm (31.5 in)
WEIGHT, UNLOADED: 15.9 kg (35 lb)
WEIGHT, WITH POWER SUPPLY: 26.8 kg (59 lb)
BARRELS: 559 mm (22 in)
RIFLING: 4 grooves, rh
FEED SYSTEM: 4000-round linked belt
CYCLIC RATE: Ca. 6000 rounds/min

IN PRODUCTION:
1963–

MARKINGS:
Identification plate bearing nomenclature, serial number, stock number, and date of manufacture, together with either "GENERAL ELECTRIC CO" or "ROCK ISLAND ARSENAL" will be found riveted to receiver body.

SAFETY:
Safety is controlled by simply cutting off power supply to breech rotor, and is a function on control box rather than a mechanism on gun.

UNLOADING:
Unloading should not be necessary, since operating system will stop ammunition supply and empty gun when trigger or firing button is released. Gun is therefore always unloaded except when actually firing.

M240B and M240G USA

After years of using the Belgian MAG as a coaxial machine gun, the US armed forces realized that the coaxial gun, known to them as the M240, was extremely reliable and set about type-classifying the M240 as a ground-mounted general-purpose machine gun to replace their ageing M60s. In 1994, the US Marine Corps started to convert redundant M240 guns for the ground role as the M240G. The M240G is virtually identical to the Belgian MAG original and operates in the same fashion. The US Army followed with the M240B, but this model differed visually by the addition of a molded handguard over the barrel area. Otherwise, the M240B and M240G are the same, although most M240Bs are manufactured from scratch. Some M240B enhancements are in the pipeline, from armor-piercing ammunition to a reduction in the cyclic fire rate. The center of production for both guns is now FN Manufacturing in the USA.

SPECIFICATION:

CARTRIDGE:
7.62 x 51 mm NATO

DIMENSIONS:
LENGTH O/A: 1232 mm (58.5 in)
WEIGHT: 12.3 kg (27 lb)
BARREL: 627 mm (24.7 in)
RIFLING: 4 grooves, rh
FEED SYSTEM: Metal link belt
RATE OF FIRE: 750 rounds/min

IN PRODUCTION:
1994–

MARKINGS:
"FN MANUFACTURING INC – COLUMBUS – SC" on right of receiver together with serial number.

SAFETY:
Push-button safety catch above trigger: push from left side to right for safe, push from right side to left to fire.

UNLOADING:
Press cover catch in front of rear sight and open cover. Lift out belt, if present. Inspect feedway and close cover. Pull cocking handle to eject any round in chamber. While holding cocking handle back, press trigger and ease cocking handle forward.

M249 SAW (Squad Automatic Weapon) USA

The M249 is the FN Minimi with sundry small changes to meet the US Army's requirements for a light machine gun. It was approved in 1982 but did not enter production until the early 1990s due to a long, drawn-out period of testing and modification before the requirements were satisfied. The changes were largely to suit US manufacturing methods and were relatively small, though nonetheless important. The principal exterior difference is the presence of a heat shield above the barrel; all other characteristics of the Minimi are unchanged. Once the original batch of M249s had been delivered from Belgium, production switched to the USA where FN Manufacturing subsequently carried out all production for the numerous M249 SAW contracts. Only the first 1000 guns carried Belgian markings.

SPECIFICATION:

CARTRIDGE:
5.56 x 45 mm NATO

DIMENSIONS:
LENGTH: 1040 mm (41 in)
WEIGHT: 6.9 kg (15 lb 2 oz)
BARREL: 523 mm (20.6 in)
RIFLING: 6 grooves, rh
FEED SYSTEM: 30-round detachable box or 200-round metal belt
CYCLIC RATE: 750 rounds/min

IN PRODUCTION:
1992–

MARKINGS:
"FN Manufacturing Inc, SC, M249." Serial number on left side of receiver.

SAFETY:
Push-through safety catch on left side of receiver: push from right to left to fire, left to right for safe.

UNLOADING:
Press in two spring catches at top rear of receiver and lift feed cover. Remove belt or magazine. Pull back cocking handle. Inspect chamber and feedway. Release cocking handle. Press trigger.

Machine Gun, Caliber 7.62 mm NATO, M60/M60E1

USA

The M60, with its modified successor the M60E1, was the standard squad general-purpose machine gun of the US Army. The original M60 had some serious drawbacks, the most noticeable being the barrel change. Each barrel had its own gas cylinder and bipod but no handle. It was, therefore, not only expensive but also unnecessarily heavy and dangerous to handle when hot. An asbestos glove formed part of the gun's equipment, and since the bipod vanished with the barrel, the gunner had to hold the gun up in the air while the barrel was changed. The later M60E1 had a simpler barrel with the gas cylinder and bipod fixed to the gun, and it also had a handle for barrel changing. A feature of both models was the Stellite lining of the barrels, which prolonged their lives beyond that normally experienced with unprotected steel.

SPECIFICATION:

CARTRIDGE:
7.62 x 51 mm NATO

DIMENSIONS:
LENGTH: 1100 mm (43.5 in)
WEIGHT: 10.5 kg (23 lb 3 oz)
BARREL: 560 mm (22 in)
RIFLING: 4 grooves, rh
FEED SYSTEM: Disintegrating link belt
CYCLIC RATE: 550 rounds/min

IN PRODUCTION:
1960–

MARKINGS:
"MACHINE GUN 7.62 MM M60 SACO DEFENSE DIVISION MAREMONT CORP USA or SACO-LOWELL SHOPS USA" or other manufacturer on top of feed cover.

SAFETY:
Two-position safety catch is on left side of receiver above pistol grip. No fire selector. This weapon fires only in automatic mode. Note: Safety catch must be in "fire" position to allow gun to be cocked.

UNLOADING:
Pull back cocking handle until bolt engages behind sear. Unlock and open top cover by lifting latch at rear right of receiver. Remove ammunition belt. Check that no rounds remain in feedway or chamber. Close cover. Pull trigger.

Machine Gun M60E3 USA

This was the further development of the M60 design, intended to produce a more handy weapon, with a forward handgrip. The barrel may be a short assault barrel or a longer and heavier one for sustained-fire missions. The feed cover has been modified to permit its being closed whether the bolt is forward or back, and the bipod is attached to the receiver. A winter trigger guard allows firing while wearing heavy gloves. The M60E3 was taken into use by the US Navy and Marine Corps and sold to several other countries.

SPECIFICATION:

CARTRIDGE:
7.62 x 51 mm NATO

DIMENSIONS:
LENGTH: 1077 mm (42.4 in)
WEIGHT: 8.8 kg (19 lb 6 oz)
BARREL: 558 mm (22 in)
RIFLING: 4 grooves, rh
FEED SYSTEM: Disintegrating link belt
CYCLIC RATE: 600 rounds/min

IN PRODUCTION:
1994–

MARKINGS:
"MACHINE GUN 7.62MM M60E3 SACO DEFENSE INC" on feed cover.

SAFETY:
Two-position safety catch on left side of receiver above pistol grip. No fire selector. This weapon fires only in automatic mode.

UNLOADING:
Unlock and open top cover by lifting latch at rear right of receiver. Remove ammunition belt. Check that no rounds remain in feedway. Pull back cocking handle to eject any round in chamber. Inspect chamber and feedway. Close cover. Release bolt. Pull trigger.

Manufacturers

This lists the "short title" used in the list of Brand Names, or the common title of the company that is used as an identifying name for their products. Against this is the full title and location of the company; a brief history is given where the firm has changed hands or titles or other distinctive features during its life, since this can often assist in approximately dating a weapon. Where there were no changes the period of the company's activity is indicated if known. Note also that the addresses given are those relevant to the period, and, particularly in central Europe, place-names can change over the years. Thus Zella St Blasii changed into Zella Mehlis, and Bohemia into Czechoslovakia into Czech Republic.

There are, of course, many omissions from this list; every country has numerous small provincial gunmakers whose name is unknown beyond a 50-mile radius, and every country has a host of "gunmakers" who purchase guns from major manufacturers and engrave their own names on them. These are difficult to discover and tabulate, so their absence must be excused. There are also custom gunmakers who build expensive rifles, shotguns, and free-style target pistols to order, and obviously their products defy listing.

Accuracy Int.	Accuracy International, Portsmouth, England
Acha	Originated as Acha Hermanos y Cia in Ermua, Spain, ca. 1915; ca. 1920 became Domingo Acha y Cia, then Fabrica de Acha Hermanos. Closed ca. 1935.
Adams	Adams Patent Small Arms Co., London (1864–93)
Adler	Adler Waffenwerke Max Hermsdorff, Zella St Blasii, Germany. Active 1905–07.
Adolph	Frederick Adolph, Genoa, N.Y., USA (ca. 1900–24)
Advantage	Advantage Arms, St Paul, Minn., USA
Aetna	Aetna Arms Co., N.Y., USA (1876–90)
Agner	Agner-Saxhoj Products, Denmark
Aguirre	Aguirre y Cia, Eibar, Spain. Also operated as Aguirre, Zamacolas y Cia (1915–30)
Alkartasuna	Soc. Anon. Alkartasuna Fabrica de Armas, Guernica, Spain. Began operating in 1915 as contractors to Gabilondo; factory burned down 1920, company liquidated 1922.
Allen	Allen & Wheelock, Worcester, Mass., USA (to 1865). Ethan Allen & Co., Worcester, Mass., USA (1865–71)
All Right	All Right Firearms Co., Lawrence, Mass., USA (1876–85)
Alpha	Alpha Arms Co., Flower Mound, Tex., USA (1983–87)
AMAC	American Military Arms Corp., Jacksonville, Ark., USA. Bought the remains of Iver Johnson (qv) in 1987. Closed 1990.
American Arms (1)	The American Arms Co., Boston Mass., and Milwaukee, Wis., USA. Founded 1882 in Boston, moved to Milwaukee 1897, closed down 1904.

American Arms (2)   American Arms Co., Garden Grove, Calif., USA (1984–85)

American Derringer   American Derringer Corp., Waco, Tex., USA (1980–)

American Firearms   American Firearms Mfg. Co. Inc., San Antonio, Tex., USA (1972–74)

American Industries   American Industries, Cleveland, Ohio, USA (ca. 1980); later reorganized to become the Calico Corp. (qv).

American Standard   American Standard Tool Co., Newark, N.J., USA (ca. 1870); successor to the Manhattan Firearms Co.

Alsop   C.R. Alsop, Middletown, Conn., USA (ca. 1870–80)

Ames   Ames Sword Co., Chicopee Falls, Mass., USA. Not a firearms company but spent 1897–1910 making the Turbiaux repeating pistol as contractor.

Ancion-Marx   L. Ancion-Marx, Liege, Belgium (1860–1914)

Anschutz   J.G. Anschutz, Zella St Blasii/Zella Mehlis, Germany (1886–1945); J.G. Anschutz GmbH, Ulm/Donau, Germany (1950–)

Apaolozo Hermanos   Apaolozo Hermanos, Zumorraga, Spain (1917–35)

Arcadia   Arcadia Machine & Tool Co., Covina, Calif., USA

Arcus   Arcus Co., Lyaskovets, Bulgaria

Arizaga   Gaspar Arizaga, Eibar, Spain (1812–1936)

Arizmendi   Began as Arizmendi y Goenaga, Eibar, Spain, in 1886. In 1914 reorganized as Francisco Arizmendi and remained in business until 1936.

Arizmendi, Zulaica   Arizmendi, Zulaica y Cia, Eibar, Spain (1916–25). Relationship with Francisco Arizmendi not known.

ArmaLite   ArmaLite Div. of Fairchild Engine & Airplane Co., Costa Mesa, Calif., USA (1954–83)

Armas de Fuego   Manufactura Arnas de Fuego, Guernica, Spain. Operated about 1920–25 and appears to have been the Alkartasuna company revived.

Armero Especialistas   Armeros Especialistas Reunidas, Eibar, Spain. A worker's cooperative that made pistols 1920–25 and thereafter became a sales agency for other makers until 1936.

Armigas   Armigas-Comega Costruzioni Mecchaniche Gardonesi Attilio Zanoletti, Gardone Val Trompia, Brescia, Italy (1961–)

Armi-Jager   Armi-Jager di Armando Piscetti, Milan, Italy.

Arminex   Arminex Inc., Scottsdale, Ariz., USA (1979–88)

Armitage   Armitage International Ltd., Seneca, S.C., USA

Arostegui   Eulogio Arostegui, Eibar, Spain (1924–36)

Arrieta   Arrieta y Cia, Elgoibar, Spain

Arrizabalaga   Hijos de Calixto Arrizabalaga, Eibar, Spain (1915–36)

Ascaso   Francisco Ascaso, Tarassa, Cataluna, Spain. Small factory that made copies of the government-issue Astra 400 for the republicans in the Spanish Civil War.

ASP   Armament Systems & Procedures, Appleton, Wis., USA

A–Square	A–Square Co., Inc., Madison, Ind., USA
A.S.T.	see American Standard
Astra-Unceta	Astra-Unceta y Cia SA, Apartado 3, Guernica (Vizcaya), Spain. Began in 1907 as Pedro Unceta y Juan Esperanza, Eibar; moved to Guernica in 1913 and became Esperanza y Unceta, adopted Astra as their principal trade-name in 1914, became Unceta y Cia in 1926 , Astra-Unceta in 1955, and Astra Gernika SA in 1994.
ATCSA	Armas de Tiro y Casa, Barcelona, Spain (1931–36)
Atkin	Atkin, Grant & Lang, London, England (1960–)
Automag	The Automag pistol has been made by various companies, listed here for convenience:
	Sanford Arms Co., Pasadena, Calif., USA. Designers and initial development only (1963–70).
	Auto-Mag Corp., Pasadena, Calif. Initial production (1970–72).
	TDE Corp., North Hollywood, Calif. (1973–77). During this period, marketing was done by the High Standard Company.
	Sanford Arms, Pasadena, Calif. (1977–80)
	Arcadia Machine & Tool Corporation, Covina, Calif., USA (1980–85)
Auto-Ordnance	Auto-Ordnance, West Hurley, N.Y., USA
Azanza y Arrizabalaga	Azanza y Arrizabalaga, Eibar, Spain (1915–19)
Bacon	Bacon Manufacturing Co., Norwich, Conn., USA. Then became Bacon Arms Co. 1862–91, when it failed and the remains were bought to form the basis of the Crescent Firearms Co. (qv).
Baford	Baford Arms, Bristol, Tenn., USA
Baker	Baker Gun & Forging Co., Batavia, N.Y., USA
Ballard	C.H. Ballard & Co., Worcester, Mass., USA
Barrett	Barrett Firearms Mfg. Co., Murfreesboro, Tenn., USA
Bar-Sto	Bar-Sto Precision Machine Co., Burbank, Calif., USA (1972–75)
Barthelmes	Fritz Barthelmes KG, Heidenheim-Oggenhause, Germany (1948–)
Bascaran	Martin A. Bascaran, Eibar, Spain (1915–31)
Bauer	Bauer Firearms Corp., Fraser, Mich., USA (1976–84)
Bayonne	Manufacture d'Armes de Bayonne, Bayonne, France (1921–88)
Beaumont	Frans Beaumont, Maastricht, The Netherlands. Patentee and manufacturer of Dutch service revolvers and rifles (1873–05).
Becker	Becker & Hollander, Suhl, Germany (ca. 1885–1945)
Beistegui	Beistegui Hermanos, Eibar, Spain (1915–36)
Benelli	Benelli Armi SpA, Urbino, Italy (ca. 1850–)

Beretta	Pietro Beretta SpA, Gardone Val Trompia, Italy (1680–)
Bergeron	L. Bergeron, St. Etienne, France
Bergmann	Th. Bergmann Waffenfabrik, Suhl, Germany (1885–1918) Bergmann's Industriewerke, Gaggenau, Germany (1918–45)
Bern	Eidgenossische Waffenfabrik Bern, Bern, Switzerland. Government arsenal since 1875. Name changed in 1993 to w + f Bern.
Bernadon-Martin	Bernadon-Martin, St. Etienne, France (1906–12)
Bernardelli	Vincenzo Bernardelli SpA, Gardone Val Trompia, (Brescia), Italy (1865–)
Bernedo	Vincenzo Bernedo y Cia, Eibar, Spain (1875–1914)
Bersa	Fabricas de Armas Bersa SA, Ramos Mejia, Argentina
Bertrand	Manufacture Generale d'Armes et Munitions Jules Bertrand, Liege, Belgium (ca. 1885–1914)
Bertuzzi	Bertuzzi, Brescia, Italy
Bighorn	Bighorn Rifle Co., Orem, Utah, USA; Bighorn Rifle Co., American Fork, Utah, USA
Bighorn Arms	Bighorn Arms Co., Watertown, S. Dak., USA
Billings	Billings & Spencer, Hartford, Conn., USA (ca. 1865)
Bingham	Bingham Ltd., Norcross, Ga., USA (1976–85). Makers of .22RF caliber imitations of the Kalashnikov rifle, Soviet PPSh submachine gun, and similar weapons.
Blake	J.H. Blake, New York, N.Y., USA (1890–1912)
Bland	Thomas Bland, London, England (1876–). Gunmaker; name found on revolvers, rifles, and shotguns of his own make and on other makes sold by him.
Blaser	Blaser-Jagdwaffen GmbH, Isny/Allgau, Switzerland (1978–)
Bliss	Franklin D. Bliss, New Haven, Conn., USA (ca. 1870)
Bock	Otto Bock, Berlin, Germany (ca. 1900–15)
Bolumburu	Gregorio Bolumburu, Eibar, Spain (1908–36)
Boss	Boss & Co., London, England (1832–)
Boswell	Charles Boswell, London, England (1884–)
Braendlin	Braendlin Armoury, Birmingham, England (1871–89)
Brenneke	Wilhelm Brenneke, Leipzig, and Berlin, Germany (ca. 1920–45) W. Brenneke GmbH, Berlin, Germany (ca. 1950–).
Britarms	This name has passed between several companies; it appears to have originated with the Berdan Group of Aylesbury, Bucks., England in about 1973, and thereafter went through various hands before ending with Westlake Engineering of Bordon, Hants., England in the mid-1980s.
Brixia	Metallurgica Bresciana Tempini, Brescia, Italy (1908–15)
Brooklyn Arms	Brooklyn Arms Co., Brooklyn, N.Y., USA (ca. 1865)
Brown	Brown Precision Inc., Los Molinos, Calif., USA
Browning	Browning Arms Co., Morgan, Utah, USA

Bruchet	P. Bruchet, St. Etienne, France. Began manufacturing shotguns on the Darne system in 1982.
Bryco	Bryco Firearms, Carson City, Nev., USA
BSA	Birmingham Small Arms Co. Ltd. (1861–75) Birmingham Small Arms & Metal Co. Ltd. (1875–1919) BSA Guns Ltd. (1919–86)
Bullard	Bullard Repeating Arms Co., Springfield, Mass., USA (1883–90)
Burgsmuller	Hugo Burgsmuller & Sohn, Kreiensen, Germany (ca. 1880–1914)
Cadillac Gage	Cadillac Gage Corp., Warren, Mich., USA
Century	Century Arms, Evansville, Ind., USA (1976–85) Century Mfg. Corp., Greenfield, Ind., USA (1986–)
Century Int'l	Century International Arms, St. Albans, V., USA
Champlin	Champlin-Haskins Firearms Co., Enid, Okla., USA (1966–70). Champlin Firearms Inc., Enid, Okla., USA (1971–)
Charlier	Fabrique d'Armes Charlier et Cie, Liege, Belgium (pre-1914)
Charter Arms	Charter Arms Corp., Bridgeport, Conn., USA (1964–82); then at Stratford, Conn. (1982–)
Chipmunk	Chipmunk Mfg. Corp., Medford, Ore., USA
Christ	Albert Christ, California, Ohio, USA
Churchill	E.J. Churchill Ltd., London, England (1892–)
Classic	Classic Rifle Co., Charleroi, Pa., USA
Classic Arms	A division of Navy Arms (qv)
Clement	Charles Clement, Liege, Belgium (1900–14)
Cobray	Cobray Industries, Atlanta, Ga., USA. Made semiautomatic copies of the Ingram M10 submachine gun.
Cogswell	Cogswell & Harrison, London, England (1863–)
Colt	Colt's Patent Firearms Mfg. Co., Hartford, Conn., USA (1847–1947); Colt's Mfg. Co. (1947–55); Colt's Patent Firearms Mfg. Co. (1955–64); Firearms Div. of Colt Industries (1964–89); Colt Mfg Corp. (1990–); Colt Canada, Kitchener, Ontario, Canada (formerly DIEMACO).
Columbia	Columbia Armory, Columbia, Tenn., USA. A fictitious company invented for sales purposes by Maltby, Henley & Co. of New York in the 1885–1900 period and marked on pistols made by the Norwich Falls Pistol Co.
Competition	Competition Arms, Tucson, Ariz., USA
Conn Arms	Connecticut Arms Co, Norwich, Conn., USA (ca. 1855–70)
Conn Mfg.	Connecticut Arms & Manufacturing Co., Naubuc, Conn., USA
Coonan	Coonan Arms, St. Paul, Minn., USA
Copeland	T. Copeland, Worcester, Mass., USA

Cowles	Cowles & Son, Chicopee, Mass., USA
Cranston	Cranston Arms Co., Providence, R.I., USA. A "paper company" formed by Universal Windings Co. of Providence to manufacture the Johnson automatic rifle in 1941–42 since, at that time, the Johnson Automatics Co. had no manufacturing capability. The factory was located in Cranston, a suburb of Providence.
Crescent Firearms	Crescent Firearms Co., Norwich, Conn., USA (1892–?)
Crucelegui	Crucelegui Hermanos, Eibar, Spain (1900–25)
Cummings	O.S. Cummings, Lowell, Mass., USA (ca. 1866–75) Cummings & Wheeler, Lowell, Mass., USA (ca. 1875–85)
CZ	Ceska Zbrojovka a.s., Prague, Czechoslovakia (1921–)
Daewoo	Daewoo Precision Industries, Pusan, South Korea
Daffini	Libero Daffini, Montini, Brescia, Italy
Daisy	Daisy Mfg Co., Rogers, Ark., USA
Dakin	Dakin Gun Co., San Francisco, Calif., USA (1960s). Shotguns.
Dakota	Dakota Arms Inc., Sturgis, S. Dak., USA (1987–)
Dan Wesson	Dan Wesson Arms, Monson, Mass., USA (1968–)
Dardick	Dardick Corp, Hamden, Conn., USA (1950–62)
Darne	Darne SA, St. Etienne, France (1881–1979)
Davenport	Davenport Firearms Co., Norwich, Conn., USA (1880–1910)
Davis	Davis Industries, Chino, Calif., USA (1986–)
Davis-Warner	Davis-Warner Corp., Assonet, Mass., USA (1917–19)
Decker	Wilhelm Decker, Zella St. Blasii, Germany (1910–14)
Deringer	Deringer Rifle & Pistol Works, Philadelphia, Pa., USA Deringer Revolver & Pistol Co., Philadelphia, Pa., USA
Detonics	Detonics Associates, Seattle, Washington, USA (ca. 1972–88) Detonics Inc., Bellevue, Wash., USA (1988–)
Deutsche Werke	Deutsche Werke AG, Erfurt, Germany. Manufactured the Ortgies pistol 1921–39.
Diana	Mayer & Grammelspacher, Rastatt, Germany (1890–)
Dickinson	E.L. & J. Dickinson, Springfield, Mass., USA (ca. 1860–85)
Dickson	John Dickson & Sons, Edinburgh, Scotland
Dornaus	Dornaus & Dixon, Huntington Beach, Calif., USA (1980–86)
Dornheim	G.C. Dornheim, Suhl, Germany. Marketed pistols made by other firms, also made an automatic pistol and rifles under their own name. Bought out by Albrecht Kind in 1940.
Doumoulin	Doumoulin et Fils, Liege, Belgium
Drulov	Dilo Svratouch, Litomysl, Czechslovakia
DuBiel	DuBiel Arms Co., Sherman, Tex., USA (1975–90)
Dumoulin	Dumoulin Freres & Cie, Liege, Belgium
Dusek	Frantisek Dusek, Opocno, Czechoslovakia. From about 1926 until absorbed by CZ in about 1947.
DWM	Deutsche Waffen und Munitionsfabrik, Berlin (1897–1945)

Echave y Arizmendi	Echave y Arizmendi y Compania SA, Eibar, Spain (1911–79)
Echeverria	Bonifacio Echeverria y Cia, Eibar, Spain (1908–)
Eiler	Eiler, Pecs, Hungary
Em-Ge	Em-Ge Sportgerate GmbH & Co. KG; Gerstenberger & Eberwein; Gerstetten-Gussenstadt, Germany. (Formerly known as Moritz & Gerstenberger, from which came the Em-Ge trademark.)
Encom	Encom-America Inc., Atlanta, Ga., USA
Enfield	Royal Small Arms Factory, Enfield Lock, England (1854–1988). Operation then purchased by British Aerospace (Royal Ordnance) and transferred to the Royal Ordnance Factory, Nottingham, England.
Erma	Erma-Werke, B. Giepel GmbH, Erfurt, Germany (1919–45). Erma-Werke GmbH, Munchen-Dachau, Germany (1949–)
Erquiaga	Erquiaga y Cia, Eibar, Spain (1915–19); then Erquiaga, Muguruzu y Cia, Eibar (until ca. 1935)
Errasti	Antonio Errasti, Eibar, Spain (1904–36)
Escodin	Manoel Escodin, Eibar, Spain (ca. 1920–33)
Esprin	Esprin Hermanos, Eibar, Spain (1906–17)
Evans	Evans Rifle Mfg. Co., Mechanic Falls, Maine, USA (1871–80)
Fabarm	Fabricca di Armi Brescia, Brescia, Italy
Fajen	Reinhart Fajen Mfg. Co., Warsaw, Mo., USA
Falcon	Falcon Firearms Mfg. Corp., Granada Hills, Calif., USA. Made left-handed versions of the Colt M1911 pistol (1986–89).
FAMAE	Fabrica de Material de Ejercito, Santiago, Chile. Previously known as Fabrica de Material de Guerra.
Farrow	Farrow Arms Co, Holyoke, Mass., USA (1885–1900)
FAS	Fabbrica Armi Sportive Srl, Settimo Milanese, Italy. Took over the business of IGI (qv) in 1973.
FAVS	Fabbrica Armi Valle Susa, Vilaforchado, Turin, Italy
Feather	Feather Industries Inc., Boulder, Colo., USA (1986–)
Federal	Federal Engineering Corp., Chicago, Ill., USA (1984–)
Federal Ordnance	Federal Ordnance Inc., South El Monte, Calif., USA (ca. 1985–)
FEG	see Fegyver
Fegyver	Fegyver es Gepgyar Reszvenytarsasag, Budapest, Hungary (ca. 1880–1945); then became Femaru es Szerszam-gepgyar NV until ca. 1985, when it became the FEG Arms & Gas Appliances Factory.
Feinwerkbau	Feinwerkbau Westinger & Altenburger GmbH & Co. KG, Oberndorf/Neckar, Germany (1948–)
Fiala	Fiala Arms & Equipment Co., New Haven, Conn., USA (1920–23)
Firearms	Firearms Co. Ltd., Bridgewater, England

Firearms Int'l	Firearms International Corp., Washington, D.C., USA (ca. 1962–74)
FN HERSTAL	Fabrique National de Armes de Guerre, Herstal, Liege, Belgium (1889–1945)
	Fabrique National SA, Herstal, Liege, Belgium (1949–90). It was then purchased by Giat (qv) and became FN Nouvelle Herstal SA, Liege, Belgium (1990–96). Giat got into financial difficulties and FN was repurchased by the Walloon local authorities and became FN Herstal SA, Liege, Belgium (1996–).
FNM	FN Manufacturing LLC, Columbia, S. Ca., USA
Foehl & Weeks	Foehl & Weeks Firearms Mfg. Co., Philadelphia, Pa., USA. Pistol manufacturer, 1890–94.
Forehand	Forehand & Wadsworth, Worcester, Mass., USA (1871–90)
	Forehand Arms Co., Worcester, Mass., USA (1890–1902). Taken over by Hopkins & Allen 1902.
Fort	Science-Industrial Association, Vinnitsa, Ukraine
Fox	Fox Gun Co., Philadelphia, Pa., USA (1903–30). Acquired by the Savage company, who continued making shotguns with the Fox name until 1942.
Franchi	Luigi Franchi SpA, Fornaci, Brescia, Italy
Francotte	August Francotte & Cie, Herstal, Belgium (1805–)
Franklin	C.W. Franklin, Liege, Belgium (ca. 1885–1914)
Franconia	Waffen-Franconia, Wurzburg, Germany
Fraser	Daniel Fraser & Co, Edinburgh, Scotland (ca. 1871–1914)
Freedom	Freedom Arms, Freedom, Wyo., USA
Fyrberg	Andrew Fyrberg, Hopkinton, Mass., USA (1880–1910). Principally a patentee of various firearms items, which he licensed to other makers. He entered the pistol business under his own name between 1903 and 1910 producing the Fyrberg revolver.
Gabbett-Fairfax	Hugh Gabbett-Fairfax, Leamington Spa, England. Patentee of the Mars automatic pistol 1895–1904.
Gabilondo	Founded at Eibar, Spain, in 1904 as Gabilondos y Urresti; one of the Gabilondo brothers left in 1909 and it then became Gabilondo y Urresti until 1920, when the firm moved to Elgoeibar and became Gabilondo y Cia. In 1936 it changed its name to Llama-Gabilondo y Cia, and in 1940 moved to Vitoria.
Galand	Charles Francoise Galand, Liege Belgium (ca. 1870– 1914)
Galesi	Industria Armi Galesi, Collebeato, Brescia, Italy. Also known, at various times, as Armi Galesi; Rino Galesi; Soc Italiana Fili Galesi.
Garate	Garate Hermanos, Eibar, Spain (ca. 1910–27)
Garate Anitua	Garate, Anitua y Cia, Eibar, Spain (1900–36)

Gasser	Leopold Gasser, Vienna, Austria (1880–1914)
Gatling	Gatling Arms & Ammunition Co., Birmingham, England. Formed in 1888 to market the Gatling machine gun in Europe and manufactured the Dimancea revolver until liquidated in 1890.
Gavage	Fabrique d'Armes de Guerre de Haute Precision Armand Gavage, Liege, Belgium (ca. 1934–44)
Gaztanaga	Isidro Gaztanaga, Eibar, Spain (1904–36). During this period he also traded as Gaztanaga, Trocaoloa y Ibarzabal making and selling pistols.
Gehmann	Walter Gehmann, Karlsruhe, Germany
Genschow	Gustav Genschow AG, Hamburg, Germany. Primarily an ammunition company (Geco), now part of Dynamit Nobel, but prior to 1914 marketed pistols under the Geco name.
GIAT	Groupement Industriel des Armamentes Terrestres, Saint-Cloud, France (1950–1990). During this period, it was a government agency coordinating the activities of all French munition factories. In 1990 it was privatized and became GIAT Industries, at the same address and doing the same job, but as a private industry it was able to purchase a number of munitions companies (e.g., FN, Matra, Manurhin) that would otherwise have gone to the wall.
Gibbs	George Gibbs, Bristol, England (ca. 1900–40)
Gibbs	Gibbs Rifle Co. Inc., Martinsburg, W.Va., USA (1992–). This company, a subsidiary of Navy Arms Co., acquired the rights to the Parker-Hale rifle designs and manufactures them under the Parker-Hale name.
Gibbs	Gibbs Guns Inc., Greenback, Tenn., USA. Made a semi-automatic copy of the Thomson submachine gun 1985–88.
Glaser	W. Glaser, Zurich, Switzerland (ca. 1925–50)
Glock	Glock GmbH, Deutsch-Wagram, Austria. Began making pistols in 1982, but had been a manufacturer of knives and edged tools for several years before.
Golden Eagle	Golden Eagle Rifles Inc., Houston, Tex., USA. Marketed rifles under this name made by Nikko of Japan (1976–82).
Golden State	Golden State Arms Corp., Pasadena Calif., USA (1960s)
Goncz	Goncz Co., North Hollywood, Calif., USA (1985–90)
Grabner	Georg Grabner, Rehberg, Austria. Manufactured the Kolibri pistol 1914–27.
Grand Precision	Fabrique d'Armes de Guerre de Grand Precision, Eibar, Spain. A trading name registered by Extezagarra y Abitua, gunmakers of Eibar, as a sales agency for pistols of their own make and those made by other small concerns in Eibar, in the period 1918–36.

Great Western	Great Western Gun Works, Pittsburgh, Penn., USA
Green	Edwinson C. Green, Cheltenham, England. Maker of pistols and sporting guns 1880–1982.
Greener	W.W. Greener, Birmingham, England. (1864–)
Greifelt	Greifelt & Co., Suhl, Germany
Grendel	Grendel Inc., Rockledge, Fla., USA
Griffin & Howe	Griffin & Howe, New York, N.Y., USA
Grunel	Grunig & Elmiger, Malters, Switzerland
Guide Lamp	Guide Lamp Division of General Motors, Detroit, Mich., USA. Made the Liberator single-shot pistol for three months in 1942.
Gunworks	Gunworks Ltd., Buffalo, N.Y., USA. Made a two-barrel Derringer pistol in 1985–86.
Haenel	C.G. Haenel Gewehr & Fahrradfabrik, Suhl, Germany (1840–1945). After this, it became one of the founders of VEB.
Hafdasa	Hispano-Argentine Fabrica de Automobiles SA, Buenos Aires, Argentina
Halger	Halbe & Gerlich (Halger-Waffenwerke), Kiel and Berlin, Germany (ca. 1923–39)
Hammerli	Hammerli AG, Lenzburg, Switzerland (1863–)
Harrington & Richardson	
	Harrington & Richardson , Worcester, Mass., USA (1874–1975); Harrington & Richardson Inc., Gardner, Mass., USA (1975–84).
Harris	Harris Gun Works, Phoenix, Ariz., USA. Took over the McMillan company in 1993 and continues to make the McMillan 0.50 heavy rifles under the Harris name.
Hartford Arms	Hartford Arms & Equipment Co., Hartford, Conn., USA. Made a 0.22RF automatic pistol 1929–1932, when they were liquidated and the remains taken over by the High Standard Company. Note that there was no connection between this firm and the earlier revolvers bearing the sales name Hartford Arms and made by the Norwich Pistol Company in the 1880s.
HDH	Henrion, Dassy & Heuschen, Liege, Belgium (ca. 1880–1914)
Hebsacker	Hege, Schwabisch Hall, Germany (1960–80)
Heckler & Koch	Heckler & Koch GmbH, Oberndorf/Neckar, Germany, from 1949. Purchased by British Aerospace in 1992.
Heinzelmann	C.E. Heinzelmann, Plochingen, Germany (1930–39)
Henry	Alexander Henry & Co., Edinburgh, Scotland
Heym	Friedrich Wilh. Heym GmbH & Co KG, Munnerstadt, Germany. Founded 1865; located in Suhl until 1945.
Higgins	J.C. Higgins, Chicago, Ill., USA. A fictitious company used

	as a sales name by Sears, Roebuck 1946–52. The weapons (shotguns, rifles, and revolvers) were made by various companies and were usually cheaper versions of their standard products.
High Standard	High Standard Inc., Hartford, Conn., USA (1926–85). Originally barrel makers, they bought the remains of the Hartford Arms Co. in 1932 and used their pistol design as a basis for their own developments.
Holland	Holland & Holland, London, England (1877–)
Holmes	Holmes Firearms, Wheeler, Ariz., USA. Made semi-automatic pistol styled as submachine guns 1985–86.
Hood	Hood Firearms Co., Norwich, Conn., USA (1873–82)
Hopkins & Allen	Hopkins & Allen, Norwich, Conn., USA (1868–1917), then absorbed into the Marlin-Rockwell Corporation. A second company of this name, owing nothing to its forebears, was formed in Hawthorne, N.J., in the early 1960s to make replica percussion pistols that it sold through the Numrich Arms Corporation, though there is some doubt whether Hopkins & Allen actually made them.
Hourat	Hourat et Vie, Pau, France (1920–40)
Howa	Howa Industries, Aichi, Japan
Hunter (1)	Hunter Arms Co., Syracuse, N.Y., USA. Reorganized name for what had been the L.C. Smith Gun Co. (1890–1948) when it became a division of Marlin.
Hunter (2)	Hy Hunter Firearms Mfg. Co., Hollywood, Calif., USA. Actually an importer and wholesaler, dealing in the cheaper European pistols such as Rigarmi, Reck, and Pyrenees, and having the Hunter name on them.
Husqvarna	Husqvarna Wapenfabrik, Huskvarna, Sweden
IGI	Italguns International, Zingone de Tressano, Italy (1972–85); acted as a sales agency for Fabbricca Armi Sportive, Settimo Milanese, Italy.
IMBEL	Industrias de Materials Belico do Brasil, Sao Paulo, Brazil
IMI	Israel Military Industries, Ramat Hasharon, Israel (1950–93, 1996–). Became Ta'as Israel Industries in 1993–96, but then reverted to the original name.
Inglis	John Inglis & Co., Toronto, Canada. Made the Browning High-Power pistol for China and Canada in 1944–45.
Interarms	Interarms, Alexandria, Va., USA (ca. 1965–)
Interdynamics	Interdynamics of America, Miami, Fla., USA. Made semi-automatic pistols styled as submachine guns 1981–85. It had links with a company of the same name set up in Sweden in the late 1970s to promote an assault rifle firing a high-powered rimfire cartridge, and it is probable that the weapon designs sold in the USA originated in Sweden.

Intratec	Intratec Inc., Miami, Fla., USA. Assumed the business of Interdynamics (above) 1985–90.
Irving	William Irving, New York, N.Y., USA (1863–70)
Ithaca	W.H. Baker & Co., Ithaca, N.Y., USA (1883–89)
	Ithaca Gun Co., Ithaca, N.Y., (1889–88)
	Ithaca Gun Co., Kingferry, N.Y. (1988–)
ITM	Industrial Technology & Machines AG, Solothurn, Switzerland (1984–89); then absorbed into Sphinx Engineering and its products known under the Sphinx name thereafter.
Izhmash	Izhmash Joint Stock Company, Izhevsk, Russia
Izhmech	Izhevsky Mekhanichesky Zavod, Izhevsk, Russia
Jacquemart	Jules Jacquemart, Liege, Belgium (1912–14)
Jager	F.Jager & Co., Suhl, Germany (1907–45)
Jager Armi	Jager-Armi di Armando Piscetta, Milan, Italy
Iver Johnson	Iver Johnson & Co., Worcester, Mass., USA (1883–91); Iver Johnson Arms & Tool Co., Fitchburg, Mass., USA (1891–1982); Iver Johnson Arms Inc., Jacksonville, Ark., USA (1982–86). Became a division of American Arms Corp. in 1987.
Jeffrey	W.J. Jeffrey, London, England (1888–89)
	Jeffrey & Davis, London, England (1889–91)
	W.J. Jeffrey & Co., London, England (1891–)
Jennings	Jennings Firearms Inc., Stateline, Nev., USA (1981–)
Johnson	Johnson Automatics Mfg. Co., Cranston, R.I., USA (1936–44)
Johnson, Bye	Johnson, Bye & Co., Worcester, Mass., USA. Founded 1871 to manufacture cheap revolvers; in 1883 Bye sold his holding to Johnson, who then reorganized the firm as Iver Johnson & Co. (qv).
Kassnar	Kassnar Imports, Harrisburg, Pa., USA. Distributes rifles made by Sabatti (qv).
KBP	KBP Instrument Design Bureau, Tula, Russia
Keberst	Keberst International, Paris, Ky., USA (1987–88)
Kessler	F.W. Kessler, Suhl, Germany (pre-1914)
Kessler	Kessler Arms Corp., Silver Creek, N.Y., USA. Shotguns (1951–53)
Kettner	Edward Kettner, Suhl, Germany. Made combination rifle/shotguns 1920–39.
Kimball	Kimball Arms Co., Detroit, Mich., USA (1955–58)
Kimber	Kimber of Oregon Inc., Clackamas, Ore., USA
Kind	Albrecht Kind AG, Nuremberg, Germany (1920–45)
	Albrecht Kind AG, Hunstig, Germany (1950–)
Kodiak	Kodiak Mfg. Co., North Haven, Conn., USA (ca. 1959–74)
Kohout	Kohout & Spolecnost, Kdyne, Czechoslovakia (1927–39)

Kolb	Henry M. Kolb, Philadephia, Pa., USA (1892–1930)
Kommer	Theodor Kommer Waffenfabrik, Zella Mehlis, Germany (1920–39)
Konchar	Konchar Arms, Zagreb, Croatia
Korriphila	Korriphila Prazisionsmechanik GmbH, Ulm/Donau, Germany
Korth	Waffenfabrik W. Korth, Ratzeburg/Holstein, Germany
Kragujevac	Yugoslavian military arsenal set up by Fabrique National of Belgium in the early 1900s. Became known as Voini Techniki Zavod (Army Technical Factory) in the 1920s. More or less destroyed 1939–45; reconstituted as Crvena Zastava, and in 1990 changed its name to Zastava Arms.
Krauser	Alfred Krauser, Zella Mehlis, Germany (1920–31)
Krico	Krico GmbH, Stuttgart, Germany
Krieghoff	Heinrich Krieghoff Waffenfabrik, Suhl, Germany (pre-1945)
	H. Krieghoff GmbH, Ulm/Donau, Germany (post-1945)
Kynoch	The Kynoch Gun Factory, Birmingham, England (1888–90). (The name is more usually associated with ammunition, but George Kynoch set up this pistol factory independently of his ammunition business in order to manufacture a pistol of his own design. He unfortunately died two years later and the factory was closed down.)
Lancaster	Charles Lancaster, London, England. Actually a trading name for Henry Thorn who had been Lancaster's apprentice, and under which name he produced various sporting weapons and pistols in the 1880–1900 period.
Langenhan	Friedrich Langenhan, Zella Mehlis, Germany (1842–1936)
Laurona	Laurona SA, Eibar, Spain
LAR	LAR Manufacturing Inc., Jordan, Utah, USA
Lebeau	Lebeau-Courally, Liege, Belgium (1910–)
Lecocq	Lecocq et Hoffmann, Liege, Belgium (?–1940; 1955–70)
Lee Arms	Lee Arms Co., Wilkes Barre, Pa., USA (ca. 1865–85)
Lefever	Lefever Arms Co., Syracuse, N.Y., USA (1884–1916) then acquired by Ithaca, who continued to make shotguns with the Lefever name until 1948. The founder was forced out by a board-room revolution in 1901 and set up a separate firm, D.M. Lefever, Sons & Co., also making shotguns, until his death in 1906, when the company folded.
Leigoise	Manufacture Liegoise d'Armes de Feu SA, Liege, Belgium
LePage	Manufacture d'Armes LePage SA, Liege, Belgium (ca. 1780–1940)
Lignose	Lignose Pulverfabrik AG, Germany. Bought the Bergmann factory in 1921 and made Bergmann and other pistols under the Lignose name until 1939.

Ljutic	Ljutic Industries, Yakima, Wash., USA (1980–88)
Llama	Llama-Gabilondo y Cia SA, Vitoria, Spain (1936–). For earlier history see Gabilondo.
Loewe	Ludwig Loewe & Co., Berlin, Germany. Founded in the 1850s as an engineering firm, began making rifles on contract, then licenced Smith & Wesson pistols for Russia and backed Borchardt and Luger in their automatic pistol designing. Amalgamated with a cartridge company in 1896 to become DWM (qv).
Lorcin	Lorcin Engineeering Co., Riverside, Calif., USA (1988–)
Lowell (1)	Lowell Arms Co., Lowell, Mass., USA. Formerly the Rollin White company, formed 1864, closed 1868.
Lowell (2)	Lowell Arms Co., Lowell, Mass., USA. Marked on Phoenix pistols made by Robar and imported into the USA ca. 1925–33. May have been an import agency, or even a fictitious name. It is unlikely that it had any connection with Lowell (1).
Lower	John P. Lower, Philadelphia, Pa., USA (ca. 1865–70)
Maadi	Maadi Military & Civil Industries Co., Cairo, Egypt
MAB	Manufacture d'Armes de Bayonne, Bayonne, France (1921–88). A private company manufacturing automatic pistols.
MAC	Miitary Armaments Corp., Atlanta, Ga., USA. Made the Ingram submachine gun ca. 1976–82.
M.A.C.	Manufacture d'Armes Chatellerault, Chatellerault, France. State arms factory, particularly noted for machine guns.
McMillan	McMillan Gun Works Inc., Phoenix, Ariz., USA. Was taken over in 1993 and became the Harris Gun Works.
Madsen	Dansk Industrie Syndikat AS "Madsen," Copenhagen, Denmark. Now known as DISA Systems, and no longer in the firearms business.
M.A.S.	Manufacture d'Armes de Ste Etienne, St. Etienne, France. State arms factory; rifles, submachine guns, pistols.
Manhattan	Manhattan Firearms Co., New York, N.Y., USA (1850–65)
Mann	Fritz Mann Werkzeugfabrik, Suhl, Germany (1919–29)
Manufrance	Manufacture Francaise d'Armes et Cycles de Saint Etienne, St. Etienne, France. Later (post-1945) adopted the name Manufrance SA.
Manurhin	Manufacture de Machines du Haut-Rhin, Mulhouse-Bourtzwiler, France. Began firearms manufacture in the early 1950s. Later changed its name to Manurhin and later to Manurhin Defense, until taken over by GIAT in 1990. It still retains its own identity within the GIAT organization and markets arms under the Manurhin name. Also a major producer of ammunition-making machinery.

Marathon	Marathon Products, Weathersfield, Conn., USA (1984–88)
Marble	Marble Manufacturing Co., Gladstone, Mich., USA. Made the Marble Game Getter, a combination rifle/shotgun. from about 1907 to 1929.
Marlin	John M. Marlin, New Haven, Conn., USA (1865–81); Marlin Firearms Co., New Haven, Conn., USA (1881–1969); Marlin Firearms Co., North Haven, Conn., USA (1969–).
Marston	W.W. Marston & Co., New York, N.Y., USA (1850–74)
Marston & Knox	Fictitious sales name used by W.W. Marston
Mateba	Macchine Termo Ballistiche, Pavia, Italy (ca. 1980–87). Manufactured the Mateba revolver.
Mauser	Gebruder Mauser, Oberndorf/Neckar, Germany (1872–74); Gebruder Mauser & Co. (1874–84); Waffenfabrik Mauser (1884–1922); Mauserwerke AG (1922–45); Mauserwerke Oberndo.
Maverick	Maverick Arms Co., Eagle Pass, Tex., USA (1989–)
Mayor	E. & F. Mayor, Lausanne, Switzerland
MBA	MB Associates, San Ramon, Calif., USA (1960–70). Made the Gyrojet pistol/rifle rocket launchers.
Menz	Waffenfabrik August Menz, Suhl, Germany (1914–37)
Meriden	Meriden Firearms Co., Meriden, Conn., USA (1895–1915). Sold revolvers under their own name and also supplied them to Sears, Roebuck.
Merkel	Gebruder Merkel & Co., Suhl, Germany (1781–1945). It was then, like all East German gunsmiths, absorbed into the state-run VEB organization but continued to produce guns for export under the Merkel name.
Merrill	The Merrill Co., Fullerton, Calif., USA
Merwin, Hulbert	Merwin and Bray, New York, N.Y., USA (1853–64); Merwin, Taylor & Simson, New York (1864–68); Merwin, Hulbert & Co, New York (1868–92); Hulbert Brothers, New York (1892–96). This company acted as an agency for various revolver makers, notably Hopkins & Allen, and owned a number of patents that were worked by various firms. Hopkins & Allen produced revolvers bearing the Merwin, Hulbert name.
Miroku	Miroku Firearms Co. KK, Kochi City, Shikoku, Japan (1965–)
Mitchell	Mitchell Arms Inc., Santa Ana, Calif., USA
MKEK	Makina ve Kimya Endustrisi Kurumu, Ankara, Turkey. Makers of the Kirrikale pistol and various licenced Heckler & Koch weapons.
MOA	MOA Corp., Dayton, Ohio, USA
Mondial	MM–Mondial, Modesto Molgora, Milan, Italy.
Moore	Moore's Patent Firearms Co., Brooklyn, N.Y., USA (1860–65). Then taken over by the National Arms Co.

Morini	Morini Competition, Lamone, Switzerland
Moritz	Heinrich Moritz, Zella-Mehlis, Germany (1920s)
Mossberg	O.F. Mossberg & Sons, New Haven, Conn., USA
Muller	Muller & Greiss, Munich, Germany (?–1914)
Musgrave	Musgrave (Pty.), Bloemfontein, South Africa. Originally an independent company founded by Musgrave, after his death it became part of the Armscor organization. Manufactures hunting rifles; ammunition bearing their name is made by PMP.
Nagant	Emile Nagant, Liege, Belgium (?–1910)
	Fabrique d'Armes Leon Nagant, Liege, Belgium (?–1910)
	Fabrique d'Armes et Automobiles Nagant Frères, Liege, Belgium (1910–14)
National	National Arms Co., Brooklyn, N.Y., USA (1865–70). Then bought out by Colt.
Navy Arms	Navy Arms Co., Ridgefield, N.J., USA (1957–)
New England	New England Firearms Co., Gardner, Mass., USA. Founded 1988 out of the remains of Harrington & Richardson.
Newton	Newton Arms Co., Buffalo, N.Y., USA (1914–18);
	Charles Newton Rifle Corp., Buffalo, N.Y., USA (1921–22);
	Buffalo-Newton Rifle Co., Buffalo, N.Y., USA (1923–24);
	Buffalo-Newton Rifle Co., Springfield, Mass., USA (1924–29);
	Lever-Bolt Rifle Co., New Haven, Conn., USA (1929–32).
Nikko	Nikko Firearms Mfg. Co., Tochigi, Japan
Noble	Noble Firearms Co., Haydenville, Mass., USA (1950–71)
Norarmco	North Armament Co., Mount Clemens, Mich., USA (1972–77)
Norinco	North China Industries Corp., Peking, China. Sales organization for the Chinese national munitions factories.
North American (1)	North American Arms Co., Quebec, Canada (1917–20). Set up for wartime production of various weapons, notable for producing a small number of Colt 0.45 auto pistols on contract.
North American (2)	North American Arms Corp., Toronto, Canada (1948–52). There is no connection between these two companies. This firm appears to have been set up solely to promote the Brigadier pistol, an enlarged Browning 1935 chambered for a special 0.45 NAACO cartridge. It failed.
North American (3)	North American Arms, Spanish Fork, Utah, USA (1975–)
Norton	Norton Arms Co., Mount Clemens, Mich., USA. Manufactured the Budischowsky pistol 1977–79.
Norwich Falls	Norwich Pistol Co., Norwich, Conn., USA (1875–81);
	Norwich Falls Pistol Co., Norwich Falls, Conn., USA (1881–87)
O.D.I.	O.D. Inc., Midland Park, N.J., USA (1981–82)

Ojanguren	Ojanguren y Marcaido, Eibar, Spain (1895–1930). Then liquidated and revived as Ojanguren y Vidosa, surviving until 1936.
Olympic	Olympic Arms Inc., Olympia, Wash., USA
Omega	Omega Firearms Co., Flower Mound, Tex., USA (1968–75)
Orbea	Orbea Hermanos, Eibar, Spain (ca. 1860–1936)
Ortgies	Heinrich Ortgies & Co., Erfurt, Germany (1919–21). Then bought out by Deutsche Werke.
Osgood	Osgood Gun Works, Norwich, Conn., USA (ca. 1878–82)
Osterreich	Osterreichische Werke Anstalt, Vienna, Austria (1920–25)
PAF	Pretoria Arms Factory, Pretoria, South Africa (1960–70)
Page-Lewis	Page-Lewis Arms Co., Chicopee Falls, Mass., USA (1920–26). Then bought out by Stevens Arms Co.
Para-Ordnance	Para-Ordnance Mfg. Inc., Scarborough, Ontario, Canada (1989–). Makes conversions and kits for M1911-type pistols.
Pardini	Fiocchi SpA, Lecco, Italy
Parker	Parker Bros, Meriden, Conn., USA (1868–1934). Then bought out by Remington. Shotguns.
Parker-Hale	Parker Hale Ltd., Birmingham, England (1880–1992). In 1992, the rights and patents to Parker-Hale rifles were sold to the Gibbs Rifle Co. (qv), who then began making rifles under the Parker-Hale name.
Pedersen	Pederson Custom Guns, North Haven, Conn., USA. This was a division of Mossberg that produced higher-quality versions of Mossberg shotguns from 1975 to 1977.
Pedersoli	Armi D. Pedersoli, Gardone Val Trompia, Brescia, Italy
Perrazi	Perazzi, Brescia, Italy. Shotguns.
Perugini	Perugini-Visoli & Co., Nuovolera, Brescia, Italy. Shotguns.
Peters-Stahl	PSW Vertriebsgesellschaft mbH, Aachen, Germany
Pfannl	F. Pfannl, Krems, Austria (1912–36)
PGM	PGM Precision, BP29, F-74334 Poisy Cedex, France
Phelps	E.F. Phelps Mfg. Co., Evansville, Ind., USA
Phoenix	Phoenix Arms Co. Fictitious sales name used by W. W. Marston.
Pickert	Friedrich Pickert Arminius Waffenwerk, Zella Mehlis, Germany (1900–39)
Pieper	Henri & Nicolas Pieper, Herstal, Belgium (1866–1905). Then became Ancien Etablissements Pieper until about 1955.
Pietta	Fabricca d'Armi Filli Pietta di Giuseppe & Co., Gussago, Italy
Pilsen	Zbrojovka Plzen, Plzen, Czechoslovakia. An offshoot of the Skoda company, set up in the 1920s to manufacture pistols and probably closed down in 1938.
Pirandelli	Pirandelli & Gasparini, Brescia, Italy. Shotguns.

Plainfield (1)	Plainfield Machine Co., Dunellen, N.J., USA Made reproduction M1 carbines ca. 1963 until 1975, when bought out by Iver Johnson.
Plainfield (2)	Plainfield Ordnance Co., Middlesex, N.J., USA. Made 0.22 and 0.25 pistols in the 1970–80 period. Their relationship to Plainfield (1) is unclear.
Pond	Lucius W. Pond, Worcester, Mass., USA
Powell	William Powell & Son, Birmingham, England (1822–)
Praga	Praga Zbojovka, Prague, Czechoslovakia (1918–26)
Prescott	E.A. Prescott, Worcester, Mass., USA (1860s)
Pretoria	Pretoria Small Arms Factory, Pretoria, South Africa (ca. 1955–60)
Protector	Protector Arms Co., Philadephia, Pa.,USA. An offshoot of the Rupertus company in the 1870s.
Providence	Providence Tool Co., Providence, R.I., USA
PSMG	P.S.M.G. Gun Co., Arlington, Mass., USA (1988–)
Purdey	James Purdey & Sons Ltd., London, England
Pyrenees	Manufacture d'Armes des Pyrenees Francaise, Hendaye, France (1923–). Principally known for the Unique range of pistols.
Quackenbush	O. Quackenbush, Herkimer, N.Y., USA (ca. 1880–1910)
Radom	Fabrika Brony w Radomu, Radom, Poland
Rahn	Rahn Gun Works, Grand Rapids, Mich., USA
Raick	Raick Freres, Liege, Belgium
Raven	Raven Arms, Industry, Calif., USA (ca. 1976–)
Reck	Reck Division, Umarex-Sportwaffen GmbH & Co. KG, Arnsberg i Neheim-Husten, Germany
Reid	James Reid, New York, N.Y., USA (ca. 1862–90). Rimfire revolvers.
Reising	Reising Arms Co., Hartford, Conn., USA (1916–24). Made a 0.22 pistol. Note that there is no connection between this firm and the Reising automatic weapons made during World War II other than the name; Reising designed these weapons, but they were made by Harrington & Richardson.
Remington	Eli Remington & Son, Ilion, N.Y., USA (1816–86) Remington Arms Co., Bridgeport, Conn., USA (1886–)
Renato Gamba	Armi Renato Gamba SA, Gardone Val Trompia, Italy Reorganized in the late 1980s and became SAB (qv).
Retolaza	Retolaza Hermanos, Eibar, Spain (1895–1936)
Reunies	Soc. Anonyme des Fabriques d'Armes Reunies, Liege, Belgium (1909–18) Fabrique d'Armes Unies, Liege, Belgium (1918–31)
Reynolds	Reynoilds, Plant & Hotchkiss, New Haven, Conn., USA (ca. 1863–70)

Rheinmetall	Rheinische Metallwaren und Maschinenfabrik, Sommerda, Germany. Began as an engineering firm in 1889; purchased the Waffenfabrik von Dreyse in 1901 and thereafter used the Dreyse name on pistols and machine guns. Amalgamated with Borsig AG in 1936 to become Rheinmetall-Borsig, reorganized after 1945 to become Rheinmetall AG. Still extant but not in the small-arms business.
Rhode Island	Rhode Island Arms Co., Hope Valley, R.I., USA (1949–53). Shotguns.
Richland	Richland Arms, Blissfield, Mich., USA. American importer and distributor of Spanish shotguns of various makes.
Rigarmi	Rigarmi di Rino Galesi, Brescia, Italy (1951–)
Rigby	John Rigby & Co., London, England (1867–)
Robar	Robar & DeKerkhove, Liege, Belgium (ca. 1890–1927); L. Robar & Cie. Liege (1927–48); Manufacture Leigoise d'Armes a Feu Robar et Cie, Liege (1948–58).
Rocky Mountain	Rocky Mountain Arms Corp., Salt Lake City, Utah, USA
Rohm	Rohm GmbH, Sontheim a.d. Brenz, Germany
Rome	Rome Revolver & Novelty Works, Rome, N.Y., USA
Romer	Romerwerke AG, Suhl, Germany (1924–27)
Ronge	J.B. Ronge et Fils, Liege, Belgium (1880–1914)
Roper	Roper Repeating Rifle Co., Amherst, Mass., USA (ca. 1870)
Ross	Ross Rifle Co., Quebec, Canada (ca. 1900–17)
Rossi	Amadeo Rossi SA, Sao Leopoldo, Brazil (1881–)
RPM	R & R Sporting Arms, La Brea, Calif., USA
Ruby	Ruby Arms Co., Eibar, Spain. Fictitious company, marked on Ruby pistols made by Gabilondo.
Ruger	Sturm, Ruger & Co. Inc., Southport, Conn., USA (1949–)
Rupertus	Rupertus Patent Pistol Mfg. Co., Philadelphia, Pa., USA
Ryan	Thomas E. Ryan, Norwich, Conn., USA
SAB	Società Armi Bresciana, Gardone Val Trompia, Italy
Sabatti	Fab. d'Armi Sabatti SpA, Gardone Val Trompia, Italy
SACM	Société Alsacienne de Constructions Mecaniques, Cholet, France (1930–40)
Safari	Safari Arms, Phoenix, Ariz., USA (1978–87). Pistols. Bought out by Olympic Arms.
S.A.G.E.M.	Société d'Applications Generales Electriques et Mecaniques, Mulhouse (?) France (ca. 1930–40)
St. Etienne	Manufacture Nationale d'Armes de Saint Etienne, St. Etienne, France
St. Etienne Automatique	
	Manufacture d'Armes Automatiques, St. Etienne, France
St. Louis	St. Louis Arms Co. (ca. 1895–1910). Fictitious name adopted by American importer of Belgian shotguns.

Sako	Oy Sako AB, Riihimaki, Finland
San Marco	Armi San Marco di Ruffoli, Brescia, Italy
San Paolo	Armi San Paolo, San Paolo, Italy
Santa Barbara	Empresa Nacional de Industrias Militares Santa Bárbara, La Coruña and Madrid, Spain. Spanish government arsenal that also makes sporting rifle actions and barrels.
Sarasqueta	Victor Sarasquete, Eibar, Spain. Shotguns.
Sauer	J.P. Sauer & Sohn GmbH, Suhl, Germany (1733–1945); J.P. Sauer & Sohn GmbH, Eckernforde, Germany (1945–).
Savage	Savage Repeating Arms Co., Utica, N.Y., USA (1893–1970). Savage Arms Corp., Westfield, Mass., USA (1970–)
Schilling	V. Chr. Schilling, Suhl, Germany (ca. 1860–1934)
Schmidt	Herbert Schmidt, Ostheim-a-d-Rhon, Germany (1955–)
Schmidt & H	Schmidt & Habermann, Suhl, Germany
Schuler	Waffenfabrik August Schuler, Suhl, Germany (?–1939)
Schutz	Schutz & Larsen, Otterup, Denmark. Sporting rifles. Active in developing taper-bore weapons in the 1930s.
Schwarzlose	Andreas W. Schwarzlose GmbH, Berlin, Germany (1893–1919)
SEAM	Fabrica d'Armes de Sociedade Espanol de Armas y Municiones, Eibar, Spain (ca. 1910–36). Principally a marketing organization for Urizar and other makers.
Sears	Sears, Roebuck Co. American mail order store; sold all types of firearms under various brand names, and also had a revolver factory in Meriden, Conn., USA, until some time in the 1930s.
Security	Security Industries, Little Ferry, N.J., USA (1973–78)
Sedgley	R.F. Sedgley Inc., Philadephia, Pa., USA (1930–38). Successors to H.M. Kolb.
Seecamp	L.W. Seecamp Inc., New Haven, Conn., USA (1980–)
Semmerling	Semmerling Corp., Newton, Mass., USA
Sempert	Sempert & Krieghoff, Suhl, Germany (?–1924). Then merged with Krieghoff.
Sharps	Christian Sharps & Co., Philadelphia, Pa., USA (1850–74); Sharps Rifle Mfg. Co., Hartford, Conn., USA (1874–)
Shattuck	C.S. Shattuck, Hatfield, Mass., USA (1880–ca. 1892)
Sheridan	Sheridan Products, Racine, Wis., USA (1953–60). Principally air and pneumatic guns, but made a .22 SS pistol.
Shilen	Shilen Arms, Ennis, Tex., USA (1961–)
Shiloh	Shiloh Products, Farmingdale, N.Y., USA (1976–83); Shiloh Rifle Mfg. Co., Big Timber, Mont., USA (1983–).
Shin Chuo Kogyo	Shin Chuo Kogyo K.K., Tokyo, Japan (1956–)
SIG	Schweizerische Industrie Gesellschaft, Neuhausen/Rheinfalls, Switzerland (1853–)
Simson	Waffenfabrik Simson & Co., Suhl, Germany (ca. 1860–1945)
Sirkis	Sirkis Industries, Ramat Gan, Israel.

S J & D	Simonis, Janssen et Doumoulin, Liege (1880–1900)
SKB	S.K.B. Arms, Tokyo, Japan. Manufacturers of shotguns since ca. 1885, and produce shotguns for various companies that claim to manufacture them. They also sell under their own name, but products for others are hard to identify.
Slough	John Slough of London, Hereford, England (1975–)
Smith (1)	Otis A. Smith, Rock Falls, Conn., USA (1873–98)
Smith (2)	L.C. Smith Gun Co., Syracuse, N.Y., USA (1877–90). Then became the Hunter Gun Co. Major U.S. shotgun maker, but equally famous for typewriters.
Smith & Wesson	Smith & Wesson, Springfield, Mass., USA (1852–)
Soc. Franc. d'Armes	Société Française d'Armes Automatiques de St. Etienne, France
Sodia	Franz Sodia, Ferlach, Austria
Sokolovsky	Sokolovsky Corp., Sunnyvale, Calif., USA (1984–89)
Spirlet	A. Spirlet, Liege, Belgium (ca. 1865–1900). Principally a designer and patentee who licensed his ideas to other makers.
Sporting	Sporting Arms Mfg. Co., Little Field, Tex., USA
Sprague	Sprague and Marston. Fictitious sales name used by W.W. Marston.
Springfield	Springfield Armory Inc., Genesee, Ill., USA (1975–94); Springfield Inc., Genesee, Ill., USA (1994–).
Squibman	Squires Bingham Mfg. Co. Inc., Manila, Philippines
Stafford	T.J. Stafford, New Haven, Conn., USA (ca. 1875–90)
Standard	Standard Arms Co., Wilmington, Delaware, USA (1906–12)
Starr	Starr Arms Co., Yonkers, N.Y., USA (1860–75)
Steel City	Steel City Arms Inc., Pittsburg, Pa., USA (1984–)
Stenda	Stendawerke Waffenfabrik GmbH, Suhl, Germany (ca. 1910–26)
Sterling (UK)	Sterling Armaments Co., Dagenham, England (1940–88)
Sterling (USA)	Sterling Arms Corp., Gasport, N.Y., USA (1953–64); Sterling Arms Corp., Lockport, N.Y., USA (1964–86).
Stevens Tool	J. Stevens & Co., Chicopee Falls, Mass., USA (1854–88); J. Stevens Arms & Tool Co., Chicopee Falls, Mass., USA (1888–1920). Then taken over by the Savage Arms Co.
Steyr	Josef Werndl, Steyr, Austria (1863–69); Osterreichische Waffenfabrik Gesellschaft GmbH, Steyr, Austria (1869–1919); Steyr-Werke AG (1919–34); Steyr-Daimler-Puch, Steyr, Austria (1934–90); Steyr-Mannnlicher GmbH, Steyr, Austria (1990–). A subsidiary company, Steyr-Solothurn AG, existed 1934–45 as a marketing organization for military weapons made by Steyr, Rheinmetall and Solothurn AG.
Stiga	Stiga AB, Tranas, Sweden
Stock	Franz Stock Maschinen und Werkbaufabrik, Berlin, Germany (1915–38)

Stoeger	Stoeger Arms Corp., South Hackensack, N.J., USA (1920–76); Stoeger Industries, South Hackensack, N.J., USA (1976–86)
Sundance	Sundance Industries Inc., North Hollywood, Calif., USA
Super Six	Super Six Industries, Elkhorn, Wis., USA
Swift	Swift Rifle Co., London, England
Swing	Swing Target Rifles, Newcastleton, Roxburgh, Scotland
Ta'as	Israel Military Industries, Ramat Hasharon, Israel (1950–93). Became Ta'as Israel Industries in 1993–96, then reverted to the original name.
Tanfoglio	Sabotti & Tanfoglio, Gardone Val Trompia, Brescia, Italy (1935–58); Fabbrica d'Armi Guiseppe Tanfoglio, Gardone Val Trompia, Brescia, Italy.
Tanner	Andre Tanner, Fulenbach, Switzerland (1955–)
Taurus	Forjas Taurus SA, Porto Alegre, Brazil
Taylor	L.B. Taylor & Co., Chicopee, Mass., USA (1860–75)
Texas	Texas Longhorn Arms Inc., Richmond, Tex., USA (1984–)
Thames	Thames Arms Co., Norwich, Conn., USA (ca. 1870–1910). May have been a marketing subsidiary of the Meriden Arms Corp.
Thayer	Thayer, Robertson & Cary, Norwich, Conn., USA (1890–1914)
Thieme & Edeler	Thieme & Edeler, Eibar, Spain (1914–16)
Thompson/Center	Thompson/Center Arms, Rochester, N.H., USA (1962–)
Tipping & Lawden	Caleb & Thomas Tipping Lawden, Birmingham, England (ca. 1845–77). Then sold to P. Webley & Son.
Tikka	Oy Tikkakoski AB, Tikkakoski, Finland (1893–)
Tomas de Urizar	Tomas de Urizar y Cia, Eibar, Spain (1903–21). Appears to have been absorbed by Garate Anitua y Cia.
Tomiska	Alois Tomiska, Pilsen, Bohemia (1902–19)
Triple-S	Triple-S Development Co. Inc., Wickliffe, Ohio, USA (1976–81)
Trocaola	Trocaoloa, Aranzabal y Cia, Eibar, Spain (1903–36)
Trompia	Brescia, Italy (1958–)
TsKIB SOO	Sporting & Hunting Guns, Central Research & Design Bureau, Tula, Russia
TSNIITOCHMASH	Central Scientific-Research Institute of Precise Mechanical Engineering, Klimovsk, Russia
Tulskii	Tulskii Oruzhenyi Zavod, Tula, Russia
Uberti	Aldo Uberti, Ponte Zanano (Brescia), Italy (1959–)
Ultra-Light	Ultra-Light Arms Inc., Granville, W.Va, USA
Unceta	See Astra-Unceta
Union	Union Firearms Co., Toledo, Ohio, USA (ca. 1900–19)

Union Arms	Union Arms Co., New York, N.Y., USA (ca. 1863–70). Possibly a sales name used by W.W. Marston.
Union, Eibar	Union des Fabricants d'Armes, Eibar, Spain (ca. 1911–14)
United States	United States Arms. Ficitious company name used by Otis A. Smith on a 0.44 revolver in the 1870s.
Universal	Universal Sporting Goods, Hialeah, Fla., USA. Made reproduction M1 carbines from 1962 to 1983, when taken over by Iver Johnson.
US Arms (1)	U.S. Arms Co., New York, N.Y., USA (ca. 1870–90)
US Arms (2)	U.S. Arms Co., Riverhead, N.Y., USA (1976–83)
Valmet	Valmet AB, Jyvaskyla, Finland. Taken over by Sako in 1992.
Varner	Varner Sporting Arms, Marietta, Ga., USA
VEB	VEB Fahrzeug und Jagdwaffenfabrik Ernst Thalmann, Suhl, (East) Germany (1945–89)
Venus	Venus Waffenwerke Oskar Will, Zella Mehlis, Germany (ca. 1900–18)
Verney-Carron	Manufacture d'Armes Verney-Carron et Cie, St. Etienne, France
Vickers	Vickers Ltd., Crayford, Kent, England (1919–39)
Victory	Victory Arms, Northampton, England (1988–92)
Voere	Voetter & Co., Schwarzwald, Germany (1950–77); Tiroler Jagd und Sportwaffenfabrik, Kufstein, Austria (1978–87); Mauserwerke, Oberndorf/Neckar, Germany (1988–), who now make the Voere rifles under the Mauser name.
Voetter	Voetter & Co., Vohrenbach, Germany
Voini Techniki Zavod see Kragujevac	
Vom Hofe	Vom Hofe & Scheinemann, Berlin, Germany (1927–45). Name adopted by Gehmann of Karlsruhe (qv) in 1955.
Wahl	Albin Wahl, Zella Mehlis, Thuringia, Germany (pre-1914)
Walther	Carl Walther Waffenfabrik, Zella Mehlis, Germany (1886–1945). Then reorganized in Ulm a.d. Donau in 1950 and now known as Carl Walther Waffenfabrik, Postfach 4325, D–7900 Ulm/Donau, Germany.
Warnant	L. & J. Warnant Frères, Hognee, Belgium (1870–1914)
Warner	Warner Arms Corp., Brooklyn, N.Y, and Norwich, Mass., USA. Set up in 1912, merged to become the Davis-Warner Corp. in 1917, liquidated 1919. Marketed the Schwarzlose 1908 automatic in the USA under their own name, then manufactured pistols for a short time.
Washington	Washington Arms Co. Fictitious sales name used by W. W. Marston.
Weatherby	Weatherby Inc., South Gate, Calif., USA (1949–)
Weaver	Weaver Arms, Escondido, Calif., USA (1983–90)

Webley	Originated as Philip Webley in 1845; P. Webley & Son (1860–97); The Webley & Scott Revolver & Arms Company (1897–1906); and finally Webley & Scott Ltd. (1906–), all of Birmingham, England. In 1958 the company was acquired by R.H. Windsor Ltd.; in 1959 the Windsor group was taken over by Arusha Industries, who later became General & Engineering Industries Ltd. In 1965 this company acquired W.W. Greener, and in 1973 sold Greener and Webley & Scott to the Harris & Sheldon Group. In 1980 firearms production ceased; the shotgun business was reestablished as W. & C. Scott and subsequently sold to Holland & Holland, and the revolver designs and tooling were sold to Pakistan in 1983. The Harris & Sheldon group still manufacture air rifles and pistols under the Webley name.
Weihrauch	Herman Weihrauch Waffenfabrik, Mellrichstadt, Germany. Founded in 1899 in Zella St. Blasii, dissolved in 1945 and reconstituted in Mellrichstadt, West Germany, in 1948 making airguns. It adopted the Arminius trade-name formerly associated with Pickert (qv) and began making firearms again in the 1960s.
Wesson	Frank Wesson, Worcester, Mass., USA (1854–65); Frank Wesson, Springfield, Mass., USA (1865–75). Co-existed with Wesson & Harrington but specialized in rifles and single-shot and double-barreled pistols, while W&H made revolvers.
Wesson & Harrington	
	Wesson & Harrington, Worcester, Mass., USA (ca. 1868–75)
Western Arms	Western Arms Co. Sales name used by W.W. Marston
Western Field	Sales name used by the Montgomery Ward mail-order company in the USA for rifles and shotguns made by various manufacturers on contract.
Westley Richards	Westley Richards & Co., London, England (1850–)
White	Rollin White, Lowell, Mass., USA (ca. 1860–64). Then the name changed to Lowell Arms.
Whitney	Whitney Firearms Co. Inc., New Haven, Conn., USA (1954–65)
Whitneyville	Whitney Arms Co., Whitneyville, Conn., USA (ca. 1840–88). Then bought out by Winchester.
Wichita	Wichita Arms, Wichita, Kans., USA (1977–)
Wiener	Wiener Waffenfabrik, Vienna, Austria. Made the Little Tom pistol 1919–25, having purchased the patents of Tomiska.
Wildey	Wildey Firearms Co. Inc., P.O. Box 447, Cheshire, Conn., USA (1972–)
Wilkinson (1)	Wilkinson Sword Co., London, England. Had revolvers made for them by Webley, 1885–1914.

Wilkinson (2)	Wilkinson Arms, Parma, Ind., USA
Wilkinson Arms	US importer's sales name for Belgian-made shotguns.
Winchester	Winchester Arms Co., New Haven, Conn., USA (1866–1977); US Repeating Arms Co., New Haven, Conn., USA (1978–).
Winkler	Benedikt Winkler, Ferlach, Austria
Winslow	Winslow Arms Co., Camden, S.C., USA (1962–89)
Wurflein	William Wurflein, Phiadelphia, Pa., USA (ca. 1852–84)
Wurthrich	W. Wurthrich, Lutzelfluh, Switzerland
Zanotti	Fabio Zanotti, Brescia, Italy. Shotguns.
Zastava Arms	Post-1990 name for Kragujevac arsenal and its successors; see Kragujevac.
Zbrojovka Brno	Ceskoslovenska Zbrojovka, Brno, Czech Republic (1919–)
Zehner	E. Zehner Waffenfabrik, Suhl, Germany (ca. 1921–27)
ZML	ZM Lucznik SA, Radom, Poland
Zoli	Antonio Zoli SpA, Gardone Val Trompia, Brescia, Italy
Zulaica	M. Zulaica y Cia, Eibar, Spain (1902–36)

Brand Names

Explanatory notes

Scope: This covers as many brand names as can be discovered from the beginning of the metallic cartridge era. Percussion pistols and peculiar cartridge weapons are not considered here, since we are primarily concerned with weapons that are likely to be used today, and for which ammunition is available. Age does not come into this: a 0.22 pistol made in 1870 can be as effective a weapon as a 0.22 pistol made in 1995.

Name: Brand names given here are those actually marked on weapons; names identifying catalogue variations or purely for factory-record purposes are not given. Weapons named for their maker will be identified from the List of Manufacturers.

Type: Rev—revolver; Pistol—semiautomatic pistol; RP—repeating pistol or multi-barreled pistol; MP—machine (automatic) pistol; MG—machine gun; SMG—submachine gun; SS—single-shot pistol; Shotg—shotgun.

Caliber: Most are obvious. Oblique strokes indicate alternative calibers. Suffixes: RF—rimfire; P—Parabellum; S—Short; B-B—Bergmann-Bayard. "Various" indicates that the full range of calibers is usually to be found in that class: e.g., 10, 12, 16, 20, and 28 bore for shotguns.

Maker: The "short title" is given: the full name, location, and other information will be found in the List of Manufacturers. Where the maker is not positively known, the country of origin or probable maker is shown in [square brackets].

Name	Type	Caliber	Maker
AAA	Pistol	6.35/7.65	Aldazabal
ABILENE	Rev	0.357	Mossberg
ABILENE	Rev	0.357/0.44	US Arms (2)
ACE	Pistol	0.22	Colt
ACME ARMS	Rev	0.22/0.32	Stevens
ACME HAMMERLESS	Rev	0.32	Hopkins & Allen
ACRA	Rifle	Various	Fajen
ACTION	Pistol	6.35/7.65	Modesto Santos
ADLER	Pistol	7.65	Engelbrecht & Wolff
AETNA	Rev	0.22/0.32	Harrington & Richardson
AG	Pistol	7.65	Gavage
AJAX ARMY	Rev	0.44RF	Meacham
AKAH	Rifle	Various	Kind
ALAMO	Rev	0.22	Stoeger
ALASKA	Rev	0.22	Hood
ALASKAN	Rifle	Various	Skinner's
ALASKAN MARK X	Rifle	Various	Zastava
ALERT	Rev	0.22	Hood
ALEXIA	Rev	0.32/0.38/0.41RF	Hopkins & Allen
ALEXIS	Rev	0.22	Hood
ALFA	Rev	0.38	Armero Especialistas
ALFA	All types	Various	Adolf Frank
ALKAR	Pistol	6.35/7.65	Alkartasuna
ALLEN	Rev	0.22	Hopkins & Allen
ALLEN	Shotg	Various	McKeown
ALLIES	Pistol	6.35/7.65	Bersaluze
ALPINE	Rifle	Various	Firearms

Name	Type	Caliber	Maker
AMERICA	Rev	0.22	Bliss & Goodyear
AMERICA	Rev	0.32RF	Norwich Falls
AMERICAN, THE	Rev	0.38	Hopkins & Allen
AMERICAN BARLOCK WONDER	Shotg	Various	Crescent Firearms
AMERICAN BOY	Rev	0.22	Bliss & Goodyear
AMERICAN BULLDOG	Rev	Various	Johnson, Bye
AMERICAN CHAMPION	Shotg	12	?
AMERICAN EAGLE	Rev	0.22/0.32	Hopkins & Allen
AMERICAN EAGLE 0.380	Pistol	9S	American Arms
AMERICAN GUN CO.	Rev/Shotg	Various	Crescent Firearms
AMERICUS	Rev	0.22	Hopkins & Allen
APACHE	Rev	0.38	Garantizada
APACHE	Pistol	6.35	Ojanguren y Vidosa
ARICO	Pistol	6.35	Pieper
ARISTOCRAT	Rev	0.22/0.32RF	Hopkins & Allen
ARISTOCRAT	Shotg	Various	Stevens
ARMINIUS (pre-1945)	Rev	Various	Pickert
ARMINIUS (post-1945)	Rev	Various	Weirauch
ARMSCOR 0.38	Rev	0.38	Squires, Bingham
ARVA	Pistol	6.35	[Spain, pre-1914]
ASIATIC	Pistol	6.35/7.65	[Spain, 1920s]
ASTRA	Pistols	Various	Astra-Unceta
ATLAS	Pistol	6.35	Domingo Acha
AUBREY	Rev	0.32/0.38	Meriden Arms/Sears
AUDAX	Pistol	6.35/7.65	Pyrenees
AURORA	Pistol	6.35	[Spain]
AUTOGARDE	Rev	7.65	SFM
AUTO-MAG	Pistol	0.44	Automag
AUTOMASTER	Pistol	0.45	Sokolovsky
AUTOMATIC	Rev	0.32/0.38	Hopkins & Allen
AUTOMATIC HAMMERLESS	Rev	0.32/0.38	Iver Johnson
AUTOMATIC LESTON	Pistol	6.35	Unceta
AUTOMATIC POLICE	Rev	0.32	Forehand & Wadsworth
AUTOMATIQUE FRANCAISE	Pistol	6.35	Soc. Franc. d'Armes
AUTO-POINTER	Shotg	12	Yamamoto
AUTOSHOT	SS	0.410	Stevens
AUTOSTAND	SS	0.22	Manufrance
AVION	Pistol	6.35	Azpiri
AYA	Shotg	Various	Aguirre y Aranzabal
AZUL	Pistol	Various	Arostegui
BABY	Pistol	6.35	FN HERSTAL
BABY BULLDOG	Rev	0.22	[USA, ca. 1885]
BABY RUSSIAN	Rev	0.38	American Arms
BACKUP	Pistol	9S	AMT
BAIKAL	Shotg/Rifle	Various	Russian State
BANG-UP	Rev	0.32RF	Bacon Arms
BARRACUDA	Rev	9P	FN HERSTAL
BASCULANT	Pistol	6.35	Aguirre Zamacolas
BASQUE	Pistol	7.65	Echave & Arizmendi
BATAVIA	Rifle/Shotg	0.22/Various	Baker
BANG-UP	Rev	0.22	Hopkins & Allen
BANTAM	Pistol	6.35	Beretta
BAYARD	All types	Various	Pieper

Name	Type	Caliber	Maker
BEHOLLA	Pistol	7.65	Becker & Hollander
BELLMORE	Shotg	Various	Crescent Arms
BENEMERITA	Pistol	6.35/7.65	Aldazabal
BENGAL NO. 1	Rev	0.22	Iver Johnson
BERSA	Pistol	0.22/0.38	Ange
B.H.	Rev	0.38	Beistegui Hermanos
BICYCLE	Rev	0.22/0.32	Harrington & Richardson
BIG BONANZA	Rev	0.22	Bacon Arms
BIG HORN	SS	0.22	Bighorn Arms
BIJOU	Rev	Various	Debouxtay
BIJOU	Pistol	6.35	Menz
BISLEY	Rev	Various	Colt
BISLEY	Rev	0.357	Ruger
BISON	Rev	0.22	Herbert Schmidt
BLACKHAWK	Rev	0.357	Ruger
BLOODHOUND	Rev	0.22	Hopkins & Allen
BLUE JACKET	Rev	0.22/0.32RF	Hopkins & Allen
BLUE WHISTLER	Rev	0.32RF	Hopkins & Allen
BOCK-FITZKOW	SS	0.22	Buchel
BOIX	Pistol	7.65	[Spain]
BOLTUN	Pistol	7.65	Francisco Arizmendi
BONANZA	Rev	0.22	Bacon Arms
BOOM	Rev	0.22	Shattuck
BORCHARDT	Pistol	7.65	Loewe/DWM
BOSTON BULLDOG	Rev	Various	Iver Johnson
BOY'S CHOICE	Rev	0.22	Hood
BREN TEN	Pistol	10 mm	Dornaus & Dixon
BRIGADIER	Pistol	9P	Beretta
BRIGADIER	Pistol	0.45	North American Arms
BRISTOL	Pistol	7.65	Bolumburu
BRITISH BULLDOG	Rev	Various	Forehand & Wadsworth
BRITISH BULLDOG	Rev	Various	Johnson, Bye
BRNO	Rifle/shotg	Various	Zbrojovka Brno
BROMPETIER	Rev	6.35/7.65	Retolaza
BRONCHO	Pistol	6.35/7.65	Errasti
BRONCO	Pistol	6.35/7.65	Echave y Arizmendi
BRON-GRAND	Rev	6/6.35/7.65	Fernando Ormachea
BRONG-PETIT	Rev	6.35	Crucelegui
BRON-SPORT	Rev	6.35/7.65/8	Crucelegui
BROW	Rev	6.35/7.65/0.38	Ojanguren & Marcaido
BROWNIE	RP	0.22	Mossberg
BROWREDUIT	Rev	6.35/7.65	Salvator Arostegui
BRUNSWIG	Pistol	7.65	Esperanza & Unceta
BRUTUS	Rev	0.22	Hood
BUCCANEER	Pistol	7.65	Pyrenees
BUCKHORN	Rev	0.357	Uberti
BUDISCHOWSKY	Pistol	0.22/0.25	Korriphila
BUFALO	Pistol	6.35/7.65	Gabilondo
BUFFALO STAND	SS	0.22	Manufrance
BULL DOZER	Rev	Various	Norwich Pistol
BULL DOZER	SS	0.22RF	Conn Mfg.
BULLDOG	Rev	Various	Forehand & Wadsworth
BULLDOG	Rev	0.44	Charter Arms
BULLDOG TRACKER	Rev	0.357	Charter Arms
BULLFIGHTER	Rev	0.300	[Belgium]
BULLSEYE	Rev	0.22	[USA, ca. 1885]

446

Name	Type	Caliber	Maker
BULWARK	Pistol	6.35/7.65	Beistegui
BURGHAM SUPERIOR	Pistol	7.65	Pyrenees
BURGO	Rev	0.22	Rohm
BUSHMASTER	Pistol/Rifle	0.223	Gwinn Arms
CADET	Rev	0.22	Maltby, Curtis
CADIX	Rev	0.22/0.32/0.38	Astra-Unceta
CAMINAL	Pistol	7.65	[Spain]
CAMPEON	Pistol	6.35/7.65	Hijos de C Arrizabalaga
CAMPER	Pistol	0.22/6.35	Astra-Unceta
CANTABRIA	Pistol/Rev	Various	Garate Hermanos
CAPITAN	Pistol	7.65	Pyrenees
CAPTAIN JACK	Rev	0.22	Hopkins & Allen
CAROLINE ARMS	Shotg	Various	Crescent Firearms
CA-SI	Pistol	7.65	Grand Precision
CASULL	Rev	0.454	Freedom Arms
CATTLEMAN	Rev	0.357/0.44	Uberti
CAVALIER	Rifle	Various	Zastava
C.D.M.	Rev	0.22	[USA, ca. 1980]
CEBRA	Pistol	6.35	Arizmendi, Zulaica
CELTA	Pistol	6.35	Urizar
CENTAUR	Pistol	6.35	Reunies
CENTENNIAL 1876	Rev	0.32/0.38RF	Derringer
CENTRAL	Shotg	Various	Stevens
CENTRAL ARMS CO.	Shotg	Various	Crescent Firearms
CENTURION	Pistol	9P	Beretta
CENTURION MODEL 100	Rifle	Various	Golden State
CESAR	Pistol	7.65	Pyrenees
J.CESAR	Pistol	6.35	Tomas de Urizar
C.H.	Rev	0.38	Crucelegui Hermanos
CHALLENGE	Rev	0.32RF	Bliss & Goodyear
CHAMPION	Pistol	0.22	Manufrance
CHANTECLER	Pistol	7.65	Pyrenees
CHANTICLER	Pistol	6.35	Isidor Charola
CHARLES LANCASTER	Rifle	Various	Atkin
CHAROLA Y ANITUA	Pistol	5/7 mm	Garate Anitua
CHEROKEE ARMS CO.	Shotg	Various	Crescent Firearms
CHESAPEAKE GUN CO.	Shotg	Various	Crescent Firearms
CHEYENNE SCOUT	Rev	0.22	Schmidt
CHICAGO ARMS CO.	Rev	0.32/0.38	Meriden
CHICAGO CUB	Rev	0.22	Reck
CHICAGO PROTECTOR	RP	0.32	Ames
CHICHESTER	Rev	0.38RF	Hopkins & Allen
CHIEFTAIN	Rev	0.32RF	Norwich Pistol
CHIMERE RENOIR	Pistol	7.65	Pyrenees
CHORERT	Rev	8 mm	[Belgium]
CHURCHILL	Rifles	Various	Kassnar
CHYLEWSKI	Pistol	6.35	SIG
CILINDRO LADEABLE	Rev	0.32	Ojanguren & Matiade
CLEMENT	Rev	0.38	Clement, Neumann
CLEMENT	Pistol	5/6.35	Clement
CLEMENT-FULGOR	Pistol	7.65	Clement
CLIMAS	Shotg	12	Stevens
COBOLD	Rev	9.4mm	HDH
COBOLT	Rev	Various	Ancion-Marx
COBRA	Pistol	7.65	[Spain]
COLON	Pistol	6.35	Azpiri

Name	Type	Caliber	Maker
COLON	Rev	0.32-20	Orbea
COLONIAL	Pistol	7.65	Pyrenees
COLONIAL	Pistol	6.35/7.65	Grand Precision
COLUMBIAN	Rev	0.38	Crescent Firearms
COLUMBIAN AUTOMATIC	Rev	0.32/0.38	Foehl & Weeks
COMANCHE	Rev	0.357	Gabilondo
COMMANDER	Pistol	0.45	Colt
COMMANDO ARMS	S/A Carbine	Various	Volunteer
COMBAT COMMANDER	Pistol	9P/0.45	Colt
COMPEER	Shotg	Various	Crescent Firearms
CONSTABLE	Pistol	7.65	Astra-Unceta
CONSTABULARY	Rev	7.5 mm	Ancion-Marx
CONSTABULARY	Rev	0.32/0.38/0.45	Robar
CONQUER0R	Rev	0.22/0.32RF	Bacon Arms
CONTINENTAL	Pistol	6.35	Bertrand
CONTINENTAL	Pistol	6.35/7.65	RWS
CONTINENTAL	Rifle/Shotg	Various	Stevens
CONTINENTAL	Rev	0.22/0.32RF	Great Western
CONTINENTAL	Rev	0.22/0.32RF	Hood
CONTINENTAL	Pistol	6.35	Tomas de Urizar
CORLA	Pistol	0.22	Zaragoza
CORRIENTES	Pistol	6.35	Modesto Santos
COSMI	Shotg	Various	Abercrombie & Fitch
COSMOPOLITE OSCILLATORY	Rev	0.38	Garate Anitua
COUGAR	Pistol	7.65/9	Beretta
COW-BOY	Pistol	6.35	Fabrique Française
COWBOY RANGER	Rev	Various	Liege United Arms
CRESCENT	Rev	0.32RF	Norwich Falls
CREEDMORE	Rev	0.22	Hopkins & Allen
CRIOLLA	Pistol	0.22	Hafdasa
CROWN JEWEL	Rev	0.32RF	Norwich Falls
CRUCERO	Pistol/Rev	7.65/0.32	Ojanguren & Vidosa
CRUSO	Rifle/Shotg	Various	Stevens
CUB PISTOL	Pistol	0.22/6.35	Astra-Unceta
CUMBERLAND ARMS CO.	Shotg	Various	Crescent Firearms
CZ	All	Various	Ceskoslovenska
CZAR	Rev	0.22	Hood
CZAR	Rev	0.22/0.32RF	Hopkins & Allen
DAISY	Rev	0.22	Bacon Arms
DAKOTA	Rev	0.38/0.45	Uberti
DANTON	Pistol	6.35/7.65	Gabilondo
DEAD SHOT	Rev	0.22	Pond
DEFENSE	Pistol	6.35	[Spain]
DEFENDER	Rev	0.22/0.32RF	Johnson, Bye
DEFENDER	Pistol	6.35	Javier Echaniz
DEFENDER 89	Rev	0.22	Iver Johnson
DEFENSE	Pistol	6.35	[Spain, 1920s]
DEFIANCE	Rev	0.22	Norwich Falls
DEK-DU	Rev	5.5/6.35	Tomas de Urizar
DELPHIAN	Shotg	Various	Stevens
DELTA	Pistol	6.35	[Spain]
DELTA ELITE	Pistol	10 mm	Colt
DE LUXE	Pistol	6.35	Bolumburu
DEMON	Pistol	7.65	Pyrenees
DEMON	Pistol	7.65	[Spain]

Name	Type	Caliber	Maker
DEMON MARINE	Pistol	7.65	Pyrenees
DEPREZ	Rev	11 mm	[Belgium]
DEPUTY ADJUSTER	Rev	0.38	Herbert Schmidt
DEPUTY MAGNUM	Rev	0.357	Herbert Schmidt
DEPUTY MARSHAL	Rev	0.38	Herbert Schmidt
DESERT EAGLE	Pistol	Various	Taas Israel Industries
DESPATCH	Rev	0.22	Hopkins & Allen
DESTROYER	Pistol	6.35/7.65	Gaztanaga
DESTRUCTOR	Pistol	6.35/7.65	Salaverria
DETECTIVE	Rev	0.32	Garate Anitua
DETECTIVE SPECIAL	Rev	0.38	Colt
DEWAF MODEL IV	Pistol	6.35	[Spain, 1920s]
DIAMOND	Shotg	Various	Stevens
DIAMONDBACK	Rev	0.22/0.38	Colt
DIANA	Pistol	6.35	[Spain]
DIANE	Pistol	6.35	Wilkinson
DIANE	Pistol	6.35	Erquiaga, Muguruzu
DICKSON BULLDOG	Rev	0.22	Weirauch
DICKSON SPECIAL AGENT	Pistol	7.65	Echave & Arizmendi
DICTATOR	Pistol	6.35	Reunies
DICTATOR	Rev	0.22/0.32RF	Hopkins & Allen
DIPLOMAT	Pistol	9S	Bernardelli
DOMINO	Pistol	0.22	Italguns
DOUBLE DEUCE	Pistol	0.22	Steel City
DOUBLE NINE	Rev	0.22	High Standard
DOUGLAS	Pistol	6.35	Lasagabaster
DREADNOUGHT	Rev	0.38	Errasti
DREADNOUGHT	Rev	0.22/0.32RF	Hopkins & Allen
DREUX	Pistol	6.35	[France]
DREYSE	Pistol	Various	Rheinmetall
DRULOV	SS	0.22	Lidove Drusztvo
DUAN	Pistol	6.35	Ormachea
DUC	Pistol	6.35	[France?]
DUCO	Rev	7.5 mm	Dumoulin
DUO	Pistol	6.35	Dusek
DUPLEX	Rev	0.22/0.32RF	Osgood
DURABEL	Pistol	6.35	Warnant
DURA-MATIC	Pistol	0.22	High Standard
DURANGO	Rev	0.22	High Standard
E.A.	Pistol	6.35	Echave y Arizmendi
E.A.	Pistol	6.35	Arostegui
EAGLE 1	Rev	0.45	Phelps
EAGLE 0.380	Pistol	9S	American Arms (2)
EAGLE ARMS CO.	Rev	Various	Johnson, Bye
EARL HOOD	Rev	0.32RF	Dickinson
EARTHQUAKE	Rev	0.32RF	Dickinson
EASTERN	Shotg	Various	Stevens
EASTERN ARMS CO.	Rev	0.32/0.38	Meriden/Sears
E.B.A.C.	Pistol	6.35	Pyrenees
ECHASA	Pistol	0.22/6.35/7.65	Echave y Arizmendi
ECIA	Pistol	7.65	Esperanza y Cia
ECLIPSE	SS	0.22/0.25/0.32RF	Johnson, Bye
EICHEL	Rifle	Various	Kind
EIG	Rev	0.22	Rohm
EL BLANCO	Rev	0.22	Ojanguren & Matiade
EL CANO	Rev	0.32	Arana y Cia

Name	Type	Caliber	Maker
EL CID	Pistol	6.35	Casimir Santos
ELECTOR	Rev	0.22/0.32RF	Hopkins & Allen
ELECTRIC	Rev	0.32RF	Forehand & Wadsworth
ELES	Pistol	6.35	[Spain]
ELEY	Pistol	6.35	[Spain]
ELGIN ARMS CO.	Shotg	Various	Crescent Firearms
ELITE	Pistol	7.65	Pyrenees
EL LUNAR LEBEL RAPIDE	Rev	8	Garate Anitua
EL PERRO	Pistol	6.35	Lascuraren & Olasolo
EM-GE	Rev	0.22	Gerstenberger
EMPIRE	Rev	0.22/0.38/0.41RF	Rupertus
EMPIRE	Rifle	0.22	Vickers
EMPIRE ARMS	Rev	0.32/0.38	Meriden
EMPIRE ARMS CO.	Shotg	Various	Crescent Firearms
EMPIRE STATE	Rev	0.32/0.38	Meriden
EMPRESS	Rev	0.32RF	Rupertus
ENCORE	Rev	0.22/0.32/0.38RF	Johnson, Bye
ENDERS OAKLEAF	Shotg	Various	Crescent Firearms
ENDERS ROYAL SERVICE	Shotg	Various	Crescent Firearms
ENFORCER	Pistol	0.45	Safari Arms
ERIKA	Pistol	4.25	Pfannl
ERMA	All	Various	Ermawerke
ERMUA 1924	Pistol	6.35	Acha
ERMUA 1925	Pistol	6.35	Ormachea
E.S.A.	Pistol	6.35/7.65	[Spain, 1920s]
ESCORT	Pistol	0.22	Echeverria
ESPECIAL	Pistol	6.35	Arrizabalaga
ESPINGARDA	Rev	0.38	Machado
ESSEX	Shotg	Various	Crescent Firearms
ESSEX	Rifle/Shotg	Various	Stevens
ESTRELA	Pistol	6.35/7.65	Echeverria
ETAI	Pistol	6.35	[Spain]
ETNA	Pistol	6.35	Salaberrin
EUREKA	Rev	0.22	Johnson, Bye
EUSKARO	Rev	0.38/0.44	Esprin Hermanos
EUSTA	Pistol	7.65/9S	[West Germany]
EXCELSIOR	Rev	0.32RF	Norwich Pistol
EXCELSIOR	Rev	9.1 mm	S J & D
EXPRESS	Rev	0.22	Bacon Arms
EXPRESS	Pistol	6.35/7.65	Urizar
EXTRACTEUR	Rev	7.5 mm	Ancion Marx
F.A.	Rev	0.32	Francisco Arizmendi
F.A.G.	Rev	7.62/8	Arizmendi & Goenaga
FALCON	Pistol	7.65	Astra-Unceta
FAST	Pistol	Various	Echave y Arizmendi
FAULTLESS	Shotg	Various	Crescent
FAVORIT	Pistol	6.35	[Spain]
FAVORIT	Rifle	Various	Frankonia
FAVORIT SAFARI	Rifle	Various	Frankonia
FAVORITE	Rev	0.22/0.32/ 0.38/0.41RF	Johnson, Bye
FAVORITE NAVY	Rev	0.44RF	Johnson, Bye
FEDERAL ARMS	Rev	0.32/0.38	Meriden
F.E.G.	Pistol	Various	Femaru
FIEL	Pistol	6.35/7.65	Erquiaga, Muguruzu
FIELD KING	Pistol	0.22	High Standard

Name	Type	Caliber	Maker
FINNISH LION	Rifle	0.22	Valmet
FIREBALL	SS	0.221	Remington
FIREBIRD	Pistol	9P	Femaru
FLITE-KING	Pistol	0.22	High Standard
FLORIA	Pistol	6.35	[Spain]
FME	Pistol	6.35	FAMAE
FORBES	Shotg	Various	Crescent
FOREHAND 1901	Rev	0.32	Hopkins & Allen
FORT	Pistol	9 mm Mak	Fort Co
FORTUNA	Pistol	7.65	Unceta
FORTY-NINER	Rev	0.22	Harrington & Richardson
FOUR ACES	Rev	0.22	Svendsen
FOUR ACES	RP	0.22	ESFAC
FOX	Pistol	6.35	Tomiska
FRANCAISE	Pistol	6.35	Soc. Franc. d'Armes
FRANCO	Pistol	6.35	Manufrance
FREEHAND	Rev	0.38	[Germany?]
FRONTIER	Rev	0.32RF	Norwich Falls
FRONTIER ARMY	Rev	0.44	Ronge
FURIA	Pistol	7.65	Ojanguren & Vidosa
FUROR	Pistol	7.65	Pyrenees
G.A.C. FIREARMS MFG. CO.	Rev	0.32-20	Garate Anitua
GALEF	Pistol	7.65	[Spain]
GALEF STALLION	Rev	0.22/0.357	[Italy]
GALLIA	Pistol	7.65	Pyrenees
GALLUS	Pistol	6.35	Retolaza
GAME GETTER	Rifle/Shotg	0.22/0.410	Marble
GARRISON	Rev	0.22	Hopkins & Allen
GARRUCHA	DB Pistol	0.22	Amadeo Rossi
GAUCHO	Pistol	0.22	[Argentine]
GAULOIS	Rep Pist	8	Manufrance
G & E	Rev	0.22	Gerstenberger
GECADO	Pistol	6.35	Dornheim
GECO	Rev	6.35/7.65	Genschow
GECO	Shotg	12	Genschow
GEM	Rev	0.22	Bacon Arms
GEM	SS	0.22/0.30RF	Stevens Tool
GERMAN BULLDOG	Rev	0.32/0.38	Genschow
G.H.	Rev	0.38	Guisasola Hermanos
GIBRALTAR	Rrev	0.32/0.38	Meriden
GIRALDA	Pistol	7.65	Bolumburu
GLENFIELD	Rifle	0.30-30	Marlin
GLORIA	Pistol	6.35/7.65	Bolumburu
G.M.C.	Pistol	0.22	Garb, Moretti & Co.
GOLDEN BISON	Rev	0.45-70	Super Six
GOLDEN EAGLE	Rifle	Various	Nikko
GOLIAT	Rev	0.32	Errasti
GOOSE GUN	Shotg	Various	Stevens
GOVERNOR	Rev	0.22	Bacon Arms
GP-100	Rev	0.357	Ruger
GRACH	Pistol	9 mm P	Tsniitochmash
GRAND	Rev	0.357/0.38	Zbrojovka Brno
GRIZZLY	Pistol	Various	LAR
GRUENEL	Rifle	Various	Gruenig & Elmiger
G.S.M.	Pistl	7.65	[Hungary]
GUARDIAN	Rev	0.22/0.32RF	Bacon Arms

Name	Type	Caliber	Maker
GUEURE	Pistol	6.35	Arizmendi
GYROJET	Pistol	13 mm	MBA
HAKIM	Rifle	7.92	Maadi
HALF-BREED	Rev	0.32RF	Hopkins & Allen
HAMADA	Pistol	7.65	Japan Gun Co.
HANDY MODEL 1917	Pistol	9S	[Spain]
HARDBALLER	Pistol	0.45	AMT
HARD PAN	Rev	0.22/0.32RF	Hood
HARTFORD ARMS CO.	Rev	0.32RF	Norwich Falls
HARTFORD ARMS CO.	Shotg	Various	Crescent Firearms
HARVARD	Shotg	Various	Crescent Firearms
HAWES WESTERN MARSHAL	Rev	Various	Sauer
HAWES SILVER CITY	Rev	0.22	Sauer
HAWES CHIEF MARSHAL	Rev	Various	Sauer
H&D	Rev	Various	Henrion & Dassy
HEGE	Pistol/Combo	Various	Hebsacker
HEIM	Pistol	6.35	Heinzelmann
HELFRICHT	Pistol	6.35	Krauser
HELKRA	Pistol	6.35	Krauser
HELVICE (or HELVECE)	Pistol	6.35	Grand Precision
HE-MO	Pistol	7.65	Moritz
HERCULES	Shotg	Various	Stevens
HERITAGE 1	Rev	0.45	Phelps
HERMAN	Pistol	6.35	[Belgium]
HERMETIC	Pistol	7.65	Bernadon-Martin
HERMITAGE	Shotg	Various	Stevens
HERMITAGE ARMS CO.	Shotg	Various	Crescent Firearms
HERMITAGE GUN CO.	Shotg	Various	Crescent Firearms
HERO	Rev	0.22/0.32 0.38/0.41RF	Rupertus
HEROLD	Rifle	0.22	Jager
HERTER	Rev	0.357	[Germany]
HEYM	Rev	0.22	[Germany]
HIGHLANDER	Rifle	Various	Kassnar
HIGH SIERRA	Rev	0.22	High Standard
HIJO	Pistol	6.35/7.65	Galesi
HIJO QUICK-BREAK	Rev	0.22/0.32/0.38	Iver Johnson
HOPKINS, C.W.	Rev	0.32/0.38RF	Bacon Mfg. Co.
HORSE DESTROYER	Rev	0.38	Gaztanaga
HOWARD ARMS	Rev	0.32/0.38	Meriden
HOWARD ARMS	Shotg	Various	Crescent Firearms
H.R.	SS	0.22	Haidurov
H.S.	Rev	0.22	Schmidt
HUDSON	Pistol	6.35	[Spain]
HUNTER	SS	Various	Wichita
HUNTER'S PET	SS	0.22/0.25/0.32RF	Stevens
H.V.	Pistol	6.35	Hourat
HY HUNTER	Rev	0.22	Rohm
HY-SCORE	Rev	0.22	Rohm
I.A.G.	Pistol	7.65	Galesi
IDEAL	SS	0.22	Buchel
IDEAL	Pistol	6.35	Dusek
ILLINOIS ARMS CO.	Rev	6.35	Pickert
IMPERATO	Pistol	6.35/7.65	Heckler & Koch
IMPERIAL	Pistol	6.35	Tomas de Urizar

Name	Type	Caliber	Maker
IMPERIAL	Rev	0.22/0.32RF	[USA]
IMPERIAL ARMS	Rev	0.32/0.38RF	Hopkins & Allen
INDIAN	Pistol	7.65	Gaztanaga
INDISPENSABLE	Rev	5.5 mm	[Belgium]
INFALLIBLE	Pistol	7.65	Davis-Warner
INGRAM	SMG	9/0.45	MAC
INSPECTOR	Rev	0.38	Uberti
INTERNATIONAL	Rev	0.22/0.32RF	Hood
INTERNATIONAL	SS	Various	Wichita
INTERSTATE ARMS CO.	Shotg	Various	Crescent Firearms
INVICTA	Pistol	7.65	Salaberrin
IRIQUOIS	Rev	0.22	Remington
IRIS Rev	0.32-20	Ojanguren	
ISARD	Pistol	9B-B	[Spain]
IXOR	Pistol	7.65	Pyrenees
IZARRA	Pistol	7.65	Echeverria
JACKRABBIT	Rifle/Shotg	Various	Continental Arms
JACKSON ARMS CO.	Shotg	Various	Crescent Firearms
JAGA	Pistol	6.35	Dusek
J.CESAR	Pistol	6.35	Urizar
JENKINS SPECIAL	Pistol	6.35	[Spain]
JERICHO	Pistol	9P	Ta'as
JETFIRE	Pistol	6.35	Beretta
JEWEL	Rev	0.22	Hood
J.G.A.	Rev	7.65	Anschutz
JIEFFECO	Pistol	6.35/7.65	Robar
JOHA	Pistol	6.35/7.65	[Spain]
JO-LO-AR	Pistol	7.65	Arrizabalaga
JUBALA	Pistol	6.35	Larranaga & Elartza
JUBILEE	Rifle	0.22	Vickers
JUNIOR	Pistol	6.35	PAF
JUNIOR	Pistl	0.22/6.35	Colt
JUPITER	Pistol	7.65	Grand Precision
JUPITER	Rev	5.5 mm	Francotte
KABA SPEZIAL	Pistol	7.65	Menz
KABA SPECIAL	Pistol	6.35/7.65	Arizmendi
KAPITAIN	Pistol	7.65	Alkartasuna
KAPPORA	Pistol	6.35	[Spain]
KEBLER	Pistol	7.65	[Spain]
KING COBRA	Rev	0.357	Colt
KINGLAND SPECIAL	Shotg	Various	Crescent Firearms
KINGLAND 10-STAR	Shotg	Various	Crescent Firearms
KING NITRO	Rifle/Shotg	Various	Stevens
KIRRIKALE	Pistol	9S	MKEK
KITTEMAUG	Rev	0.32RF	[USA]
KITU	Pistol	6.35	[Spain]
KLESZEZEWSKI	Pistol	6.35	[Spain]
KNICKERBOCKER	Shotg	Various	Crescent Firearms
KNOCKABOUT	Shotg	Various	Stevens
KNOCKABOUT	SS	0.22	Sheridan
KNOXALL	Shotg	Various	Crescent Firearms
KOBOLD	Rev	Various	Raick
KOBRA	Pistol	6.35	[Germany]
KOLIBRI	Pistol	3 mm	Grabner
KOLIBRI	Pistol	6.35	Arizaga
KRAUSER	Pistol	0.22	Manurhin

Name	Type	Caliber	Maker
LA BASQUE	Pistol	6.35	[Spain]
LA's DEPUTY	Rev	0.22	Schmidt
LADYSMITH	Rev	0.32/0.38	Smith & Wesson
LA FURY	Pistol	6.35	Reck
LA INDUSTRIA	Pistol	7.65	Orbea Hermanos
LA LIRA	Pistol	7.65	Garate Anitua
LAMPO	RP	8 mm	Tribuzio
LANCER	Pistol	0.22	Echeverria
LA SALLE	Shotg	Various	Manufrance
LAWMAN	Rev	0.357	Colt
L.E.	Rev	0.32	Larranaga y Elartza
LE AGENT	Rev	8 mm	Manufrance
LE BASQUE	Pistol	7.65	Urizar
LE BRONG	Rev	5/6.35/7.65	Crucelegui
LE CAVALIER	Pistol	7.65/9S	Bayonne
LE CHASSEUR	Pistol	11	Bayonne
L'ECLAIR	Rev	6 mm	Garate Anitua
LE COLONIAL	Rev	8 mm	Manufrance
LE DRAGON	Pistol	6.35	Urizar
LE FRANCAIS	Pistol	Various	Manufrance
LE GENDARME	Pistol	9S	Bayonne
LEGITIMO TANQUE	Rev	0.38	Ojanguren & Vidosa
LE MAJESTIC	Pistol	7.65	Pyrenees
LE MARTINY	Pistol	6.35	[Belgium]
LE METEORE	Pistol	6.35	[Belgium]
LE MILITAIRE	Pistol	9P	Bayonne
LE MONOBLOC	Pistol	6.35	Jacquemart
LE NOVO	Rev	6.35	Galand
LE PETIT FORMIDABLE	Rev	6.35	Manufrance
LE PROTECTOR	RP	6 mm	Turbiaux
LE RAPIDE	Pistol	6.35	Bertrand
LE SANS PARIEL	Pistol	6.35	Pyrenees
LE SECOURS	Pistol	6.35	Grand Precision
LE SECOURS	Pistol	7.65	Tomas de Urizar
LE STEPH	Pistol	6.35	Bergeron
LE TOUT ACIER	Pistol	6.35/7.65	Pyrenees
LEADER	Rev	0.22/0.32RF	Hopkins & Allen
LEADER GUN CO.	Shotg	Various	Crescent Firearms
LEE SPECIAL	Shotg	Various	Crescent Firearms
LEE'S MUNNER SPECIAL	Shotg	Various	Crescent Firearms
LEFT WHEELER	Rev	0.32	HDH
LEGIA	Pistol	6.35	Pieper
LEONHARDT	Pistol	7.65	Gering
LEPCO	Pistol	6.35	[Spain]
L.E.S.	Pistol	9P	Steyr-Mannlicher
LESTON	Pistol	6.35	Unceta
L.H.	Pistol	6.35	[Germany]
LIBERATOR	SS	0.45	Guide Lamp
LIBERTI	Pistol	7.65	[Spain]
LIBERTY	Rev	0.22/0.32RF	Hood
LIBERTY	Pistol	6.35/7.65	Retolaza
LIBERTY-11	Rev	0.22	Schmidt
LIBERTY RG-12	Rev	0.22	Rohm
LIBERTY CHIEF	Rev	0.38	Miroku
LIBIA	Pistol	6.35/7.65	Beistegui
LIEGOISE D'ARMES A FEU	Pistol	6.35/7.65	Robar

Name	Type	Caliber	Maker
LIGHTNING	Pistol	6.35	Echave y Arizmendi
LILIPUT	PIstol	4.25/6.35	Menz
LILIPUT	Pistol	6.35	Fegyver
LINCOLN	Rev	0.32	Ancion Marx
LINCOLN	Rev	0.22/0.32RF	HDH
LINCOLN BOSSU	Rev	5.5/6.35	HDH
LINCOLN BULLDOG	Rev	0.32	Robar
LINCOLN HAMMERLESS	Rev	0.320	Robar
LINDA	Pistol	0.22	Wilkinson (2)
LION	Rev	0.22/0.32/ 0.38/0.41RF	Johnson, Bye
LITTLE ALL RIGHT	Rev	0.22	All Right
LITTLE GIANT	Rev	0.22	Bacon Arms
LITTLE JOHN	Rev	0.22	Hood
LITTLE JOKER	Rev	0.22	Marlin
LITTLE PET	Shotg	Various	Stevens
LITTLE TOM	Pistol	6.35/7.65	Tomiska
LITTLE TOM	Pistol	6.35	Wiener
LLAMA	Pistol	Various	Gabilondo
LLANERO	Rev	0.22	[Argentina]
LOBO	Pistol	6.35	[Spain]
LONGHORN	Rev	0.22	High Standard
LONGINES	Pistol	7.65	Cooperativa Orbea
LONG RANGE WONDER	Shotg	Various	Sears
LONG TOM	Shotg	Various	Stevens
LOOKING GLASS	Pistol	6.35/7.65	Acha
LOSADA	Pistol	7.65	[Germany]
LUGER	Pistol	7.65P/9P	Stoeger
LUNA	SS	0.22	Buchel
LUR-PANZER	Pistol	0.22	Echave y Arizmendi
LUSITANIA	Pistol	7.65	[Spain]
LUTETIA	Pistol	6.35	[Spain]
LYNX	Rev	0.357	[South Africa, ca. 1979]
M & H	Rev	0.44-40	Hopkins & Allen
MAB	Pistol	Various	Bayonne
MAJESTIC	Pistol	6.35	[Spain]
MAGMATIC	Pistol	0.44Mag	Powers
MALTBY, HENLEY & CO.	Rev	0.22/0.32/0.38	Columbia
MAMBA	Pistol	9P	Relay Products
MAMBA	Pistol	9P	Navy Arms
MARINA	Pistol	6.35	Bolumburu
MARKE	Pistol	6.35	Bascaran
MARK X	Rifle	Various	Zastava
MARQUIS OF LORNE	Rev	0.22/0.32RF	Hood
MARS	Pistol	6.35/7.65	Kohout
MARS	Pistol	9/0.45	Webley
MARS	Pistol	9BB	Pieper
MARS	Pistol	7.65	Pyrenees
MARSHWOOD	Shotg	Various	Stevens
MARTE	Pistol	6.35	Erquiaga, Muguruzu
MARTIAL	Rev	0.357	Gabilondo
MARTIAN	Pistol	6.35/7.65	Martin A Bascaran
MARTIGNY	Pistol	6.35	Jorge Bascaran
MASSACHUSETTS ARMS	Shotg	Various	Stevens
MAXIM	Pistol	6.35	Galesi
MAXIMUM	SS	Various	MOA

Name	Type	Caliber	Maker
MELIOR	Pistol	Various	Robar
MENTA	Pistol	6.35/7.65	Menz
MERCURY	Pistol/Shotg	Various	Robar
MERKE	Pistol	6.35	Ormachea
MERKUR	Rifle	Various	Kind
MERVEILLEAUX	RP	6 mm	[France]
METEOR	Rifle	0.22	Stevens
METROPOLITAN	Shotg	Various	Crescent Firearms
METROPOLITAN POLICE	Rev	0.32RF	Norwich Falls
MIDLAND GUN CO.	Rifle	Various	Parker-Hale
MIKROS	Pistol	Various	Pyrenees
MILADY	Rev	7.65	Ancion-Marx
MILADY	Rev	8 mm	Jannsen Fils
MILITARY	Pistol	6.35	Retolaza
MILITARY MODEL 1914	Pistol	7.65	Retolaza
MILITAR Y POLICIA	Rev	0.38	Ojanguren & Vidosa
MILITAR Y POLICIAS	Rev	0.38	Ojanguren & Matiade
MINERVA	Pistol	6.35	Grand Precision
MINIMA	Pistol	6.35	Boyer
MINX	Pistol	6.35	Beretta
MISSISSIPPI VALLEY	Shotg	Various	Crescent Firearms
MITRAILLEUSE	RP	8	St. Etienne
MITRAILLEUSE	Pistol	6.35	[Spain]
ML	Pistol	6.35/7.65	Robar
MOHAWK	Shotg	Various	Crescent Firearms
MOHEGAN	Rev	0.32RF	Hood
MONARCH	Rev	0.22/0.32/0.38/0.41RF	Hopkins & Allen
MONDIAL	Pistol	6.35	Arrizaga
MONITOR	Shotg	Various	Stevens
MONOBLOC	Pistol	6.35	Jacquemart
M.S.	Pistol	6.35/7.65	Modesto Santos
MOSSER	Pistol	6.35	[Spain]
MOUNTAIN EAGLE	Rev	0.32RF	Hopkins & Allen
MUELLER SPECIAL	Rev	6.35	Decker
MUGICA	Pistol	Various	Gabilondo
MUNICIPAL	Rev	8 mm	HDH
MUSEUM	Pistol	6.35	Echeverria
MUSTANG	Pistol	9S	Colt
MUSTANG POCKETLITE	Pistol	9S	Colt
MUXI	Pistol	6.35	[Spain]
NALAVA	Pistol	6.35	Eiler
NAPOLEON	Rev	0.22/0.32RF	Ryan
NATIONAL	Rev	0.32/0.38RF	Norwich Falls
NATIONAL	SS	0.41RF	Norwich Falls
NATIONAL ARMS CO.	Shotg	Various	Crescent Firearms
NERO	Rev	0.22/0.32RF	Rupertus
NERO	Rev	0.22/0.32RF	Hopkins & Allen
NEVER MISS	Rev	0.22/0.32/0.41RF	Marlin
NEW ACE	Pistol	0.22	Colt
NEW BABY	Rev	0.22	Kolb
NEW CHIEFTAIN	Shotg	Various	Stevens
NEW JAGUAR	Pistol	0.22/7.65	Beretta
NEW NAMBU	Rev/Pistol	Various	Shin Chuo Kogyo
NEW RIVAL	Shotg	Various	Crescent Firearms
NEW YORK ARMS CO.	Shotg/Rev	Various	Crescent Firearms

Name	Type	Caliber	Maker
NEW YORK PISTOL CO.	Rev	0.22	Hood
NEWPORT	Shotg	Various	Stevens
NIGHTHAWK	Pistol	9P	Weaver
NITRO PROOF	Shotg	Various	Stevens
NIVA	Pistol	6.35	Kohout
NOMAD	Pistol	0.22	Browning Arms
NONPARIEL	Rev	0.32RF	Norwich Falls
NORTHWESTERNER	Rifle/Shotg	0.22/Various	Stevens
NORWICH ARMS CO.	Shotg	Various	Crescent Firearms
NORWICH ARMS CO.	Rev	0.22/0.32RF	Norwich Falls
NOT-NAC MFG. CO.	Shotg	Various	Crescent Firearms
NOVELTY	RP	0.32	Mossberg
OAK LEAF	Shotg	Various	Stevens
OBREGON	Pistol	0.45	Fab de Armas Mexico
OCULTO	Rev	0.32/0.38	Orueta Hermanos
OFF-DUTY	Rev	0.38	Charter Arms
O.H.	Rev	0.22/0.32/0.38	Orbea
OICET	Rev	0.38	Errasti
O.K.	SS	0.22	Marlin
OKZET	Pistol	6.35	Menz
OLD TIMER	Shotg	Various	Stevens
OLYMPIA	Pistol	6.35/7.65	SEAM
OLYMPIC	Shotg	Various	Stevens
O.M.	Rev	Various	Ojanguren y Matiade
OMEGA	Pistol	6.35/7.65	Armero Especialistas
OMEGA	Pistol	10 mm	Springfield
OMEGA	Rev	0.22	Gerstenberger
OMEGA	Rev	0.32	Weirauch
OMEGA III	Rifle	Various	Hi-Shear
OMNI	Pistol	0.45/9P	Gabilondo
ONANDIA	Rev	0.32	Onandia Hermanos
OREA	Rifle	Various	Orechowsky
ORTGIES	Pistol	Various	Deutsche Werke
OSCILLANT AZUL	Rev	0.38	Arostegui
O.V.	Rev	0.32	Ojanguren & Vidosa
OWA	Pistol	6.35	Osterreich
OXFORD ARMS	Shotg	Various	Stevens
OXFORD ARMS CO.	Shotg	Various	Crescent Firearms
OYEZ	Pistol	6.35	[Belgium]
PADRE	Pistol	7.65	Galesi
P.A.F.	Pistol	6.35	PAF
PAGE-LEWIS ARMS CO.	Shotg	Various	Stevens
PALMETTO	Shotg	Various	Stevens
PANTAX	Pistol	0.22	Woerther
PARAGON	Shotg	Various	Stevens
PARAMOUNT	Pistol	6.35/7.65	Retolaza
PARKER SAFETY HAMMERLESS	Rev	0.32	Columbia
PAROLE	Rev	0.22	Hopkins & Allen
PATENT	Pistol	6.35	[Spain]
PATHFINDER	Rev	0.22	Charter Arms
PATHFINDER	Pistol	6.35	Echave & Arizmendi
PATRIOT	Rev	0.32RF	Norwich Falls
PEACEKEEPER	Rev	0.357	Colt
PEERLESS	Rifle	0.22	Stevens
PEERLESS	Shotg	Various	Crescent Firearms

Name	Type	Caliber	Maker
PEERLESS	Rev	0.32RF	Hood
PENETRATOR	Rev	0.32RF	Norwich Falls
PERFECT	Rev	0.38	Foehl & Weeks
PERFECT	Pistol	7.65	Pyrenees
PERFECTION	Shotg	Various	Crescent Firearms
PERFECTION AUTOMATIC	Rev	0.32	Forehand Arms
PERFECTIONNE	Rev	8 mm	Pieper
PERFECTO	Rev	0.32	Orbea
PERLA	Pistol	6.35	Dusek
PETITE	Rev	0.22 Short	Iver Johnson
PEUGOT	Pistol	6.35	[France]
PHOENIX	Pistol	6.35	Robar
PHOENIX	Pistol	6.35	Urizar
PHOENIX ARMS CO.	Pistol	6.35	Lowell
PICCOLO	Rev	0.38	Gabilondo
PIEDMONT	Shotg	Various	Crescent Firearms
PILSEN	Pistol	7.65	Zrojovka Plzen
PINAFORE	Rev	0.22	Norwich Falls
PINKERTON	Pistol	6.35	Gaspar Arizaga
PIONEER	Rev	0.22/0.38RF	[USA]
PIONEER	Rifle	0.22	Stevens
PIONEER ARMS CO.	Shotg	Various	Crescent Firearms
PISTOLET AUTOMATIQUE	Pistol	6.35	Arizmendi
PLUS ULTRA	Pistol	7.65	Gabilondo
POLICE BULLDOG	Rev	0.44	Charter Arms
POLICE SERVICE SIX	Rev	0.357	Ruger
POLICE UNDERCOVER	Rev	0.32/0.38	Charter Arms
POLICEMAN	Pistol	6.35	Manufrance
PONY	Pistol	9S	Iver Johnson
POPULAIRE	SS	0.22	Manufrance
PORTSIDER	Pistol	0.45	Falcon
POSSE	Rev	0.22	High Standard
POWERMASTER	SS	0.22	Wamo Mfg. Co.
PRAGA	Pistol	7.65	SEAM
PRAGA	Pistol	6.35	Novotny
PRAIRIE KING	Rev	0.22	Norwich Falls
PRATIC	Pistol	6.35	[Spain]
PRECISION	Pistol	6.0.357.65	Grand Precision
PREMIER	Pistol	6.35/7.65	Urizar
PREMIER	Rifle	0.22	Stevens
PREMIER	Rev	0.22/0.38RF	Ryan
PREMIER TRAIL BLAZER	Rifle	0.22	Stevens
PRICE J.W.	Shotg	Various	Stevens
PRIMA	Pistol	6.35	Pyrenees
PRINCE	SS	0.50RF	Iver Johnson
PRINCEPS	Pistol	7.65	Urizar
PRINCESS	Rev	0.22	[USA]
PRINCIPE	Pistol	6.35	Urizar
PROTECTOR	Pistol	6.35	Echave & Arizmendi
PROTECTOR	Pistol	6.35	Santiago Salaberrin
PROTECTOR	Rev	0.22/0.32RF	Norwich Falls
PROTECTOR	Rev	0.22	Protector
PUMA	Pistol	0.22	Beretta
PUMA	Pistol	6.35	Urizar
PUPPET	Pistol	7.65	Ojanguren & Vidosa
PUPPET	Rev	6.35	Ojanguren & Vidosa

Name	Type	Caliber	Maker
PUPPY	Rev	5 mm	Crucelegui
PUPPY	Rev	5 mm	Retolaza
PUPPY	Rev	5.5 mm	Francisco Arizmendi
PUPPY	Rev	0.22	Izidro Gaztanaga
PUPPY	Rev	0.22	Ojanguren & Marcaido
PUPPY	Rev	Various	HDH
PYTHON	Rev	0.357	Colt
P.Z.K.	Pistol	6.35	Kohout
QUAIL	Shotg	Various	Crescent Firearms
QUAILS FARGO	Shotg	Various	Dakin
QUEEN CITY	Shotg	Various	Crescent Firearms
RADIUM	Pistol	6.35	Gabilondo
RANGER	Pistol	0.22	Pyrenees
RANGER	Rev	0.32RF	Dickinson
RANGER	Rifle/Shotg	Various	Stevens
RANGER NO. 2	Rev	0.32RF	Dickinson
RANGER NO. 2	Rev	0.22/0.32RF	Hopkins & Allen
RAPID-MAXIMA	Pistol	7.65	Pyrenees
RAVEN	Pistol	6.35	Dornheim
RAYON	Pistol	6.35	[Spain]
R.E.	Pistol	9BB	Republica Espana
RECKY	Rev	0.22	Reck
REDHAWK	Rev	0.44	Ruger
RECORD	SS	0.22	Anschutz
RED CLOUD	Rev	0.32RF	[USA]
RED JACKET	Rev	0.22/0.32RF	Lee Arms
REFORM	RP	6.35	Schuler
REFORM	Pistol	6.35	[Spain]
REGENT	Pistol	6.35/7.65	Bolumburu
REGENT	Rev	0.22	Burgsmuller
REGENT	Rifle	Various	Kassnar
REGINA	Pistol	6.35/7.65	Bolumburu
REGNUM	RP	6.35	Menz
REID PATENT	Rev	0.22/0.32/0.41RF	Irving
REIFGRABER	Pistol	7.65	Union Arms
REIMS	Pistol	6.35/7.65	Azanza y Arrizabalaga
REINA	Pistol	7.65	Pyrenees
RENARD	Pistol	6.35	Echave & Arizmendi
REPUBLIC	Pistol	7.65	Azanza y Arrizabalaga
RETRIEVER	Rev	0.32RF	Ryan
REV-O-NOC	Shotg	Various	Crescent Firearms
REX	Pistol	6.35/7.65/9S	Bolumburu
RG	Rev	Various	Rohm
RICKARD ARMS	Shotg	Various	Crescent Firearms
RIGARMI	Pistol	0.22/6.35/7.65	Galesi
RIVAL	Pistol	6.35	Union, Eibar
ROBIN HOOD	Rev	0.22/0.32RF	Hood
ROLAND	Pistol	6.35/7.65	Arizmendi
ROME	Rev	0.22	Rome
ROMO	Rev	0.22	Rohm
ROWNHNES	Pistol	7.65	[Spain]
ROYAL	Rev	0.22/0.32RF	Hopkins & Allen
ROYAL	Rev	0.38	[Spain]
ROYAL	Pistol	Various	Zulaica
ROYAL NOVELTY	Pistol	6.35/7.65	Zulaica
RUBI	Pistol	0.22	Venturini

Name	Type	Caliber	Maker
RUBY	Pistol	Various	Gabilondo
RUBY EXTRA	Rev	Various	Gabilondo
RUMMEL	Shotg	Various	Crescent Firearms
RURAL	Rev	0.32	Garantizada
S.A.	Pistol	6.35	Soc. Franc. d'Armes
S & A	Rev	0.38	Suinaga & Aramperri
SABLE BABY	Rev	0.22	[Belgium]
S.A.C.M.	Pistol	7.65 Longue	SACM
SAFETY POLICE	Rev	0.32	Hopkins & Allen
ST HUBERT	Pistol	7.65	Pyrenees
SALSO	Pistol	6.35	Unceta
SALVAJE	Pistol	6.35	Ojanguren & Vidosa
SATA	Pistol	0.22/6.35	Sabotti & Tanfoglio
SATURN	Rifle	Various	Kind
SCARAB SCORPION	Pistol	9P	Armitage
SCHMEISSER	Pistol	6.35	Haenel
SCHONBERGER	Pistol	8 mm	Steyr-Mannlicher
SCHOUBOE	Pistol	7.65	Madsen
SCHUTZMANN	Rifle	Various	Kind
SCORPIO	Rev	0.38	Gabilondo
SCOTT ARMS CO.	Rev	0.32RF	Norwich Falls
SCOTT REVOLVER-RIFLE	Rev/Rifle	0.38RF	Hopkins & Allen
SCOUT	Shotg	Various	Stevens
SCOUT	Rev	0.32RF	Hood
SECRET SERVICE SPECIAL	Rev	0.32/0.38	Iver Johnson
SECURITAS	Pistol	6.35	St. Etienne Automatique
SECURITY SIX	Rev	0.357	Ruger
SELECTA	Pistol	6.35/7.65	Echave & Arizmendi
SELECTA	Pistol	7.65	Pyrenees
SELF	Pistol	6.35/7.65	[Spain]
SENTINEL	Rev	0.22/0.357	High Standard
SHARP-SHOOTER	Pistol	6.35/7.65/9S	Azanza y Arrizabalaga
SHERRY	Pistol	0.22	Wilkinson
SILESIA	Pistol	6.35	SEAM
SILHOUETTE	SS	Various	Wichita
SILHOUETTE	Pistol	0.44	Automag
SIMPLEX	Pistol	8 mm	Bergmann
SINGER	Pistol	6.35/7.65	Arizmendi & Goenaga
SINGER	Pistol	6.35	Dusek
SINGLE SIX	Rev	0.22	Ruger
SIVISPACEM	Pistol	7.65	SEAM
SIVISPACEM PARABELLUM	Pistol	6.35	Thieme & Edeler
SLAVIA	Pistol	6.35	Vilimec
SLOCUM	Rev	0.32RF	Brooklyn Arms
S.M.	Pistol	6.35	[Spain]
SMITH AMERICANO	Rec	0.32/0.38/0.44	Errasti
SMOK	Pistol	6.35	Nakulski
SMOKER	Rev	0.22/0.32/ 0.38/0.41RF	Johnson, Bye
SNAKE CHARMER	Shotg	0.410	Sporting
SOUTHERN ARMS CO.	Shotg	Various	Crescent Firearms
SPEED SIX	Rev	0.357	Ruger
SPENCER GUN CO.	Shotg	Various	Crescent Firearms
SPENCER SAFETY	Rev	0.38	Columbia
SPITFIRE	Pistol	9P	Slough
SPORT KING	Pistol	0.22	High Standard

Name	Type	Caliber	Maker
SPORTSMAN	Shotg	Various	Stevens
SPORTSMAN	Shotg	Various	Crescent Firearms
SPORTSMAN BUSH & FIELD	Rifle	Various	Marathon
SPRINGFIELD ARMS	Shotg	Various	Crescent Firearms
SPRINTER	Pistol	6.35	Bolumburu
SPY	Rev	0.22	Norwich Falls
SQUARE DEAL	Shotg	Various	Crescent Firearms
SQUIBMAN	All	Various	Squires, Bingham
STALLION	Rev	Various	Uberti
STAR	Pistol	Various	Echeverria
STARLET	Pistol	6.35	Echeverria
STAR VESTOPKCET	Rev	0.22/0.32RF	Johnson, Bye
STATE ARMS CO.	Shotg	Various	Crescent Firearms
STENDA	Pistol	7.65	Stendawerke
STERN	SS	0.22	Buchel
STERN-PISTOLE	Pistol	6.35	Wahl
STINGRAY	Rev	0.22	Rohm
STOSEL	Pistol	6.35/7.65	Retolaza
SULLIVAN ARMS CO.	Shotg	Various	Crescent Firearms
SUPER AZUL	MP	7.63	Arostegui
SUPER BLACKHAWK	Rev	0.44	Ruger
SUPER COMANCHE	Rev	0.357/0.44	Gabilondo
SUPER DESTROYER	Pistol	7.65	Gaztanaga, Trocaola
SUPERIOR	Pistol	6.35	[Spain]
SUPER REDHAWK	Rev	0.44	Ruger
SUPERMATIC	Pistol	0.22	High Standard
SURETE	Pistol	7.65	Gaztanaga
SWAMP ANGEL	Rev	0.41RF	Forehand & Wadsworth
SWIFT	Rev	0.38	Iver Johnson
SYMPATHIQUE	Pistol	7.65	Pyrenees
T.A.C.	Rev	Various	Trocaola
TANARMI	Pistol	0.22	Tanfoglio
TANKE	Rev	0.38	Orueta Hermanos
TANNE	Rifle	Various	Kind
TANQUE	Pistol	6.35	Ojanguren & Vidosa
TARGA	Pistol	Various	Tanfoglio
TARGET BULLDOG	Rev	0.357/0.44	Charter Arms
TARN	Pistol	9P	Swift
TATRA	Pistol	6.35	Alkartasuna
TATRA	Pistol	6.35	SEAM
TAULER	Pistol	Various	Gabilondo
T.E.	Pistol	7.65	Thieme & Edeler
TED WILLIAMS	Shotguns	Various	Sears
TELL	SS	0.22	Buchel
TERRIBLE	Pistol	6.35	Azanza y Arrizabalaga
TERRIER	Rev	0.22/0.32/ 0.38/0.41RF	Rupertus
TERRIER ONE	Rev	0.32	[Germany]
TERROR	Rev	0.32RF	Forehand & Wadsworth
TEUF-TEUF	Pistol	6.35	Arizmendi & Goenaga
TEUF-TEUF	Pistol	6.35	[Belgium]
TEXAS LONGHORN	Rev	Various	Texas
TEXAS MARSHAL	Rev	0.45	Sauer
TEXAS RANGER	Rev	0.38	Unies de Liege
TEXAS RANGER	Shotg	12/16	Stevens

Name	Type	Caliber	Maker
THALCO	Rev	0.22	Rohm
THAMES AUTOMATIC	Rev	0.22/0.32/0.38	Thames
THE VICTORY	Pistol	6.35	Zulaica
THOMAS	Pistol	0.45	James Ordnance
THOMPSON	SMG	0.45	Auto-Ordnance
THUNDER	Pistol	6.35	Bascaran
THUNDER CHIEF	Rev	0.22	Squibman
TIGER	Shotg	Various	Crescent Firearms
TIGER	Rev	0.32RF	[USA]
TIGRE	Pistol	6.35	Garate Anitua
TIKKA	Rifle	Various	Tikkakoski
TIRO AL BLANCO	Rev	0.38	Ojanguren & Matiade
TISAN	Pistol	6.,35	Salaberrin
TITAN	Pistol	6.35	Armigas
TITAN	Pistol	7.65	Retolaza
TITAN	Pistol	6.35	Tanfoglio
TITANIC	Pistol	6.35/7.65	Retolaza
TIWA	Pistol	6.35	[Spain]
TOKAGYPT	Pistol	9P	Femaru
TOMPKINS	SS	0.22	Varsity Mfg. Co.
TORPILLE	Pistol	7.65	[Spain]
TOURISTE	Pistol	7.65	Pyrenees
TOWERS POLICE SAFETY	Rev	0.38RF	Hopkins & Allen
TOZ	Pistol	6.34	Tulskii
TRAILSMAN	Rev	0.22	Iver Johnson
TRAMP'S TERROR	Rev	0.22	Hopkins & Allen
TRIDENT	Rev	0.38	Renato Gamba
TRIFIRE	Pistol	0.45	Arminex
TRIOMPHE	Pistol	6.35	Apaolozo Hermanos
TRIOMPHE FRANCAISE	Pistol	7.65	Pyrenees
TRIPLEX	Pistol	6.35	Domingo Acha
TRIUMPH	Pistol	7.65	Garate Anitua
TROOPER	Rev	0.22/0.357	Colt
TRUE BLUE	Rev	0.32RF	Norwich Falls
TRUST	Pistol	6.35/7.65	Grand Precision
TRUST SUPRA	Pistol	6.35	Grand Precision
TTIBAR	Pistol	0.22	S.R.L.
TUE-TUE	Rev	Various	Galand
TURNER & ROSS	Rev	0.22	Hood
TWO-BIT	Pistol	6.35	Steel City
TYCOON	Rev	All RF	Johnson, Bye
U.A.E.	Pistol	6.35	Union Armera Eibarens
U.A.Z.	SS	0.22	Anschutz
U.C.	Pistol	6.35	Urrejola & Co.
U.M.C. ARMS CO.	Rev	0.32RF	Norwich Falls
UNCLE SAM	SS	0.50RF	Iver Johnson
UNDERCOVER	Rev	0.38	Charter Arms
UNDERCOVERETTE	Rev	0.32	Charter Arms
UNION	Pistol	7.65	Fabrique Française
UNION	Pistol	6.35/7.65	Seytres
UNION	Pistol	6.35/7.65	Unceta
UNION	Pistol	6.35	Tomas de Urizar
UNION ARMERA	Pistol	6.35	Union Armera Eibarens
UNION JACK	Rev	0.22/0.32RF	Hood

Name	Type	Caliber	Maker
UNION SALES CO.	Rev	9RF	[Germany]
UNIQUE	Rev/RP	0.32/0.38RF	Shattuck
UNIQUE	Pistol	Various	Pyrenees
UNIQUE CORSAIR	Pistol	0.22	Echeverria
UNIQUE ESCORT	Pistol	0.22	Echeverria
UNIS	Pistol	7.65	Pyrenees
UNIS	Pistol	6.35	Santiago Salaberrin
UNIVERSAL	Rev	0.32	Hopkins & Allen
U.S. ARMS CO.	Shotg	Various	Crescent Firearms
U.S. ARMS CO.	Rev	0.22/0.32/ 0.38/0.41RF	US Arms
U.S. REVOLVER CO.	Rev	0.22/0.32/0.38	Iver Johnson
VAINQUER	Pistol	6.35	Aurelio Mendiola
VALIANT	Rifle	0.22	Stevens
VALOR	Rev	0.22	Rohm
VELO-BROM	Rev	6 mm/8 mm	Retolaza
VELO-DOG	Rev	5 mm	Galand (and many others)
VELO-MITH	Rev	6.35	Crucelegui
VELO-MITH	Rev	6.35	Ojanguren & Marcaido
VELO-MITH	Rev	7.65	Retolaza
VELO-MITH ARTIAN	Rev	6.35	Arizmendi
VELO-SMITH	Rev	6.35	[Spain]
VELO-STARK	Rev	6/6.35	Garate Hermanos
VENCEDOR	Pistol	6.35	Casimir Santos
VENUS	Pistol	7.65	Urizar
VENUS	Pistol	7.65	Venus Waffenwerke
VER-CAR	Pistol	6.35	Verney-Carron
VESTA	Pistol	6.35/7.65	Hijos de A Echeverria
VESTPOCKET	Rev	0.22	Rohm
VETERAN	Rev	0.32RF	Norwich Falls
VETO	Rev	0.32RF	[USA]
VICI	Pistol	6.35	[Belgium]
VICTOR	Pistol	6.35/7.65	Francisco Arizmendi
VICTOR	SS	0.38RF	Marlin
VICTOR	Rev	0.22/0.32	Harrrington & Richardson
VICTOR	Shotg	Various	Crescent Firearms
VICTOR, THE	Pistol	0.22	High Standard
VICTOR NO. 1	Rev	0.22/0.32	Harrington & Richardson
VICTOR SPECIAL	Shotg	Various	Crescent Firearms
VICTORIA	Rev	0.32RF	Hood
VICTORIA	Pistol	6.35/7.65	Esperanza & Unceta
VICTORY	Pistol	6.35	Zulaica
VIKING	Pistol	0.45	ODI
VILAR	Pistol	7.65	[Spain]
VINCITOR	Pistol	6.35/7.65	Zulaica
VINDEX	Pistol	7.65	Pyrenees
VIRGINIA ARMS CO.	Shotg	Various	Crescent Firearms
VIRGINIAN DRAGOON	Rev	Various	Interarms
VITE	Pistol	6.35/7.65	Echave & Arizmendi
VOLUNTEER	Shotg	Various	Stevens
VULCAN ARMS CO.	Shotg	Various	Crescent Firearms
VULCAIN	Pistol	6.35	[Spain]
VULKAN	Pistol	6.35	Pfannl

Name	Type	Caliber	Maker
WACO	Pistol	6.35	SEAM
WALAM	Pistol	7.65	Femaru
WALDMAN	Pistol	6.35/7.65	Arizmendi & Goenaga
WALKY	Pistol	6.35	[Spain]
WALMAN	Pistol	6.35/7.65/9S	Arizmendi & Goenaga
WARWINCK	Pistol	7.65	Arizaga
WEGRIA-CHARLIER	Pistol	6.35	Charlier
WELTWAFFEN	Pistol	7.65	MKEK
WESTERN BULLDOG	Rev	0.44	[Belgium]
WESTERN FIELD NO. 5	SS	0.22	Pyrenees
WESTERN SIX-SHOOTER	Rev	Various	Weirauch
WESTERN STYLE	Rev	0.22	Rohm
WHEELER	RP	0.41RF	American Arms
WHITE STAR	Rev	0.32	[USA]
WICKLIFFE	Rifle	Various	Triple-S
WIDE AWAKE	Rev	0.32RF	Hood
WINFIELD	Pistol	9S/9P	Bayonne
WINFIELD ARMS CO.	Rev	0.32RF	Norwich Falls
WINOCA ARMS CO.	Shotg	Various	Crescent Firearms
WITTES HARDWARE CO.	Shotg	Various	Stevens
W.L.GRANT	Rev	0.22/0.32RF	Lower
WOLF PATENT	Pistol	7.65	[Spain]
WOLVERINE	Pistol	0.22	Whitney
WOLVERINE ARMS CO.	Shotg	Various	Crescent Firearms
WOODSMAN	Pistol	0.22	Colt
WORTHINGTON ARMS	Shotg	Various	Stevens
WORTHINGTON, GEORGE	Shotg	Various	Stevens
XL	Rev	0.22/0.32/0.38	Hopkins & Allen
XL BULLDOG	Rev	0.38	Hopkins & Allen
XX STANDARD	Rev	0.22/0.32/0.38	Marlin
YATO	Pistol	7.65	Hamada Arsenal
YDEAL	Pistol	6.35/7.65	Francisco Arizmendi
YOU BET	Rev	0.22	Hopkins & Allen
YOUNG AMERICA	Rev	Various	Harrington & Richardson
YOVANOVITCH	Pistol	6.35/7.65/9S	Kragujevac
Z	Pistol	6.35	CZ
ZALDUN	Pistol	6.35	[Spain]
ZB	Rifle/MG	Various	Zbrojovka Brno
ZENTRUM	SS	0.22	VEB
ZEPHYR	Shotg	Various	Stoeger
ZEPHYR	Rev	0.22	Rohm
ZOLI	Pistol	6.35	Tanfoglio
ZONDA	SS	0.22	Hafdasa

Name	Type	Caliber	Maker
UNION SALES CO.	Rev	9RF	[Germany]
UNIQUE	Rev/RP	0.32/0.38RF	Shattuck
UNIQUE	Pistol	Various	Pyrenees
UNIQUE CORSAIR	Pistol	0.22	Echeverria
UNIQUE ESCORT	Pistol	0.22	Echeverria
UNIS	Pistol	7.65	Pyrenees
UNIS	Pistol	6.35	Santiago Salaberrin
UNIVERSAL	Rev	0.32	Hopkins & Allen
U.S. ARMS CO.	Shotg	Various	Crescent Firearms
U.S. ARMS CO.	Rev	0.22/0.32/ 0.38/0.41RF	US Arms
U.S. REVOLVER CO.	Rev	0.22/0.32/0.38	Iver Johnson
VAINQUER	Pistol	6.35	Aurelio Mendiola
VALIANT	Rifle	0.22	Stevens
VALOR	Rev	0.22	Rohm
VELO-BROM	Rev	6 mm/8 mm	Retolaza
VELO-DOG	Rev	5 mm	Galand (and many others)
VELO-MITH	Rev	6.35	Crucelegui
VELO-MITH	Rev	6.35	Ojanguren & Marcaido
VELO-MITH	Rev	7.65	Retolaza
VELO-MITH ARTIAN	Rev	6.35	Arizmendi
VELO-SMITH	Rev	6.35	[Spain]
VELO-STARK	Rev	6/6.35	Garate Hermanos
VENCEDOR	Pistol	6.35	Casimir Santos
VENUS	Pistol	7.65	Urizar
VENUS	Pistol	7.65	Venus Waffenwerke
VER-CAR	Pistol	6.35	Verney-Carron
VESTA	Pistol	6.35/7.65	Hijos de A Echeverria
VESTPOCKET	Rev	0.22	Rohm
VETERAN	Rev	0.32RF	Norwich Falls
VETO	Rev	0.32RF	[USA]
VICI	Pistol	6.35	[Belgium]
VICTOR	Pistol	6.35/7.65	Francisco Arizmendi
VICTOR	SS	0.38RF	Marlin
VICTOR	Rev	0.22/0.32	Harrrington & Richardson
VICTOR	Shotg	Various	Crescent Firearms
VICTOR, THE	Pistol	0.22	High Standard
VICTOR NO. 1	Rev	0.22/0.32	Harrington & Richardson
VICTOR SPECIAL	Shotg	Various	Crescent Firearms
VICTORIA	Rev	0.32RF	Hood
VICTORIA	Pistol	6.35/7.65	Esperanza & Unceta
VICTORY	Pistol	6.35	Zulaica
VIKING	Pistol	0.45	ODI
VILAR	Pistol	7.65	[Spain]
VINCITOR	Pistol	6.35/7.65	Zulaica
VINDEX	Pistol	7.65	Pyrenees
VIRGINIA ARMS CO.	Shotg	Various	Crescent Firearms
VIRGINIAN DRAGOON	Rev	Various	Interarms
VITE	Pistol	6.35/7.65	Echave & Arizmendi
VOLUNTEER	Shotg	Various	Stevens
VULCAN ARMS CO.	Shotg	Various	Crescent Firearms
VULCAIN	Pistol	6.35	[Spain]
VULKAN	Pistol	6.35	Pfannl

Name	Type	Caliber	Maker
WACO	Pistol	6.35	SEAM
WALAM	Pistol	7.65	Femaru
WALDMAN	Pistol	6.35/7.65	Arizmendi & Goenaga
WALKY	Pistol	6.35	[Spain]
WALMAN	Pistol	6.35/7.65/9S	Arizmendi & Goenaga
WARWINCK	Pistol	7.65	Arizaga
WEGRIA-CHARLIER	Pistol	6.35	Charlier
WELTWAFFEN	Pistol	7.65	MKEK
WESTERN BULLDOG	Rev	0.44	[Belgium]
WESTERN FIELD NO. 5	SS	0.22	Pyrenees
WESTERN SIX-SHOOTER	Rev	Various	Weirauch
WESTERN STYLE	Rev	0.22	Rohm
WHEELER	RP	0.41RF	American Arms
WHITE STAR	Rev	0.32	[USA]
WICKLIFFE	Rifle	Various	Triple-S
WIDE AWAKE	Rev	0.32RF	Hood
WINFIELD	Pistol	9S/9P	Bayonne
WINFIELD ARMS CO.	Rev	0.32RF	Norwich Falls
WINOCA ARMS CO.	Shotg	Various	Crescent Firearms
WITTES HARDWARE CO.	Shotg	Various	Stevens
W.L.GRANT	Rev	0.22/0.32RF	Lower
WOLF PATENT	Pistol	7.65	[Spain]
WOLVERINE	Pistol	0.22	Whitney
WOLVERINE ARMS CO.	Shotg	Various	Crescent Firearms
WOODSMAN	Pistol	0.22	Colt
WORTHINGTON ARMS	Shotg	Various	Stevens
WORTHINGTON, GEORGE	Shotg	Various	Stevens
XL	Rev	0.22/0.32/0.38	Hopkins & Allen
XL BULLDOG	Rev	0.38	Hopkins & Allen
XX STANDARD	Rev	0.22/0.32/0.38	Marlin
YATO	Pistol	7.65	Hamada Arsenal
YDEAL	Pistol	6.35/7.65	Francisco Arizmendi
YOU BET	Rev	0.22	Hopkins & Allen
YOUNG AMERICA	Rev	Various	Harrington & Richardson
YOVANOVITCH	Pistol	6.35/7.65/9S	Kragujevac
Z	Pistol	6.35	CZ
ZALDUN	Pistol	6.35	[Spain]
ZB	Rifle/MG	Various	Zbrojovka Brno
ZENTRUM	SS	0.22	VEB
ZEPHYR	Shotg	Various	Stoeger
ZEPHYR	Rev	0.22	Rohm
ZOLI	Pistol	6.35	Tanfoglio
ZONDA	SS	0.22	Hafdasa